Patrick White within the Western Literary Tradition

John Beston

SYDNEY UNIVERSITY PRESS

Published 2010 by Sydney University Press

SYDNEY UNIVERSITY PRESS
University of Sydney Library
sydney.edu.au/sup

Sydney University Press
Fisher Library F03
University of Sydney NSW 2006 AUSTRALIA
Email: sup.info@sydney.edu.au

National Library of Australia Cataloguing-in-Publication entry

Author: Beston, John, 1930-
Title: Patrick White within the western literary tradition / John Beston.
ISBN: 9781920899370 (pbk.)
Notes: Includes bibliographical references.
Subjects: White, Patrick, 1912-1990--Criticism and interpretation
Authors, Australian--20th century--History and criticism.
Literature--20th century--History and criticism.
Dewey Number:
A823.3

Cover image: *Burke and Wills at Mount Hopeless,* watercolour on paper by George W Lambert (1907), purchased 1960, Bendigo Art Gallery. Image courtesy of Bendigo Art Gallery

Cover design by Court Williams, University Publishing Service

Contents

SECTION 3: STUDIES OF WHITE'S MAJOR NOVELS

SECTION 4: THEMATIC STUDIES OF WHITE'S NOVELS

FOREWORD

John Beston writes literary criticism that is clear, erudite and accessible. This is a rare talent these days, where critics often attempt to be as inscrutable as possible. But I do not find inscrutability to be a sign of sophistication or higher learning; on the contrary, the good critic is the one who wears his erudition lightly, and who has integrated his cultural sources and theories so thoroughly that he no longer has to display them like war medallions. The student of literature and the general reader will find much to admire and value in the pages of this impressive volume. Here we have twenty-two chapters which explore the vast continent that is the imagination and literary contribution of Patrick White, Australia's only Nobel Prize winning author. This volume not only sits well beside existing works of White criticism, but signals a new direction in the field: here the critic is urbane without being showy, theoretical without being theory-driven, and completely at home with the cultural sources and languages from which Patrick White drew.

Beston puts forward an irrefutable case for placing Patrick White's fiction in the context of the Western literary tradition. White, who was born and partly educated in Europe, is larger than Australia and best seen in a context that goes beyond its borders. White is so thoroughly European that it is high time that a book such as this appeared. Beston is well placed to author such a work, with his extensive knowledge of French, German, American and English languages and literatures. White studied French and German at Cambridge University and throughout his long career he returned to these sources to revive and revitalise his interests. Flaubert, Stendhal, Rimbaud, Joyce and Lawrence were among the sources from which he drew, not only for imaginative content and thematic structure but for stylistic influence. It has to be said that Beston's final chapter on White's style is among the most important and original in this volume, and represents a landmark in White criticism. Beston's sensitivity to style, and alertness to aesthetic considerations in literature, mark this book as one in which White's language receives as much attention as his 'themes', 'myths' and narrative content. Finally, we have a White criticism which is attuned to the musicality of his writing, to its aesthetic complexities and subtleties, and not one which is tone-deaf.

Australian critics have generally been shy of exploring White's 'Europeanness', mainly because our critics have been schooled in English language traditions and have been unable to explore the full range of White's continental influences. His Europeanness has not been fashionable for another reason: critics here have been keen to explore White's 'Australianness' and to see him as an artist of Australian experience. Much of the focus has been on how White has engaged in mythmaking in the Australian context, how he takes aspects of Australian history and culture and develops these to build his fictional worlds. But Beston points out that much of this mythmaking is European in origin and transplanted into a new regional context. Although Australians may want to nationalise Patrick White and make him an 'Aussie', Beston reminds us that White had a fiercely ambivalent relationship with things Australian, and we should not get carried away by our need to turn him into a national monument. White belongs to the wider world of culture and discourse, and he was only stationed, as it were, in Australia. He once referred to himself not as an Australian citizen, but as a 'citizen of the universe'. Beston shows how much this is the case, elucidating the international influences that come together and converge in the figure of Patrick White.

It is true that White hated certain aspects of Australian life and society. He despised its apparent vulgarity and coarseness, its celebration of the average, its esteem for the mediocre. White feared that in such an environment the mind was 'the least of possessions', as he wrote in his 1958 essay, 'The Prodigal Son'. At times White invests Australian society not only with mediocrity and vulgarity, but with a sense of evil that is positively demonic. This is found most clearly in *Riders in the Chariot*, where a circle of suburban women act as notorious witches who orchestrate the persecution and crucifixion of those who are spiritually inclined. Indeed, it is hard to know how Australians can show nationalistic pride in Patrick White when he reveals their society in such a jaundiced manner. Despite an attempt of the literary establishment to nationalise our Nobel laureate and make him an Aussie hero, the majority of ordinary Australians have maintained a respectful distance from Patrick White, sensing that he is not a supporter of national values, assumptions or attitudes. Dorothy Green once said he is the 'conscience of the nation', but even that assessment makes him seem too Australian. He is quite simply the archetypal outsider, whose only hope is that the mind and spirit are not crushed in what he described as 'the march of material ugliness'.

Barry Humphries, whose fame at home and abroad as social satirist exceeds that of White, said that Patrick needed to hate Australia with as much venom as he could summon. This appears to be true for two reasons. First, as Beston is keen to point out, his negative response to Australian society provided him with the basis for his biting social satire, which is a theme running through several of the essays of this volume. This is an aspect of White's work that has not received much critical attention until now. Beston is able to deal with this satire partly because, as an international citizen himself, he seems not too identified with the Australian ethos or national character. He is able to accept White's social satire without feeling nationally offended or personally hurt. Second, White's negative construction of Australian society provided the impetus to explore his signature terrain: the internal realm of imagination and fantasy. White is dependent on a crude social and exterior world to enable him to withdraw into an intensely imagined interior world. His most important characters, from Theodora Goodman, to Stan Parker, Voss, Himmelfarb, Miss Hare and Ellen Roxburgh, retreat from Australian banality to explore the interior realm of psychic or spiritual reality. As they go deeper into this world, into depths that are at times paralleled by geographical journeying, they encounter mythic forces and figures that link them to universal patterns of human experience. It is this hidden, invisible Australia, the 'Australia of the mind', that White is chiefly concerned with. For him the external society is useful merely as a foil, or as a negative stimulus to compel his sensitive characters to explore realms of mind in which they are themselves the chief pioneers.

White's central characters are fictional, and the realm they explore is symbolic and invented, and yet this realm seems more real to Patrick White than the superficial world that common sense refers to as 'reality'. John Beston and I have mutual interests in this interior reality, which have taken both of us into the complex and controversial fields of psychoanalysis. Beston is a Freudian and I am a Jungian, but we agree that interior reality is as 'real' as the external world. In Europe and North America, Freudians and Jungians are hostile to each other and attempt to shoot each other down. In Australia, the situation is different. There is so little intellectual complexity here, and so little evidence of the existence—or rivalry between—psychoanalytic traditions, that Freudians and Jungians are likely to support each other in a bid to defend against the general antipathy to 'European' thought. European psychoanalytic traditions are often seen as decadent, foreign and un-Australian. They are contemptible in making ordinary life more complicated than it should be. Hence in this country, as in no other, a Jungian such as myself can write a preface for a book by a Freudian, and heartily recommend it to the reading audience.

There are, however, some differences in our points of view, if the reader chooses to compare my book on White with the present volume. I see unconscious factors playing a larger role in the creative process than Beston does. I construct White as an 'unconscious genius' who was never able to master his muse. Beston tends to emphasise the control and discipline of White's craft and literary skill, whereas I focus on the archetypal symbols and myths that appear to be in control of White himself. For me, White wrestles with a creative demon which is stronger than he is, and Beston sees him as a writer whose consummate skill is manifest in a variety of ways, and most powerfully in his masterpieces, *The Aunt's Story* and *Voss*. Beston and I agree on which are the best, and which are the worst, novels. Our differences are clearly and fairly delineated in chapter twenty-one of this volume, 'Mythmaking in Patrick White's Novels'.

Beston and I also see the mother as the central figure in White's psychic and fictional universe. She is the prime instigator of narrative action in White's novels, the paradoxical goddess who repels and wounds with her wickedness and self-centredness, and who attracts and enchants with her feminine mystique and charm. White can never decide whether he hates or loves the mother, but in the final analysis he seems to hate and love at the same time. If the negative side of the mother is experienced through society, banality, suburban women and mind-crushing materialism, the positive side of the mother is conveyed through the Australian landscape. He finds the land nurturing, mysterious and supportive. As early as the 1940s, when he was stationed in the Middle East and Europe, White experienced what he called 'the terrible nostalgia of the desert landscapes', and it was this 'longing to return to the scenes of childhood' that encouraged him to settle in Australia. White lives in a Manichean universe, based on the splitting of the experience of the mother into good and evil, a phenomenon discussed by Freud and Melanie Klein. Society is a crushing evil and landscape a redemptive good, and I believe that White would have projected this dualism onto any country in which he lived. This psychological fact makes his condemnation of Australian society much less convincing.

Society produces materialism and landscape engenders mysticism. As White's elect retreat from social banality and evil, they encounter forces in the natural world that can only be described as spiritual. Whether we are referring to Theodora Goodman wandering in New Mexico, Elyot Standish at the seashore in England, Voss in the deserts of Australia, or Miss Hare in her secret garden, nature is the nurturing force that supports life and allows feelings of elation and erotic excitation. Sometimes these trysts with the earth mother end in ecstatic moments of unity and epiphany, as with Stan Parker, and at other times they lead to madness and disintegration, as with Voss and Theodora. But whether the earth is crushing the human spirit or allowing it to be elevated, the central characters always experience this as orgasmic, releasing and transformative. Beston gives these epiphanies a Freudian interpretation, and for me they suggest a powerful mythic pattern of mother/son in which White is held and unable to break free. White is a great writer, and a master of literary style, but he is not a full genius because he is the victim of a complex which he never manages to overcome. Indeed, the mother complex overcomes him, as is painfully evident in his last two novels, *The Twyborn Affair* and *Memoirs of Many in One*. When a complex takes over, and can no longer be disguised by symbols or spiritual feelings, the fiction degenerates and the creative novelist loses his powers.

White reached his artistic and creative peak when he camouflaged his personal obsession for the mother with symbolism and the mythologisation of nature. As he was tempted to dismantle his mythopoeic universe to reveal the personal drives which underlay it, the writing becomes flat, prosaic and dull. This decline begins with *The Vivisector* and continues to the last work, with only the wonderful *A Fringe of Leaves* to interrupt the descent. The highly poetic and intensely symbolic writing of his major novels disappears, along with the Joycean epiphanies, and all we find are depictions of sons who are desperate to unite with their mothers. These sons cannot engage in heterosexual activity because only the mother will do. The movement from *Riders in the Chariot* to *The*

Twyborn Affair is one of steady decline, as Beston makes clear. To me, this unfortunate trajectory points to a psychoanalytic truth: sexual energies are most powerful, interesting and creative when they are sublimated into cultural forms and mythic constructs.

When the mythmaking collapses and the symbolism falls away, the bare elements of oedipal incestuous desire are not interesting. There is nothing gripping about a son who wants to bed the mother, but there is much splendour and enchantment for the reader when he enacts this ritual process in symbolic forms. It is the grand poetic themes and spiritual gestures, when sustained across large narrative spaces, that command our interest and respect. When the heightened tension is released and raw impulses are exposed, the horizons are narrowed and mystery subsides. A certain degree of repression is good for art and culture, and the career of Patrick White reveals an epic journey in the attempt to sublimate and transform the incestuous feeling that a son has for the mother. It is symbolic fantasy, not sexual reality, that reveals Patrick White at his best. I welcome this book and award it a special place in the history of White criticism.

David Tacey
Reader in Literature and Associate Professor in Psychoanalytic Studies
La Trobe University

August 2010

Author's Preface

The essays on Patrick White presented in this collection have been selected from some thirty essays published over a period of thirty-five years, initially through the support of a generous Postdoctoral Fellowship from the University of Queensland. They were published in a number of overseas countries as well as in Australia—in the US, Canada, England, France and India—the early ones in accordance with my intention then to make White better known throughout the world. While that may have helped to establish White's reputation outside Australia, it had the disadvantage that many of these articles, valid now as then, have become inaccessible outside major libraries. Collected in this volume, they give access to the varied body of my work on White.

Over the years I have broadened my work on White from specific, focused aspects of individual novels like the struggle between Voss and Laura for dominance in *Voss* to broader aspects of his work, like his preoccupation with epiphanies at the conclusions of his novels. Most of my studies have centred on his major novels, those that I believe will stand the test of time: *The Aunt's Story*, *The Tree of Man*, and *Voss*. Although there is clearly a first-rate mind at work in *Riders in the Chariot*, *The Eye of the Storm*, and *A Fringe of Leaves*, these novels will always be handicapped by one failing or another: the inadequate central symbol in *Riders in the Chariot*, the sheer negativism in *The Eye of the Storm*, the lack of a strong controlling theme in *A Fringe of Leaves*. My work on White culminates here with two long, previously unpublished essays, both with broad and important themes: 'Mythmaking in Patrick White's Novels' and 'White's Style', a linguistic study of White's style as it kept changing over his career in accordance with his changing interests, themes and mood.

All my work on White has been carefully edited by my wife Rose Marie, who collaborated with me on a number of articles in this collection. I would be happier if her name were on the cover, but that is not her wish, so I can do no more than emphasise that my work would be greatly inferior without her contributions, suggestions and corrections. She is the *sine qua non* of my existence and of the publication of this collection of essays.

Section 1
Patrick White within the Western Literary Tradition

Introduction
The Raison d'Être of this Book

Patrick White's novels do not belong simply to Australian literature but, more widely, to the literature of the West. The prime element in White's intellectual development was his study of French and German literatures during his formative years at Cambridge University from 1932 to 1935, when he was in his early twenties. British and British Commonwealth universities in those days did not venture far into the twentieth century in their study of literature, hence White studied chiefly nineteenth-century writers. His closest affinities remained with nineteenth-century Continental novelists, as he acknowledged when he said 'I am a nineteenth-century novelist.' He was influenced chiefly by such nineteenth-century writers as Flaubert, Stendhal, Rimbaud and Goethe. Only two works by Continental writers who influenced him significantly belong to the twentieth century, Thomas Mann's *Buddenbrooks* (1901) and Alain-Fournier's *Le Grand Meaulnes* (1913), both published before World War I.

White's residence in England during his years at Cambridge and then in London exposed him to British literature, which also left its mark upon his work. One can detect the influence of James Joyce, stylistically and thematically. Another Irish novelist whom White admired, George Moore (1852–1933), had been responsible for the Europeanisation of English-language literature, thereby providing White with a model for his own Europeanisation of Australian literature. Moore, asserted his chief critic, Jean-Claude Noël, 'fut un des principaux agents de diffusion en pays de langue anglaise de diverses attitudes esthétiques du continent européen' [was one of the main writers to disseminate various aesthetic attitudes of the Continent throughout English-speaking countries].[1]

White's acquaintance with American literature began with his reading Steinbeck in England during the 1930s. He picked up a number of story strands for *Happy Valley* from Steinbeck's *The Pastures of Heaven*, published in England in 1933, and that may well be the reason for his travelling to the USA to find a publisher for *Happy Valley*. His stay in the US from 1939 to 1940 enabled him to become further acquainted with American literature when it was little known in other English-speaking countries. There he became acquainted with Willa Cather's work; her novels of the 1920s influenced him from *The Aunt's Story* on. Cather's chief contribution was to provide in *My Antonia* (1918) a model for the pioneer novel *The Tree of Man* (published in 1955 in the US and 1956 in the UK). *My Antonia* and *The Tree of Man* are the classic pioneer novels of their respective countries.

White's origins in Australia and his residence in Europe and in America are reflected in his first masterpiece, *The Aunt's Story* (1948): part One is set in New South Wales, part Two ('Jardin Exotique') in southern France and part Three ('Holstius') in the American Midwest and Southwest. The 'Jardin Exotique' section is more deeply immersed in Continental European culture than anything previous in Australian literature. And the final section of the novel gives a varied picture of America, its enormous productivity along with its abandoned settlements, as Theodora travels by train from Chicago to Taos in New Mexico.

From first to last, one finds in White's novels continual evidence of his exposure to European culture, a culture that he wanted to incorpo-

[1] Noël (1966).

rate into Australian literature. Sometimes the European influence comes from a medium outside literature, like the Goyaesque images that recur throughout his work. Through these images he links the newest of worlds to the oldest in a harsh reminder to Australians that the violence of Europe can irrupt in their sheltered land. There is a score or more of such scenes as the crucifixion scenes in *Happy Valley* and *Riders in the Chariot*, the bloated body of a dog floating in the water in *The Living and the Dead* and *The Eye of the Storm*, the drowned man in the tree in *The Tree of Man*, Voss' decapitation, the spearing of Palfreyman in *Voss* and of Austin Roxburgh in *The Eye of the Storm*, the bird impaled on the bough in *The Eye of the Storm*, the dog tearing off Waldo's penis in *The Solid Mandala*. (Goya is mentioned twice in *The Vivisector*.) These scenes appear to express a latent, lingering antagonism in White to Australia; it is as if he wanted to remind Australians that it was not an idyllic land.

During most of White's lifetime (1912–1990), Australians had a very uncertain sense of national identity, a fact that younger Australians living in the confident and prosperous country that has emerged would hardly be aware of. When White was in his twenties, in the 1930s, ambitious Australians fled to Europe to acquire another, more prestigious identity and to absorb an older and more developed culture. White was part of this movement. Until the second half of last century, too, Australians had a very diffident attitude towards their literature: the literature was not widely read by the general public and was rarely studied in school or university. Some people even boasted perversely of never having read an Australian work. Things began to change radically only in the 1970s as Australia became a more prosperous country.

White took a negative idea of Australia to England with him when he attended secondary school and later university there, and had that notion confirmed and reinforced by his English associates; most of them looked with condescension on Australia. Ruth White, his mother, like Hurtle's mother in *The Vivisector*, 'always said Australia was common' (p. 185);

Ruth chose to spend her last years in England. The young Patrick absorbed her viewpoint, for he made vulgarity and lack of education one of the chief targets of his satire, pretty much equating them with evil in the persons of Mrs Jolley and Mrs Flack in *Riders in the Chariot*; he never portrayed any vulgar Europeans. Before his return to Australia in 1946 he was not committed to Australia and did not feel that he belonged in it. When he was in the US in the late 1930s, he thought of living there, in Cooperstown in upstate New York, but the war intervened and his life changed. After the war, he thought of living in Greece, but was discouraged by Manoly Lascaris, his lifelong partner, who didn't want to confront his family with his relationship with Patrick. Even in the late 1940s his doubts about returning to Australia can be seen in his reluctance to have Theodora return to it at the end of *The Aunt's Story*: she tears up her return ticket and opts for a mental home in New Mexico.

But he *did* return in 1946 and found its culture in his terms mediocre and lacking in spirituality. Years later, in 1958, in his essay 'The Prodigal Son', White told of his disdain for the Australia he returned to. At the very end of *Memoirs of Many in One* (1986) he wrote of our 'Philistine environment and bourgeois habits'—four years before his death. In his old age he failed to update his image of Australia, in which he had lived continuously for forty years. After he recovered from his disappointment at the public reception of *The Aunt's Story*, however, he made a deep commitment to Australia and undertook the enormously ambitious task of raising its culture. He did that under the influence of what he had absorbed primarily from European and secondarily from American culture.

Against this Euro-American version of White that I have presented here is the fact that seven of his twelve novels are set wholly in Australia and another four partly in Australia. Why doesn't that tip the balance towards affiliating him with Australia? The main reason is his lack of feeling for the country: there is no sense that it is a beautiful country with a breathtaking coastline, or that there are people of integrity, aspiration and achievement within it. (The idyllic presentation of Rhine Towers in *Voss* is a concession to his early memories of the White family estate of Belltrees in the Hunter Valley.) He chose to hold himself apart from it and never quite belonged here. Born in England, White seems to have felt adopted into Australia, a changeling like Hurtle Duffield in *The Vivisector*. The commitment that he felt towards it was to its cultural advancement, quite like Voss' determination to make the map of Australia. When Mr Bonner asks him if he has studied the map of Australia, Voss replies, 'The map? … I will first make it' (p. 19). White did not study Australian literature: he wanted to create it. His way of doing so was through what he absorbed primarily from European and secondarily from American culture, and it is through those traditions that we should approach him.

All the diverse influences I discuss in this collection of essays constitute a statement of where he lived, when he lived, and the nature of his education. All three of these aspects embrace areas outside Australia, and they are an essential part of his identity as a novelist who was always oriented towards a wider world. That is why I have entitled this book *Patrick White within the Western Literary Tradition*. In a recent essay on *Voss*, the German critic Henrike Wenzel wrote

> Whites Verbindung zu europäischer Literaturtradition wird … in der Konzeption seines Protagonisten [Voss] deutlich. In seinem Verlangen nach Erkenntnis gleicht er dem Faust, der die Grenzen des Menschlichen durch Erkenntnis überwinden will; in der Rast- und scheinbaren Ziellosigkeit seiner Wanderung dem Odysseus, dessen Schicksal die Suche ist.[2]

---

[2] [White's connection to European literature is … made clear in his conception of his protagonist (Voss). In his ardent desire for knowledge and understanding he resembles both Faust, who would overstep the limits of humankind, and

My overall approach in this collection is twofold in its emphasis. On the one hand I am concerned with White's evocation of dimensions other than material reality (in my essays on *Voss*, White and Cather, and his preoccupation with epiphanies and mythmaking). And on the other hand I offer a series of analytical studies of his themes and characters in his major novels (in my essays on *The Aunt's Story*, *The Tree of Man* and *Voss*), and even of the man himself (in my discussion of the importance of White's oedipal relationship to his mother in my essay on White and Rimbaud). It has been said that if Freud is rarely found in the analyst's rooms today, he is everywhere in literary criticism, and he frequently helps to illuminate it.

Odysseus, who in the restlessness and apparently undefined goal of his wandering is fated to quest forever.]

1
A Survey of White's Life and Novels

Patrick White (1912–1990), winner of the Nobel Prize in Literature in 1973, is widely regarded as one of the major writers in English of the twentieth century. He wrote in nearly all the chief literary genres—eight plays, three books of short stories, an autobiography, and two early short books of poems as well as his twelve novels—but it is only in the novel that his reputation is likely to endure. Critical assessment of his work other than in the novel has rarely been enthusiastic, even during his lifetime, when his overwhelming presence, both as a literary giant and as a formidable, domineering figure, made it difficult to scant anything he wrote. The current attitude is that his nonfictional work has to be taken account of insofar as it bears upon his work in the novel, but it attracts few readers other than White specialists. It is his novels that this book is concerned with, for it is within them that his extraordinary talents most fully express themselves and that his main preoccupations are clearest.

Patrick White was born in London in 1912 to Victor ('Dick') and Ruth White, both from pastoralist families in the Hunter Valley area of New South Wales, during their two-year stay in England.[1] He was brought back to Australia as a baby, where a sister, Suzanne, was born in 1915. He was raised as a child in Sydney, his father having essentially sold out his share in the wealthy Belltrees estate near Muswellbrook. His early school-

[1] Beston (1974b), pp. 16–29.

ing was at the hands of governesses and at a prestigious private school; for his high school education he was sent to a boarding school in England. He returned from England to work as a jackeroo first in the Monaro district in southern New South Wales, then out west near Walgett. Life as a pastoralist did not attract him, however, and he persuaded his father to let him return to England to study French and German at Cambridge University. His readings in these languages profoundly influenced his writing—more than his readings in English literature—and largely account for characteristics in his style that some readers find difficult. To those who read those languages fluently, however, his style is an exciting experience very like that of reading French and German, extending the possibilities of English. A.D. Hope's well-known attack upon the style of *The Tree of Man* as 'pretentious and illiterate verbal sludge'[2] comes primarily from his very different ideal of style: Hope writes in a Classical style like that of Alexander Pope, while White writes in a Romantic style like that of Rimbaud.

Settled in London after his graduation from Cambridge, White wrote his first novel, *Happy Valley* (1939), set in the Monaro district in which he had worked as a jackeroo. (Part 2 of *The Twyborn Affair*, forty years later, was also to be set there.) His second novel, *The Living and the Dead*, was largely written while he was in America in 1939 and 1940, trying to get *Happy Valley* published there. The outbreak of World War II forced him to reduce the scope of *The Living and the Dead* (1941), but like its predecessor, it is an apprentice novel, and it is doubtful that it would have become a much livelier work with further revision. Set in London, it has nothing at all of Australia in it. But his experiences in England and continental Europe immediately before and after the war led him ultimately to think of Europe as decadent, even as he had not yet resolved to return to Australia. His feelings towards Europe and Australia at that time are

---

[2] Hope (1956), p. 15.

reflected in parts 2 and 3 of *The Aunt's Story*, in which Theodora Goodman experiences Europe and rejects it before travelling on to America, where she opts for life in a protected mental home rather than return to Australia. The most enduring effect of his experiences of America was his setting part 3 of *The Aunt's Story* in New Mexico; and it was probably there that he read Willa Cather, whose influence is visible in *The Tree of Man*, *The Eye of the Storm*, and *The Twyborn Affair.*[3]

Still in America when the war broke out, White returned to England and enlisted. He was assigned to the intelligence section of the air force and stationed in North Africa and Greece. When the war ended, while he was waiting in Alexandria to be demobilised, he began *The Aunt's Story*, finishing it on his return to Australia in 1946. Published in 1948, *The Aunt's Story* is White's first masterpiece. It is the story of a lonely spinster, Theodora Goodman, so damaged early in life by her destructive mother that she is unable even to begin her quest for a meaningful life of her own until her mother dies. Her journey takes her to France and America, but the real quest takes place in her mind. The central section of the novel, set in the cactus garden of a French hotel, attempts something highly original in the genre of the novel—though not in cinema, for it takes its inspiration in the German silent film, *The Cabinet of Dr Caligari.*[4] *Dr Caligari* deals with bizarre happenings in a German village, happenings that are finally revealed to be the fantasies of a deranged man who is promptly confined to an asylum. Theodora, too, fantasises a series of experiences in which she is centrally involved with the other residents of a French hotel, and at the end of the novel is taken to an asylum in New Mexico. *The Aunt's Story* was too experimental to have attracted a wide Australian audience of the time. White remarked how the condition of library copies of the book indicated that people stopped reading it early

---

[3] Beston (2006b), see chapter 7 in this edition.

[4] Beston (2004c), see p. 116 in chapter 9 in this edition.

in the 'Jardin Exotique' section.[5] Discouraged by the reception of the novel, he abandoned writing for some years, but returned to it in *The Tree of Man*, an archetypal story of a pioneering family inland from Sydney. He laboured mightily over the work, beset by frequent attacks of asthma. A severe asthma attack is a frightening experience, and the condition, normally a lifelong affliction, is depressing—which may help to explain the original title for *The Tree of Man* as 'A Life Sentence upon Earth'. (There are a number of poorly motivated suicides in White's works, too, suggesting periodic depression in the author.) White's efforts with *The Tree of Man* were rewarded when it was heralded as 'a timeless work of art' in the *New York Times* Book Review. *The Tree of Man* (1955) and his following novel, *Voss* (1957), established his reputation as a writer of the first rank. *Riders in the Chariot* (1961) was the fourth in a series of major novels. From 1948 to 1961 White published an unbroken series of great novels, an achievement hardly matched by any other English-language novelist of the latter half of the twentieth century. He was not to produce work of first-rate quality again until twelve years later with two successive novels, *The Eye of the Storm* (1973) and *A Fringe of Leaves* (1976). The intervening novels, *The Solid Mandala* (1966) and *The Vivisector* (1970), are abrasive in mood and deal with generally unattractive characters. This wedge between the four major novels that precede them and the two major novels that follow them constitutes an anomaly; it would seem that the 1960s were a time when White was alienated and alienating.

As a portrait of a creative artist, *The Vivisector* is the most autobiographical of White's novels. It is a long drawn-out depiction of the frustrations of being a creative artist, a series of accusations of himself and others, chiefly people who prostitute themselves to his genius in the hope of owning some of it. It has a central importance in White's work in

---

[5] Marr (1992), p. 258.

its revelations of his tormented attitude to himself and his art. The vivisector of the title is most immediately the main character Hurtle Duffield, who sees with the clarity of a vivisector, a clarity that separates him from the rest of humankind. White extends the concept, however, to the creative artist generally, and it is this representation of the artist that most alienated his readers, to make *The Vivisector* the least popular of his mature novels.

The Vivisector is beset by questions and ambivalence. White pushes beyond the creative artist, who is both vivisector and vivisected, to ask repeatedly, who is the ultimate vivisector? Is it God, who bestowed the creative impulse? Or is it Hurtle's controlling adoptive mother, Mrs Courtney, who drove him further into the refuge of art? Was the ultimate cause, that is, of supernatural or of psychological origin? Did Hurtle's alienation lead to his creativity or did his creativity lead to his alienation?[6] White tended to be weak on causation. He was not much interested in psychological theory, but did read some Jung.[7]

Through the prostitute Nance, White raises the question whether it is possible to be a human being and an artist at the same time: 'You aren't a 'uman being', she accuses Hurtle, to which he retorts, 'I'm an artist' (p. 203). Hurtle has only his art to give significance to his life, but he is largely in rejection even of his art. If the book were merely a self-portrait, it could perhaps be respected for its scarifying honesty. But it demeans creative artists generally, and that was what offended the Nobel committee which was considering White for the Nobel Prize that year.[8]

White took heed of the reprimand from the Nobel Prize committee: his next novel, *The Eye of the Storm,* is one of his finest works and brought him the delayed Nobel Prize. The citation of the Nobel Prize, on

---

[6] Beston (1971a), p. 171.
[7] Marr (1992), p. 452.
[8] Ibid., p. 534.

display now at the State Library of New South Wales, declares that it was awarded to White 'for an epic and psychological narrative art which has introduced a new continent into literature.' No doubt feeling more self-assured, he went on to write his most perfect novel, *A Fringe of Leaves*.

White's last two novels, *The Twyborn Affair* (1979) and *Memoirs of Many in One* (1986), seem from this distance in time to be two weak works enclosing his major novels, bookends to the two apprentice novels, *Happy Valley* and *The Living and the Dead*, with which he began his career. These late works prolonged his literary career, but added little to his stature. Coming at the end of his illustrious career, however, the two novels have received an attention that the early books have not.

The vogue of *The Twyborn Affair* was no doubt helped by the fact that as a novel treating transvestitism and homosexuality, it was taken up by a Sydney which was fast becoming as relentlessly liberal as it had previously been relentlessly illiberal. Ironically, transvestitism and homosexuality are given only superficial treatment in the novel: we never really see into Eddie's mind to understand his sexual identity or behaviour. Here again, as in *The Vivisector*, White is weak in causation. Sex between males occurs off-stage (between Eddie/Eadith and Gravenor's nephew) or is indicated as briefly and coyly as in a 1940s movie (in the rape, if rape it is, of Eddie by Don Prowse and later of Don Prowse by Eddie); the attraction between Eddie/Eadith and Gravenor is never consummated. The aspect of transvestism did not receive any critical attention, but it seems to have a function in part 1, where Eddie/Eudoxia lives as a woman in a sort of marriage to Angelos Vatatzes. Vatatzes is modelled upon Manoly Lascaris, White's Greek lover of nearly forty years;[9] they have, notably, similar Byzantine connections. White is varyingly deferential and dismissive towards the Byzantine connections of

[9] Birns (1999), p. 223.

Vatatzes/Lascaris;[10] and if there is something of White himself in Eddie/Eudoxia, then he likewise flatters himself by making himself young and attractive and mocks himself by highlighting his feminine side, in drag. White's thinly disguised representation here of his relationship with Lascaris, preceding his open acknowledgement of his homosexuality three years later in *Flaws in the Glass*, seems to have provided him with a sort of release valve for his mixed attitudes towards the relationship.

Memoirs of Many in One (1986), White's last novel, is more remarkable as an exercise in game-playing and self-mockery than as a literary endeavour. The fiction in which Patrick is the editor of the memoirs of Alex Xenophon Demirjian Gray, a narrative device previously used by such writers as Jorge Borges and John Barth, has its moments of humour but keeps interrupting the narrative. It is a novel that at once asserts and makes fun of White's literary stature. At the age of seventy-four, unassailably established as the giant of Australian literature but in declining health, White was prone to make fun of himself, a tendency already there in *The Twyborn Affair.*

By nature a private person, White pushed himself to become a political activist in the last twenty years or so of his life. The threat to destroy neighbouring Moore Park and to bulldoze houses in his area in order to create a State Sports Centre drove him in 1972 to appear on TV in protest. In later years, he spoke or marched in support of the Whitlam government, to protest mining on Fraser Island, to campaign against the Fraser government, and to promote nuclear disarmament. If his public appearances and speeches were little more than an irritant to the prevailing government, they do give us a broader sense of the man and his most cherished values: White was more committed to abstract principles than he could ever allow himself to be to people.

---

[10] Riemer (1980), pp. 14–16.

White resists simple classification, even in the matter of his national identity. Although he was born in England, he was brought back as a child of two to Australia and lived here until he was sent to England for his high school and university education. After a brief stint in Australia as a jackeroo, he returned to England to become a writer, visited America, and did his war service in North Africa. He returned to Australia in 1946 and lived here continuously until his death in 1990. Much of his early background, then, and his education in particular, is European. Even as he lived in England, he was immersed in French and German literature, travelling at times to the Continent in pursuance of those interests. Part 2 of *The Aunt's Story* and part 1 of *The Twyborn Affair* are set in France, and the Himmelfarb section of *Riders in the Chariot* is set mainly in Germany. Other novels are set wholly or in part in England: *The Living and the Dead* almost entirely; the parts that deal with Ruth Godbold's early life in *Riders in the Chariot*, Sir Basil's professional life in *The Eye of the Storm*, and Ellen Roxburgh's early life in *A Fringe of Leaves*; and part 3 of *The Twyborn Affair*. Hurtle and Hero visit White's beloved Greece in *The Vivisector*, and Alex Gray visits it as a nun in *Memoirs of Many in One*. The only novels set entirely in Australia are *Happy Valley*, *The Tree of Man*, *Voss*, and *The Solid Mandala*. White's known lovers indeed were from countries other than Australia; culturally, he oriented himself chiefly to Europe. And it is White's non-Australian/Australian identity that has prevented him from ever being fully accepted by Australians.

White's cultural orientation to Europe remained as an overlay in the area of his most enduring commitment to Australia: his desire to raise its cultural level above the mediocrity that he saw there. (It was by no means as mediocre as he asserted, but few critics then dared to contradict White.) He stated his aim to elevate Australian culture in his early essay 'The Prodigal Son' (1958), in association with an account of his writing of *The Tree of Man* and *Voss*. It was an aim that was to continue through to *The Eye of the Storm* and *A Fringe of Leaves*, but he did not find it appropriate to make any further statement to that effect.

It was especially through mythmaking, in both its thematic and stylistic aspects, that White sought to elevate the dignity of his narratives. He does not actually create myths of his own, but takes archetypal stories from ancient and modern times, and infuses them with a high seriousness and formal dignity. To speak of White's mythmaking is to imply both the archetypal nature of the stories that he draws upon and the ways in which he raises those stories to mythic status. He draws upon ancient myths (from the Bible, from ancient Greece, and the Middle Ages) and modern myths (archetypal stories from recent history). Taken from ancient myths, we find Ezekiel's chariot as a central symbol in *Riders in the Chariot*, the *Odyssey* underlying the journey of Theodora in *The Aunt's Story* and of Ellen in *A Fringe of Leaves*, and the medieval story of Tristan and Iseult linking the early romantic dreams of Ellen and their later crude realisation in *A Fringe of Leaves*. It was modern myths, however, stories of the exploration and settlement of Australia, that most engaged White's imagination, leading him to write of a pioneer community from around 1875 to the early 1940s in *The Tree of Man*, of exploration of Australia in the late 1840s in *Voss*, and of an historical shipwreck and a white woman survivor living with an Aboriginal tribe in the mid-1830s in *A Fringe of Leaves*. All these novels are narrated in a highly poetic style in which he makes use of techniques appropriate to myth.

If White's national identity is difficult to classify, how much more are his novels! One can group them by their broad themes, but it is difficult to trace how one novel led to another. Some critics have stressed his historical novels, others his religious novels. None has called him a social satirist, although satire constitutes a large part of his writing.

It is as a historical novelist, in *The Tree of Man*, *Voss*, and *A Fringe of Leaves*, that White most securely established his reputation. Once he returned to Australia in 1946 with the intention of remaining here, Australia and its history were in his blood again. His family, after all, had been in Australia for four generations. *The Tree of Man*, his first novel written in Australia, tells the story of a young couple, the first settlers in a rural area near Sydney. They experience flood, drought and fire as their area acquires a place name, then grows more populated on its way to becoming an outlying suburb of Sydney. The novel ends in the early 1940s, but neither World War II nor the rapid industrialisation of Australia at that time is mentioned: White wanted to keep the illusion of a pre-industrial country. *Voss* is set in the late 1840s, the expedition that it tells of being modelled upon that of Ludwig Leichhardt in 1848; but White was less interested in the story of exploration than in the theme of an over-reacher who, like himself, was bent on moulding Australia according to his own will. The novel reflects both White's own ambition and his fear of that ambition. It was not until after he had been awarded the Nobel Prize that White returned to a historical subject in *A Fringe of Leaves*, set in 1836, some ten or twelve years before the time of *Voss*. It embraces early nineteenth-century Australia more completely than *Voss*, looking at Aboriginal people and at convict life more directly. In *Voss* the only Aboriginal person to receive much attention is the boy Jackie, while Judd's convict days are in the past, alluded to only briefly. In *A Fringe of Leaves* Ellen is fully engaged in the life of the Aboriginal tribe she lives with, and her life with an escaped convict is treated intimately.

If White is not thought of as primarily a historical novelist then he is likely to be considered a religious novelist. From his interview with Craig McGregor in 1969[11] until shortly before his death, in his 'Credo',[12] he continued to state and represent his belief in a deity. Of all his statements of faith, perhaps the main single one is 'I believe that God does intervene.' While religion underlies most of his novels, there are really only three novels in which it has importance as a theme, *The Tree of Man*, *Voss*, and *Riders in the Chariot*—but it is an importance that increases from one

---

[11] White (1989), pp. 19–23.

[12] Ibid., p. 197.

novel to the other. *The Tree of Man* devotes a chapter to a Communion Service in which White examines what the members of the congregation derive from the Sacrament. Stan emerges as the most exalted, preparing us for his epiphany at the end of the novel, the revelation of overarching unity: 'One is the answer to all sums.' The novel is suffused with a sense of destiny, a belief in the role of divine guidance in our lives. *Voss* abounds in explicit references to God and destiny; the major theme, for both Laura Trevelyan and Voss, is that of man returning to God after renouncing his arrogant assumption of Godhood in himself. It is Laura who articulates that theme during her illness: 'How important it is to understand the three stages. Of God into man. Man. And man returning into God' (p. 411). Of all White's novels, *Voss* is the most directly concerned with the question of salvation. *Riders in the Chariot* is his most spiritually embracing work, presenting four visionaries of very different faiths as parallel to the four living creatures who bear the Throne of God in Ezekiel: a Jew recently arrived from Palestine, a pantheist, a Methodist, and an Aboriginal man whose faith is expressed through his art. They all lead solitary lives, connected by fleeting chance encounters but more by their interest in the recurring image of the chariot. Each has a different concept of the chariot, but each understands it as a manifestation of the immanence of God. The most spiritually elevated of the visionaries is Himmelfarb, acknowledged as a *zaddik*, one of thirty-six 'holy men who go secretly about the world, healing, interpreting, doing their good deeds' (p. 173); he is the central figure to whom the other visionaries are drawn. Through Himmelfarb, who arrives in Australia in 1946, relocated from a decadent Europe to a land of new possibilities, White may well have been reliving something of his own return to Australia in that year. Both men found translated there a spiritual dimension that had been assigned to the Old World and the Old Testament. In the newest of New Worlds, in a Sydney suburb, Himmelfarb becomes the Christ figure in the restaging of the Crucifixion and deposition. *Riders* represents White's strongest claim for a spiritual vitality in Australia (even if that is most evident in those who are marginalised), a claim from which he retreated during the next twelve years.

White returned in *The Eye of the Storm* to the subject of salvation, not as a resumption of his interest in it in *Voss*, but because the figure he was portraying, Elizabeth Hunter, was based upon his own mother, to whose eternal fate he could not be indifferent. By no means a saintly character, Elizabeth nonetheless commands respect; she is more than once compared to Stendhal's Sanseverina, the most dazzling figure in the court of Parma. If her soul is the flaw in an emerald, then it is in the nature of emeralds to contain a flaw (pp. 225, 424). That she is saved is clear from her bestowing a transfiguration upon her worthiest acolyte the morning after her death.

There is another interest of White's, however, that recurs more frequently than his historical or religious interests: his fondness for social satire. His satire is witty and trenchant, but it is also frequently mocking and sarcastic, and can be quite inappropriate. Thus the visionary *Riders* ends with a derisive account of three society ladies at a luncheon that is a prolonged exercise in mockery. When the luncheon ends, their social prominence is dismissed with some contempt: 'each of the three tried to remember where she should go next' (p. 545). At times in scenes of Australian society White seems to enjoy humiliating a character, as when he tells in *The Eye of the Storm* how Cherry Cheeseman, an old schoolfriend of Dorothy Hunter's, becomes so drunk at her own party that she falls on her bathroom floor, taking the curtains with her (p. 296). Critics have averted their eyes from this aspect of his work, so that in all the volume of critical writings on White, there is no study of him as a satirist. While it is in these scenes of social satire that White's dramatic gifts find fullest expression, more than in his actual plays, it is here too that his alienation from fellow-feeling is most evident. Australian satire often has a crude and merciless quality to it, evident in its most famous exponent, Barry Humphries, born in 1934 and so younger than White but a product of the same society in those slower-moving times.

If one tries to evaluate White's novels, one is struck by the fact that his best novels are those that are most poetically written: *The Aunt's Story*, *The Tree of Man*, *Voss*, *Riders in the Chariot*, *The Eye of the Storm*, and *A Fringe of Leaves*. And his weakest novels are the most prosaic: the first two apprentice novels, the two mid-career novels, *The Solid Mandala* and *The Vivisector*, finally his last two novels, *The Twyborn Affair* and *Memoirs of Many in One*. As one travels through the poetic landscape of White's work, one finds that the lush abundance of the major novels with their beautiful images, haunting rhythms, and memorable cryptic utterances alternates with the semi-desert terrain of the weaker works. The change in the stylistic landscape is especially noticeable in the two novels written in the 1960s, *The Solid Mandala* and *The Vivisector*, a long, fairly unproductive stretch for White: there is hardly a poetic sentence in either work. In *The Twyborn Affair* White attempts to forge a different style but it betrays a loss of control rather than the opening of new possibilities near the end of his career. He is not infrequently guilty of passages that are overwritten rather than poetic: 'His own languor did not prevent him forcing himself at his discipline of interrogating La Rochefoucauld, the words tasting musty to a furred tongue, the thought rising like baroque remains in a tropic jungle' (p. 136). At times, too, his syntax can be shaky or wrong: 'the road was one with which Mrs Golson was less familiar than most of those which formed the surrounding network' (p. 41). White's last great stylistic achievement and last major work was *A Fringe of Leaves*.

But *Voss* is his masterpiece, containing within itself the qualities that constitute his legacy to Australian literature—or, as he would have it, to Australian culture. It successfully fuses his historical interests and his religious concerns, and in drawing upon Australian myths it comes close to creating a myth of its own. It is written in a sustainedly dignified style, is indeed one of the stylistic masterpieces of the English language, most striking in its sententious or cryptic observations, like 'No official personage has experienced the inferno of love' (p. 469). After the Governor's representative is driven away from the obligatory farewell ceremony for Voss, 'a horse neighed, dropped its fragrant dung, and life was resumed' (p. 122). When Dr Badgery, trying to elicit an indication of interest from Laura, is met with a blunt rejection because of her very hopelessness, we are told that

> Even the dependable Dr Badgery could not have rescued her from that sea, however much she might have wished it. That she did wish, must be recorded, out of respect for her rational judgment and his worthiness. But man is a rational judge only fleetingly, and worthiness is too little, or too much. (p. 349)

Certain passages can thrill through their sheer beauty. As Laura and Belle are clasped in an embrace, watching Voss' ship sail north, 'the light, touching the kumquats on the little bamboo table, turned these into precious stones, the perfection of which gave further cause for hope' (p. 131). At Rose's burial, 'the thin young clergyman was strewing words' upon the grave (p. 251). *Voss* will always be the great Australian novel: it has the scope of a great theme, the passionate intensity, the quintessential Australianness of wanting to control or yield to the country, to be an essential part of it even if after death like Voss or White: 'Whether dreams breed, or the earth responds to a pint of blood, the instant of death does not tell' (p. 419). Taken all in all, we shall not see its like again.

SECTION 2
EUROPEAN AND AMERICAN INFLUENCES ON WHITE

2

THE INFLUENCE OF *MADAME BOVARY* ON *THE TREE OF MAN*[1]

One of the most powerful influences working on Patrick White's early novels, and on *The Tree of Man* in particular, is Flaubert's *Madame Bovary*. White would certainly have read *Madame Bovary* in his studies of modern languages, which he pursued at Cambridge. During an interview with Craig McGregor in 1969, he mentioned re-reading the novel, and exclaimed how impressed he was: 'it really knocked me right over.'[2] Usually one re-reads what one was impressed by on first reading—and *Madame Bovary* is not the kind of novel that one easily forgets. It would have been hard for White to be quite free from the influence of *Madame Bovary* in writing of a frustrated woman driven into a fantasy life, and in fact Emma Bovary lies to an extent behind Vic Moriarty in *Happy Valley* and Theodora Goodman in *The Aunt's Story*. But it is Amy Parker in *The Tree of Man*, who most bears the traces of her distinguished forebear, that I am most concerned with here.

Although I will endeavour to demonstrate that there are discernible links between *Madame Bovary* and *The Tree of Man*, I would not maintain that White was consciously trying to write a twentieth-century

[1] First published in 1972, *Revue de Litterature Comparee*, 46: 555–68.
[2] McGregor (1969), p. 221.

Australian *Madame Bovary.* But beyond the common concept of the dreaming of a frustrated woman, there are some striking parallels in situation and in the makeup of the two heroines that would suggest in White the memory of the French work.

The most remarkable parallel in the two novels is the situation of Emma at the ball at the Château de la Vaubyessard and Amy at the party at Glastonbury. Not only are the two situations parallel, but they are thematically central in both novels. For both heroines it is the high spot in their lives, the threshold that they never cross into a way of life they so much want. When in the ballroom 'madame Bovary tourna la tête et aperçut dans le jardin, contre les carreaux, des faces de paysans qui regardaient',[3] we are reminded of Amy among the gardenias looking in upon the company and Madeleine in particular, who 'robbed the lamp even of its light' (p. 160). The fact that Emma is on the inside looking out and that Amy is on the outside looking in is an appropriate reflection of the social and educational gap that separates them and that determines some of the differences between the two novels. Amy's dreams have to be externalised in the figure of Madeleine, for she cannot centre them around herself as Emma can: they are constantly checked by the isolation and bare realities of her existence. But for Emma and Amy alike entrance into the world they dream of is equally closed. La Vaubyessard and Glastonbury remain permanently in their minds. Emma calls her child Berthe because at the ball she heard the marquis call a young woman Berthe (p. 407),[4] and the image of Madeleine with a rose covering the cleft of her

---

[3] [Madame Bovary turned her head and saw in the garden the peasants' faces against the window-panes looking on]. Flaubert (1951), p. 372. All page references are to this edition and all translations are my own.

[4] Léon suggests the name Madeleine to Emma for her daughter as 'excessivement à la mode maintenant' (p. 406), with strong romantic associations. Madeleine in *The Tree of Man* is the focus for Amy's romantic fantasies. Is this perhaps another instance of White's memory at work?

breasts (p. 161) recurs to Amy as an old woman of about sixty watching *Hamlet*:

> She could see a naked woman, was it ? with a bunch of violets in her breasts ... Then Amy Parker ... began to be certain it was Madeleine. It was the violets that Madeleine had never worn but should have, in the nest of leaves. (pp. 415, 417)

Because the world of la Vaubyessard and Glastonbury means so much to them, neither Emma nor Amy will see reality even when it is in front of them. Emma's eyes, we are told, return again and again, 'comme sur quelque chose d'extraordinaire et d'auguste',[5] to the old Duc de Laverdière, reputed to have been the lover of Marie Antoinette:

> Il avait mené une vie bruyante de débauches, pleine de duels, de paris, de femmes enlevées, avait dévoré sa fortune et effrayé toute sa famille. (p. 369)[6]

Now he eats 'courbé sur son assiette remplie et la serviette nouée dans le dos comme un enfant',[7] letting drops of sauce fall from his mouth. A servant shouts into his ear the names of the various dishes that the Duc points to stammering, but for Emma it is important only that 'Il avait vécu à la Cour et couché dans le lit des reines' (p. 370).[8] Amy's celebrations at Glastonbury are confined to a glass of wine in the kitchen—the first that she has ever drunk. Like Emma with the Duc, she is intoxicated with Madeleine, ignoring Mrs Frisby's hints that all is not well with Madeleine: 'She's out of tune. It's all in the eye with Madeleine' (p. 164). Mrs Frisby assures Amy that she will not miss anything by never speaking

---

[5] [as on something extraordinary, something awe-inspiring].

[6] [He had led a riotous life of debauchery, filled with duels, gambling, women abducted; he had devoured his fortune and alarmed his whole family].

[7] [bent over his heaping plate with his serviette tied around his neck like a child].

[8] [He had lived at Court and slept in the bed of queens].

to Madeleine, an unwelcome reminder of reality that no doubt plays its part in Amy's consequent rejection of Mrs Frisby's gift of corned beef:

> Amy Parker ... threw the parcel of cold corned beef into some bushes near the front gate. (p. 165)

The world of reality was unattractive to Emma too: on her return home she angrily dismissed Charles' old servant for being late with the dinner and for answering back. Amy does not wilfully hurt anyone, only herself. Constantly we are faced with the difference in viewpoint, that White does not alienate us from his heroine as Flaubert does from his.

With the private world of la Vaubyessard and Glastonbury closed to them, Emma and Amy find in the public gaiety of Rouen and Sydney an occasion for dreams. The trip that the Parkers make to Sydney is remarkably similar to that of the Bovarys to Rouen, and again suggests memory at work in White. In the city, both Emma and Amy see a theatrical performance in which they find a relevance to their own lives. Emma finds that the opera, *Lucie de Lammermoor*, 'ne lui semblait être que ... quelque chose même de sa vie' (p. 530).[9] When she watches Lucie approach her wedding pale and fainting, she recalls her own wedding, but with considerable distortion:

> Pourquoi donc n'avait-elle pas, comme celle-là, résisté, supplié? Elle était joyeuse, au contraire, sans s'apercevoir de l'abîme où elle se précipitait ... Ah! si, dans la fraîcheur de sa beauté, avant les souillures du mariage et la désillusion de l'adultère, elle avait pu placer sa vie sur quelque grand cœur solide, alors la vertu, la tendresse, les voluptés et le devoir se confondant, jamais elle ne serait descendue d'une félicité si haute. (p. 531)[10]

---

[9] [just seemed to her something out of her own life].

[10] [Why hadn't she resisted or begged like that woman? She'd been content instead with no idea of the abyss to which she was rushing. Oh, if only in the first glow of her beauty before she experienced the imperfections of marriage and the disillu-

Amy watching *Hamlet* is likewise troubled by thoughts of what marriage has failed to give her. She too has been through 'la désillusion de l'adultère': 'That man, that bugger. And acting as if you did not want it' (p. 419). The resignation she appears to have attained is suddenly seen as a desperate attempt to fill her emptiness:

> Well, you got over it ... There is a time when you do not want anything ... Or ... a time when you want everything and do not know what this is. I want Stan, I want Ray, said the queen, and I am not sure that I have had anything, that I know to have.

Although the situation of the heroine watching a theatrical performance during her one visit to a city with her husband is a conspicuous parallel in the two novels, the external similarity highlights a fundamental difference in White's outlook from that of Flaubert, a difference that keeps recurring and that illuminates White's aims in writing *The Tree of Man*. He is as surely inviting sympathy for Amy in her need for love as Flaubert is discouraging sympathy for Emma in hers. We respond to Amy's misery as she stirs in the theatre 'for the closeness of her husband in the dark' (p. 419), the darkness of life itself, but we are deterred by Emma's utter self-concern in her fantasies about the tenor who sings the role of Edgar. In these fantasies, Emma sees herself as the adored rather than the adoring one:

> Avec lui, par tous les royaumes de l'Europe, elle aurait voyagé de capital en capital, partageant ses fatigues et son orgueil, ramassant les fleurs qu'on lui jetait, brodant elle-même ses costumes; puis chaque soir, au fond d'une loge, derrière la grille à treillis

---

sionment of adultery, she'd been able to entrust her life to some great noble heart! Then as virtue and tenderness and sensual delights and duty mingled with one another, she would never have fallen from such a height of happiness.]

d'or, elle eût recueilli, béante, les expansions de cette âme qui n'aurait chanté que pour elle seule. (p. 532)[11]

Emma's concept of a lover is unrealistic, for there never was or will be such a man; and she spurns love where it is most available, from Charles. Amy's love, we are told (told rather than convincingly shown), is devouring;[12] it is disastrous that she is married to a man so afraid of emotion. White sympathises with her in that she seeks a love she has never had in her life; but at the same time he sees her search for love as threateningly greedy. Many readers will find her quest for love understandable, however, and her expectations from love reasonable. At any rate, if White's picture of Amy is ambiguous and ambivalent, Flaubert's portrait of Emma is decidedly unattractive.

There is another parallel situation that is important in both novels: Emma's reception of Extreme Unction before her death and Amy's attendance at the Communion Service with Stan. Both scenes come near the end of the novel, and highlight the heroine's basic search in life. Emma's kissing the crucifix 'de toute sa force expirante' with 'le plus grand baiser

---

[11] [Together with him throughout all the kingdoms of Europe she would have travelled from capital to capital, sharing his fatigues and his successes, picking up the flowers that were thrown to him, embroidering his costumes herself; then every evening at the back of her box in the theatre, behind the golden trellis, she would have breathed in with open mouth the expansions of that soul that would have sung for her alone.]

[12] Amy is described early as 'rather greedy for bread, and, once discovered, for [Stan's] love' (p. 27). Forgetting this remark, White repeats 100 pages later, 'By this time Amy Parker had grown greedy for love. She had not succeeded in eating her husband' (p. 126). The strange incident of the boy that they adopt and lose during the floods in chapter 7 is probably meant to reflect on the devouring quality of her love. But since she is not shown as doing anything more than giving him kindly reassurance, the incident does not provide evidence of her love as overbearing.

d'amour qu'elle eût jamais donné' (pp. 621–22)[13] reminds us that her whole life has been a search for

> un être fort et beau, une nature valeureuse, pleine à la fois d'exaltation et de raffinements, un cœur de poète sous une forme d'ange. (p. 584)[14]

This is Emma's third affair with religion, following her convent days and her recovery after Rodolphe's abandonment of her. We are aware that God is only another lover to Emma; indeed after her affair with Rodolphe, when she prays, 'elle adressait au Seigneur les mêmes paroles de suavité qu'elle murmurait jadis à son amant, dans les épanchements de l'adultère' (p. 522).[15] Had Emma recovered from the poison, her third affair with religion would not have lasted; directly after she has kissed the crucifix and been anointed, she asks for a mirror and weeps at the sight of herself. The scene reminds us that Emma's search for the great lover is bound to be unsuccessful, for her dreams are wholly unrealistic; perhaps God as an abstract notion has the best chance of meeting her expectations but even 'les meilleurs baisers',[16] like that she bestowed upon the crucifix 'ne vous laissaient sur la lèvre qu'une irréalisable envie d'une volupté plus haute' (p. 584).[17]

In the Communion Service in *The Tree of Man*, we see Amy in the last of her lifelong attempts to get close to someone. During Leo's third visit, she had been driven to realise 'that she was not to come closer to this man … or perhaps to anyone. Each one was wrapped in his mystery' (p.

---

[13] [with all her dying strength] ; [the greatest kiss of love she had ever given].

[14] [a strong and fine being, a valorous nature full at once of ardour and refinement, the heart of a poet within the form of an angel.]

[15] [she addressed to the Lord the same sweet words that she had murmured to her lover in the outpourings of adultery].

[16] [the most ardent kisses].

[17] [only left upon your lips the unattainable desire of a greater pleasure.]

329). At the Communion Service, however, she makes her last attempt to get close to Stan by entering into his world of religion. Stan has always shut Amy out; despite his deep wish to open himself to others, he cannot do so. Amy in response lives out a confused and resentful life. As she drinks the Communion wine she thinks of the wine that poisoned Gertrude in Hamlet:

> They poisoned the queen, who had had her conscience as well, working in her for some time. The wine worked. I have hated, said the old woman. Do I love or hate? She was confused … It was the wine.[18] It is Stan, she said, again with love or hatred, ah, look at me, Stan, but he cannot of course, now. Then she realised it was finally between herself and God, and that it was quite possible she would never succeed in opening her husband and looking inside. (pp. 431–32)

Her train of thinking suggests that she regards Stan as having poisoned her life: 'Now she went grumbling … He has made me like this, she said' (p. 429). And although White defends Stan with a partial disclaimer, that Amy 'liked to blame other people for herself', she is not entirely in the wrong of it, for she is married to a man who cannot open himself to love. Shut out by Stan against his own conscious wish, Amy is a more sympathetic figure than Emma, who contemptuously shuts out the loving Charles.

In one chief aspect of their makeup, Emma and Amy strongly resemble one another: their hope of an outside event that will fill their lives for them. In Emma the hope amounts almost to a belief that she has a right to have her problems taken magically away and her life made supremely happy. She is accordingly either sullenly resentful or violently angry when

---

[18] Here Amy seems to be recalling Gertrude's dying words, 'the drink,—O my dear Hamlet! The drink, the drink; I am poison'd.'

her expectations are disappointed. Early in the novel, after her return from La Vaubyessard, she

> attendait un événement. Comme les matelots en détresse, elle promenait sur la solitude de sa vie des yeux désespérés, cherchant au loin quelque voile blanche dans les brumes de l'horizon. Elle ne savait pas quel serait ce hazard. ... chargé d'angoisses ou plein de félicités ... Mais, chaque matin, à son réveil, elle l'espérait pour la journée ... puis, au coucher du soleil toujours plus triste, désirait être au lendemain. (p. 382)[19]

Disappointed, she abandons her interest in things that had given her pleasure—reading, sewing and embroidery, sketching, and the piano: 'A quoi bon? A quoi bon? ... Et elle restait à faire rougir les pincettes, ou regardant la pluie tomber' (p. 383).[20] Towards the end of the novel, with ruin hovering over her, she still maintains her hope that an outside event will save her:

> Advienne que pourra! se disait-elle. Et puis, qui sait? pourquoi, d'un moment à l'autre, ne surgirait-il pas un événement extraordinaire? Lheureux même pouvait mourir. (p. 599)[21]

When she herself takes a course of action, as when she visits Léon and Rodolphe to ask for money, it is with the wholly unreasonable expecta-

---

[19] [was waiting for something to happen. Like sailors in distress, she would cast desperate eyes upon the loneliness of her life, seeking in the distance some white sail or other in the mists of the horizon. She did not know what this chance would be ... whether charged with anguish or full of happiness ... But every morning when she woke up she hoped it would be that day ... then at sunset, each one sadder than the one before, she wanted it to be the next day.]

[20] [What's the use? What's the use? ... And she kept heating the curling-irons or looking at the rain falling.]

[21] [Come what may! she said to herself. Besides, who knows, why couldn't some extraordinary event happen from one moment to the next? Lheureux could even die.]

tion that they will remove from her responsibility for her own actions. Although she tells them what she would do in their place (pp. 596, 610), she does not do it herself. Necessarily disappointed in her expectations, she reacts with a violent hatred of men, as if they were to blame for her ruin: 'Elle aurait voulu battre les hommes, leur cracher au visage, les broyer tous'. (p. 603)[22]

Amy too is filled with 'a private yearning for ... immeasurable events' (p. 49). With her the hope 'If something were to happen' is an indication of the sadness and emptiness of her life. It lacks the petulant quality that accompanies Emma's expectations. In Emma the expectation of 'un événement extraordinaire' fosters unreasonable demands of life and of men; in Amy the hope that something might happen produces a quiet, ingrown unhappiness, for she can never quite believe in her own hope or quite let it go. Constantly she represses the allure of her dreams with a disapproval of them as silly, and immerses herself in the practical details of work; in that way, she achieves enough balance to endure her life. One senses a bravery in Amy that Emma lacks: Emma dreams wildly in spite of reality, whereas Amy tries to check her dreams because she knows the reality. One incident in particular shows Amy first dreaming and then resorting to her characteristic defenses when disappointed: walking with Stan one night, she begins to move close to him, feeling that

> He should, by rights, have been chained by her power of soft darkness. But tonight he was not. It might have been hard daylight in which they walked. So she said, in a voice that blamed him for it, 'I am going in, Stan. We can't walk about like lunatics all night. There are things to do.' (p.149)

She does feel spasms of resentment against Stan's inability to match her dreams, but her resentment is mild compared to Emma's brutal con-

[22] [She would have liked to beat men, to spit on their faces, to crush them all.]

tempt of Charles and anger against men generally.[23] Amy is more prone to vague hope than to brutality:

> Then great sadness invaded the house, or was it just the silence that she was listening to ... If something were to happen—what, she did not dare to think—would she conduct herself with delicacy, or that brutality that sometimes threatened her? ... Or a letter would arrive ... Stan is waiting for me, said the heavy woman ... She went out then without any further thought or silliness, though looking about, in case somebody might come, asking for directions, or to tell some news. (pp. 301–02)

Silly or not, her dreams persist. When her brief extramarital affair with Leo ends, she is left lonely and discouraged, inclined to abandon her search for a fuller emotional life:

> Whatever is to happen now will happen in spite of me, she realised ... Then she ... gave way to her own solitariness. (p. 330)

During the remainder of the novel,

> What she did expect, in fact, was that some enlightenment would come from without. But it did not. (p. 342)

---

[23] There is a major difference between Emma's attitude to Charles expressed after his unsuccessful operation on Hippolyte and Amy's to Stan expressed to Mrs Fisher during her visit. Emma 'ne partageait pas son humiliation, elle en éprouvait une autre: c'était de s'être imaginé qu'un pareil homme pût valoir quelque chose' [did not share his humiliation but felt another one, from having imagined that a man like that could have been worth anything], pp. 494–95. When Charles turns to her for comfort she rejects him furiously: 'Laisse-moi! fit-elle, toute rouge de colère.' ['Leave me alone!' she said, quite red with anger.]
Amy's resentment against Stan is not contemptuous, and is allowed only indirect expression. When she complains to Mrs Fisher about Stan's habit of lighting fires, she is really complaining about his (and Leo's) having lit the fire of sexual passion in her only to leave her unsatisfied: 'it is a habit of most men, I think, to stand around a fire and look into it, once they have got it going', p. 449.

As an old woman, about to attend the Communion Service with Stan, she is still expecting salvation from without:

> She would have been ashamed to admit she was looking for miracles, like some young girls. (p. 426)

The heroine's waiting for an extraordinary event is rarely so explicit and so pervasive as in *Madame Bovary* and *The Tree of Man*. This does suggest the influence of one novel on the other, but again also significant is the difference between Emma and Amy within a similar framework. Emma strikes us as hard and demanding, Amy as sad but struggling.

In addition to parallel situations that are thematically important in the two novels, there are correspondences in name and incident that are thematically unimportant but that strongly reinforce the impression of the memory of *Madame Bovary* influencing White during his composition of *The Tree of Man*. The names Emma and Amy show some degree of correspondence, as do those of their lovers, Léon and Leo. Leo further appears to acquire aspects of Lheureux, the merchant who brings various articles to Emma's house on his first visit there. Leo also brings a range of dress materials to Amy (though as far as the story is concerned he could equally well have brought kitchenware). It is interesting that when Leo shows her his materials, he points out that they are French. Like Lheureux, Leo is a calm salesman: the one enjoins 'mais rien ne presse, quand vous voudrez' (pp. 419–20),[24] while the other invites 'But take your time, lady. Have a look … We've got all day' (p. 307). Neither Emma nor Amy, however, buys anything on this occasion, the one refusing with 'Je n'ai besoin de rien',[25] the other with 'I am sorry. I have everything. There is nothing I want.'

Similarities between the two novels do suggest themselves, then. But what in the first place would have awakened in White the memory of

---

[24] [but there's no hurry, whenever you want].

[25] [I don't need anything].

Madame Bovary to influence him? Most immediately, the situation of a frustrated woman driven to a fantasy life fascinated White between *Happy Valley* and *The Tree of Man*—and the depiction of fantasy is his forte. But Flaubert and he were interested in that theme because of something more basic, the kinship in their personalities. Both novelists are incurable dreamers, their lives dedicated to the consciously controlled dreaming of literary creation. At the same time they do not feel convinced of the ability of dreaming, of fantasy, to deal with the realities of life. Their novels reveal considerable ambivalence in their attitudes towards dreaming. On the one hand they fear the allure of dreaming as almost irresistible in the temptation it offers them to sink themselves in it and become absorbed. On the other hand neither Flaubert nor White goes so far as to show the dreaming as actually destructive: neither Emma nor Amy is ruined by dreaming. If dreaming threatens one with self-annihilation, they are saying, it need not actually be destructive.

Flaubert, remarks Martin Turnell, 'attempted a dispassionate analysis of the Romantic malady in the unconscious hope of curing himself of its ravages.'[26] White sees dreaming as potentially culminating in a desire for annihilation of one's life in the ordinary world. Amy's most extravagant fantasy is of offering her throat in abandonment to the knife of the Romantic Lover (p. 108). If Emma Bovary represents much of Flaubert, as he is reported to have said, perhaps Amy Parker represents much of White.[27] Because both writers are so strongly attracted to dreaming, they shield themselves from it defensively, presenting it in an unfavourable light. The figures that Emma and Amy build their dreams upon are

---

[26] See Turnell (1950), p. 259. Levin (1963), also writes of 'the latent romanticist which Flaubert had suppressed', p. 248.

[27] To Craig McGregor, White confessed 'Of course, all artists are terrible egoists. Unconsciously you are largely writing about yourself. I could never write anything factual; I only have confidence in myself when I am another character. All the characters in my book are myself, but they are a kind of disguise', p. 221.

shown by Flaubert and White as failing the dreamer. Rodolphe and Léon fail Emma, partly because they are weak, but largely too because her expectations of them are unrealistic.[28] Madeleine and Leo fall far short of Amy's dreams because of the kind of people they are, the one shallow ('it's all in the eye with Madeleine'), the other 'flash' and physically unattractive. White himself gives an extra twist to the knives he thrusts into Madeleine and Leo by suggesting that they both come to an inglorious end: there are suggestions that Leo's stomach trouble may be cancerous, and Madeleine's death is barely recorded because she is not important enough to anyone.

Despite the dangerous allure of dreams, neither Flaubert nor White quite sees them as destructive. It is not Emma's dreams but her debts that bring about her ruin, and her extravagance is not integrally related to her dreaming. Her dreams, though unrealistic, do at least give her a certain refinement: one recalls how, at the opera in Rouen, 'elle se cambra la taille avec une désinvolture de duchesse' (p. 528).[29] Amy is not destroyed in any case, but survives to the end. White is even more disposed than Flaubert to see a positive function in his heroine's dreams: without them her life is empty. Amy's tragedy is not that her dreams prevent her from coming to grips with reality but that they do not enable her to transcend reality. The Communion Service which she attends near the end of the novel focuses her feeling of failure when the Communion wine which should have afforded her an entrance into the intoxicating world of the spirit turns instead into the wine that poisoned Gertrude in *Hamlet:* 'The crimson

---

[28] Emma must have expected Léon to marry; he does not betray her. Rodolphe was weak in not rejecting at the outset Emma's unrealistic request to take her and Berthe away. But he is generous enough: Flaubert tells us that he would have given Emma the money she asked for if he had it, 'bien qu'il soit généralement désagréable de faire de si belles actions' [although it's generally unpleasant to make such fine gestures], p. 609.

[29] [she arched her back with the elegance of a Duchess].

wine sounded and looked intolerable as it was flowing through her' (p. 432). Part of the kinship in personality that would have drawn White to Flaubert, too, lies in certain misanthropic tendencies that they share. These tendencies are not nearly so marked in White as in Flaubert, but they do recur throughout his writing. During his career, White has first followed Flaubert in his dislike of people (in *Happy Valley* and *The Living and the Dead),* then largely rejected misanthropy in his greatest works *(The Aunt's Story* through *Riders in the Chariot)* only to return to it in his works of the 1960s, culminating in his alienated *The Vivisector.*[30] But even his works from *The Aunt's Story* to *Riders in the Chariot* are not totally free from misanthropic traits: there is a constant tension in them between compassion and misanthropy. In *The Tree of Man,* for instance, White shows compassion for Stan and Amy; the distaste that he feels for people in general is transferred away from them to the Forsdykes, to whom he takes an unaccountably strong dislike. If we hesitate to accept White's prejudice against them, they emerge on purely factual evidence as harmless enough people, no worse than many of us. A brief survey here of White's development up to *The Tree of Man* will make clearer the tension in him between compassion and misanthropy and give a more definite place to *The Tree of Man* in his thinking. To some degree, the shadow of Flaubert hangs over all these early novels, but most of all over *The Tree of Man.*

White's first novel, *Happy Valley,* already has an Emma figure in the vain Vic Moriarty. Like Emma, she is filled with romantic longings, hates the *mœurs de campagne*, is involved in an extramarital affair, and runs up heavy debts. The portrait of Vic is an unsympathetic and an uncomplex one; the fact that she is killed by her husband may indicate something of White's own feelings towards her. He is at this stage a follower of Flaubert rather than a creator of an Emma Bovary in his own mould. The charac-

---

[30] White's alienation is the subject Beston (1971a).

ters in *The Living and the Dead,* with the exception of Connie Tiarks, are not attractive. But in *The Aunt's Story* and *The Tree of Man,* White presents portraits of dreamers that are both fuller and more compassionate than we find elsewhere in his writings. Since *Happy Valley* on the one hand and *The Tree of Man* on the other are both under the influence of *Madame Bovary,* what would account for the more sympathetic portrait of Amy Parker? There are, I think, a number of factors at work:

First, the portrait of Vic is only lightly sketched, not far removed from caricature, whereas in *The Aunt's Story* and *The Tree of Man* White is writing at the peak of his powers. It would seem that the confidence born of his sense of control plays a part in softening his attitude towards Theodora and Amy.

Second, in his portraits of Theodora and Amy, White deals with an area that Flaubert had hardly looked at: the reasons why certain people turn to a life of dreams. What motivation Flaubert provides for Emma's dreaming is hardly adequate: he shows it as a result of her reading, her convent training, her marriage to a man like Charles, and—vaguest of all—of something within her own makeup. White shows the causes of Theodora and Amy's retreat into a silent but active dream life with considerable penetration, and along with his understanding of the reasons for their dreaming comes compassion for their suffering. White's ability to motivate the dreaming of his characters is an area in which he surpasses Flaubert.

Third, White seems to have wanted after his first two novels to check the propensities within himself towards alienation, an alienation which is so marked in Flaubert. The excesses of *Madame Bovary* are softened in *The Tree of Man.* After his initial attraction to the kind of negativism that we find in Flaubert White seems to have turned from it as offering few possibilities of growth.[31] After the series of frustrated dreamers in *Happy Valley* and the unhappy characters in *The Living and the Dead,* White portrays in *The Aunt's Story* and *The Tree of Man* central characters who invite sympathy, if not positive affection.

Fourth, White seems to have balked at showing dreaming quite as unsympathetically as Flaubert had presented it and as he himself showed it in Vic Moriarty. Beginning with *The Aunt's Story,* White is increasingly inclined to see dreaming as serving a positive purpose in a life that is otherwise isolated and empty.[32] Neither Theodora's nor Amy's dreams are destructive, the damage that was wrought upon them having taken place before their entry into a fantasy world. Theodora's dreams provide her with an alternative existence to a shattered life, and Amy's do help to fill her emptiness.

Ultimately, the chief complaint of both Flaubert and White would be not with dreaming but with life itself. Both *Madame Bovary* and *The Tree of Man* are expressions of a view of life as frustrating: since life is so empty, one must dream. The emptiness of life for Emma and Amy is connected with lovelessness and the difficulty in communication, of loving and being loved. Both novelists set their dreamers in an environ-

---

[31] A misanthropic vision does limit a work's greatness, as a number of critics point out in their assessment of Flaubert. Thus Bart (1966) maintains that 'the really great books of the western tradition counsel the understanding of life and urge terms in which it may be accepted. They go beyond the bitter taste of irony to some form of love', p. 197. And Martin Turnell (1950) charges that Flaubert's 'preoccupation with the negative states almost certainly reflects his own inability to penetrate deeply into the content of experience', p. 263. Tillet (1961) is most reasonable when she asserts that 'The major flaw in Flaubert's work is undoubtedly that he produces not one wholly likeable character; and no amount of explanation can alter the fact that this is a weakness in a novelist', pp. 127–28.

[32] To White, the highest form of dreaming that can give significance to an empty life is the dreaming that expresses itself in artistic creation. This is a theme in his novel *The Vivisector.*

ment that reflects, though it does not cause, their isolation. For Emma the town of Yonville is slightly more congenial than the village of Tostes, but it is doubtful that she would have been much happier in Paris (indeed, we are told that she would have liked simultaneously to die and to live in Paris, an indication of an unresolved conflict within herself). White's dreamers are especially isolated. *The Tree of Man* is set in a remote area around Sydney, initially without even a place name. The lives of the Parkers barely touch those of others. In this respect, the characters of *The Tree of Man* are still more isolated than those of *Happy Valley* and *The Aunt's Story*. *Happy Valley*, though a small community, resembles Yonville rather than Tostes in that the lives of the characters there interweave, and *The Aunt's Story* shifts from Meroë to Sydney to France and then to the U.S. Unlike the Bovarys, who each have one parent surviving, Stan and Amy are without parents. They begin and end their married life in *The Tree of Man* alone.

What do we learn then about White's aims and his thinking in *The Tree of Man* from looking at it in its relationship to *Madame Bovary*?

For all the similarities between the two novels, White's starting point is different from Flaubert's. White is interested in 'burnt ones', unhappy people leading lonely, isolated lives. When in their unhappiness they enter a dream world then they resemble Emma Bovary. But Amy's dreaming is more precisely motivated and from different reasons than Emma's. Primarily she dreams from a sense of deprivation, of having missed out on something in life without being quite sure what it was, a feeling 'that some mystery was withheld from her' (p. 326). Flaubert partly blames Emma's reading for her extravagant dreams: he uses her to attack the literary tradition that feeds her dreams. But it is not possible to accept Flaubert's motivation as adequate: reading may reinforce preexisting personality traits but does not cause them. Amy's dreaming also takes a different course from Emma's. Emma's dreams take love for granted; she is even the inspiration of the love she receives. Amy's dreams can hardly aspire to the concept of herself as loved. They are directed to the attainment of her substitute for love, the getting close to someone, whether Madeleine (in her fantasy conveyed to Mrs Frisby, pp. 163–64), Con the Greek, Leo, or Stan. In motivating Amy's dreaming, and integrating it within her total personality, White makes her a softer and sadder character than Emma.

Amy is softer in a number of ways. For one thing, she is a timid dreamer, as befits her deprivation:

> she wondered what kind of children she would have made with the Greek. But her courage did not dare pursue this road very far. (p. 236)

Her dreams are restricted, especially in comparison to Emma's. Amy is unusually deprived; she is even orphaned earlier than Stan. She has nothing to build dreams upon, whether love, education, social rank, or religious faith. At the time of her meeting Stan, 'Amy had not yet been loved' and 'had not yet felt affection for any human being' (p. 16). The world of fantasy opened by education is closed to her; Emma on the other hand had had a convent education and read avidly. Amy has read only the Bible and four unnamed books (p. 32). Amy's Bible and Emma's *Paul et Virginie* stand as symbols of the gap that separates the two heroines. Even Amy's religion, evidently an evangelical one stemming from nineteenth-century England, is bare compared to Emma's—contrast the severe Communion Service of *The Tree of Man* (pp. 426–33) with Emma's reception of Communion after Rodolphe's abandonment of her (p. 520).

Amy even wins our sympathy more than White may perhaps have intended. Although he speaks early of Stan's love for her and her love for Stan, we see little persuasive evidence of love; and he continues to speak of their love long after it has clearly deteriorated to a stage, for instance, where 'Habit comforted them, like warm drinks and slippers, and even went disguised as love' (p. 342). Never having experienced love before marriage, Amy knows little of it within marriage or the raising of children: Ray is hostile and Thelma thin-souled. Emma was loved by Charles and by her lovers. She is hard in her attitude to Charles, and predictably invites rejection by her lovers because of her demands, thereby deflecting our sympathy. Flaubert never presented love or marriage favourably, and has no likeable character in his works. White portrays at least one attractive character, Doll Quigley, in *The Tree of Man*, and he softens still further in the novel that follows *The Tree of Man, Voss:* there we find a number of attractive characters, and two quite successful marriages, those of the Sandersons and the Bonners. Finally White is not so negative, not so unqualifiedly misanthropic as Flaubert. There are likeable characters in his works, and sympathetic characters. Neither Flaubert nor White seems to have accepted himself personally or humankind at large,[33] and so each found his chief satisfaction in his art.[34] Flaubert has so renounced the possibility of love as to abandon cynically any search for it, but one always feels that White, though not strongly hopeful, is still-searching sadly for love.

This study of *The Tree of Man* in relation to *Madame Bovary* shifts the emphasis in the novel away from Stan to Amy, where I feel it properly belongs. Some previous studies, like J.F. Burrows' article on Stan Parker's *Tree of Man* or Brian Kiernan's essay on White in *Images of Society and*

---

[33] Bart (1966) points out that 'It is Flaubert's reiterated contention in his letters that life is hateful, farcical, grotesque; that it consists of ignominy and stupidity', p. 196. Such a view of life goes hand in hand with self-hatred. And White's self-vindication to McGregor (1969) is less than convincing: 'I wouldn't call myself a humanist: I am indifferent to people in general. But I have always been gregarious. This myth that I'm not has been put about by bitches that I wouldn't have in my house [sic!]. I'm not isolated.' White (1989), pp. 22–23.

[34] Bart (1966) quotes Flaubert, 'through all the hideousness of existence, we must always contemplate the great blue vault of poetry', p. 196. Hurtle Duffield, thought by many to be a voice for White, says in *The Vivisector*, 'I believe … in art … I have my painting.', p. 474.

Nature,[35] have concentrated upon Stan. Stan is less a dreamer than Amy, being too repressed to dream, and because of his repression cannot well carry the burden of central significance.

The kinship that emerges in the personality of Flaubert and White helps to explain the blackness of the novels that follow his three masterpieces. Without the support of a powerful creative impulse and a strong sense of control, White has not resisted well the pull of a Flaubert-like misanthropy in the works that follow *Voss*.

Most important, this study provides one focus for *The Tree of Man*. As with most of White's novels, it is hard to say exactly what *The Tree of Man* is about; but when it is seen alongside *Madame Bovary* it appears as a step in White's search for a life value not in experience but within the imagination. Like its predecessors and successors, *The Tree of Man* deals with the attempt to find meaning in a life which is already pretty badly burnt. If White endeavoured to write a 'universal novel', as his early language indicates when he speaks of 'the man' and 'the woman', and as his introduction of drought, fire and flood also suggests, he departed early from this attempt and wrote instead a Flaubert-like novel about a frustrated woman driven to a life within the imagination.

---

35 Burrows (1969). Kiernan (1971) discusses *The Tree of Man* on pp. 97–113 of his book.

3
PATRICK WHITE AND RIMBAUD[1]

Patrick White acknowledged, 'I am, indeed, soaked in Rimbaud, and it could well be that that comes out'.[2] It was no doubt during his study of French and German at Cambridge University in the early 1930s that he became familiar with Rimbaud, who was to be a strong influence on his themes and style from *The Tree of Man* in 1955 through *The Eye of the Storm* in 1973, the year in which he received the Nobel Prize in Literature. There are five poems in his novels which show Rimbaud's influence, one in *The Tree of Man* (1955), three in *Voss* (1957), and one in *The Eye of the Storm* (1973). They are the poem that Stan's grandson envisions on the last page of *The Tree of Man* (p. 499), Le Mesurier's two companion poems 'Childhood' and 'Conclusion' in *Voss* (pp. 313–17), Voss' song as he leaves Jildra (pp. 202–03), and Lottie Lippmann's song as she dances for Elizabeth Hunter in *The Eye of the Storm* (pp. 444–46); the last two are in German.[3] It is unfortunate that these poems have not attracted critical attention in the fifty or so years that have passed since the publication of *The Tree of Man* and *Voss,* for they provide the best

[1] First published in 2005, *Commonwealth*, 27(2): 99–110.

[2] Marr (1994), p. 217.

[3] I have corrected an error in German in Voss' song, however ('der edler Rock' should read 'der edle Rock'), and another in Lottie Lippmann's song ('Manage' in the first line should read 'Manege').

insight into the nature and extent of Rimbaud's influence. Although White's poems show Rimbaud influence stylistically, what is of prime importance, and the subject of this article, is the fact that these poems—the only ones in White's novels—are linked thematically to Rimbaud and to one another.

White's repetition of themes in these poems means that they have special significance to him, and they do indeed reveal a good deal about Patrick White the artist while bringing into focus certain themes in his novels that would else be less clear. The main idea running through the poems is the child's sense of manipulation by his mother, and his need to escape by resorting to the life of his imagination—the child being a projection of the young Patrick White. And that is a main theme also in Rimbaud: the escaping of a constrictive mother by fleeing into the imagination. It is the principal theme of his early 'Les Poètes de Sept Ans' and recurs in later poems like 'Mémoire'. Writing was for both Rimbaud and White an assertion of their freedom and independence.

A second important theme in White's poems also has its counterpart in Rimbaud. Running alongside the theme of flight into the imagination and following on from it is the notion of the proneness of the imagination to run out of control into areas from which one has to retreat in failure and frustration. Even in White's first poem, the one growing within the mind of Stan's grandson, the boy becomes increasingly excited as his fantasies grow until he suddenly becomes afraid of their power to take over his mind and abandons them in frustration. The same process takes place in Rimbaud's mind in 'Les Poètes de Sept Ans' and the virtual continuation of that poem in 'Le Bateau Ivre'. In the early poem he flees into the imagination from his authoritarian mother, and in 'Le Bateau Ivre' he allows his imagination free licence as the boat sails down the river, perhaps the Mississippi, to the open sea (neither of which he had ever seen). There his bravado gives way to fear as he is overwhelmed by strange new experiences, and he retreats, defeated, to the childhood memory of sailing a paper boat in a cold, dark puddle.

White's poems, like Rimbaud's, are characterised by disjunctions in thought and feeling, and these disjunctions offer him a camouflage for the expression of the themes I have been discussing. The two poems in German have the same kind of discontinuities as those in English, with the added camouflage of the foreign language. Few readers of White in the Australia of 1957, when *Voss* appeared, or of 1973, when *The Eye of the Storm* appeared, would have read German. The fact that discontinuities exist in all the poems suggests strong feelings in White, perhaps a conflict between the desire to deal with these ideas and a wariness at the uneasiness they arouse in him. White was an unusually private man who revealed little of himself to his public. Even his autobiography, *Flaws in the Glass* (1981), does not reveal a great deal about his thinking.[4] For all his stating to Craig McGregor that all his life was in his books, very little in fact was accessible to his readers until the biography of White by David Marr in 1992.[5] Marr's work provides the biographical background for interpreting White's writings.

The theme of the need to escape the mother by turning to the freedom and power of the imagination recurs in White's five poems in varying degrees of completeness, so that I will discuss the poems thematically rather than chronologically. In its full form, the notion is developed only in Le Mesurier's 'Childhood', which gives that poem a special importance. Le Mesurier does not specify the mother as manipulating a child; his poem is couched in general terms of parents manipulating children, and so provides a level of camouflage for autobiographical elements. The childhood described in Le Mesurier's poem reflects White's own, a rather privileged one lived in large houses, with education by governesses. (The companion-piece 'Conclusion' gives a glimpse of White's more adult life in the affluent social circle of his

---

[4] White (1981).

[5] McGregor (1969), pp. 219–20, 222. Marr (1992).

parents: 'I shall recall with amazement the visions of love, of trampling horses, of drowning candles, of hungry emeralds'.) In its accusations of parents, 'Childhood' is startling in its directness, all the more for being in English:

> When they had opened us with knives, they took out our hearts. Some wore them in their hats, some pressed them to keep forever, some were eating them as if they had been roses, all with joy, until it was realised the flesh had begun to putrefy. (p. 313)

The children compensate for their sense of powerlessness by fantasising powers of their own, like the ability to fly:

> It is not known that we shall rise above the trees any afternoon we choose. We are only waiting to pin the calico wings on our backs. Parents and governesses assemble to watch, and some old people, who do perhaps see. We run, and flap, and crow, and rise—one foot? Everyone applauds, and pretends, and disperses, unaware that we have flown above the pointed trees. We enjoy the immense freedom of dreams ... (p. 314)

The dreams are left at this point in Le Mesurier's poem, however; they are the dreams of children generally. The carrying of dreams into poetic expression by a gifted child was explored earlier in the fantasies of Stan's grandson at the end of *The Tree of Man*. Two Rimbaud poems deal with the same theme as Le Mesurier's 'Childhood', 'Les Poètes de Sept Ans' and 'Mémoire'.[6] The first poem shows the boy fleeing from the mother, his soul 'livrée aux répugnances',[7] into the life of the imagination; alone in his bare room with closed shutters, 'Il lisait son roman sans cesse médité'.[8] Lying on the floor on pieces of unbleached cloth, he conjures up

---

[6] I quote from the Pléiade edition of Rimbaud's *Oeuvres Complètes*, edited by Antoine Adam (1972).

[7] [Given over to loathing].

[8] [He would read the novel that he was constantly thinking about], p. 45.

a sail ('pressentant violemment la voile!') in vivid anticipation of what was to become his most famous poem, 'Le Bateau Ivre'. The second poem shows the boy fleeing from the rigid figure of 'Madame' as she stands 'trop debout dans la prairie',[9] crushing the flower heads of a chervil-like plant ('foulant l'ombelle'), twirling her parasol with her fingers but disdaining to avail herself of its shade ('trop fière pour elle'). As he escapes 'par delà la montagne',[10] she is forced to run after him (p. 87). 'Mémoire' has its roots in Rimbaud's first flight to Paris in 1870, when he was sixteen, but his record of the fact explodes in an ecstatic fantasy of freedom when he portrays himself in his flight as like 'mille anges blancs qui se séparent sur la route'.[11]

Since we never see Stan's grandson with his mother Elsie in *The Tree of Man*, it could seem that there is no implication that the boy's flight into fantasy is to escape a controlling parent—and yet there are hints of an uneasy relationship with his mother and grandmother Amy. He has left the house where they are in order to contemplate his projected poem in solitude among the gum trees, and when he abandons the poem in frustration at his inability to realise it yet, he returns to their company, 'taking with him his greatness, which was still a secret' (p. 499). Years before, when Amy asked him what he would write, he would not answer,

---

[9] [Unnaturally straight in the meadow].

[10] [Beyond the mountain].

[11] [A thousand white angels flying in different directions over the road]. There has been some disagreement among critics whether the 'Lui' who flees from 'Madame' is the young Arthur or his father, who separated from Madame Rimbaud in 1864. Berrichot (1897), Rimbaud's brother-in-law, declared that it referred to the young Arthur, and that is the interpretation I favour. The date 1864 seems too long ago for the immediacy of this poem: Rimbaud was nothing if not intense. Futhermore, the reference to 'Lui … [qui] s'éloigne par delà la montagne' as resembling 'mille anges blancs qui se séparent sur la route' makes good sense if one interprets it as an explosion of Arthur's joy at the potential of freedom and recognition in Paris.

but picked at the woodwork (p. 400). White appears to be wary of indicating what in his own background led him to write. Rimbaud, intense, angry and accusatory, did not have the same need for camouflage in writing of his childhood; in 'Angoisse' (in *Illuminations)* he refers to his mother as 'la Vampire qui nous rend gentils' (p. 143).[12] In 'Les Poètes de Sept Ans' he tells how 'Tout le jour il suait d'obéissance',[13] so that his mother can go off smugly while he presses his clenched fists into his groin in anger, 'et dans ses yeux fermés voyait des points'.[14] He retires to the outhouse, opening his nostrils wide to savour what to him is fresh air compared to the air that surrounds his mother. There he sits undisturbed, his mind free to roam: 'Il pensait, tranquille'.[15]

Stan's grandson in *The Tree of Man* goes into the imagination more extensively if less dramatically than Le Mesurier in his 'Childhood': his poem will be on a grand scale, embracing all life and death, 'what he did not know, but knew'. To the young boy and to Patrick White, the creative imagination is a unique way of looking at the world, through a piece of stained glass from a former church, hence both romantic and spiritual. The boy's poem is envisioned as he lies on his back on the sandy earth, looking through the glass 'at the crimson mystery of the world' (p. 498). The imagined poem grows within him until it becomes too much for his youth and inexperience and he abandons it with a feeling of impotence. Although, as said, there is no suggestion in the context of this poem that the boy has entered into the world of the imagination to escape a manipulative parent—his mother Elsie is a shadowy figure who makes only a few brief appearances—the poem has striking resemblances to 'Les Poètes de Sept Ans', in which the seven-year-old Arthur Rimbaud rejects

---

[12] [The bloodsucker who makes us behave ourselves].

[13] [All day he sweated obedience].

[14] [And closed his eyes so tightly that he saw black dots].

[15] [He would think quietly].

the immediate presence of his strict mother for a fantasy life in which he can compose romances 'sur la vie/Du grand désert, où luit la Liberté ravie,/Forêts, soleils, rives, savanes!'[16] As *The Tree of Man* ends, White is not interested in the boy's relationship with his mother, for he is intoxicated with the concept of the poem that the boy will write:

> Long words wired for the occasion, marble words of dictionaries, paper words in rat traps would decorate his poem. He was a bit frightened of it ... he would write a poem of life, of all life ... Of all people, even the closed ones, who do open on asphalt and in trains. He would make the trains run on silver lines, the people still dreaming on their shelves, who will wake up soon enough and feel for their money and their teeth. Little bits of coloured thought, that he had suddenly and would look at for a long time, would go into his poem, and urgent telegrams, and the pieces of torn letters that fall out of metal baskets. He would put the windows that he had looked inside. Sleep, of course, that blue eiderdown that divides life from life. His poem was growing. It would have the smell of bread, and the rather grey wisdom of youth, and his grandmother's kumquats, and girls with yellow plaits exchanging love-talk behind their hands, and the blood thumping like a drum, and red apples, and a little wisp of white cloud that will swell into a horse and trample the whole sky once it gets the wind inside it.[17] (p. 499)

Since the boy here is not preoccupied with a yearning for freedom, he is able to concern himself with aspects of technique that are not yet accessible to him: 'Long words wired for the occasion, marble words in dictionaries, paper words in rat traps'. Rimbaud in his poem is oppressed

[16] [About life/In the desert, where Liberty, having been stolen thence, shines resplendent,/Forests, other suns, alongside rivers, savannas!]
[17] I have done an exegesis of this poem elsewhere in this collection: see chapter 15.

with a sense of confinement and filled with a passionate desire for places 'où luit la Liberté ravie', places that he invests with a naïve exoticism.

It was not until *The Eye of the Storm*, when White was in his early sixties, that he dropped his protective camouflage to write his most autobiographical novel, in which the artist's relationship with his mother, portrayed in the story of Sir Basil and Elizabeth Hunter, is the central theme.[18] Lottie's song 'Wenn Mutter in die Manege ritt'[19] is the most explicit of White's poems dealing with the situation of a controlling mother and her child. The first half of the poem (vv. 1–14) deals with the child's reaction to 'Mutter', while the second (vv. 15–25) reflects upon the relationship from the viewpoint of the same child, now an adult. The song has no personal meaning to Lottie—she sings it as if it were a performance in a German Kabarett—but it does have a strong personal meaning to the artist Patrick White, who wrote it. It begins by tracing the child's transition from an initial excitement at his mother's performances to disillusionment, and to contempt for her admiring audience:

> Wenn Mutter in die Manege ritt,
> Wie jauchzt' mein Herz auf Scritt und Tritt
> Hoppla, hoppla, tripp, trap, trap!
> Bis mir die Schuppen von den Augen fielen
> Ich sah den Dreck in allen Dielen

---

[18] Ruth Withycombe, who was to be White's mother, lived in the Hunter Valley in New South Wales, married neighbour Victor White (whom everyone called 'Dick'), had two children, a boy and a girl, and died at the age of 86, half-blind. Elizabeth Salkeld in *The Eye of the Storm* married Alfred Hunter (whom everyone called 'Bill'), had two children, a boy and a girl, and died at the age of 86, half-blind. The first element in the women's maiden names, 'withy' and 'salk', means 'willow', the former word being of Germanic origin, the latter of Romance origin. There are other reasons to link the two women.

[19] [When Mother rode into the circus ring].

Hoppla, hoppla, tripp, trap, trap!
Es ist das alte, fade Lied
Nichts macht mehr einen Unterschied
Es ist 'ne Welt für leere Laffen,
Ein Zirkus mit dressierten Affen
Die Löwen und die Löwenkätzchen
Die Dame ohne Unterleib,
Die Hohe Schul' mit allen Mätzchen,
Was ist es schon? Ein Zeitvertreib! (p. 444)[20]

This first part of the poem, which does not look at the child's reaction to his mother beyond his disillusionment, may seem to be an exception to the pattern of the child's fleeing into a compensatory fantasy life—until we relate the central figures of the poem to their real referents, Elizabeth ('Mutter') and Basil ('ich'). Basil does not become a writer, but his choice of a career as an actor is another form of living in the world of fantasy. Willa Cather once wrote that an actor is an author who writes a novel every night upon the stage. So we have again the pattern found in

[20] [When mother rode into the circus ring,
how my heart would cheer at every step
—clip clop, clippety clop, clip clop!
Until the scales fell from my eyes and
I saw the dirt on all the floorboards.
Clip clop, clippety clop, clip clop!
It's the same old song—
nothing makes any difference any more.
It's a world fit for stupid morons,
a circus for trained monkeys,
the lions and the lion cubs,
the lady with no underwear,
the training school with its goings on.
So what's it all about? A way of passing time!]

White's other poems and in Rimbaud of the child of a controlling mother finding a defence within his imaginative life.

There is, I suggested earlier, a second theme in the poems of White and Rimbaud: the proneness of the imagination to run out of control, followed by a need to retreat, ending in frustration and failure. This outcome of flights of fancy appears so regularly in White and Rimbaud that, for them, it evidently constitutes a conviction. It is an outcome, however, that seems less than inevitable to readers now, so that some explanation seems called for.

White's first poem, the one conceived by Stan's grandson, can seem rather exciting as it grows in the boy's mind, beginning as a wisp of white cloud that swells into a horse that tramples the whole sky, but the boy cuts it short at the point where he feels it to be getting out of control, and abandons it in frustration. His scribbling upon the trees seems sullen rather than acceptant,[21] rather like the boy in Rimbaud's 'Les Poètes de Sept Ans', who had a taste for gloomy things: 'dans la chambre nue aux persiennes closes,/ Il lisait son roman sans cesse médité …'.[22] The sullenness of the two boys suggests a brooding anger; their fantasies, they have found, have not led to the freedom that they sought. Voss' German song 'Eine blosse Seele ritt hinaus'[23] picks up the image that concludes the projected poem of Stan's grandson, the wisp of cloud that swells into a

[21] The 'already scribbled trees' that the boy scribbles on are scribbly gums, a kind of eucalyptus that attracts insects whose larvae nibble beneath the bark, leaving permanent scribble-like traces. White's botanical knowledge here surpassed that of commentators, for none of them picked this up. The detail has it importance, however, for it graphically illustrates the boy's 'impotence' (White's word) at being unable to achieve his grand concept: his writing is indistinguishable from the tracks left by insects.

[22] [In the bare room with the shutters closed / He would read the novel that he was constantly thinking about].

[23] [A bare soul rode out].

horse trampling the whole sky once it gets the wind (the breath of inspiration) inside it. Leaving Jildra, the last outpost of white civilisation, Voss bursts into an impromptu song in which he sees himself magically riding his steed into the blue sky:

> Eine blosse Seele ritt hinaus
> Dem Blau' entgegen.
> Sein Rock flog frei.
> Sein Schimmel mit den Wolken
> Um die Ehre ran.
> Nur der edle Rock zu Schaden kam,
> Die Fetzen fielen
> Den Himmel entlang. (pp. 202–03)[24]

The image of Voss on a white steed that flies into the blue, aiming to outrace the clouds, informs us that his expedition represents the indulgence of a fantasy so overreaching that he himself knows must end in failure. Immediately before bursting into song, Voss jibes Dugald for bringing his 'fine coat', which to Dugald would represent a veneer of European civilisation: 'You were foolish to bring along that fine coat … Now, if you lose your life, you will lose your coat too' (p. 202). The sequence of ideas here is strange—'if you lose your life, you will lose your coat!—but makes sense if we consider what Voss' own 'edle Rock'[25] means to him: it is a veneer for him too, the camouflage that he needs in

---

[24] [A bare soul rode out
into the blue.
Its coat flew free.
Its white horse was trying to outrace the clouds.
But the fine coat came to grief,
its tatters falling along the sky].

[25] [Fine coat].

order to conceal his megalomania from his patrons and from himself. His death, of which he has a premonition here, would strip his soul of all covering as the tatters of the coat fall along the sky, exposing his delusions for what they were. Voss' song has a visionary quality to it, like a number of Rimbaud poems; erupting from him almost without his intention and without his comprehension, it is as close as he can get at this point to facing a grim reality. But he and we already know that the price he will pay for the living out of excessive fantasies is failure.

Le Mesurier's poem 'Conclusion' leaps from alluding to children's excited fantasies of flying in 'Childhood' to depicting vividly the delusions of grandeur of one man, Voss:

> Man is King. They hung a robe upon him, of blue sky … He rode across his kingdom of dust, which paid homage to him for a season, with jasmine, and lilies, and visions of water … He continued to eat distance, and to raise up the sun in the morning, and the moon was his slave by night. Fevers turned him from Man into God. (p. 315)

The fantasy that carries a man from delusions of royal power to God-like power is of course the force that drives Voss on his expedition; Le Mesurier's poem records his own visionary insight into Voss' psyche and his awareness of the disastrous conclusion of the journey. In order to re-establish one's humanity, Le Mesurier asserts, it is necessary to abandon such fantasies completely and embrace humility: 'Humility is my brigalow, that must I remember' (p. 316). But Le Mesurier's concept of humility is virtually a form of self-annihilation, itself an excessive notion: 'Now that I am nothing, I am …' (p. 316).

Rimbaud warns against the excesses of the imagination in 'Le Bateau Ivre'. In that poem the boat, a symbol for Rimbaud himself, is borne along a river, being successively freed of its restraints until it enters the open sea. There unforeseen threats menace it—it is choked by seaweed in shallow bays, and a hurricane even makes it airborne for a time. It ends waterlogged, not even worth being fished out by passing vessels of other countries and other times, so that it looks back longingly to the safety of its beginnings:

> Et je voguais, lorsqu'à travers mes liens frêles
> Des noyés descendaient dormir, à reculons! ...
> Or moi, bateau perdu sous les cheveux des anses,
> Jeté par l'ouragan dans l'éther sans oiseau ...
> Je regrette l'Europe aux anciens parapets! (p. 68)[26]

Rimbaud's poem, like Le Mesurier's later, ends in a sense of personal failure: Rimbaud leaves the dangers and excitement of the open sea for the safety of the boat's beginnings as a paper boat that he sailed as a child in a cold, dark puddle:

> Si je désire une eau d'Europe, c'est la flache
> Noire et froide où vers le crépuscule embaumé
> Un enfant accroupi plein de tristesses, lâche
> Un bateau frêle comme un papillon de mai. (p. 69)[27]

This sense of failure and frustration is common in Rimbaud's poetry and is characteristic of all White's poems except 'Childhood', which is in any case the first half of a total conception, 'Childhood'/'Conclusion',— and 'Conclusion' ends in failure.

---

[26] [And I sailed on, and through my frail lines
drowned men sank down backwards to sleep! ...
Now, a boat lost among the hairy seaweed,
Thrown by the hurricane into the air empty of birds ...
I miss Europe with its ancient parapets!]

[27] [If I would like one of Europe's watery stretches, it's the cold,
Dark puddle where, as a fragrant dusk sets in,
A sad child, squatting down, releases
A boat frail as a May butterfly.]

Lottie's song in *The Eye of the Storm,* White's last poem, was written some sixteen years later than the poems in *Voss.* It is the only poem in which the child of the controlling mother is not shown fleeing into a life within the imagination, but that situation had been thoroughly explored in the earlier poems in *Voss.* The poems in *The Tree of Man* and *Voss* offered White the camouflage he sought for his most profound self-revelation. When he came to *The Eye of the Storm,* he no longer felt the same need for camouflage, and brought into the centre of the novel itself the situation of children fleeing from their controlling mother into a life of fantasy. Both Basil and Dorothy live a life of fantasy in a foreign country, away from Elizabeth, and their lives end in a stalemate. Basil's whole career is a continuing exploration of the imagination, the limit being set at playing King Lear, which he cannot do, partly because his mother represents a daunting Queen Lear, and there his career is stuck; his achievements are essentially behind him. Dorothy for her part has adopted another language and another culture, but her marriage is a failure and she belongs neither in France nor in Australia. Both Basil and Dorothy have gained titles—he has been knighted and she is by marriage Princesse de Lascabanes—but in Australia their titles elicit awkwardness rather than respect. Like the figures of the poems in *The Tree of Man* and *Voss,* they pursue great ambitions in order to achieve a sense of their own worth, which is never quite achieved, not having been won from their mother in their childhood, the time when it mattered most. This is the situation that Alice Miller writes of and it seems to reflect the personal situation of Rimbaud and White.[28]

---

[28] Miller (1979) maintains in her opening chapter that gifted children of controlling mothers often feel they have failed to live up to some standard expected of them and go through life afflicted with anxiety or deep feelings of guilt and shame.

Elizabeth Hunter and the 'Mutter' of Lottie's poem are both commanding, manipulative women, and there is no need to distinguish between them for the purposes of interpretation. In Lottie's song however, the reaction of the child, who in the second half of the song has advanced to adulthood, is very different from that of Basil and Dorothy. The 'ich' of the song, who speaks early of 'mein Herz' rejoicing at every step as his mother enters the circus ring but who later laments that 'meine Seele' has lost its innocence, is pretty clearly Patrick White, first as child then as adult, in the same way that the figures in the earlier poems are also projections or representations of himself.[29] It is an extraordinarily self-revealing poem, covering a wide range of emotions. The first half records the reactions of one who passes from child to early adolescent, from excitement at his mother's repeated performances to boredom, world-weariness, and disgust:

> Bis mir die Schuppen von den Augen fielen …
> Es ist das alte, fade Lied
> Nichts macht mehr einen Unterschied …
> Die Hohe Schul' mit allen Maetzchen,
> Was ist es schon? Ein Zeitvertreib! (p.444)[30]

The second half is sadder and calmer, recording the state of mind of a mature adult. It confesses to a sense of abiding guilt and pleads for understanding, for lack of judgement:

---

[29] In two other articles I have discussed Stan's grandson as a projection of White as a child and both Le Mesurier and Voss as projections of White as an adult writing *Voss*. See chapter 15 in this collection.

[30] [Until the scales fell from my eyes …
It's the same old song—
nothing makes any difference any more …
the training school with its goings on.
So what's it all about? A way of passing time!]

Jede Nacht, seit ich geboren,
Hat mein Seel' ihre Unschuld verloren.
Verdammt sie nicht, versteht es nur,
Sie war zu schwach in der Struktur
So geht's enimal in der Natur. (p. 445)[31]

Patrick White here is in an unwontedly gentle, meditative mood, himself refraining from harsh judgement upon others. The poem ends twice voicing the notion of rebirth, of carnations springing up where others have died down, and roses being constantly reborn:

Am selben Platz wo sie verwelken,
Da wachsen wieder andere Nelken.
Sie gehen nie verloren,
Sind ewig neugeboren.
Die Rosen können nie vergehen,
Die Liebe lässt sie neuerstehen. (pp. 445–46)[32]

The carnations appear to refer to other literary figures, whose works will continue to appear after White's own, so that he is acknowledging his own passing glory; but the roses refer specifically to his mother's

[31] [Every night since I was born
my soul has lost its innocence.
Don't condemn it, just understand,
it was too weak in its make-up,
that's the way things are].

[32] [In the same place where carnations wither,
others grow.
They are never lost but born again,
over and over.
Roses can never die,
love lets them rise again].

irrepressible personality. The roses that cannot die represent a final tribute to her, a tribute that is repeated at the end of the novel when de Santis gathers roses in the early morning after Elizabeth has died.

The Eye of the Storm, then, shows two reactions to a powerful mother one (in the novel itself) the familiar flight into the life of the imagination that ends in failure, the other (in Lottie's song) an acknowledgement of defeat before a stronger figure. *The Eye of the Storm* is White's last word on his own drama as the gifted child of a powerful mother, and if there is ambivalence within the resolution that he comes to here, that may be as far as the resolution can go. Having finally conceded that his mother was a worthy opponent, White turns in his later novels to other subjects.

The poems of both White and Rimbaud show artists turning from a powerful mother to an inward world of the imagination, which they explored to what they felt were its limits, at which point they became fearful and completely retreated, with a sense of having failed. This sense of failure can strike a modern reader as strange. In turning from the freedom of the imagination, the artists betray signs of fear and guilt from having rejected the mother's principles too completely, necessitating a return to her, and that is the ultimate cause of their sense of failure. Certainly the life of the imagination, which seemed to offer such freedom, brings them no lasting happiness. Rimbaud's sailing a paper boat in a puddle at the end of his grand fantasy in 'Le Bateau Ivre' does suggest that. And a sense of guilt weighs heavily over the latter half of Lottie's song in *The Eye of the Storm:* 'Jede Nacht seit ich geboren/Hat meine Seel' ihre Unschuld verloren.' In that song there is a sad acknowledgement of the author's weakness, 'So geht's einmal in der Natur', that precedes a tribute to his mother's enduring vitality, a claim to which he does not make for himself. If White and Rimbaud did not succeed in leaving their childhood behind, then they have left memorable poetic evidence of one aspect of the human condition.

4

OUT OF CHILDHOOD: THE LOVE STORY IN *LE GRAND MEAULNES* AND *VOSS*

> 'If it be love indeed, tell me how much?' *Antony and Cleopatra* (1.1)

Before his return to Australia in 1946, after World War II, Patrick White had spent more than half his life abroad. His high school years were spent in England, at Cheltenham, and he returned to England to study French and German literature at Cambridge University from 1935 to 1939. His stay in England and his readings in British literature left their mark upon his work: one can variously detect the influence of D.H. Lawrence, James Joyce and T.S. Eliot. Even his short stay in the United States between 1939 and 1941 left him receptive to Willa Cather and John Steinbeck.[1] But the chief influences upon him came from French literature, from Flaubert and Rimbaud and Stendhal, writers he specifically admired. One can discern debts to Goethe and Thomas Mann, too, but memories of the recent war against Germany probably inhibited him from embracing more of German culture.[2] White never fully accepted Australian culture:

---

[1] See chapters 6 and 7 in this collection.

[2] See chapters 2, 3 and 5 in this collection. For the influence of Goethe see note 7 in this essay.

although most of his novels are set wholly or in part in Australia, there is almost no significant influence from Australian literature in his work. White's strongest literary affiliations are with Europe, and discussion of these affiliations is necessary to understand his place in the Western literary tradition. It is an aspect of White that I have repeatedly interested myself in over the last thirty-five years.

In this essay I turn to another of his favourite French writers, Alain-Fournier. White twice mentioned Alain-Fournier's *Le Grand Meaulnes* [Big Meaulnes] (1913) as one of his favourite novels.[3] It is not surprising then that its influence should appear in his own novels, most notably in *Voss* (1957). The theme of a quest in which fantasised relationships play a larger part than real relationships, the very essence of *Le Grand Meaulnes*, appears in *The Aunt's Story* (1948) and *The Tree of Man* (1955), but is a leading theme in *Voss*. Theodora Goodman's series of fantasised relationships with the figures in the 'Jardin Exotique' of the French hotel represent a quest to establish an identity of her own by giving free rein to her imagination after her mother's death. And Amy Parker's sexual fantasies when she kisses Stan passionately under the mulberry tree and when she contemplates Tom Armstrong and Madeleine at the estate of Glastonbury (names rich in romantic associations) represent a quest to see herself as a romantic figure.

But *Le Grand Meaulnes* exercised a much more powerful and direct influence upon *Voss*: it provided White with a model for his portrayal of the Voss-Laura relationship, one that like the Meaulnes-Yvonne relation-

---

[3] Quoted by Marr (1991), p. 127, and also recorded in an interview with Herring & Wilkes (1973). *Le Grand Meaulnes* was one of the enduring cult novels in Europe during the twentieth century, and almost 100 years later still sells 200,000 copies a year in France alone. There are at least five translations of the novel into English. Gibson (2005) gives an account of its rise to fame. The edition of *Le Grand Meaulnes* that I quote from in this chapter is the *Livre de Poche* published by Fayard (Paris, 1971).

ship is based upon fantasy. Both these stories fail to show intimations of love when the couple are together but take on a highly romantic, dream-like quality when the couple are separated. The Voss-Laura story is a strange love story, which in a novel of lesser stature might simply be passed over as a puzzling or unsuccessful element in the story; but it lies at the heart of the Great Australian Novel, so that an explanation of it represents a contribution to understanding one of the icons of Australian literature. And certain aspects of *Le Grand Meaulnes* too will become clearer in the course of this comparative study than they would otherwise.

My concern in this essay is with showing how the love story in *Le Grand Meaulnes* throws light upon the Voss-Laura love story and how its quest themes helped to shape the quest themes in *Voss*. Alain-Fournier's *Le Grand Meaulnes* deals essentially with two quests, the quest for a beautiful woman met briefly but memorably and a quest for the 'Domaine inconnu' [unknown domain] that she inhabits—a special land, it is implied, that is difficult of access and unlike any other.[4] Patrick White's *Voss* also deals with two quests, a quest for a strong-minded woman met briefly but memorably, and a quest to explore the unknown interior of Australia.[5] In both novels, the two quests fluctuate, blur and at times merge into one another, for they are essentially aspects of the same quest. My emphasis is on the love story, for it is more revealing about the creative impulses that underlie both quests.

Both novels tell highly unusual but very similar love stories. In their infrequent meetings with the heroine early in the story, both Meaulnes

[4] There is a third quest, Meaulnes' quest on behalf of Frantz, which reinforces the quest theme, but is a quite separate story.

[5] Although Voss' territorial quest to explore Australia occupies most of the novel, it does not engage White's interest as the love story does. The direction Voss travels and the distance he covers are never clearly indicated, and we know less of the terrain than of the climatic changes it undergoes.

and Voss are gauche or ineffective, behaving in ways more likely to alienate the woman than to attract her. And yet these meetings provide the basis for their quest of a love that is at the heart of both novels.

Meaulnes meets Yvonne de Galais only twice before his sudden proposal to her. On the first meeting, his persistence drives her to remonstrate with him mildly: 'nous avons fait une folie' [we've been foolish] (p. 100). She leaves open, however, the possibility of future meetings: 'Je vous attendrai' [I will expect you] (p. 100). During the second meeting nearly three years later, Meaulnes is unfailingly sullen and tactless, slow even to present himself to Yvonne. It is only late in the day that he speaks to her, and that is when she has detached herself from the group she is with in order to seek him out. He continually harks back to their first meeting in a way that almost holds her responsible for the changes that have taken place in the family property, now only a shadow of its former self, so that she is driven to acknowledge, with considerable embarrassment, 'Nous sommes devenus pauvres' [We are poor now] (p. 236). By the time they part at the end of the evening, he has found an outlet for his disappointment in his exaggerated anger over the accident to her horse, and uses that as an excuse not to look at her: 'il prenait un plaisir amer et désespéré à aggraver la situation, à tout briser à jamais' [he took a bitter, desperate pleasure in making the situation worse, in ruining everything for ever] (p. 240).

The sense of distance between Meaulnes and Yvonne at the 'partie de plaisir' [picnic], their second meeting, is paralleled by the sense of distance between Voss and Laura on a similar occasion, the picnic at Point Piper (chapter 3). Indeed, the picnic scene in *Voss* appears to be modelled, perhaps in unconscious memory, upon the 'partie de plaisir' in *Le Grand Meaulnes*. Voss and Laura had met once before, at the very beginning of the novel, but that meeting was not especially significant: its main purpose was to establish them as the central figures, linked to one another and to the expedition. There is nothing in it to prepare us for Laura's suddenly flinging down the gauntlet at the picnic, announcing imperiously, 'This expedition, Mr Voss ... this expedition of yours ... I do not believe that I fully understand you. But I will' (pp. 74–75). From the outset, Laura and Voss are conceived of as engaged in a contest. Laura's announcement is an accusation and a warning, a bid for dominance that flares out as a full-scale clash the next time they meet, in Mr Bonner's garden. Their conversation in the garden is essentially a clash of wills, instigated by Laura but accepted by Voss: her going into the garden is an invitation to him to follow her, and he understands it as such. She repeats there her claim to him, 'I think I can enter into the minds of most men', and he takes her up on it, 'And in my instance, what does your imagination find?' (p. 93). 'That it would take place', says White, 'they both knew now' (p. 94), and it is scarifying.[6] Laura is appropriately represented in this scene as destructive: she is shown casually tearing the camellias 'as if they had not been flesh' (p. 94)—alive and sentient, that is, not just beautiful.

So Laura begins the attack:

> You are so vast and ugly ... I can imagine some desert, with rocks, rocks of prejudice, and, yes, even hatred. You are so isolated. That is why you are fascinated by the prospect of desert places ... Human emotions, when you have them, are quite flattering to you ... But most flattering, I think, when you experience it, is the hatred, or even the irritation of weaker characters. (p. 94)

Voss responds with a counterattack, that she is *atheistisch*, one of those 'so lacking in magnificence that they cannot conceive the idea of a Divine Power ... *Atheismus* is self-murder' (p. 95).[7]

---

[6] I have written at some length of this scene and indeed the whole relationship of Voss and Laura in chapter 19 in this collection.

[7] The discussion of religious beliefs between Voss and Laura in Mr Bonner's garden points to White's memory of a similar discussion between Faust and

The scene in the garden is charged with sexual imagery as Voss and Laura perform, in vicarious form, a kind of mutual rape. Attack is met by counterattack in this antagonistic exchange until it reaches its climax (one might almost say orgasm) in mutual recrimination: 'It is for our pride that each of us is probably damned', said Laura. Then he shook her off ... He was wiping his lips, which had begun to twitch' (p. 96).

The exchange, which exhausts both parties, ends in 'a clumsy contentment of the flesh' (p. 97), and Voss shows signs of a post-coital tiredness, as it were: 'The man yawned again ... He, too, was rather exhausted by what had happened' (p. 98). A psychic rape, even if mutual, makes an odd beginning to what is intended to become a love story. Many readers accordingly have been unwilling to recognise or remember the assaults Voss and Laura make upon each other in this scene, and no one hitherto has drawn attention to the sexual imagery in their exchange.[8]

In their last meeting, on the wharf as Voss' ship is about to leave, Laura and Voss do not enter into conversation. She speaks instead to the gentler Palfreyman, and drops her whip, temporarily chastened after the contest in the garden, unwilling to continue it so soon. When she recalls

---

Gretchen in Marthe's garden, and links Voss the overreacher to Faust. There are suggestions throughout the novel that White was tempted to make Laura an agent in Voss' salvation like Gretchen in Faust's, but he was always held back from the notion by his dislike and fear of a strong woman like Laura. After Voss' death he reduces Laura to a schoolmarm, commanding of attention but also slightly ludicrous.

[8] David Malouf in his libretto and Richard Meale in his opera *Voss* (1986) represented the Voss-Laura love story as one of closeness. Such a taming of the love story diminishes the power of the novel, and neither libretto nor music succeeds in exciting one's imagination. The opera has not been revived. Alban Berg would have been the ideal composer of an opera from *Voss*, and White may have sensed that as he repeatedly listened to Berg's violin concerto while writing *Voss*; Marr (1991), p. 306. But Berg died in 1935.

the 'incident' in the garden a little later, 'there came into her mouth a bad taste, as of blood oozing, as if she had lost a tooth' (p. 130).

Meaulnes' and Voss' proposals, both unexpected, born of sudden impulse rather than mature deliberation, again link the two novels. Both proposals are poorly timed and reveal conflicting emotions. Meaulnes' proposal to Yvonne comes almost in desperation. It is only as he is being driven away from the 'partie de plaisir' that he impulsively jumps out of the carriage and runs to the château to propose to her, sobbing—sobs that express regret, conflict, guilt, helplessness, and fear rather than love. There is a disquieting sense of his forcing himself to do what he does not want to do, and this holding back introduces a sense of distance from her that never quite leaves their relationship henceforth. We witness almost nothing of their courtship over the next five months. It is summarised in a single short paragraph:

> Les fiançailles ont duré cinq mois. Elles ont été paisibles, aussi paisibles que la première entrevue avait été mouvementée. Meaulnes est venu très souvent aux Sablonnières, à bicyclette ou en voiture. Plus de deux fois par semaine, cousant ou lisant près de la grande fenêtre qui donne sur la lande et les sapins, Mlle de Galais a vu tout d'un coup sa haute silhouette rapide passer derrière le rideau, car il vient toujours par l'allée détournée qu'il a prise autrefois. Mais c'est la seule allusion— tacite—qu'il fasse au passé. Le bonheur semble avoir endormi son étrange tourment. (p. 244)[9]

[9] [The engagement lasted five months. It was peaceful, as peaceful as their first meeting had been agitated. Meaulnes came very often to Les Sablonnières, by bicycle or by car. More than twice a week Mlle de Galais, sewing or reading near the large window overlooking the moor and fir-trees, would suddenly see his tall shadow pass quickly across the curtain, for he always came by the side-road that he took on the first occasion. But that was the only reference—an unspoken one—that he made to the past. Happiness seemed to have lulled his strange anxiety.]

We see the two again, at a distance from us and from one another, on their wedding night. That is their only night together, for the following morning Meaulnes departs on a third and unrelated quest, to fulfil a schoolboy promise made to Yvonne's brother Frantz. When Meaulnes leaves, he and Yvonne are completely removed from one another, for Meaulnes never attempts to communicate with her during the more than twenty months of his absence. The woman of his fantasy, she to whom he said 'Vous êtes belle' at the 'fête étrange' [strange party], no longer existed when he married the woman who inspired the fantasy.

Voss' proposal, like Meaulnes', is made in a sort of desperation, at the last opportunity for him to write and receive an answer before moving into the interior. He has been softened by his observation of the Sandersons' fruitful marriage at Rhine Towers,[10] but his letter of proposal (pp. 163–64) is still uncompromising and self-assertive: 'That which I am intended to fulfil, must be fulfilled.' He makes no declaration of love, asking only for 'a companion of strength and judgment' to join him on the throne of victory when he returns from the expedition. Laura in her answer does not accept a secondary role: rather, she continually strives to establish herself and Voss on the same level. They are both, she says, flawed by arrogance and mutual hatefulness (pp. 197–99). (Laura characteristically accuses herself of a serious failing in order to accuse Voss of the same failing.) Both write further letters, but the letters go astray,[11]

---

[10] At Rhine Towers, a novelised version of his parents' estate of Belltrees inland from Newcastle, White is close to home; Marr (1991), p. 13. This is one suggestion of a link between Laura and Patrick White's mother. White remarked to me in May 1973 that the more thousand miles there were between him and his mother the better, a strong statement for a casual conversation.

[11] When he wrote about the genesis of *Voss* (1957) in his well-known essay 'The Prodigal Son' (1989), White mentioned his work as a censor in World War II, reading the letters of servicemen to their loved ones, an experience that did indeed contribute to his portrayal of the love between Voss and Laura, but less than did

suggesting that their relationship has nowhere to go in reality, only in fantasy. In both novels the role of fantasy is an important indication of the relationship that the lovers seek.

Fantasy plays a less direct part in *Le Grand Meaulnes* than in *Voss*. Meaulnes is clearly haunted by Yvonne's image, but it is frozen in his memory, resisting any change (that is why he is so upset when he is called upon to modify it at the 'partie de plaisir'). We can assume closeness to her after the 'fête étrange' because of his preoccupation with finding her; but we never see him engaged in a fantasy of her, and indeed cannot, since the story is told by a third person, Meaulnes' friend François Seurel. Whatever fantasy is in his mind therefore can appear only in indirect form. So we witness the fantasy and the quest itself displaced from the person to the place as he continues to search for the 'Domaine inconnu': that is where he will find Yvonne. The sense of closeness vanishes when he is in Yvonne's company again, and he quite disintegrates when he proposes to her. We are told that their courtship is a 'temps paisible' [peaceful time], but 'paisible' is not quite the adjective we might hope for, in that it can suggest the latent possibility of strife, as if Meaulnes is fighting against himself. After the wedding, the love story effectively disappears from the novel; we learn later of Meaulnes' adventures but not of any longing he feels for Yvonne.

Fantasies, often in the form of dreams or feverish images, are an important indication in *Voss* of what is going on in Voss' inner life and his relationship to Laura at a particular time. The fantasies develop in several broad stages, closely related to the main stages in Voss' personal development once he leaves Sydney. It is a development that represents his progressive renunciation of aspirations to godhood in favour of human-

---

his reading of *Le Grand Meaulnes*. Although Voss and Laura write several letters to one another, only his proposal and her tentative acceptance are actually received.

ity. The first stage of Voss' fantasies reveals him as moving towards his proposal to Laura. At the Sandersons' at Rhine Towers, he has a dream that combines aspects of his meetings with Laura in Mr Bonner's garden and at the wharf. It is in this dream that he first reveals signs of a sexual interest in Laura: 'the hills were enfolding him … So he was touching those same hills, and was not surprised at their suave flesh … That is the hill of love, his voice said' (p. 149). His sexual interest becomes more overt after he receives her acceptance letter. That is when he dreams of Palfreyman's lily, 'a big, dreamy lily propped in a tin mug', with seeds like testes 'attached to the rather virginal flower': 'Now [he and Laura] were swimming so close they were joined together at the waist' (p. 200). Laura's acceptance letter is the agent that propels him into the second and most important stage of his development, his struggle between continuing to strive for godhood with its 'crown of fire' or accepting 'the ring of gentle gold' (p. 227).

Voss' third stage of development is shorter and simpler. Captured by Aborigines along with the two remaining members of his expedition, he abandons all delusion of godhood ('I am no longer your Lord, Harry') (p. 360). Weak and powerless, he derives comfort from frequent fantasies of Laura riding alongside, treating his wounds, nourishing him or receiving nourishment along with him (pp. 387, 390, 407–09, 417–18). Given the unpromising beginnings to their relationship, it is hard to accept these fantasies of an exhausted man as testifying to the achievement of an intimate mutual relationship.[12] For her part, Laura is seen still wrestling with Voss' image some 20 years later. She is extremely reluctant even to discuss him with Colonel Hebden, and when she delivers her final, per-

---

[12] There is the one instance of telepathy, 'I shall not fail you … Even if there are times when you wish me to, I shall not fail you' (pp. 353, 358), but it is highly ambiguous in its meaning, able to suggest competition rather than closeness. See chapter 19 in this collection.

emptory verdict upon Voss, it is to disparage him: 'I am convinced that Voss had in him a little of Christ, like other men. If he was composed of evil along with the good, he struggled with that evil. And failed' (p. 474).

The role of fantasy is important in both love stories as a way of controlling the man's relationship with the woman. For Meaulnes it is a way of enshrining the woman in a fixed, unchanging form of his determination. For Voss it is a way of reducing the threat of Laura as a rival: he transforms her in his late fantasies into a loving companion and a ministering angel, an image that the real Laura counters in her two meetings with Colonel Hebden near the end of the novel (pp. 437–41, 469–74). For both Meaulnes and Voss, the fantasies help to deal with their fear of the woman.

For it is fear. Late in the novel, Yvonne identifies Meaulnes' fear to the narrator as the fear of a dream realised:

> Nous lui avons dit: 'Voici le bonheur, voici ce que tu as cherché pendant toute ta jeunesse, voici la jeune fille qui était à la fin de tous tes rêves!' Comment … n'aurait-il pas été saisi d'hésitation, puis de crainte, puis d'épouvante, et n'aurait-il pas cédé à la tentation de s'enfuir! (p. 273)[13]

Once he has attained the object of his fantasy, neither he nor the fantasy has anywhere to go: it will not accommodate reality. Yvonne's observation here concerning Meaulnes is not inaccurate, but it serves to shield her, and the reader, from the more disturbing realisation that his essential fear is of a woman. That fear is exposed in the unseemly speed with which Meaulnes embarks upon his quest on behalf of Frantz, on the

---

[13] [We said to him, 'Here is the happiness, here's what you've been looking for all your youth, here is the girl who was the goal of all your dreams!' Why wouldn't he have been seized with hesitation and fear, finally terror! And why wouldn't he have yielded to the temptation to flee!]

morning after the marriage: he clearly cannot sustain a sexual relationship in marriage to Yvonne. Having no way of dealing with it, he flees.

Voss, we have seen, does have sexual fantasies in his dreams: 'That which would have been reprehensible, nauseating, *frightening in life*, was permissible, even desirable, in sleep' (p. 149; my italics). He too has a deep-seated fear of women, but deals with it very differently from Meaulnes: along with Laura, he displaces the thrusting and counter-thrusting of sexual activity with the thrust and counterthrust of a struggle for dominance. Voss and Laura are contestants rather than lovers, and it is difficult to imagine them locked in a loving embrace.

There is a link between the two novels that points to the origin of the fear of women in the two heroes: the fact that the two women are presented early surrounded by children, thereby coming to represent mother figures and becoming associated with oedipal impulses.[14] The oedipal impulses prompt guilt simultaneously with desire, an admixture fraught with frustration and irresolution. They arise early in childhood, and it is this origin in childhood that the two novels give evidence of.

The 'fête étrange' where Meaulnes first meets Yvonne is essentially a celebration held for children. The wedding, which is the occasion, is mentioned but not stressed and does not take place, and indeed such an event would propel the novel out of a world of children into an adult world. The celebration takes place in a faery world ruled by children, and it is in this world of childhood fantasies that Meaulnes meets Yvonne and photographs her image in his mind, to become the object of his quest.[15]

[14] Maclean (1973) writes of Meaulnes' 'peur sub-consciente de l'inceste occasionnée par le rapprochement d'Yvonne et de la figure maternelle' [unconscious fear of incest occasioned by the linking of Yvonne to the figure of the mother], p. 145.

[15] The quest of exploration of a land is also a fantasy formed in childhood. That is clearest in *Voss* in the two prose poems of Le Mesurier, 'Childhood' and 'Conclusion'. In 'Childhood' he writes generally of children's fantasies and then in 'Conclusion' immediately leaps to his vision of Voss' expedition as an extended

Meaulnes witnesses groups of children before he sees Yvonne, and overhears them talk about their day free of adult restraints: 'Est-ce que nous n'avons pas toutes les permissions? … Même celle de nous faire mal, s'il nous plaît' [Don't we have permission to do whatever we want to? … Even to hurt ourselves, if we like.] (p. 72).[16] When he speaks to Yvonne, she interrupts her brief conversation with him to join the children and organise their games, 'puisqu'ils sont les maîtres aujourd'hui' [since they're in charge today] (p. 98). At the 'partie de plaisir' later she is also surrounded by young people, from whom she has to separate herself in order to speak with Meaulnes (p. 232). On both occasions as her attention is divided between Meaulnes and the children it is as if she has to turn her attention to a single child versus a group of children. (One may wonder at such times if the title *Le Grand Meaulnes* rather than just *Meaulnes* sprang from an attempt by Alain-Fournier to claim a maturity for Meaulnes that he fails to invest Meaulnes with.) There is an echo of this second meeting of Meaulnes and Yvonne at the 'partie de plaisir' in the picnic at Point Piper in *Voss* (chapter 3), the occasion of the second meeting of Laura and Voss. There Laura is engaged with the eleven Pringle children and their games, and so, like Yvonne, is presented early in a maternal role and can adopt that role also towards Voss. She reappears notably in a maternal role late in the novel when we see her as a headmistress surrounded by children.

---

fantasy, pp. 313–17. At 'the feast of children' in the first poem, 'We run, and flap, and crow, and rise—one foot? Everyone applauds, and pretends, and disperses, unaware that we have flown above the pointed trees.' There is no great difference between this fantasy and the image of Voss' fantasy that opens 'Conclusion': 'Man is King. They hung a robe upon him, of blue sky.'

[16] Does this remark, which appears casual and insignificant, imply in Alain-Fournier's mind permission (normally withheld) for Meaulnes to indicate strong attraction to Yvonne—even if it could hurt him? That would again suggest the oedipal nature of the love story.

But nowhere are the two heroines so clearly mother figures and the heroes so represented as children as when the heroines interpret or evaluate the heroes. Yvonne is a gentle, shadowlike character, who defers always to Meaulnes. She offers only the one analysis of him (previously quoted, p. 273), but in doing so, she shows a maturity beyond that of Meaulnes, who acts always on impulse, without thinking. In their very first meeting, it is she who remarks with a certain poise that they have behaved like 'deux enfants' [two children] (p. 100), and directs him not to follow her. Laura interprets Voss extensively and commandingly in Mr Bonner's garden (pp. 94–97), having threatened to do so earlier at the picnic (pp. 74–75). Her analysis sets her above him and makes him answerable to her: '*You* are *my* desert!' And he finishes their contest as a 'tired child' (p. 98).

If, as said, the heroes of these two novels are prompted by oedipal impulses in these stories, why does it matter? How do these impulses affect the course and content of the stories, the relationship of the lovers to the people around them, the resolution of these troubled love stories? In fact, the oedipal undercurrents account for both the attraction and the frustration that we ourselves feel in reading the novels, and provide an explanation of many of the stranger features of the love stories.

The guilt associated with oedipal impulses explains the secrecy with which the lovers guard their love and the strange mixture of attraction and repulsion that the men feel towards the woman they seek. It explains Meaulnes' flight from Yvonne once she becomes accessible as a real person and a lover: he cannot even befriend her, as François Seurel does—but François meets her as a young woman in a normal social context from the beginning (pp. 204–08). It explains, too, the struggle for dominance between Voss and Laura for as long as they are in contact, and their allowing themselves an indulgence in sympathetic fantasy when they are apart. And it explains, finally, Laura's sudden resumption of the contest when Voss is discussed as a public figure some twenty years later. To Laura Hebden represents a stand-in for Voss, and she resumes her contest with Voss through this symbolic figure. If the course of true love never did run smooth, still less did the course of an oedipally prompted love.

Meaulnes locks away his experience at the 'Domaine inconnu' (not just his encounter with Yvonne) on the unspoken assumption that no one else would understand and sympathise with it. But the narrator easily guesses it (p. 54) and others among his schoolmates must also. Meaulnes makes it a forbidden subject. Voss and Laura maintain a secrecy about their relationship that is hard to explain other than in terms of guilt. Laura tells no one of Voss' proposal, not even her sympathetic cousin Belle. She closes her secret tight within her, as if it were shameful. Yet she adopts Mercy, knowing that rumour will prevail that Mercy is her own illegitimate daughter; that rumour, it seems, is for Laura the lesser of two sources of shame. Voss too says nothing of Laura to the members of his expedition. He could have acknowledged her to Palfreyman when he makes a verbal slip, 'So my wife speaks' (p. 278), but when Palfreyman quickly asks if he is married, he wiggles his way out of it by suggesting faulty English grammar, the use of present tense for conditional. What Meaulnes, Voss and Laura have in common is a strange fear of being accused of loving someone, a fear that I have endeavoured to explain.

The oedipal origins of their love explain the heroes' ambivalence to it: the reluctance to express it in the presence of the woman loved, the escape to less threatening fantasies, the impossibility of ever resolving it. Meaulnes flees from the marriage he sought; Voss, who would be more persistent, is punished for his presumption—indeed, he is killed for it. The form of his death, decapitation instead of spearing, is so unexpected that it invites speculation: is his head a substitute for the more fundamental penis? Marie Maclean, citing the number of head wounds in *Le Grand Meaulnes*—to Yvonne, to Frantz, and the baby—wondered, with good reason, if these could be interpreted as an expression of a castration fear in that novel (p. 147). Voss also has his head scored badly by a tree branch when his horse shies at a snake (p. 221–22), and very shortly after that is kicked in the stomach by one of the mules (p. 225), another likely castration symbol.

Above all, it is the impossibility of resolving the oedipal love story that presents problems for the author. He must try to bring contradictions into harmony: he has to engage our sympathetic interest in the story while denying it a happy ending. There can be no happy ending to such a story.[17] How did Alain-Fournier and White contrive to make these love stories attractive in spite of their problematic content? Certainly the romantic glow (in Yvonne's case) or the powerful aura (in Laura's case) that they cast around the woman helps. For the man the pursuit of love is associated with an out of the world experience (the 'fête étrange' for Meaulnes) or an out of the world undertaking to make another land one's own (for Voss). So the oedipal quest for the mother figure becomes vindicated, dignified, and elevated by its association with another quest theme, the conquering of another land. In these two novels, the quest for the dreamworld of the 'Domaine inconnu' or the mapping of the interior of Australia is part of the quest for the elusive, inaccessible woman, the source of inspiration. My stress in this essay has been on the quest for the woman. Each quest heightens the other, but neither can succeed, for they both spring from unrealisable impulses metamorphosed into romantic ideals.

What struck White in Alain-Fournier's novel, and what he reproduced in his, was the elusive, dreamlike nature of the double quest of the woman and the land she inhabits (a special land, it is implied, that is not quite like any other). White too portrays the increasing remoteness in the lovers' relationship even as they seek togetherness, the sense of a quest

---

[17] Cf. Maclean (1973): 'cet amour sans issu possible … [a] fourni la tension spirituelle qui permettait la création du *Grand Meaulnes*, qui la rendait même indispensable' [this love without any possible resolution furnished the spiritual tension that allowed the creation of *Le Grand Meaulnes*, even making it essential], p. 167.

moving further and further from realisation even as it is pursued. If there seems to be something sacred in the pursuit of the quests, there is something sacred too, one senses, that is being violated by the quests. Fear and confusion hang over the quests, even if not articulated. The quest itself, not the fulfilment, is the goal, and it ends almost inevitably in a death, Yvonne's in the one novel, Voss' in the other. In both novels, there are plenty of signs that death is waiting in the wings.

The theme of the quest for an inaccessible woman in or from a strange land in*Le Grand Meaulnes* and *Voss* so links these novels as to suggest influence of one on the other. While it is true that this theme has its roots in a long and distinguished literary tradition,[18] no other work comes as close to White's novel as Alain-Fournier's does; and both at times approach the mystical. White twice mentioned it as one of his favourite works because it stayed in his mind: he no doubt had a photographic memory, like the memory he attributed to Basil Hunter, one of his personas, in *The Eye of the Storm*.[19]

It would have been the sense of mystery that most attracted White to Alain-Fournier's novel. Marie Maclean in her book on Alain-Fournier listed his favourite concepts as revealed in his vocabulary, words like 'aventure', 'charme', 'chimère', 'cérémonie', 'enchanteur', 'étrange', 'fantasque', 'idéal', 'illusion', 'image', 'imaginer', 'jeu' [game], 'merveille', 'magique', 'mystérieux', 'perfection', 'reflet' [reflection], 'rêve' [dream], 'représentation', 'revenant' [ghost], 'romantique', 'souvenir', 'silhouette', tourbillon'

---

[18] In Alain-Fournier's immediate past one can recognise works like Flaubert's *L'Education Sentimentale* (1869), Bédier's *Tristan et Iseut* (1900), Maeterlinck's *Pelléas et Mélisande* (1892) and Debussy's opera based upon it (1902), which Alain-Fournier saw twice. In White's past one can recognise, among other works, Goethe's *Faust* (1808) and also Bédier's *Tristan*, which he used again in *A Fringe of Leaves*.

[19] Basil 'had a phenomenal memory. As a boy, he could recite whole scenes from Shakespeare' (p. 100). On White's memory, see chapter 7 in this collection.

[whirlwind], 'troupe', and 'vision' (p. 167). Geneviève Laigle likewise in her long study of *Le Sens du Mystère dans l'Oeuvre Romanesque de Patrick White* (1989) listed White's favourite concepts as revealed in his vocabulary, and they are strikingly similar to Alain-Fournier's: words like 'dream', 'expedition', 'mystery', 'magic', 'perfection', 'secret', 'secretive', 'strange', 'supernatural', 'supernal', 'esoteric', and 'recollection' (Avant-Propos 2). Alain-Fournier indirectly made a contribution to Australian literature by providing White with a model for the double quest that is the theme of *Voss* and by helping him to add a dimension of mystery to it. It was through the suggestion of dimensions beyond the everyday that White sought to invest Australia with a spirituality he found lacking in it. And it was through his great admiration of European literature and the culture it reflected that White sought to elevate Australian culture above the mediocrity he found in it in the 1950s.[20] That was his most enduring goal, almost impossible for one person to achieve—and yet he did just that.

[20] See White (1968).

5

THREE CONCLUSIONS: *BUDDENBROOKS*, *THE AUNT'S STORY* AND *VOSS*[1]

John Docker's recent attempt to link White with an Australian literary tradition of romantic idealism[2] is insular and distorts his literary orientation. White's real connections are with the European literary tradition: with Flaubert, Rimbaud, Alain-Fournier, Mann, and Dostoevsky on the Continent, with Joyce and Lawrence in the United Kingdom.[3] I would like here to demonstrate something of the influence of Mann's *Buddenbrooks,* which White has told me he read in the early 1930s, when he was studying modern languages at Cambridge.

The family backgrounds of Mann and White are quite similar: both writers represent the fourth generation of people with business acumen ending in artistic sensibility. White seems to have felt some identification with Mann accordingly. Mann's family was urban, located in Lübeck, while White's family was pastoral, located in the Upper Hunter Valley. Mann and White both appear to have felt some guilt about not being able to follow the family tradition, or even wanting to do so, for they see the artistic sensibility as a form of decadence. The development of a family from commercial success to the appearance of artistic talent, a

---

[1] First published in 1979, *Literary Half-Yearly*, 20(1): 134–41.

[2] Docker (1974).

[3] See chapter 2 in this collection.

development seen as symptomatic of a decline, is a leading theme in *Buddenbrooks,* subtitled 'The Decline of a Family', and is reflected palely in the history of the Parker family in *The Tree of Man.*[4]

But I am concerned specifically with the influence of *Buddenbrooks* on White where it is clearest: on *The Aunt's Story* and, particularly, on *Voss.* It is in the final half-pages of the three novels that the resemblances are most striking. All three novels end with a forceful assertion of the superiority of a world of the spirit to the ordinary world in which most people live. The assertion is made in each case by a spinster who is a somewhat ludicrous figure physically or a failure socially: Sesemi Weichbrodt, Theodora Goodman, and Laura Trevelyan. Both Mann and White make a strong contrast between this pathetic figure and her spiritual convictions.

Before we consider these points more closely, let me quote here the basic text in my comparison, the conclusion of *Buddenbrooks.* The translation is my own.

> 'Hanno, little Hanno,' went on Frau Permaneder, with tears flowing over the down and the lifeless skin of her cheeks. 'Tom, father, grandfather, and all the others. Where are they gone to? One sees them no more. Oh, it is so hard and sad!'
>
> 'There will be a reunion,' said Friederike Buddenbrook, clasping her hands in her lap, casting down her eyes and lifting her nose in the air.

[4] *The Tree of Man* is unusual as a saga of an early Australian family, dealing with decadence rather than development—a notion closer to Mann than to the optimism one might expect of a Great Australian Novel. Like Mann, White tells his story of the rise and decline of a family within one lifetime, that of the main male character. The highest point in the Parkers' material success is reached when Thelma is invited to dine at Government House. The family turns to decadence in Ray's son, who in the final chapter shows an artistic sensibility accompanied by a neurotic tension.

> 'Yes, so they say ... Oh, there are hours, Friederike, when there is no comfort, may God forgive me—when one begins to doubt justice, goodness, and everything. Life breaks so many of us to pieces; it lets so many beliefs come to ruin. A reunion ... if only there were!'
>
> But then Sesemi Weichbrodt raised herself at the table, as high as ever she could. She stood on tiptoe, stretched her neck, and rapped on the table. The cap trembled on her head.
>
> '*It is so*!' she said with her whole strength and looked at them all defiantly.
>
> She stood there, a victor in the good fight that she had fought all her life against the onslaughts of reason in her role as a teacher—humpbacked and quivering with conviction, a tiny, admonishing, inspired prophetess.

In *Buddenbrooks* the superiority that Sesemi claims so strongly for the spiritual world lies primarily in the reunion that it offers, a reunion that makes unimportant any decline within the Buddenbrook family. The four generations that are represented by Hanno, Tom, Johann, and the old Johann are all accorded equal value in a world that is beyond mutability. In *The Aunt's Story* the superiority of the world of the spirit to the ordinary world is suggested even more forcefully, paradoxically by the very failure to discuss the values of the ordinary world—these values are not considered worthy of discussion.[5] There are only disdainful references to 'the pathetic presumption of the white room' where Theodora will spend the rest of her days, and to the people who look after her as limited, even if admirable. The spiritual world in *The Aunt's Story* is one where irreconcilable contraries are accepted and peace is attained.

[5] The situation is analogous to a comic strip in Peanuts, in which Snoopy is to write on the theme, 'Why Dogs are Superior to Cats'. After much thought, he writes 'They just are and that's that.'

(The reconciling of contraries is itself a strong Mann preoccupation.) The contraries are those described by Holstius when he tells Theodora that she is torn in two:

> 'What is it,' she asked in agony, 'you expect me to do or say?'
>
> 'I expect you to accept the two irreconcilable halves ... You cannot reconcile joy and sorrow ... Or flesh and marble, or illusion and reality, or life and death. For this reason, Theodora Goodman, you must accept.' (p. 293)

In her world of the spirit Theodora will also be free from the consequences of mutability. Her mistake, Holstius tells her, has been to assume that permanence is a property of pyramids, whereas true permanence is rather a state of multiplication and division (p. 299). Henceforth there will be no end to the lives of Theodora Goodman, which will continue to meet and part and interchange. In *Voss* the world of the spirit is for Laura Trevelyan one of special insight. At the end of the novel she is portrayed as a prophetess, like Sesemi, declaring her strong faith in Australia's destiny ('we are in every way provided for, by God and nature, and consequently, must survive') and in Voss' permanent achievement. When asked about Voss, 'the German fellow who died', she states emphatically that he did not die:

> 'He is there still, it is said, in the country, and always will be. His legend will be written down, eventually, by those who have been troubled by it.'
>
> 'Come, come. If we are not certain of the facts, how is it possible to give the answers?'
>
> 'The air will tell us,' Miss Trevelyan said. (p. 478)

Thus she corroborates Le Mesurier's vision in his poem 'Conclusion': 'Where is his spirit? ... It has gone out, it has gone away, it is everywhere' (p. 316). For Voss, then, the world of the spirit is a world where he has become one with God and nature and is therefore, like Theodora and the Buddenbrooks, free from mutability.

In all three novels there is a contrast between the social or physical misfit and the noble sentiment that she expresses. Sesemi Weichbrodt in particular rises to a moral height that is out of all proportion to her physical stature. Theodora, with her downy complexion (recalling Frau Permaneder's) and general physical ugliness, cuts an odd figure for one about to enter an exalted physical plane. Laura, now a middle-aged woman, has become positively ugly and her appearance is not helped any by her 'truly hideous dress' (p. 465). Immediately after uttering her firm assurance that 'The air will tell us' what became of Voss, she dissolves into insecurity: 'By which time she had grown hoarse and fell to wondering aloud whether she had brought her lozenges'. White's concluding lines, which present Laura's statement of faith and then follow it by a suggestion of frailty, strikingly resemble Mann's concluding lines, which present Sesemi's grand declaration of faith and also follow it by a reminder of her vulnerability. And Laura, like Sesemi earlier, is the headmistress of a school.

All three women, Sesemi, Theodora, and Laura have a ludicrous quality in their final appearance, and could be laughed at by an unsympathetic onlooker. Neither Mann nor White does laugh at them, but they do make us aware that they could be considered laughable. Mann and White alike use the ludicrous quality of their characters to contrast with, and so heighten, their spiritual exaltedness compared with the spiritual commonplaceness of the people around them.

Mann and White even use their character's family name to reinforce the contrast between the strength of her conviction and her social eccentricity. 'Weichbrodt' is a plebeian name meaning 'soft bread', and the first name 'Sesemi' suggests sesame seed; the whole name is ludicrous. Theodora's family name, 'Goodman', has a middle-class commonplaceness and puritan quality that contrast with the exceptional nature of her imaginative life; and her assumed name, 'Pilkington', has an old-maidish quality that intensifies our awareness of her as a spinster (whoever heard of a Mrs Pilkington?). Laura's spinsterdom is emphasised by the fact that over the last ten pages or so of the novel she is referred to only as 'Miss Trevelyan', never as Laura. Her name, moreover, has a formal dignity about it that discourages familiarity.

While the conclusion of *Voss* is much closer to the conclusion of *Buddenbrooks* than is the end of *The Aunt's Story*, there is one detail in the final picture of Theodora that suggests memory of Sesemi operating in White. As Theodora prepares to leave for the mental home where she will lead her life of the spirit, she dons her hat: 'The hat sat straight, but the doubtful rose trembled and glittered, leading a life of its own' (p. 303). Likewise, as Sesemi raises herself to her full height, the cap trembles on her head. A couple of sentences later, the reason for its trembling is spelled out: that Sesemi herself is quivering with conviction. With Theodora the rose on her hat becomes a symbol of her life within the spirit, uncertain but glorious, trembling but glittering; it is set in opposition to the hat itself, which symbolises her external physical existence ('The hat sat straight'). A small detail, perhaps, but it is in such small details that memory is prone to show itself.

For all the protestation made by their characters, Mann and White seem incompletely convinced of the higher world of the spirit. There is a defensiveness in Sesemi and Laura that points to an unsureness within the author himself. Sesemi looks defiantly at the company when she proclaims '*It is so!*' as if she would allay their doubts by the force of her will alone. Laura grows conveniently hoarse when she announces 'The air will tell us', thereby precluding further discussion.

There is however a difference in the form and degree of defensiveness between Mann and White. Mann clearly admires Sesemi; one detects a warmth and sympathy in his treatment of her that is missing in White's presentation of Theodora and Laura. Sesemi is not set totally apart from the Buddenbrook ladies: their faith is weaker, as Friederike indicates, but it is not fundamentally different from hers. White is more concerned with shielding Theodora and Laura from criticism and bolstering their uncertain superiority than with presenting them sympathetically. He sets them apart from and above the people around them, to whom they adopt a patronising attitude. Theodora's remark, 'You Americans … make life positively pneumatic' (p. 303), has a sharp edge to it, implying that a catering to material comfort is the limit of their achievement: they would not understand her higher life. Laura too, is condescending, with her sarcastic '*So you see,* we are in every way provided for' (my italics), and her dismissive 'The air will tell us' (p. 478). One can feel little empathy with White's characters. White's conclusions, then, leave us with a radically different impression from Mann's: they are deeply impressive, but do not have the enduring sadness that characterises Mann's conclusion.

6

The Influence of John Steinbeck's *The Pastures of Heaven* on Patrick White[1]

In re-reading *The Solid Mandala* recently, I was struck by situations in it parallel to situations in Steinbeck's *Of Mice and Men*. The fat, retarded, physically powerful Arthur Brown recalls Steinbeck's Lennie, and the mutual dependence of the Brown brothers resembles that of George and Lennie. Arthur's request to stroke Mrs Poulter's hair suggests Lennie's fascination with hair, and the shooting of the Browns' old dogs parallels the shooting of Candy's old dog. The end of *The Solid Mandala*, too, in which Mrs Poulter revitalises Arthur with her life spirit, resembles the end of another of Steinbeck's novels, *The Grapes of Wrath*, in which Rosasharn nurses an old man back to life, becoming herself a sort of earth mother.

White would not have been influenced by Steinbeck, as those parallels suggest, without feeling some affinity with him. One can point to their common interest in mystical themes and in the Christ figure, and their fondness for people simple of mind and heart. And from Steinbeck's preoccupation with underdogs it is no great step to White's preoccupation with burnt ones, lonely people who lead lives apart. This affinity between the two writers, combined with a general but undefined Steinbeck quality to *Happy Valley*, led me to look elsewhere in Steinbeck

[1] First published in 1974, *Australian Literary Studies*, 6(3): 317–19.

for possible influence upon this first White novel (1939). The obvious Steinbeck work in which to seek such influence was *The Pastures of Heaven* (1932), whose title resembles that of *Happy Valley. The Pastures of Heaven* does indeed appear to have influenced *Happy Valley,* and also *The Solid Mandala;* it shows more influence on White than does any other Steinbeck novel. Its present rarity in Australia (my copy came on loan from Monash University) is no comment on its literary merit. Many Steinbeck critics think highly of it, and at least one, Maxwell Geismar,[2] regards it as his masterpiece. In any case, White has acknowledged reading Steinbeck in England in the 1930s, when Steinbeck's reputation was at its height.

It is especially in theme that *Happy Valley* resembles *The Pastures of Heaven.* Both novels reject the notion of a utopia: their titles are ironic. Alys Browne's fantasy in White's novel of her pastures of heaven as lying in California particularly suggests memory of Steinbeck's novel at work in White; Alys concludes, like Steinbeck, that life has its difficulties wherever one is. White's rejection of a utopia is stronger than Steinbeck's, for his valley is cold and grey, while Steinbeck's 'sweet valley' is sheltered and verdant. Both novels deal with the failure to fulfil one's dreams and its shattering of one's illusions. Steinbeck's Whitesides, for instance, when they migrate to the California valley, do not multiply and prosper, and their fine old house is burned down. And Pat Humbert's dream of winning Mae Munroe by refurnishing his house in Vermont is shattered when he learns on its completion of Mae's approaching wedding. White's Oliver Halliday does not become a poet, Alys Browne does not go to California, the two do not leave for a new life together, and Vic Moriarty does not get to live in Sydney with a maid of her own. There is a personal disintegration in *The Pastures of Heaven* when Molly Morgan has her delusions about her father dispelled, and in *Happy Valley* when Mrs Furlow's plans for Sidney's marriage fall through.

---

[2] Geismar (1942).

The physical difference between the idyllic Californian valley and the bleak Australian valley focuses the difference in mood between the two authors. Steinbeck's novel, in spite of its severely realistic content, is basically accepting of life and affirmative. His characters are saddened by the death of their dreams, but are not driven into withdrawal. Pat Humbert and Molly Morgan may appear to be exceptions to this observation, but Pat's retreat into psychosis was inevitable, and Molly's disintegration, one feels, is only temporary—she seems fundamentally stable enough to recover the necessary balance to lead a meaningful life again. White's novel is negative. All his characters deal with the death of their dreams by adopting a course of withdrawal, from emotion in general ('all those passions that sweep down through negligence or design to consume and desolate', as Oliver puts it on the final page) and from personal relationships. Steinbeck's characters draw sustenance from one another, White's from themselves alone: 'your existence in Happy Valley must be sufficient in itself' (p. 116).

The biracial society of *The Pastures of Heaven* and *Happy Valley* is a point of more similarity between the two novels than may at first appear. The presence of two Chinese families in an isolated community in the Australian snow region is rather surprising, especially since the Quongs are largely extraneous to the story. They do provide White with an opportunity to show the racism within Australia, but I suspect that they may be present largely as White's equivalent of Steinbeck's paisanos (in *The Pastures of Heaven,* the Lopez sisters).

A closer parallel in character and situation is that between Shark Wicks in *The Pastures of Heaven* and Mr Belper in *Happy Valley.* Shark speculates in shares (though only on paper) and is respected as an affluent man until he is unmasked as poor when he cannot post bail for himself; his shattered image is repaired by his wife's faith and love. Mr Belper, one of the two rich men in *Happy Valley,* speculates in shares and loses all his savings on them; his damaged image is also repaired by his wife's acceptance of the loss.

The Pastures of Heaven and *Happy Valley* have a similarly loose structure: every so often the lives of the characters touch, but the connections are weak. On the whole, the lives of the characters in *The Pastures of Heaven* link more extensively than do those of the characters in *Happy Valley*. Steinbeck's characters may not often meet, but they are shown as communicating well with one another; in White the sets of characters linked by the one person (e.g., the Furlows and the Moriartys linked by Hagan) are on barely more than nodding terms. There is a sense of community in *The Pastures of Heaven* that is absent in *Happy Valley*. The difference is pointed up by the fact that Pat Humbert has somewhere to go every night after the death of his parents, whereas 'There never was co-operation in Happy Valley, not even in the matter of living … In Happy Valley the people existed in spite of each other' (p. 28). White is above all the novelist of aloneness, from this first novel to his last.

The Pastures of Heaven did not influence *Happy Valley* alone among White's works. The final scene in *The Solid Mandala* where Mrs Poulter takes Arthur's head in her hands and strokes it, declaring 'I believe in you', is strikingly similar to the scene in *The Pastures of Heaven* (chapter 3), where Katherine Wicks takes Shark's head in her hands and strokes it, also declaring 'I believe in you'. Both women act as a sort of life force to revitalise the shattered man, working themselves into a state of exaltation and imparting a religious quality to the scene. Steinbeck himself liked the scene enough to use it again for the end of *The Grapes of Wrath*. There are traces of both Steinbeck scenes in the end of *The Solid Mandala*.

I do not wish to lose a sense of proportion in pointing to Steinbeck's influence on White. Even on *Happy Valley*, his is not the only influence operative: the Sidney Furlow story, for instance, is strongly reminiscent of D.H. Lawrence. The three Steinbeck novels I have mentioned are not so important as Dostoevsky's *The Idiot* and *The Brothers Karamazov* in assisting interpretation of *The Solid Mandala*. Nevertheless, Steinbeck's influence is important enough for his name to be added to the list of those writers who influenced White. Until now it has been missing.

7
WILLA CATHER AND PATRICK WHITE[1]

White visited America in 1939, hoping to find a publisher for *Happy Valley*. During the course of his stay, he spent three weeks in New Mexico, with the intention of making a sort of pilgrimage to the shrine of D.H. Lawrence near Taos. In Taos he met Spud Johnson, a member of the artistic circle surrounding Mabel Dodge Luhan. Spud and Patrick became lovers in a brief, intense affair, and Spud very probably accompanied him to meet Frieda Lawrence. The Lawrences had originally stayed with Mabel Dodge Luhan at her invitation in 1923, but later moved to their own ranch some twenty miles from Taos, where White visited Frieda. A number of important writers had stayed with Mabel: Aldous Huxley and his wife in 1937, Willa Cather in 1925. Spud had met Willa Cather, whose reputation, already high in the 1920s and 1930s, has continued to grow, establishing her as one of the most enduring American writers of her time. The Lawrences also met Willa. Frieda liked her and got on well with her, but Lawrence may have felt a little threatened, for he somewhat contradictorily accused her of 'literariness', suggesting a feminine sensibility, and of being 'heavyfooted', implying a masculine deportment.

If by chance White was not already familiar with Cather's works before he visited America, he would certainly have heard of her during his

[1] First published in 2006, *Antipodes*, 20(2): 164–68.

stay. And Spud Johnson would have urged him to read *Death Comes for the Archbishop*,[2] then as now the classic novel of New Mexico. That White read it before he wrote *The Tree of Man* is clear from a borrowing from its most beautiful scene—and there is another, more extended borrowing from the very same scene in *The Eye of the Storm*. White knew a good scene when he encountered it, and it could stay in his mind to be reworked years later.

Once White had read *Death Comes for the Archbishop*, it would have been natural for him to go on to other Cather masterpieces. He read *O Pioneers!*,[3] and was so moved by the tragic death of Cather's lovers under the mulberry tree that he borrowed from it to create his own scene under the mulberry tree in *The Tree of Man*, where Stan's failure to respond to Amy's passionate kiss spells the death of passion for them. He would have read *My Antonia*,[4] first published in 1918, too before writing *The Tree of Man*, but did not borrow from it; he found in it, rather, a model for his own pioneer novel.[5] And at some stage he read *A Lost Lady*, whose most famous scene—Niel's overhearing Frank Ellinger and Mrs Forrester in her bedroom—he reworked nearly twenty years later in *The Twyborn Affair*.[6]

In the course of this essay, I propose to discuss White's borrowings from the Cather novels mentioned above. The cumulative evidence of his borrowings is stronger than that of any one instance. White's debt to Cather has not been hitherto recognised, for few White critics know Cather well, and few Cather critics know White. Both writers grew up in essentially pioneer times in their respective countries and both of them could have claimed, as Cather did indirectly in quoting Virgil, '*Primus*

[2] Cather (1927). Page references in this chapter are to this edition.
[3] Cather (1913). Page references in this chapter are to this edition.
[4] Cather (1946). Page references in this chapter are to this edition.
[5] See chapter 14 in this collection.
[6] Cather (1923). Page references in this chapter are to this edition.

ego in patriam mecum ... deducam Musas'; [I am the first ... to bring the Muses with me into my land] (3.2).[7] For Cather the *patria* was Nebraska; for White it was Australia.

THE MULBERRY TREE IN *O PIONEERS!* AND *THE TREE OF MAN*: FROM OVID THROUGH CATHER TO WHITE

The episode in *The Tree of Man* in which Amy kisses Stan under a mulberry tree is the most romantic instance of sexual passion in Patrick White's novels (pp. 149–51), so powerfully evocative that even though Amy's passion is not reciprocated, the scene stays vividly in one's mind. The image of the couple in their prime of life sampling the abundant purple berries in the dappled light beneath the opulent, large-leaved tree is breathtaking, the kind of exquisite image one would expect to find in Flaubert, but does not. In fact the tree has no progenitor in nineteenth- or twentieth-century European literature: its roots are far older, originally in Asia, and within White's lifetime its most notable scion is found outside Europe, in America. The tree's ultimate ancestor is found in Ovid's Babylon (*Metamorphoses*)[8] and mentioned again in Shakespeare's Athens (*A Midsummer Night's Dream*), but its most splendid scion is found in Willa Cather's Nebraska (*O Pioneers!*) —all in association with the story of Pyramus and Thisbe. White's story is one more instance of unfulfilled love associated with the mulberry tree, but without the Pyramus-Thisbe connection. The incident is an important milestone in the relationship of Stan and Amy, never really close and destined henceforth to grow more distant. If only Stan had been able to respond to Amy's passionate impulse, the mulberry tree in White's Durilgai could have extended and revitalised the family tree in another continent. As it is, the tree retains its association with a strong romantic impulse ending in

---

[7] Cather (1946).

[8] All references are to the George Lafaye's translation (1946).

unfulfilled love. Ovid's story of the Babylonian lovers Pyramus and Thisbe in Book 4 of his *Metamorphoses* is well known and does not need retelling. If it is not known to White's readers directly from Ovid, it is familiar to them in outline as the story that Bottom and his crew of mechanicals perform and mangle as a play at the wedding of Duke Theseus in *A Midsummer Night's Dream*. The mulberry tree is of central importance in Ovid, for it is the lovers' blood falling upon the white berries and turning them purple henceforth that is the metamorphosis in this particular story. The mulberry tree is mentioned in Shakespeare, but only fleetingly as an item in the location where the lovers have agreed to meet: Thisbe draws her lover's dagger and dies 'in mulberry shade' (5.1). Ovid's tale is not tragic, not even particularly touching: he tells it factually, as an interesting story that ends unhappily. The only romantic touch, other than the metamorphosis of the tree, is the lovers' communication through the crack in the wall. They plan their meeting under the mulberry tree by the tomb of Ninus with the straightforward practicality of teenagers sneaking out on their parents. Ovid is neither startled nor admiring when Pyramus takes his own life; he seems to look upon the lovers' suicide as precipitate rather than horrifying. It is probably because of Ovid's casual attitude that Shakespeare felt free to present a farcical version of the story.

But Cather, a Latin scholar at the University of Nebraska in Lincoln, and a Latin teacher at a Pittsburgh high school from 1900 to 1902, took Ovid's tale very seriously and went on to refashion it in *O Pioneers!* Cather was, of course, strongly influenced by her study of Latin literature, just as White was influenced by his study of French and German. If Virgil helped to heighten her interest in the rural vegetation and landscapes around her—they were both precise botanists—Ovid taught her how to create memorable scenes and images by means of a metamorphosis, a transformation. Where Cather surpasses Ovid is in her ability to make the transformation moving rather than wondrous, and in doing so, she provided a model for White in his scenes of transformation.

It is in part 4 of *O Pioneers!* ('The White Mulberry Tree') that the mulberry tree and the lovers most get sympathetic attention. The ill-starred lovers Marie and Emil die beneath the tree, shot by Marie's jealous husband, and their blood, like that of Ovid's lovers, stains the white mulberries purple. Cather's metamorphosis, however, lies not in a permanent change in the colour of the mulberries but in the transformation of the lovers' souls into white butterflies that float above their bodies:

> the stained, slippery grass, the darkened mulberries, told only half the story. Above Marie and Emil, two white butterflies from Frank's field were fluttering in and out among the interlacing shadows; diving and soaring, now close together, now far apart; and in the long grass by the fence the last wild roses of the year opened their pink hearts to die. (4.8)

Transformation plays a large part in Cather as in Ovid, but Cather's images of transformation concentrate in themselves the ecstasy and the sadness of human life, whereas they are more a playful fancy in Ovid. It is Cather's admixture of happiness and sadness that I believe stayed in White's mind, the emotions along with the setting, as he conceived the incident of Amy's passionate kiss and Stan's stoniness, prompting him to a compassion rare in his works. Where White is compassionate, it is usually under the literary influence of another author, in this case Cather.

Stan and Amy both call to mind at the same time the kiss under the mulberry tree after they walk through their garden one summer night, caressed by the shrubs and flowers, a night when Stan 'should, by rights, have been chained by her power of soft darkness. But … it might have been hard daylight in which they walked' (p. 149). Irritated and resentful at Stan's now characteristic unresponsiveness Amy leaves him and goes inside. As she begins to wind wool her mind goes back to the time when his lack of response hurt her most deeply, a memory she would clearly like to repress but cannot:

> as she wound she thought recklessly of the moment at the mulberry tree. She had been gathering mulberries, and was stained by them. Big glistening leaves waved upon their stalks as she worked. There was a continual opening and closing of the tree, an interplay of sky and leaves, of light and shade, so that she was mottled with it, as well as stained by the juice. Then her husband had come, and they stood together, inside the envelope of the shining tree, talking, and laughing at nothing, and gathering fruit. Then she had kissed him suddenly on his surprised mouth, with such vehemence, she remembered the impact of their teeth, destroying the soft ripeness of mulberries. And he laughed and looked almost shaken; *he did not hold with kissing by daylight.* So that she began again quietly to gather the fruit, ashamed of her ripeness and her purple hands. (pp. 149–50; my italics)

Her anger at Stan's unresponsiveness quickly shrivels the romantic aspects of her memory:

> How flat the leaves were afterwards. Some fruit had little maggoty things, but frankly, these would cook up. Her husband had continued to gather with her for a little while. He was drying up, as the result of working hard for many years in the sun … His muscles, which had been developed by work, were beginning to look too obvious, at times even ludicrous. So they gathered fruit together, and after a while he went. (p. 150)

The power of White's scene under the mulberry tree comes not from tragic death as in Cather but from the enduring hurt it inflicts upon Amy in an idyllic situation. The purple stain on her hands suggests both the blood of sexual passion and blood flowing from her emotional wound. She is aware that her passionate kiss ought to have aroused Stan but it did not and will not, for Stan is 'at best kind, at worst cold, but always closed to her' (p. 150).

Stan's memory of the scene under the mulberry tree occurs at the same time as Amy's, for he has sensed the same disappointment in her as when they separated under the mulberry tree. Now she implicitly accuses him: 'I am going in, Stan. We can't walk about like lunatics all night. There are things to do' (p. 149). His memory of the incident under the mulberry tree and his reaction to it are very different from Amy's. His feeling for her was friendly, not sexual: he enjoyed gathering the fruit with her. When they were physically close, he was surprised to notice her 'burnt beauty', probably catching something sexual looming, and was startled at her sudden kiss. He immediately cancelled out any intimacy: 'the desire to grapple with the unknown woman, who was also his wife, quickly dried up' (p. 151). His problem was to get out of the situation without embarrassment: 'She went on gathering fruit. And he, after gathering a few more handfuls, to make it appear more natural, went back up the path, wondering' (p. 151). For Stan the mulberry tree episode represents an embarrassment he can easily live with; for Amy it represents a chronic wound. There was no purple stain on Stan's hands.

When one surveys these stories of blighted love associated with a mulberry tree, it becomes clear why the authors have found the tree so congenial a symbol. The tree itself, generous in its spread and embrace, thickly foliaged with large healthy leaves, seems welcoming and protective towards the lovers. In its keen responsiveness to their pain, it has almost a spiritual presence. Whether its white berries are stained by the lovers' blood or its purple berries point to the wound of unfulfilled love, it is the ideal location for a meeting of lovers who should have had such happiness open to them, but who find that possibility cut abruptly, even violently short.

A Benison in the Garden: *Death Comes for the Archbishop, The Tree of Man* and *The Eye of the Storm*

That White knew and was indebted to *Death Comes for the Archbishop* is clear from two passages in his novels, one in *The Tree of Man* and one nearly twenty years later in *The Eye of the Storm*, that strikingly resemble one of the most memorable scenes in Cather's novel. All three scenes are scenes of transformation, even transfiguration, and suggest a benison.

The passage in *Death Comes for the Archbishop* shows the two priests, Bishop Latour and his vicar Joseph Vaillant, in their garden one May, when Magdalena, the woman who saved them and whom they in turn saved from her murderous consort, appears there to feed the doves and to gather flowers:

> She advanced in a whirlwind of gleaming wings, and Tranquilino dropped his spade and stood watching her. At one moment the whole flock of doves caught the light in such a way that they all became invisible at once, dissolved in light, and disappeared as salt dissolves in water. The next moment they flashed around, black and silver against the sun. They settled upon Magdalena's arms and shoulders, ate from her hand … A handsome woman she had grown to be, with her comely figure and the deep claret colour under the golden brown of her cheeks …
>
> 'Who would think, to look at her now, that we took her from a place where every vileness of cruelty and lust was practised!' murmured Father Vaillant … 'Can I ever forget it! But her very body has changed. She was then a shapeless, cringing creature. I thought her half-witted … Here she is safe and happy.' Father Vaillant sat up and called to her. 'Magdalena, Magdalena, my child, come here and talk to us for a little. Two men grow lonely when they see nobody but each other.' (7.1)

The same linking of flowers and birds and light in a garden to a transformation and a blessing occurs at the beginning of chapter 9 in *The Tree of Man*, where Amy carries her new baby around in her garden:

> She walked about on the shady borders of the house, and now indeed she was the centre of the universe. Light converged on the white cocoon she was holding in her arms; the course of birds invested it with mystical importance as they hovered above it, almost, in fussy flight; flowers and leaves inclined above the head of the woman with the child or gave blessings with long, benevolent wands when there was a breeze. (p. 112)

Cather's scene is not easily forgotten, but White may well have read it again years later to boost his own inspiration for the closing scene of *The Eye of the Storm*. There Sister de Santis comes down into the garden early in the morning after Elizabeth Hunter has died, in order to feed the birds. Blessed by the still lingering spirit of Elizabeth, she undergoes a dramatic transfiguration:

> as she filled the birds' dishes … her arms were rounded [query: surrounded?] by increasing light. In the street an early worker stared as he passed, but looked away on recognising a ceremony. A solitary rose, tight crimson, emerged in the lower garden; it would probably open later in the day. Light was strewing the park as she performed her rites. Birds followed her, battering the air … At the topmost step it occurred to her that she must take this first and last rose to her patient Irene Fletcher …
>
> She poured the remainder of the seed into the dish on the upper terrace. The birds already clutching the terracotta rim, scattered as she blundered amongst them, then wheeled back, clashing, curving, descending and ascending, shaking the tassels of light or seed suspended from the dish. She could feel claws snatching for a hold in her hair. She ducked, to escape from this prism of dew and light, this tumult of wings and her own unmanageable joy. Once she raised an arm to brush aside a blue wedge of pigeon's feathers. The light she could not ward off: it was by now too solid; herself possessed. Shortly after she went inside the house. In the hall she bowed her head, amazed and not a little frightened by what she saw in Elizabeth Hunter's looking glass. (p. 608)

Using the same essential materials—birds, a garden, light, a suggestion of omens—as in the scene of Amy's transfiguration in *The Tree of Man*, materials that Cather used before him, White achieves here his most memorable depiction of a transfiguration, a metamorphosis that awes the person to whom it is granted (she was 'not a little frightened by what she saw').

The Loss of an Illusion in *A Lost Lady*, *The Tree of Man*, and *The Twyborn Affair*

White's last borrowing from Cather, from *A Lost Lady*, comes late in his career, in *The Twyborn Affair*. The scene he adapted from *A Lost Lady* is the famous one in which Niel, stooping to leave a bunch of wild roses outside one of the French windows opening from Mrs Forrester's bedroom, overhears her laughter—'impatient, indulgent, teasing, eager'—and that of her lover, Frank Ellinger—'fat and lazy' (p. 86). In that instant, we are told, 'he had lost one of the most beautiful things in his life', an admiration 'that had been like a bloom on his existence' (p. 86). Cather is careful to confine Niel's disillusionment to throwing the roses, now a 'prickly bunch', into a mud-hole that the cattle had trampled, for 'It was not a moral scruple she had outraged, but an aesthetic ideal' (p. 87). In keeping with the loss of an ideal rather than a personal betrayal, the sentiment that comes to Niel's mind as he flees is from literature and not from life, which he has not experienced at its rawest. It is from Shakespeare's *Othello*: 'lilies that fester small far worse than weeds'. Cather does not allow Niel to descend into rage: she never ruins a moving scene by coarsening it in any way. So she shows a more matured Niel retaining an affection and concern for Mrs Forrester; later he saves her reputation by cutting the telephone wire as she is on the verge of betraying the nature of her relationship with Frank to the inevitable listener.

White's borrowing from Cather has none of the delicacy with which she shows the disillusionment of an idealistic young man. When Eddie goes up to Marcia Lushington's house, it is not, like Niel, to offer a token of his admiration, but to appease her displeasure at certain negligences of his, 'or perhaps on overcoming that displeasure, to prove to himself that she was still his mistress' (p. 287). For he has already had sex with her on two occasions, failed to respond to her advances on one occasion, and failed to have her respond to his on another. What strikes one as he approaches the house is his overall indifference—to his negligence, to

Marcia, and especially to the possibility of sex. The scene that follows, in which he overhears Marcia and Don Prowse just as Niel overheard Mrs Forrester and Frank Ellinger, is still one of disillusionment, but it is a disillusionment that springs essentially from sexual jealousy and not from the loss of an ideal. It is obvious to Eddie that Marcia and Don have possessed each other, just as they have possessed him (Marcia had led him to her bed and Don had penetrated him sexually only a few days before). Feeling jealous—of Marcia rather than of Don—he withdraws from the scene. He had approached the house feeling that 'It was most important that he should decide how much of his life was serious and how much farce' (p. 287), but leaves it in confusion, retreating to his own room, where he begins to masturbate. There is an in-your-face quality in the late White that has taken him far from Willa Cather; nevertheless, this scene has its inspiration in *A Lost Lady*.

The scene that follows Eddie's overhearing of Marcia and Don Prowse is also borrowed from Cather. But it is a minor borrowing whose chief importance lies in its corroboration of the fact that White had indeed read A *Lost Lady*.

The next day Eddie again goes up to the house, where Marcia receives him in an old cane chaise longue, part of a set of dilapidated cane furniture. She is seductive in manner, but he ignores her encouragement, even engaging briefly in recrimination, as Don Prowse did the previous night. Everything is in decline: the furniture, the stale cake, Marcia, afflicted by a heavy cold, in her old gray skirt and scuffed shoes. The situation will recall the scene in *A Lost Lady* where Niel visits the Forresters, just two chapters later than the scene of his disillusionment (2.2). Mrs Forrester receives him lying in a hammock, and is quite seductive, but Niel, in his essential decency and lingering naïveté, responds only to her charm, not her sexuality: 'He stepped forward and caught her suspended figure, hammock and all, in his arms. How light and alive she was! like a bird caught in a net.' Early in the conversation, Mrs Forrester introduces the subject of financial distress: the Forresters have had to rent the marsh to the conniving Ivy Peters. The emphasis is on decline: Niel has become a little prim, Mrs Forrester has lost some of the bloom of her complexion ('her skin was no longer like white lilacs, —it had the ivory tint of gardenias that have just begun to fade'), and there are strained lines about the corners of her mouth. What White picked up from Cather is the idea of decline following disillusionment—but he again turns it towards the unpleasant rather than the touching.

White had much to learn from Cather and might have learned more but for the limitations of his human sympathies. Although he very probably became acquainted with her work in America, it was not until he was back in Australia that his thoughts returned to her as he began to write his own pioneer novel. The most immediate affinity he would find with Cather was in her constant sense of a spiritual dimension beyond the material world, her sense of the extraordinary beyond the ordinary that he sought to achieve in his Australian novels.[9]

The two borrowings from Cather in *The Tree of Man*—the scene under the mulberry tree, whose berries attract the blood of those wounded by love (like Marie and Emil in *O Pioneers!*), and the transfiguration of Amy in the garden with her firstborn (like that of Magdalena in the Bishop's garden in *Death Comes for the Archbishop*)—freed a wellspring of sympathy that makes *The Tree of Man* one of White's most approachable novels. It was a well that he was unable to draw upon for long, however. When he again adapted the scene of transfiguration in the garden in *Death Comes for the Archbishop* in order to confirm the salvation of Elizabeth Hunter in *The Eye of the Storm*, he achieved a tour de force but did not convey the sympathy that Cather showed for all the characters in her scene. White's scene is a reassertion of life as Sister de Santis is portrayed as 'throbbing with life' following Elizabeth's death the night before. Her resolution to take the rose to her new patient is not so

[9] White (1968).

much an outburst of sympathy as a timid expression of 'love *as she had come to understand it*' (p. 607; my italics). When White portrayed Eddie's disillusionment in *The Twyborn Affair*, modelled upon the experience of Niel in *A Lost Lady*, he was a man of sixty-seven; he had written the abrasive *The Solid Mandala* (1966) and *The Vivisector* (1970) and would go on to write the self-deprecating *Flaws in the Glass* (1982) and *Memoirs of Many in One* (1986). The well of his sympathy, never really deep, had run dry, and he depicted the sordid rather than the sad: what Niel overhears is the laughter of sexually satisfied lovers, but what Eddie overhears is the mutual recrimination of lovers who finally manage to set aside their antagonism in order to relieve the sexual urgencies that have driven them together there.

White has never conformed to anyone's image of what an Australian novelist should be. Although he read fairly widely in Australian literature, he shows almost no influence of other Australian authors. His works reflect rather his education in England, his readings in French and German literature, and his travels in France, Germany, and Greece. He spent only a short time in America, from late 1939 into 1941, but shows more influence from American literature than from Australian. I have demonstrated elsewhere the influence of Steinbeck upon his early work,[10] and we can now add to that the stronger influence of Willa Cather.

[10] See chapter 6 in this collection.

8

Patrick White and Theodora Goodman in New Mexico[1]

In June 1939, shortly before the outbreak of World War II, Patrick White was in New Mexico for several weeks.[2] Nine years later, in his third novel, *The Aunt's Story* (1948), he told the story of a spinster, Theodora Goodman, who is returning from France to Australia through America when, apparently on whim, she gets off the train in a small pueblo and tears up her return tickets. The novel ends with her being taken to a mental home, where she will spend the rest of her days. The novel is set in 1939, the year White was in the United States, and the place is New Mexico.

Having crossed the continent from New York to Los Angeles, White stopped in New Mexico on his way back east in order to make a sort of pilgrimage to D.H. Lawrence's shrine at his ranch north of Taos.[3] He would have had to change trains at Lamy and take a branch line to Santa Fe eighteen miles away, for Santa Fe was not directly on the transconti-

[1] First published in 2004, *Antipodes*, 18(2): 171–73.

[2] Marr (1991), p. 185.

[3] Marr (1991), p. 183.

nental rail line.[4] He would have taken a bus north to Taos, for Taos has never had a rail connection. It is clearly Taos, however, where Theodora is to be pictured getting off the train, though no train has ever gone there: White modified the geography for artistic effect. A small settlement, Taos was already a notable art colony in the 1920s, centred around Mabel Dodge Luhan, not around Lawrence as Marr suggests.[5] Mabel, a wealthy New Yorker, had moved to Taos in 1917, embracing Indian culture when she married a local Indian, Tony Luhan. Her colony of artist friends was well established before she invited Lawrence there in November 1921. He accepted and arrived in Taos in September 1922. Taos as seen through Theodora's eyes is 'pink, mostly, of baked mud, an earth pink' (p. 275). Adobe-style houses in terracotta colours are the most distinctive characteristic of New Mexican architecture. The first human presence that Theodora encounters is a 'thin, dark, perhaps an Indian woman, or a Mexican.' Shortly afterwards a woman who notices Theodora sitting there directs her to a guesthouse 'with individual cabins, where people went, and artists … and an Indian pueblo' (p. 276), the famous multi-storeyed pueblo of Taos, the oldest continuously inhabited community in the United States. ('Pueblo', incidentally, is a New Mexican word; it is not used in Arizona.)

White was most immediately attracted to New Mexico through his interest in D.H. Lawrence, who spent three years there (1922 through 1925); but Patrick and Theodora are also linked in important ways to the New Mexico of Aldous Huxley's *Brave New World* (1932).[6] Huxley had not yet visited New Mexico when he set part of *Brave New World* there—he got his information from his friend D.H. Lawrence and from his own

---

[4] Howard Bryson, in 'the Coming of the Railroad', records that New Mexico was linked by rail to both coasts in 1880, but the Atchison Topeka and the Santa Fe never passed through Atchison, Topeka, or Santa Fe. Scheck (1989), pp. 2–4.

[5] Marr (1991), p. 183.

[6] All page references in this chapter are to the 1965 New York edition.

reading—but he and his wife Maria did spend several weeks with Lawrence's widow Frieda at her ranch, San Cristóbal, in 1937, just two years before White visited the area.[7]

Lawrence's ranch is not easy to get to, being some twenty miles further north of Taos. In order to ensure access to Lawrence's shrine, where his ashes are embedded in concrete to prevent theft, White must have had some means of introduction, whether to Frieda Lawrence, or, likely enough, to Spud Johnson. Spud was an important literary figure in Mabel Dodge Luhan's circle of artists, who all knew Lawrence well; Spud had accompanied Lawrence in Mexico City when he visited it in 1923.[8] Joseph Foster, in *D.H. Lawrence in Taos*, says that Spud was an ideal companion for Lawrence since he never said anything to disagree with the strong-minded Lawrence: 'Spud was the only living man who did not annoy Lawrence ... Spud was a sweet, faintly poetic soul'.[9] White was a young man of twenty-seven, still unpublished (he was in America in search of a publisher for *Happy Valley*), and was no doubt impressed by the fact that Spud, fifteen years his senior, was an intimate of Lawrence. Spud and Patrick quickly became lovers, and even though their brief, intense affair did not survive separation, they maintained a correspondence until 1945. According to Marr, it was Dorothy Brett, another member of Mabel's circle and an old friend of Lawrence's, who took Patrick to San Cristóbal to meet Frieda.[10] But Huxley reported Brett as profoundly deaf in 1937, two years previously,[11] so it is likely that someone else went with them to help communication, perhaps Spud himself.

---

[7] Lawrence and Huxley became friends in 1915 when they met at Garsington Manor, the home of Lady Ottoline Morrell in Oxfordshire, Murray (2003). They also became acquainted there with Dorothy Brett, who preceded them to Taos.

[8] Udall (1994).

[9] Foster (1972), pp. 68–69.

[10] Marr (1991), p. 183.

[11] Murray (2003), p. 305.

Frieda, when she learned that Patrick was a writer, would almost certainly have mentioned the Huxleys' visit in 1937.

Although White spent much more time in New York and Massachusetts, it was New Mexico that stayed in his mind and that he returned to in *The Aunt's Story*. It was because New Mexico had such vivid memories and stimulating experiences for him that Theodora got off the train there and not elsewhere. White saw topological similarities between the New Mexican landscape and the Monaro district south of Canberra where he worked as a jackeroo before returning to England in 1932,[12] and so Theodora too is made to feel an affinity between the New Mexican landscape and the black volcanic hills of Meroë, her father's estate in Australia.[13] She elects to stay in the New Mexican Meroë rather than return to 'Abyssinia' (a homonym for the abyss in ya), the term she uses for Australia in a letter to her sister Fanny (p. 271), but she is no longer capable of finding peace anywhere.

But was it just to visit the Lawrence ranch that White stopped in New Mexico? Or was his curiosity also whetted by his reading of *Brave New World*, in which New Mexico plays an important role? The life lived in the isolated Indian pueblo of Malpais, where unhappiness is accepted as part of life and sexual commitment and marriage are respected, is offered

---

[12] A jackeroo is 'a young man (usually English and of independent means) gaining experience by working as a supernumerary on a sheep or cattle station'. *Australian Oxford Dictionary*. Ed. Bruce Moore. Melbourne: Oxford University Press, 1999.

[13] Meroë was the capital city of the kingdom, which flourished between the sixth century B.C. and the fourth century A.D. It was located on the Nile, in what is now northern Sudan. White was in that area during World War II. When I wrote in 1974 asking him 'Why the name Meroë?' he answered rather vaguely that it was one of those dark, mysterious-sounding names that appealed to him. It sounds like a Greek word, and it may be that his ultimate association was with Greece, where he would have elected to stay, like Theodora in New Mexico, if Manoly Lascaris, his companion in life, had not persuaded him to return to Australia.

as the alternative to the tranquilised, sexually unrestrained, consumer-oriented society of Huxley's *Brave New World.* John Savage, removed from Malpais and brought into the wider world, is so repelled by its values that he commits suicide. His situation is reflected in Theodora's at the end of *The Aunt's Story*. Unable to function in the ordinary world, she is reduced to a symbol, the black rose on her hat, capable perhaps of glittering and trembling at times (p. 303).

One could assume that White read the Huxley novel in the 1930s, for it was famous and enormously popular; but the assumption becomes fact through an unmistakable verbal link, Theodora's use of the word 'pneumatic' in the Huxleyan sense as she is about to be taken away to a mental home: 'You Americans … make life positively pneumatic' (p. 303). This use of the word, applied to anything well padded, links Theodora's future life to the somatised world of Huxley's novel, where 'pneumatic' is almost a leitmotif. Huxley uses the word especially of a slightly plump woman, well padded for a comfortable (if empty) sexual experience.[14] Theodora, and her creator Patrick White, use the word to mean a well-cushioned lifestyle, sharing Huxley's strong reservations about the kind of comfort offered.

The Taos that Theodora steps into and remains in, then, is the Taos that Patrick White experienced, which was essentially the Taos cultural colony that Mabel Dodge Luhan created. Among her friends was, most notably for Patrick, Spud Johnson, who became Patrick's lover, who was intimate with D.H. Lawrence, who had met Aldous Huxley in 1937 and Willa Cather when she visited Mabel back in 1925, and who was a close friend of Georgia O'Keeffe. O'Keeffe, originally a New Yorker like Mabel,

---

[14] Huxley took up the word from T.S. Eliot's 'Whispers of Immortality': 'Uncorseted, her friendly bust / Gives promise of pneumatic bliss', Eliot (1920). But Eliot used it just the once, whereas Huxley made it famous. What Eliot and Huxley have in common, under their surface amused tolerance, is a discernible sexual distaste.

observed 'Once you have experienced New Mexico, it will continue to itch at you for the rest of your life.'

It was Lawrence's accounts of New Mexico that captured Huxley's imagination and led him to locate the alternative to his dystopic utopia there in *Brave New World* (6.2). Not having been to New Mexico, Huxley makes many mistakes. For instance, he locates his reservation in Malpais, which did not exist as a pueblo, and describes Easter ceremonies that belonged to the New Mexican Penitentes and to Sicily, but not to the indigenous Indians, as taking place in summer. But these things do not matter, other than pointing to Huxley's limited knowledge of New Mexico, which interested him mostly for its literary possibilities of suggesting an alternative to the horror of his utopia. After he encountered New Mexico firsthand during his three-week stay with Frieda, Huxley did not use it again in any of his novels.

But there is something special about New Mexico that led all three writers, White, Lawrence, and Huxley, to exempt it from their general criticism of American culture. In 1925, Lawrence recorded his impression of American culture as superficial and the people as suspicious. In *Jesting Pilate*, Huxley referred to Los Angeles as Joy City, and White in *The Aunt's Story* depicted an America preoccupied with making money. Theodora's fellow passenger on the train, we are told, scrabbles on the surface of life as he relates his rise from poverty to financial security and reels off statistics of population growth and increasing production: 'he talked, and heard his own voice made small' (p. 269). The corn song that Theodora imagines, reading off its notation in the telephone wires as the train advances, represents a confident trumpeting of the nation itself and its people (p. 269).

But whatever the nature of their disapproval of American culture, Lawrence loved New Mexico and his ashes were returned to Taos from Venice, where he died in the company of the Huxleys; Huxley did settle permanently in America after he went on to Hollywood from Frieda's ranch; and White remarked that he might well have stayed in America but for the outbreak of World War II.[15] What New Mexico chiefly represented for these writers was an alternative to the decadence of an exhausted Europe and to the empty materialism of America. Theodora's abandonment of Europe after consigning it to a vast conflagration of her imagining was an expression of White's own disillusionment with his life there. Still uncertain himself about returning to a culturally immature Australia as he was writing *The Aunt's Story* in 1946, White allowed Theodora to remain in her New Mexican Meroë.

---

[15] Marr (1991), pp. 190–91.

9

FILMS AND PATRICK WHITE[1]

Certain images from films leave an indelible image in the minds of their audiences—for instance, the image in Alfred Hitchcock's *Rebecca* (1940) of the housekeeper who, having set alight to a mansion, Mandelay, appears at the window of the burning house, choosing to die with the past. The image reappears in *The Aunt's Story* (1948), as Mrs Rapallo appears at the window of the burning Hôtel du Midi before she is consumed with the building:

> The window had become quite encrusted with fire ... For a moment Mrs Rapallo looked out, as if she were not watched, but watching something that was taking place ... From the window she contemplated, only vaguely, the vague evidence of faces. Fire is fiercer ... Then, she turned and withdrew, and there was the windowful of smoke ... (pp. 261–62)

For Australians, the scene may have been the more memorable in that the role of the housekeeper in *Rebecca* was played by Judith Anderson, one of the first Australians to make a movie career for herself.

It was this clear instance of a Hollywood film influencing Patrick White that led me to think about other signs of films in White's novels—and I did not have to look far or long. The very framework of the 'Jardin Exotique' section of *The Aunt's Story*, for example, may be indebted to

---

[1] First published in 2004, *Southerly*, 64(3): 176–79.

Marcel Carné's *Hôtel du Nord* (1938) in its offering a collection of people's lives, intersecting at times, within the confines of a hotel. (White told David Marr that he saw everything of Marcel Carné and Jean Renoir when their films came to England.)[2] Carné's *Hôtel du Nord* may have suggested the name of the hotel in *The Aunt's Story*, Hôtel du Midi (Hotel of the South), the name being changed with a mind to Australia; in *The Aunt's Story*, Australia is never quite abandoned for Europe, for Theodora's past is all around her. In Carné's celebrated film the two female leads were played by Annabella, the most famous French actress of her time, and Arletty, who first created an international reputation for herself in this film. (Arletty appeared later in *Les Visiteurs du Soir* and *Les Enfants du Paradis*, among other films.) Annabella and Arletty never acquired a last name, like Madeleine in *The Tree of Man* (1955); their romantic image was heightened by its very absence, as is Madeleine's. All three convey the image of a classically beautiful, icy woman, an image dear to French cinematographers that extends to Catherine Deneuve in our own times. As the housekeeper says of Madeleine in *The Tree of Man*, 'It's all in the eye with Madeleine' (p. 164). Madeleine at Glastonbury is essentially a French film star in a novel.

The influence of the famous German expressionist film, Robert Wiene's *The Cabinet of Dr Caligari* (1922), is clear in *The Aunt's Story*. (Note: Marr reports White as mentioning *Dr Caligari* with enthusiasm.)[3] Both works portray 'a world of chaos ... where the individual existence is overshadowed by fear of its own past experience and the hostile powers embodied within the establishment' (Spiros Gangas in his review of the film in the Edinburgh University Film Society Program 1993–94). One suspects sooner in White's novel than in the German film that various incidents take place only in the mind of the protagonist, but in neither

---

[2] Marr (1991), p. 124.

[3] Ibid.

work is the connection with reality ever quite certain. In both works the fantasies get wilder and wilder, until the director in one case, the author in the other, provides evidence that the incidents come from the mind of a schizophrenic person in a real place surrounded by real people. White's novel most closely approaches the dream quality of the German film in Theodora's fantasy of Mrs Rapallo and Sokolnikov (Theodora's parents, resurrected) fighting for possession of the nautilus (Theodora's soul) and destroying it in the process (p. 255).

David Selznick's *Gone with the Wind* (1939) influenced White in one of his most vivid scenes in *The Tree of Man*, where Stan carries Madeleine down the staircase of Glastonbury, out of the fire. When asked which film this reminds them of, everyone answers, *Gone with the Wind*, thinking of the scene where Rhett carries Scarlett up the staircase of Tara, two steps at a time. The direction, whether up or down the staircase, does not matter: it is the dramatic quality of the incident that makes it memorable.

From Jean Epstein's *La chute de la maison Usher*,[4] a film version of the Edgar Allan Poe short story and one of the last great silent films (1928), White took the idea he used in *Riders in the Chariot* (1961) of a mansion falling into decay, crumbling completely when the owner, last of the family line, dies. The Epstein film in turn is widely considered to have influenced Orson Welles' *Citizen Kane* (1941) in its scenes of Kane's great hall in Xanadu, the palatial mansion he builds in Florida. Xanadu, the lavish house built by Mary Hare's father in *Riders in the Chariot*, gets its name from Kane's mansion Xanadu. It is on Miss Hare's dining room that White focuses to record the crumbling of Xanadu, like both Epstein and Welles: 'At that hour, descending the stairs at Xanadu, Miss Hare saw the marble shudder, the crack widen a little farther. She waited for the structure to fall. But it did not' (p. 461). White had a fond-

---

[4] [The Fall of the House of Usher].

ness for the Gothic, with its sense of immanent but unspecified danger, and indulged it in *Riders in the Chariot* more than elsewhere.

Jean Renoir's film of *Madame Bovary* (1934) may have contributed along with Flaubert's novel to White's scene in *A Fringe of Leaves* (1976) in which Garnet Roxburgh has sex with Ellen. In White's novel as well as in Flaubert's and in Renoir's film the heroine and her would-be lover ride out in the countryside and make love in a deserted clearing when she is thrown from her horse. The incident occurs of course in Flaubert's novel, but given White's interest in Renoir as well as Flaubert, it is possible that the French director influenced White's scene, which is recounted with a sexual reticence that belongs to Renoir's 1930s rather than to the explicit 1970s (pp. 116–17). The quick flashes that White gives us of a disarranged bosom, the bare flesh of a thigh, and a man's weight pressing down on Ellen are cinematic rather than novelistic in technique. Writing to James Stern in 1958, White remarked that Renoir was 'the only man I have always felt might translate [my work] into film'.[5]

There are other scenes in White that suggest a film, and tease one's memory. Other readers, perhaps, may be able to identify them. Isn't there a film, for instance, in which a horse is ridden down a staircase, much as the overwrought and feverish Voss imagines riding his horse down a basalt staircase in the Bonners' deserted house? (p. 382). Or one in which a man rides a horse up a marble staircase, as we are told that Norbert Hare did at Xanadu (p. 15)? I have merely been able to indicate that films did influence White and to show that he is therefore a product of popular culture as well as literary culture.

---

[5] Marr (1991), p. 343.

Section 3
Studies of White's Major Novels

10
THE SEVERAL LIVES OF THEODORA GOODMAN: THE 'JARDIN EXOTIQUE' SECTION OF PATRICK WHITE'S *THE AUNT'S STORY*[1]

Part 2 of *The Aunt's Story*, 'Jardin Exotique', is in sharp contrast to part 1, the account of Theodora Goodman's childhood at Meroë and life with her mother in Sydney. White sharpens the contrast through Theodora's conversations with Pearl and Lou at the end of part 1. In the former, she sums up her last thirty years or so with the assurance that 'There is nothing to tell ... I am forty-five ... and very little has happened ... I am an aunt ... I suppose there is at least that' (p. 131). Her conversation with Lou endorses her statement of her unimportance as one of 'the people who do not have many stories to tell' (p. 136). There may indeed be 'the people as empty as a filigree ball', but Theodora is not one of them. In the cactus garden of a small hotel in southern France, this staid Australian spinster's imagination flares forth with the violence of sudden fire.

The figures and events of the 'Jardin Exotique' section take place, we will demonstrate, entirely within Theodora's mind.[2] At least initially, most

[1] Co-written with Rose Marie Beston and first published in 1975, *Journal of Commonwealth Literature*, 9(3): 1–13.

[2] Theodora does make a journey to France, and stays at an hotel that has a cactus garden. But there reality ends. Even the fire is fantasised by Theodora: her state-

readers are startled and somewhat confused by a side to Theodora which has hardly been indicated, and by the complete change in tone and technique. Part 1 shows Theodora only once engaging in fantasy outside events she has experienced, as she relives the snowy night with her father and the Man Who Was Given his Dinner, and that is within the common range of human experience. But there is a strong hint early that Theodora is living in a strange and somewhat disturbing world of her own, as she goes about the daily routine of caring for her murderous mother. People passing her 'stopped to look, sensing something strange … People mopping their heads wondered uneasily into what they sank in Theodora Goodman's eyes. People casually looking were sucked in by some disturbance that was dark and strange' (p. 100).

No human being, of course, can be so totally repressed as Theodora has appeared to be. Her silences have been her defence against her mother's destructiveness. Set 'free' by her mother's death, she compensates (through an exotic fantasy-life) for her wasted years and for a sense of the insignificance of her life. The difference between her life in part 1 and her fantasy life in part 2 is expressed partly in terms of colour: whereas yellow and black and brown predominate in 'Meroë' the crimson and magenta and orange shades predominate in 'Jardin Exotique'. But if Theodora's imagination is set free in the *jardin*, it still preoccupies itself with the figures and events of her life at Meroë and in Sydney, in the disguises of conscious daydreaming and, on one occasion, of actual dreaming. And apart from some brief, tentative romanticising of herself as Varvara, Sokolnikov's sweetheart, and as Gloria, Principessa dell'Isola Grande (Australia), her self-image remains sadly distorted. When Mrs

---

ment as a schoolgirl that she would like to write about 'fire. A river of fire. And a burning house', p. 54, prepares us for the conflagration. And when Lieselotte proclaims that 'We must destroy everything, everything, even ourselves', p. 176, Theodora retreats, '*because she knew that this was not yet her crisis*' (our italics).

Rapallo first appears in the dining room, she advances with 'a pomp of cathedrals and of circuses' (p. 162) that the colourless Theodora would wish for herself; but there is a garishness in the description of Mrs Rapallo, put together 'rashly, ritually, crimson over purple', that is ludicrously inappropriate for the personality of the sallow spinster.

We should probably be unwise to assume that the 'Jardin Exotique' represents Theodora's first major excursion into the world of fantasy. She has deliberately chosen the Hôtel du Midi[3] for its garden, which she has felt to be an ideal environment for her indulgence in fantasy: 'in the 'Jardin Exotique' … the soul, left with little to hide behind, must forsake its queer opaque manner of life and come out into the open' (p. 146). She approaches the garden eagerly, and wastes no time in setting the stage on her entrance into it. She is the master puppeteer, with a good sense of the right time and place for the appearance of her various personages. Entering the garden on the morning of her arrival, 'Even though she had not yet seen them, Theodora could feel that the hotel was full of people, and she waited to touch their hands' (p. 147). Her waiting is a signal for the action to begin. Now, 'A slight breeze began to play with the cactus fingers', and Katina runs into the garden. The various figures appear before Theodora at her unexpressed wish as she sits there: 'Theodora sat. Confident her intuition would identify, she waited for Lieselotte to appear' (p. 174). And Lieselotte does. Later that night, as she prepares for bed, 'she knew she did not really control her bones, and that the curtain of her flesh must blow, like walls which are no longer walls. She … waited for the rose wall to fall' (p. 206). It begins to palpitate and she is forthwith an

---

[3] White may have derived the idea for the Hôtel du Midi from the sanatorium in Mann's *The Magic Mountain*, which he has told me (2 August 1972) that he read in English around 1932. The sanatorium and the hotel both contain an international group of occupants, and represent a miniature of a decadent Europe just before the outbreak of a world war. The restaurant is an important meeting place in both novels.

audience to a conversation between Wetherby and Lieselotte. But perhaps the most striking evidence of Theodora's proneness to fantasy is that almost immediately after Katina's entrance into the garden, Theodora is already involved in a fantasy experience of the earthquake with Katina, in a time and place removed from the actual garden—fantasy within fantasy!

Theodora's eagerness to enter the garden is one indication that it is to be the domain for her fantasy. There are other and stronger indications that the figures and events there occur only in her mind. Quite striking, for one thing, is the readiness of the various personages to recognise her and to admit her centrally to their lives. (It is unlikely that the retiring spinster, who cannot even maintain a conversation with the travelling salesman in her trip across the western United States, would speak at length to any of the guests in the Hôtel.) The confidences that Theodora elicits and the experiences she shares are all the more extraordinary when one considers that the events of chapters 7, 8 and 9 take place on the first morning, afternoon, and night respectively of her stay at the Hôtel—except, of course, for the fantasies within fantasy, like the earthquake experienced with Katina, or her experiences as Ludmilla with Sokolnikov. Minutes after she has entered the garden, Theodora is addressed by Katina as a kind of aunt:

> 'Dear Miss Theodora, would you mind ? ... I would like better to have a talk. About life and things ...'
>
> Theodora ... *could not often mind*, because with Katina ... it was like that. (p. 149; our italics)

When Marthe Bloch, who follows Katina in appearance, speaks, Theodora hardly turns 'to discover whose voice had taken possession of her situation' (p. 152), and does not find Marthe's highly personal observation on her unwashed hands remarkable. At lunch, Sokolnikov writes her a note, in which he throws himself 'on your sympathy and understanding, which I can sense across the dining room, and suggest that some time we discuss each other' (p. 156). Mrs Rapallo likewise welcomes Theodora, 'You and I shall be friends as well as companions' (p. 165). It all takes place within hours of Theodora's arrival by the morning train, and the afternoon continues in similar style. After lunch Wetherby introduces himself in the garden and launches into a brief intimate biography. Lieselotte does not introduce herself, for it is unnecessary; indeed, Theodora informs her that Wetherby has been calling her. Thus with each of the major figures at the Hôtel, Theodora assigns herself an importance that she has never been accorded in her real life, and that she has never accorded herself (indeed, on a conscious level, she has sought anonymity). The title of the book points up her tenuous importance in the ordinary world; as she says to Pearl, 'I am an aunt ... I suppose there is at least that' (p. 131).

The names of the guests at the Hôtel are more international than one can readily believe. It is appropriate for the richness of Theodora's fantasies, however, that the characters should be as international as they are: Greek (Katina Pavlou), Russian (Sokolnikov), Dutch American (Elsie van Tuyl, who marries an Italian American), English (Wetherby), German (Lieselotte), and possibly Swiss (the Misses Bloch). One can posit persuasive reasons for Theodora's choice of some of the nationalities. Katina's Greek nationality defers to Mrs Goodman's knowledge of Greek literature and the Russian characters acknowledge Mrs Goodman's ability to read Russian. The other names probably proceed from Theodora's travels in Italy, England, Germany and France (p. 145).

As befits a fantasy world, Theodora's jardin is free from many of the restrictions that govern the ordinary world. There, the normal laws of time and place, of matter and even gravity do not always apply; and these same fantastic properties are extended to the Hôtel itself. Sitting in the garden or the dining-room, Theodora is transported from a Riviera morning to a Greek night, and is addressed in America by a suitor of a younger Mrs Rapallo, Elsie van Tuyl. Likewise, as Varvara she makes a brief excursion to St Petersburg and visits Anna Stepanovna's estate. As

Ludmilla, she flees through the pine forests of Russia with Sokolnikov during the Russian Revolution. Her Varvara fantasy exists almost out of time, as she and Sokolnikov watch a snail's progress in the garden (pp. 176–77, 179, 181) at intervals in their visits to Russia. Within a matter of weeks,[4] Katina ages from a child of about Lou's age to a girl of sixteen. Walls dissolve so that she can overhear Wetherby and Lieselotte, Sokolnikov's flesh becomes rubber, and the glass of the pagoda that Lieselotte smashes does not fall. Besides these considerations, which indeed place the events of the 'Jardin Exotique' within Theodora's mind, there is additional evidence from White speaking as author that the events in this section belong to the world of fantasy. Signing the hotel register, Theodora is afraid that she might meet too soon, 'before she had washed her hands, on the stairs, for instance, Mrs Rapallo, *on whose face she had not yet decided*' (p. 143; our italics). Katina, who makes the first entry into the garden, is not merely young: 'the girl had not yet remained anywhere very long' (p. 147). During the fire, Theodora maintains control over life and death, so can assure Miss Grigg that Katina will emerge safely, and she announces Katina's appearance 'with the certainty of certainty that fire will open' (p. 263). She does not expect Wetherby or Lieselotte to survive ('Because fevers consume, or are consumed'), or Monsieur Durand, *le petit*, or Henriette ('They too must have destroyed each other'). But Sokolnikov is deathless:

---

[4] Time in *The Aunt's Story* (as also in *The Magic Mountain*) is deliberately obscured as ordinary reality is suspended. We do not know exactly how long Theodora stays at the Hôtel du Midi. It is probably only a matter of a few weeks; at any rate, we see her folding the receipt 'for another week' at the beginning of chapter 11. White uses regular time in the 'Jardin Exotique' as a symbol of the ordinary world. As Theodora waits in the hall of the Hôtel on her arrival, the two worlds of reality and fantasy are thus opposed: 'A clock ticked, prim and slow … Somehow, Theodora remembered, there would also be the jardin exotique', p. 142.

> 'It was no miracle, Alyosha Sergei', said Theodora, 'that you failed to burn.' Her affection could not have allowed it. (p. 262)

Most importantly, however, we are told in the last few pages of the novel that 'the created lives of Theodora Goodman were interchangeable, the lives into which she had entered, making them momentarily dependent for love or hate, owing her this portion of their fluctuating personalities' (p. 300).

Since the happenings in the 'Jardin Exotique' demonstrably belong to fantasy, what has made so many readers reluctant to see them as such? The chief difficulty seems to lie in gauging where reality ends and fantasy begins. There are of course other guests in the Hôtel, who would presumably appear at times in the garden, so it is possible that there may be, at least initially, some minor incidents to touch off Theodora's fantasies. Perhaps a girl does run into the garden shortly after Theodora's first entry and drop her handkerchief there, thus serving as the 'small round white flint' (p. 149) that sets off the Katina episode. But even if it is so, the chances are that Theodora needs less and less encouragement to set a train of fantasy in motion. She has predestined the jardin to be her domain of fantasy before she even entered it: indeed, her first question on registering at the desk concerns its whereabouts. And, as we have remarked, it is difficult to imagine Theodora, a restrained conversationalist at the end of part 1 and a non-conversationalist at the beginning of part 3, engaged in meaningful conversation with any of the guests in part 2. Conversation, Sokolnikov tells her, is one indication of reality (p. 213), and conversation is not Theodora's forte.[5] Further, these European guests speak an extraordinarily idiomatic English just as Theodora speaks and comprehends a very correct French—no doubt all in fantasy.

---

[5] Even as a schoolgirl, Theodora is severely constrained in her conversation with Miss Spofforth. The meeting between them is one of like with like, but Theodora is right when she concludes 'I shall never overcome the distances', p. 51.

The question of what is fact and what is fantasy is also complicated by the presence of fantasies within fantasies: Theodora's experiencing the earthquake with Katina, her conversation with the suitor of the not yet married Elsie Van Tuyl, her flight as Ludmilla, her visit as Varvara to Anna Stepanovna, the brief appearance of Edith Sokolnikov. These twice-removed fantasies have a somewhat baffling effect on the reader, who may well force the outer fantasy into the realm of reality in his endeavour to find stable ground. Most confusing in part 2 is Theodora's first night at the Hôtel, chapter 9, where the fantasies fluctuate wildly as she dozes over the acts of the Apostles in various stages of waking and sleeping ('Her head lolled'). She is already asleep as she pictures herself entering Mrs Rapallo's room to take the nautilus, for distance lengthens ('Theodora ... considered which path to pick. They all wound ... It is an exceedingly long way, Theodora sighed') and the near at hand becomes unreachable ('she had begun to doubt whether she could reach') in ways that occur only in dreams and not in day-dreams. Obstacles outside the realm of conscious fantasy also arise:

> Sometimes it was the perplexed objects of darkness which obstructed, sometimes a dream stirred and threatened to form ... Whether the pampas of the darkness would allow, and its great clouds of grass, heavy as breath, that she parted with her ineffectual hands ... The dull and usually unresponsive tails of pampas grass flumped against her fixed eyes. (pp. 221–23)

Substance, too, becomes insubstantial in this section. We find this elsewhere in part 2 when Theodora is awake, but far more frequently in these few pages:

> Her cheek rubbed against some greater depth of sleep ... Mrs Rapallo had finally dissolved the marble groups ... Theodora ... also doubted whether the nautilus was substance enough, or whether it would blow. (pp. 221–22)

These experiences are different in kind from Theodora's previous daydreams, and testify to White's singular ability to record the full range of human fantasy.

The figures in the 'Jardin Exotique' are fantasy figures, then. Like any fantasy creations, they do have meaning, the meaning proceeding from the personality and experiences of their creator. They are all aspects either of Theodora herself or of people in her past life. For most readers the natural error will be to identify the figures of the 'Jardin Exotique' with one character or at the least with characters of the same sex. The truth is far more complex. Except for the Misses Bloch,[6] all the characters, both women and men, are at some time aspects of Theodora or have undergone her experiences. White himself has indicated it is so: 'the faces, whether Katina Pavlou, or Sokolnikov, or Mrs Rapallo, or Wetherby, [are] only slightly different aspects of the same state' (p. 188). It is particularly appropriate that Theodora Goodman, whose very name suggests Victorian middle-class respectability (born ca. 1885?),[7] should assume the guises of people with such exotic names as Ludmilla, Varvara, Sokolnikov, Lieselotte, or Elsie Rapallo (née van Tuyl). No character is one specific personage from Theodora's past: all have multiple identities, sometimes simultaneously. When, for instance, Lieselotte gives an ac-

---

[6] The function of the Misses Bloch is difficult to interpret. Perhaps in their continual losing of things (a stylo, a toothbrush, a doily, finally all their possessions) they are meant to serve as a kind of chorus, warning of the increasing loss of control, vague threats to come. But it is just as likely that they have only a tenuous relevance to the other characters, like the scavenger women in *The Ham Funeral*, and provide a kind of comic relief.

[7] The chronology of the novel is confused. Fanny completes a piece of embroidery in 1899, p. 30, presumably at about the age of ten; Theodora, the elder of the two, would accordingly have been born around 1885–87. How then can she be forty-three while dating Huntly shortly after World War I, and forty-five just before the outbreak of World War II?

count of her life with Rudi, she is re-presenting both Theodora's relationship with Huntly and a romanticised version of Theodora's cultural life with her father at Meroë. The Huntly relationship (especially as we have seen it in connection with Moraïtis) is clear in Lieselotte's description of people coming 'to the castle to hear the music that Rudi ordered as his duty towards *Kunst* … We caught the sickness of the violins … Finally Rudi sent me away … Because I am decadent' (p. 175). Even though it is Theodora who brings the Huntly relationship to an end, she seems to regard the termination as evidence of his rejection. Theodora's life with her father is romanticised to compensate for the sad reality when she tells how

> In the summer evenings, by torchlight, in the yard of the castle, we listened to more myths … We accepted the myth of love … Rudi is one of the men … who see the world through water, or through music, and grow drunk on *Ewigkeit*. Tristan and Siegfried, I think, were this way.

The ineffectual dreamer George Goodman has become transformed into a Rudi and associated with Tristan! Sometimes the opposite process happens, and the same person is split between two simultaneously appearing characters. Thus Varvara and Ludmilla appear together, Varvara being Sokolnikov's sweetheart, Ludmilla his sister. But both women are projections of Theodora, Varvara representing the girl she would have liked to be with her father, Ludmilla more the girl she was. 'Varvara comes to me in the morning, when I am young', says Sokolnikov. 'You don't take over till the small hours, Ludmilla, right at the end. All day you nurse your sense of duty and listen to the clocks' (pp. 177–78).

Identities also change from time to time. On her first appearance, Katina, for instance, represents Theodora at boarding school, but later Lou and Violet Adams. When Katina approaches at the beginning of chapter 10, Theodora knows that she has written a poem in purple ink, like those so dear to Violet. In Theodora's pocket there is a letter from Lou, also in purple ink, telling of a friendship with a nun very like her own former friendship with Violet (pp. 227–28). Mrs Rapallo, predominantly a projection of Mrs Goodman, as we will see, but sometimes also of Theodora, also shows traits of Violet Adams, especially in her fondness for secrets:

> our rooms have a communicating door, through which we can share secrets, and discuss the proposals that are made to me by rich young men … Let us take our things and go to the shack. Just the two of us. Alone. We shall walk in the lanes, and gather blueberries … Incidentally … I have news. (pp. 165–67)

Faced with such complexity, it is not particularly profitable to sort out the identities of the individual characters in the 'Jardin Exotique'. Rather let us see how Theodora and her past life appear in them, and how such figures as her mother and father, 'only apparently deceased', continue to haunt her beyond the grave.

Something of Theodora appears in all the major figures in the jardin. Katina, the first to make her appearance there, represents Theodora at boarding school about to return home.[8] Her reference to an earthquake and a black island that shook may suggest the other 'upheaval of mythic origin' that once shook the earth in the formation of Meroë, and may again. Like Theodora, too, Katina has gambling, travelling parents who abandon her as it suits them, thereby effecting the first destruction of trust:

> it left Katina Pavlou sitting with the kitten in her lap. The kitten's nose, smudged with first blood, sniffed at some fresh dubiousness in a revised universe. (p. 186)

Sokolnikov's confession of his desire as a little boy to experience everything and put it in a box (p. 158) directly repeats Theodora's wish as a

---

[8] The motif of returning home begins and ends the 'Jardin Exotique', given voice by Katina, see pp. 147–49 and 264. On both occasions, Katina represents Theodora about to leave boarding school.

little girl to know everything and put it in a box (p. 40). Later, at the military academy, no doubt his equivalent of the Spofforths' school, he discovers, like Theodora, that 'this might not be feasible. Because everything is nothing'. Wetherby's mention of living with his widowed mother in a brick house immediately suggests Theodora's life in Sydney. At boarding school he thinks of the castrating qualities ('protruding teeth') of a mother like Mrs Goodman and fantasises ways of torturing her. His father shares Mr Goodman's removedness, separated by a closed door. His patroness, Muriel Leese-Leese, holds a lease over her protégés like Mrs Goodman. Theodora's life with her mother is represented on two other occasions. One is Ludmilla's account of keeping house for her brother (really Mrs Goodman) in St Petersburg (pp. 217–18). The other is Varvara's telescoped summary of what is really Theodora's life at Meroë after boarding school and her life in Sydney:

> 'You know, Ludmilla', said Varvara ... 'that I shall go to Staraya Russa, later in the spring, or early summer. Anna Stepanovna has sent for me. It is quite deadly, of course. We shall sit in the little summerhouse by the lake, and drink tea, and sew, and Anna Stepanovna will bring out the sketches and photographs of all the lovers she never had. But there is no choice.' (p. 179)[9]

The mention of Anna Stepanovna's lovers suggests Julia Goodman's rivalry for Huntly Clarkson's attentions; we see her once in fantasy with Huntly on her arm. The careers of Fanny and Theodora after school are outlined by Miss Grigg in her account of the de Saumarez children, Lilian (= Fanny) and 'Enry (= Theodora):

> And Lilian sat beneath the trees, as nice as nice. Lilian was lovely. She took a lord, and turned stout in the end. But what 'appened to 'Enry is something we shall never know. First 'e blows 'is fortune, then 'is brains, in a bedroom in Bayswater. (p. 235)

---

[9] White's *Russa* should read *Rossiya*.

The male guise is only superficially a problem in the identification of Theodora: we have already seen her in Sokolnikov and Wetherby, and her moustache stands as a central symbol of her ambiguous sexual identity. What is most striking in 'Enry's fate is that it is the first definite intimation in part 2 that Theodora fears some form of self-annihilation after her travels through Europe.

Three women remain who show further aspects of Theodora: Lieselotte, Mrs Rapallo, and Varvara. Lieselotte in her relationship with Wetherby represents Theodora with Huntly. Lieselotte's conversation with Wetherby near the beginning of chapter 9 makes explicit a contempt that Theodora had felt for Huntly even while she felt dependent on him. The conversation draws our attention to an hostility towards men in Theodora, stemming from her inability to relate to them. Her earlier displays of shooting ability place her in contemptuous opposition to men in a field where they are commonly granted ascendancy (cf. her remark to Wetherby, 'I am a man, and you are a man', p. 174). Ultimately Lieselotte kills Wetherby. That the Lieselotte-Wetherby conversation is a realisation of Theodora's own preoccupation with love is clear from her personalised interjection: 'Love is undoubtedly an acrostic, and *that is why I have failed*, she decided' (p. 208; our italics). Mrs Rapallo and Varvara both show a split within Theodora. Mrs Rapallo is described by Sokolnikov as 'Of great ugliness, and great cunning', but defended by the Misses Bloch as *'une femme douce, intelligente, spirituelle'*, 'most cruelly put upon' (p. 161). Her ugliness and cunning point to the self-contempt and suppressed anger bred in Theodora by her mother's treatment of her. In making Mrs Rapallo's colours so garish, 'crimson over purple', Theodora is still in fantasy capitulating to the mother who mocked her as a sallow-complexioned child for wearing yellow. Varvara is a younger and romanticised Theodora, 'pretty and talented'. Her two simultaneous fiancés, Ivanov, who is accepted by her at a ball, and Federmann, who is 'reliable though undistinguished', suggest Frank and Huntly respectively. They represent pretty much her image of what her mother (here Anna

Stepanovna) and her father (Sokolnikov) would have wanted of her, and testify to the conflict born in her of trying to please two very different parents at strife with one another. Theodora consciously adopts the role of Ludmilla, so there is no difficulty here with the interpretation. Ludmilla's wearing of boots goes back to Theodora's outings with her father at Meroë. The name Ludmilla may derive from the famous heroine of Pushkin's romantic fantasy, *Ruslan i Lyudmila.*[10]

Theodora's mother and father also appear in a number of figures in the 'Jardin Exotique'. Mrs Goodman is perhaps most fully represented by Mrs Rapallo. When as a magenta sword she opposes the rubbery Sokolnikov (p. 163), Mrs Rapallo is setting the castrating qualities of Julia against the impotence of George Goodman. In their wrangling over the nautilus, Mrs Rapallo and Sokolnikov represent Theodora's parents fighting over possession of her, the one out of a desire to possess, the other out of some affection. As the owner of the monkey Mignon, too, Mrs Rapallo is Mrs Goodman desiring to control the life of Theodora; and as the mother of the brilliantly married Gloria she points to Mrs Goodman's exalted social expectations from her daughter (cf. Anna Stepanovna's description of Varvara's fiancé Ivanov, p. 181).[11] If 'only women like Anna Stepanovna think they can regulate life' (p. 179), Mrs Rapallo and Muriel Leese-Leese are also such women, and all are versions of Julia Goodman. Lieselotte, who would like to 'whip the lions through a paper hoop' (p. 174), is another such woman; specifically, her desire recalls Julia Goodman's smashing the window with a whip in her rage. Lieselotte idly squeezing the head off an ant at the picnic, too, calls to mind Julia

[10] White has told me that he has not read this tale by Pushkin. In his admiration for Pushkin's letters, however, expressed to McGregor (1969) and again to me, he would have come across references to this work.

[11] Mrs Goodman shows conflicting notions about what she desires for Theodora. On the one hand, she would not allow her any husband, p. 99; on the other, she would wish for her a marriage of social prestige for her own glory.

Goodman's abiding desire to destroy: 'It was the great tragedy of Mrs Goodman's life that she had never done a murder' (p. 99).

Mr Goodman appears in the 'Jardin Exotique' only as Sokolnikov, with whom the phallic imagery of rubber is regularly and strongly associated. The phallic implications of rubber are unmistakable in the description of Sokolnikov advancing 'huge, domed, but never confined, increasing always with the resourcefulness of rubber, pink rubber at that' (p. 163). Beyond its qualities of tumescence[12] and erection,[13] rubber can also suggest the spinelessness of George Goodman, especially in opposition to 'the stiff slash of the magenta sword' of a woman like Mrs Rapallo, Julia Goodman: 'Then you knew that Mother had won, in spite of Father breathing hard. It was terrible, the strength of Mother' (p. 42). Theodora shows towards Sokolnikov the same ambivalence that she feels towards her father. On the one hand she finds Sokolnikov physically repulsive, 'an odious and repulsive glutton', 'a pig'; but on the other, even her fault-finding has 'a certain shabby tenderness' (p. 210). They form 'that complementary curse and blessing, a relationship' (p. 210). Her repulsion to him is limited to the physical, a broader expression of the sexual; it is not strong enough to make her sever their relationship or to lessen her need to express 'that desperate affection which she had never quite been able to give' (p. 213). She stands in the same protective role with him as with her ineffectual father: 'Alyosha Sergei, you foolish child ... this is a crisis in which even I cannot protect you' (p. 224). Theodora is in clearly oedipal relationship to Sokolnikov-George Goodman, being his sweetheart (Varvara), his devoted sister (Ludmilla), and in life his daughter—everything except the ultimate relationship, that of his wife. When Lieselotte describes her husband as falling in love a second time with 'a myth

---

[12] 'Alyosha Sergei ... had taken on a fresh lease of rubber, was swelling with young hopes, or old', p. 183; see also pp. 190, 223.

[13] 'the hard, thick thwack of rubber', p. 163.

in jackboots' (p. 174), Theodora is apparently according herself prime place in her father's affections at Meroë. And when Varvara charms her sweetheart Sokolnikov as she swims against the waltz, 'and they stood in the open doorways, applauding' (p. 178), Theodora has evidently linked her father with Frank Parrot, with whom she danced so seductively at a ball; her father is central in her affections, so that she can see other men only as an extension of him. Her final comfort in the novel is offered by an idealised father-figure, Holstius. Resting her head against Holstius' knees as she had against her dying father's (pp. 88, 293), she emends her father's death to allow him an ultimate leave-taking. Now truly as she leaves the ordinary world for a world of her own, she might say, 'Mother, I am dead, I am dead, Meroë has crumbled' (p. 88). Mrs Goodman has at last, from the grave, accomplished her life's desire to do a murder; the victim is Theodora.

In our discussion of Theodora and her parents we have outlined a method of approaching the personages and events of the 'Jardin Exotique'. Our analysis is by no means exhaustive. We have omitted some characters from Theodora's earlier life, both men and women, who appear in the garden—for instance, Fanny and Pearl Brawne, Frank, and Huntly. We have also refrained from discussing how certain incidents from her past life recur in the 'Jardin Exotique' section—for instance, the auctioning of Meroë disguised as the taking over of Anna Stepanovna's estate by the peasants. We have made these omissions because it has been our aim to establish a pattern of interpretation rather than to make a complete study of all the possible relationships between part 1 and the 'Jardin Exotique'. Several things have emerged in the course of our research: that the novel possesses an extraordinary unity of personages and events in spite of the initial impression of chaos in the central section; that the 'Jardin Exotique' is indeed an unusual realisation of the vitality of conscious fantasy and of dreams; and, most importantly, that the nature of Theodora's fantasy life underscores the reader's impression of her in part 1 as a woman of deep emotional disturbance, torn by conflicts born at Meroë and sustained throughout her adult relationships, until in part 3 she opts for total emotional retreat into schizophrenia.

White's ability to present the experience of human fantasy is one of his major contributions to the art of the novel. In more than half a century since this work was written, it is surprising that no satisfactory key to it has appeared. The reason for this neglect would appear to lie on the one hand in the resistance within Australia itself to psychological interpretations and on the other in White's relative obscurity outside Australia until the appearance of *The Tree of Man* (1955), with the consequent overlooking of this novel written seven years earlier. *The Aunt's Story*, far more than being a mere tour de force, is surely one of the important novels of the twentieth century.

11

THE BLACK VOLCANIC HILLS OF MEROË: FIRE IMAGERY IN PATRICK WHITE'S *THE AUNT'S STORY*[1]

Writing in *Southerly* of *The Aunt's Story*, Thelma Herring has complained that 'a novel cannot well bear the strain of such a complex pattern of symbolic imagery'.[2] It is quite true that the diversity of the recurrent images in the novel is often confusing. Nevertheless, of all the images in the book, none recurs more often or in such significant contexts as that of the black volcanic hills of Meroë.[3] We propose in this article to indicate how Meroë continues to appear in France and the US (in parts 2 and 3), and to study the fire imagery associated with it, for no image tells us more about the makeup of Theodora or shows more clearly the process of her disintegration. In consequence the novel is seen as a coordinated whole, unified by a set of key images, which progressively clarify the effect upon Theodora of her experiences in part 1, of which the inevitable outcome is the destruction of her identity in the ordinary world. At the end of the novel, in the western United States, Theodora returns to Meroë, to 'the lost reality of childhood' (p. 264). The motif of returning

---

[1] Co-written with Rose Marie Beston; first published in 1972, *Ariel*, 3(4): 33–43.

[2] Herring (1965), pp. 6–22.

[3] We do not find the wooden imagery, for instance, discussed by James McAuley (1959), to be as central to the meaning of the novel as the fire imagery.

home had begun and ended her fantasies in the 'Jardin Exotique'. In both cases, it is given voice by Katina Pavlou, who on these occasions is a representation of Theodora about to leave boarding school. Katina speaks the first words in the garden:

> 'I am tired of all this. I shall write and tell them I must go away ... I must go home ... Before I have quite forgotten. There was an earthquake, do you remember? ... There was a black island that shook.' (pp. 147–49)

And Katina concludes her final colloquy with Theodora by announcing 'I shall go away ... I shall go to my own country. Now I know' (p. 264).

Actually, Theodora had never left Meroë, not even in Europe. The 'Jardin Exotique' is another Meroë, as she senses when she first enters it: 'she began to be afraid she had returned to where she had begun, the paths of the garden were the same labyrinth, the cactus limbs the same aching stone' (p. 146). It is in the United States, however—in New Mexico—that she finds a final and permanent Meroë. White himself emphasises the resemblance between the US and the Australian Meroë. Kilvert's hut in the hilltop suggests the hut on one of the hills surrounding Meroë, 'the madman's folly'. The landscapes are similar—black hills, dark pines, and dead yellow grass—and Theodora transforms the similarity to identity. As she looks out at 'the black sonorous islands' around Kilvert's hut she is again among the black volcanic hills of Meroë. The dust in the deserted hut, too ('The world was dim with dust through the coated windows', p. 290), recalls the volcanic ash she had seen as coating Meroë when her father described the Abyssinian original to her.[4] Holstius, to whom she assigns ownership of the hut, is a synthesis of her father and the Man who was Given his Dinner at Meroë. Some 8000 miles from Australia, Theodora has returned home.

---

[4] Note, too, that in the Hôtel du Midi, Theodora 'saw the ash trays, which had brimmed almost over, with ash', p. 202.

Theodora identifies herself closely with Meroë, particularly with the yellow house and the black volcanic hill surmounting it. When Frank Parrott is indicating his interest in her and she feels her defence of apartness dissolving, she sees Meroë's walls as crumbling:

> she wanted him to speak more. The blood in her stone hands ran a little quicker, perhaps from fear also, that stone will crumble. Not even Father could hold up the walls of Meroë when it was time. (p. 83)

And at the death of her father, she feels that she, along with Meroë, has disintegrated: 'I am dead, I am dead, Meroë has crumbled' (p. 88). White links the yellow house and grass and the black hills of Meroë with Theodora's yellow skin and black dress or hat, and Theodora herself finds the black volcanic hills totally in harmony with her personality. Accordingly, the images connected with the black hills of Meroë, especially those of a volcano, fire, and lightning, reveal much about Theodora's personality and preoccupations. Similar to the volcano image is that of the brass filigree ball sometimes filled with fire and rolled downhill. Just as in the jardin 'the created lives of Theodora Goodman were just as interchangeable' (p. 300), so the various symbols relating to a volcano—fire and lightning—are almost interchangeable too.

Early in the novel, her father's mention of the Abyssinian Meroë is significant for Theodora in clarifying her feelings about the Meroë she knows. She immediately equates the 'dead place, in the black country of Ethiopia' (p. 23) with her own Meroë, and is disturbed at the identity. 'In this dead place that Father had described the roses were as brown as paper bags, the curtains were ashy on their rings, the eyes of the house had closed.' She goes outside 'to escape from this dead place with the suffocating cinder breath', but finds no escape as she looks

> with caution at the yellow face of the house … Even in sunlight the hills surrounding Meroë were black … So that from what she saw and sensed, the legendary landscape became a fact, and she could not break loose from the expanding terror.

> Only in time the second Meroë became a dim and accepted apprehension lying quietly at the back of the mind. (p. 23)

If 'She could not set down on the black grass of the country that was called Ethiopia their own yellow stone' house, it is not from a feeling of inappropriateness but rather from a terrifying appropriateness. The picture her father has painted is of her own deadness and the deadness of her family: 'the eyes of the house had closed.' She is preoccupied with the dead bones of Meroë, still at times filled with fire. The name Meroë, we are told, smouldered—chiefly with the murderous anger of Mrs Goodman, but also with Theodora's.

Theodora is herself a black volcano, dead yet living, capable of erupting with destructive power. The volcanic quality is what she has in common with the hawk that she comes to identify with herself, speaking of 'worlds that were brief and fierce' (p. 33). When Frank aims at the hawk in their shooting contest, she directly associates its red eye with her volcanic core: 'she quivered, and the whole hillside, in some other upheaval of mythical origin' (p. 73). Her humiliation of Frank on this occasion by outshooting him is re-enacted years later when she terminates her relationship with Huntly Clarkson by a display of sharpshooting at a gallery. As she leaves the gallery after this eruption, she recalls the hawk and the black volcanic hills of Meroë. Returning home, she erupts briefly against her mother, accusing her of having been born with an axe in her hand, but quickly contains greater eruption by self-recrimination: 'I have a core of evil in me that is altogether hateful' (p. 126). It is appropriate that she should end her relationship with Huntly with these volcanic associations, for on her first visit to him she had asked him, perhaps in unconscious warning, if he had ever seen a volcano (p. 108).

Volcanic fires and fire generally are closely linked in Theodora's mind. Even as a schoolgirl, she is obsessed with the power of fire. To Violet Adams she confessed that she would like to write a poem about 'fire. A river of fire. And a burning house' (p. 54)—a clue that the fire is to consume the Hôtel du Midi is born in Theodora's fantasy. As she lives with her mother's murderous hatred in Sydney, Theodora feels the atmosphere on fire: 'the whole air burned scarlet'. Her own volcanic core shows signs of activity as her awareness of her mother's destructiveness grows. To the fire in the atmosphere she adds her own:

> Scarlet lit her face. It ran like blood beneath her brown skin. So that people stopped to look, sensing something strange ... people mopping their heads wondered uneasily into what they sank in Theodora Goodman's eyes. (p. 100)

Directly thereafter the story of the Jack Frost murders is told, which Theodora finds difficult to discuss because they are so personal, 'Like something one has done oneself'. Later in the Hôtel du Midi, when Lieselotte destroys her pictures, proclaiming 'We must destroy everything, everything, even ourselves' (p. 176), Theodora retreats to the garden, '*because she knew that this was not yet her crisis*' [our italics]. Her crisis, we will see, is directly brought on by a feeling of hopeless sexual frustration. Then, in an angry eruption, she consumes the Hôtel with her fire and disposes of 'the figments of Mrs Rapallo, and Katina Pavlou, and Sokolnikov' (p. 292). As it rages, she considers 'the phases of the fire', presumably the fire that had burned within her. Once having in the personage of Katina 'seen the face of fire' (p. 263), she can no longer repress it and proposes to return to Meroë. In her journey across America, she no longer feels safe against the violence of her own personality, 'less controllable than fire' (p. 274), and retreats from the ordinary world around her. Just because it does not look as if it might be carried away like the Hôtel by the passions of fire, Kilvert's hut is comforting to her. When she is angry and agonised there, however, the walls bend outward 'under the pressure of the hateful fire' (p. 293) until Holstius calms her. Burnt out, she finds final peace in 'airy disintegration' (p. 100), in the annihilation of her identity in the ordinary world; henceforth only fantasy can give significance to her existence.[5]

Beyond its destructiveness, there is another important aspect of fire: its association with sexual passion.[6] Dancing with Frank, so 'close to his fire', Theodora herself 'streamed with fire' (p. 78). Her other deeply sexual experience, Moraïtis' playing of the 'cello (with which she identifies herself),[7] Theodora see primarily in volcanic terms:

> She watched him take the 'cello between his knees and wring from its body a … passionate music …
>
> The 'cello rocked, she saw. She could read the music underneath his flesh. She was close. He could breathe into her mouth. He filled her mouth with long, aching silences, between the deeper notes that reached down deep into her body … The bones of her hands … were no indication of exaltation or distress, as the music fought and struggled under a low roof, *the air thick with cold ash*. (p. 116; our italics)

---

[5] We disagree radically in the interpretation here with Burrows (1966). Burrows finds Theodora successful in achieving a genuine freedom through humility. She is clearly schizophrenic at the end of the story, having completely retreated from a reality she was never quite able to cope with.

[6] White used this association in his first novel, *Happy Valley*. In section 17, Sidney Furlow sits on a phallic horse, 'trembling between her legs', and thinks of a bushfire that has excited her: 'There was something magnificent in the progress of fire … You could feel the hot air of the flames on your face. Something you could not explain. Something fierce and irrational, in the striving of the horse, in the progress of the flame.'

[7] Compare Desmond Morris in *The Human Zoo* (1969): 'The old-fashioned guitar, with a curvaceous, waisted body, was symbolically essentially female. It was held close to the chest, its strings lovingly caressed', p. 109. As the fire rages in the Hôtel du Midi, Katina asks, 'Miss Goodman … have you ever seen a burning piano?' The piano probably represents Theodora herself, her repressed sexuality now flaring forth with a destructive violence.

If Violet Adams would write a poem about the lovely sentiments of love, Theodora would write about rivers of fire—her concept of love. Starved for love, she sees it in consuming terms, whether of a volcano or fire or lightning. As a girl, Theodora had been struck by lightning but survived. Shortly before the night of the dance with Frank, she has a dream in which the lightning again figures:

> she woke in bed and found that she was not beneath the tree. She had put out her hand to touch the face before the lightning struck, but not the tree. She was holding the faceless body that she had not yet recognized, and the lightning struck deep. (p. 80)

Lightning here is clearly associated with sexual passion.

Lightning is also associated with destructive anger. In particular, lightning is linked with Mrs Goodman's strength, and so with her rings, in which her strength is seen to lie:

> Theodora could feel the hatred in her mother's hand. She could feel the pressure of the rings … from the corner of the book her hand peered, diamond-eyed … Her rings scraped on each other. (pp. 99–100)

It is likely that Theodora sees the light that flashes from her mother's rings as a kind of concentrated lightning: 'Mother was more terrible than lightning that had struck the tree' (p. 43). As Mrs Goodman sits calmly in deadly judgement upon Pearl Brawne, 'her rings flashed' (p. 39). It is likely, too, that Theodora equates her own contained fire with her mother's garnet ring, seeing her destructiveness as similar to her mother's: as the fire begins to consume the Hôtel du Midi, she reaches for her mother's garnet ring and puts it on her finger 'In the presence of the secret, leaping emotions of the fire she was glad to have her garnet' (p. 260).

Theodora was always fascinated by the notion of destruction at the heart of things. As a child, she finds 'a small pale grub curled in the heart of the rose' in the rose garden. 'She could not look too long at the grub-thing stirring … She could not subtract it from the sum total of the garden' (p. 21). The rose stands for both Mrs Goodman,[8] who ordained the garden, and for Theodora.[9] A suppressed fire burned steadily within both, but Theodora's was normally kept under control. It first flared out when Frank shot at the red-eyed hawk that she had identified with herself. Unable to direct her anger at her would-be destroyer, she turns her rage in upon herself and shoots the bird.[10] This is the suicidal impulse of the person who feels his whole existence threatened and defiantly chooses his own way of death. Most of her fire is in fact turned in upon herself: 'I shall continue to destroy myself, right down to the last of my several lives' (pp. 74–75). Even the most 'outward' of her eruptions, the fire at the end of part 2, ends in the destruction of her several lives, the creatures of her fantasy there. That conflagration follows Theodora's abandonment of the possibility of sexuality. Through the personage of Katina, Theodora decides that sexual experience is 'nauseating and painful'. Katina's experience inside the phallic tower is clearly sexual. She had 'chosen this as the moment of experience', which Theodora, with her memory of Pearl and Tom among the nettles at Meroë, expects to be violent. Her conversation with Katina is to be understood as basically concerning sexual experience:

---

[8] Theodora recalls 'the canker of the rose mouth', with her mother's scorn and anger, when *le petit* hands her Sokolnikov's note in circumstances resembling Huntly's invitation to dinner (pp. 105, 157).

[9] Theodora identifies with her mother in such actions as wearing her garnet ring and drinking camomile tea.

[10] Whitman (1963), p. 142, finds a similar self-destructive quality in Achilles' fire, which 'finds its telos, or fulfilment, not in dislocating the world as it is, but in self-destruction … The all-destructive rage with which he assails the Trojans is directed in the last analysis against himself.' For Theodora, the fire at the Hôtel is destructive of both herself and of others—of herself because she identifies herself with Meroë (of which the Hôtel is one expression), and of others insofar as they are represented in the fantasy figures there.

> 'Have you ever been inside the tower, Miss Goodman?' Katina Pavlou asked …
>
> Theodora … dreaded, in anticipation, the scream of nettles.
>
> 'No,' said Theodora, 'I have not been inside the tower. I imagine there is very little to see.'
>
> 'There is nothing, nothing,' Katina said. 'There is a smell of rot and emptiness'.
>
> But no less painful in its emptiness, Theodora felt.
>
> 'Still, I am glad,' said Katina Pavlou, speaking through her white face. 'You know, Miss Goodman, when one is glad for something that has happened, something nauseating and painful, that one did not suspect. It is better finally to know.' (pp. 252–53; our italics)

Although she has previously tried to convince herself that sexuality is necessarily repugnant, Theodora finds no resolution now in Katina's words. Instead, hopeless and angry, she summons her forces for the great eruption. She and Katina arrive back at a blacked out Hôtel, in the calm before the tempest. As she unleashes the fire within her, she identifies her destructiveness with her mother's and dons the garnet ring:

> All the violence of fire was contained in the hotel. It tossed, whether hatefully or joyfully, it tossed restraint to smoke. Theodora ran, breathing the joy or hatred of fire. (p. 259)

One group of images, pertaining to bones, is frequently in Theodora's consciousness, complementing her preoccupation with volcanic fire. Bones to Theodora are the rib cage (especially her own), whether seen as bones themselves or in disguised form as the filigree work on the brass ball, the walls of a house, cactus spears, or the shell of a volcano. Wetherby's body is spoken as of contained in a cage of bones (p. 173), Lieselotte's within a cactus cage (p. 175). The cactus garden itself is a giant rib cage; when Theodora sits inside it she is making, like Voss, a journey into the country of the mind. Bones seem to represent to her a kind of protective defence against the outside world; from within them she can look out safely. The bone imagery, then, bespeaks her apartness and defensiveness, qualities which must somewhere be accompanied by hostility too. She is aware that her protection is vulnerable, that bones can melt and walls dissolve under either external threat (destruction from her mother or disarming affection from Frank or Katina) or internal threat (her own destructive anger) (pp. 83, 149, 293). When Theodora maintains to Lou at the end of part 1 that she does not have much to tell, that she is empty as a filigree ball, she deceives herself, for her imagination is shortly to flare forth with a violence that terrifies her. She cannot live with it finally, and settles for the calmer fantasy of a Holstius in part 3. At the end of the novel her fire is spent, and her shell is entrusted to the care of others.

Theodora has a strong attraction to a landscape of bones, whether the Australian Meroë, or Moraïtis' Greece or the 'Jardin Exotique'. Sitting on the hill at Meroë, Theodora looks down upon the bones of the earth:

> There are certain landscapes in which you can see the bones of the earth. And this was one. You could touch your own bones, which is to come a little closer to truth. (p. 161)

Since she is looking down upon 'the endlessness of bones' (p. 33), she evidently feels this dead world to be a representation of her family life:

> Theodora looked down through the distances that separate ... If I could put out my hand, she said, but I cannot ... There is no lifeline to other lives. (p. 137)

The bone imagery in the novel is particularly difficult to interpret. Not that it is especially complex or rich, but that White himself fails to provide sufficient material for interpretation. There is in the novel a dazzling variety of imagery that sometimes frustrates just because the author withholds the clues to an understanding.

There is no such difficulty in understanding the choice of the volcano/fire/lightning imagery to express Theodora's makeup. Although she is externally passive, like a chair waiting for fresh acts,[11] the fire within her is shown as burning steadily, several times threatening to erupt. Until the end of part 2, the eruptions are indirect and quickly checked, however violent the emotions involved. Her most notable eruption expresses itself in her self-destructive shooting of the hawk. In part, this is a response to what she feels as an attack by Frank upon her; but it also effectively cancels the effect of her feminine wiles in having let Frank outshoot her until then. Her second outburst, her taking of the silver paperknife away from her mother, signifies her intention to claim Frank for herself against her mother's hatred. Finally, however, her fear of the consequences wins out: while she somewhat encourages him, she also sharply discourages him. There is no doubt, we believe, that Theodora could have won Frank; her mother clearly sensed this, for in speaking later of Huntly, she confuses the two courtships and speaks instead of Frank:

> 'Why won't you take him?' Mrs Goodman said … 'I remember the other evening he rode across the bridge. Well … Fanny has been happy. It was different when one waited for the sound of horses' feet.' (p. 127)

When she has effectively sent Frank to Fanny, Theodora feels defeated and returns the knife to her mother in capitulation:

> 'I'm sorry,' she said … 'You see. You were right.' … Mrs Goodman took up the paper-knife in her small hand on which the garnets shone … Theodora waited. She waited to see if there was anything else she would be expected to give. She had come for this purpose. To her mother. (p. 86)

Her performance at the shooting gallery seems to be a hostile retaliation upon Huntly for bringing into the open her inability to marry. Directly after it, she erupts briefly against the cause of her inability, her destructive mother. The same night that she accuses her mother of a need to destroy Theodora is tempted to kill her, and guilt is as strong as if she

[11] For chair imagery associated with Theodora see pp. 92, 112, 141, 227.

had actually gone through with the murder: 'it is the same thing, blood is only an accompaniment' (p. 128).

The fire that consumes the Hôtel du Midi is precipitated, we have shown, by Theodora's angry abandonment of the possibility of sexuality. As the fire devours the Hôtel, the plants in the garden take on the colour of zinc, thereby recalling the sink from which Theodora had picked up the knife to kill her mother and the 'morning the colour of zinc old Mrs Goodman died' (p. 134). In destroying the creations of her fantasy through the fire, Theodora becomes frightened of her own violence. Unable to live in a 'Jardin Exotique' or in the ordinary world around her, she creates in Holstius a calming blend of various father-figures. Her conversations with him prepare her finally to live in a world of her own, removed from people, without a lifeline to others lives.

The Aunt's Story is White's most detailed study of the disintegration of a personality. This disintegration is not shown by means of significant action, for Theodora is a passive character who goes through life waiting 'with something of the superior acceptance of mahogany for fresh acts' (p. 141). It is shown rather by the recurrence of a group of central images that betray the obsessions eating deeper into her personality. At the end, she has no country, no family, not even a name. Her life, in sad irony, has fulfilled Gertie Stepper's aspirations for her own old age:

> 'When I am old all I shall want is a cup of tea, and die.'
>
> It made Theodora laugh. As if it could ever happen this way. (p. 42)

But it does. We last see Theodora thanking the doctor who has come to take her to a mental home:

> she held her head on one side as she had seen ladies do on receiving and thanking for a cup of tea.
>
> Then they all laughed. (p. 303)

12
LOVE AND SEX IN A STAID SPINSTER: *THE AUNT'S STORY*[1]

Sexual experience in Patrick White's two masterpieces, *The Aunt's Story* and *Voss,* is presented only in fantasy or in dreams or through natural symbols. Direct sexual experience itself does not take place at all: Theodora, Voss and Laura live and die without ever experiencing intercourse, and so in these two novels White is exempted from dealing with an area in which he is noticeably weak. He never succeeded in integrating direct sexual experience with the total personality of his figures as an enriching part of their lives. Indeed, he rarely attempted to record sexual experience at all. When he does record it, early or late, he usually presents it as something indifferent (like the affair of Oliver Halliday and Alys Browne in *Happy Valley,* or the sexual lives of Stan and Amy Parker in *The Tree of Man)* or even as something unpleasant (like Hurtle Duffield's 'bleak orgasms'). *The Vivisector,* which records sexual activity more frequently and more fully than any of White's earlier works, is infected with sexual nausea. But although White failed to create characters whose sexual lives are active and fulfilling, he is in firm control in conveying the sexual fantasies of his characters, and never more so than in intimating the

---

[1] First published in 1971, *Quadrant*, 15(5): 22–27.

fantasies of his most repressed and also most completely portrayed character, Theodora Goodman.

On the surface, this staid spinster seems unbothered by her apparent asexuality. As a child, however, she was fascinated by the Pearl Brawne-Tom Wilcocks affair, 'one of the things that happened, and which it was still not possible to explain'; it reinforced her determination to 'know everything', especially 'a lot that isn't for little girls' (p. 39). We will see that problems of love and sex preoccupy her increasingly in her fantasy life in the 'Jardin Exotique'. Some resolution of her problems, if only that of a total retreat from them, abandonment, is necessary before she can accept even the minimal physical existence that is to be hers in the western United States.[2] The need to experience love, of which sex is part, is central in Theodora's makeup. It is because she has been deprived of love that she is so puzzled as a child: 'There was always a great deal that never got explained' (p. 39). At boarding school, she states her resolution to see, not to marry, presumably in the hope that an ability to see, to understand, will give her some control over her insecure position. In abandoning the possibility of marriage, she kindles within herself a smouldering anger that expresses itself henceforth in the recurring images of volcanic fire.[3] The fire images that are associated with Theodora

---

[2] Gertie Stepper's remark, 'When I am old all I shall want is a cup of tea, and die', p. 40, made Theodora laugh as a child—'As if it could ever happen this way.' But it turns out to be an accurate description of Theodora's life at the end of the novel: 'And she held her head on one side as she had seen ladies do on receiving and thanking for a cup of tea.
Then they all laughed.
"Shall we be getting along then?" Rafferty asked.
"Yes, Doctor," Theodora agreed.' (p. 309)

[3] In part 1, at the Miss Spofforths', Theodora expresses her wish to write a poem about 'A river of fire. And a burning house', p. 54. At the end of part 2 the Hôtel du Midi does go up in flames, destroying with it the fantasy life Theodora has

throughout the novel provide a focus for both her anger and her suppressed sexuality. Better, indeed, to marry than to burn, if there is a choice; but Theodora had already given up the possibility of marrying while still a child.

Theodora shows considerable conflict over how to give vent to her need for love and her feelings of sexual desire. Chiefly by means of Katina Pavlou, a fantasy creation,[4] she attempts to work through her conflicts. When Katina says she has never been in love (p. 231) but would like to fall in love (p. 185), she is restating Theodora's own need to express 'that desperate affection which she had never quite been able to give' (p. 213). Katina's assurance to Sokolnikov, 'you shall sit beside me, because I love you' (p. 238) is the only unequivocal expression of affection in the novel, representing as it does Theodora's love for her father. Like her creator, Katina is more at ease in bestowing love than in accepting it. Doubtful of her own lovability, she does not expect a return of love:

> 'I should love you, Katina,' Wetherby said ...
>
> 'There is no need,' said Katina Pavlou. 'If you will let me, I shall love you enough.' (p. 240)

Theodora accordingly sees her as 'waiting to give some token of love, or even to receive hurt' (p. 240). Katina is also chosen to undergo vicarious sexual experience, without which Theodora has felt incomplete. At boarding school, Theodora's reflection in the mirror was not complete—

---

created for herself there. In part 3 she finds the violence of her own personality even less controllable than fire, p. 274, and takes leave of the ordinary world.

[4] The figures of the 'Jardin Exotique' section, which takes place entirely within Theodora's mind, all represent aspects of Theodora herself, or of people in her past life (especially her parents). Most have multiple identities but it is a useful starting point to regard Katina as a projection of Theodora, Sokolnikov of her father, and Mrs Rapallo of her mother.

'It was a vessel waiting for experience to fill it' (p. 52). That the experience is to be primarily sexual in nature is clear from Sokolnikov's remark on Katina going to the tower with Wetherby, whom she has chosen to be the instrument of her sexual experience: 'It does not matter whether it is he. Because she has chosen. She has chosen this as the moment of experience' (p. 249).[5] Theodora had decided 'It was necessary that Katina Pavlou should discover fire' (p. 238), the fire of sexuality. But she had also decided long before that Katina's experience in the tower should be 'something nauseating and painful' (p. 253)—necessarily, to confirm her own feelings of deprivation. It is the impossibility of arriving at a fully satisfying resolution of her conflicts over love and sex that provokes Theodora shortly thereafter into destroying the Hôtel du Midi through the fire of her hopeless anger.

All the women in the 'Jardin Exotique' section show a distinct pattern of an unsatisfactory relationship with men. Since they are all creations of Theodora's fantasy, they necessarily reveal much of her outlook. Two of them, Mrs Rapallo and Edith Sokolnikov, are living apart from their husbands, with considerable provocation to do so (pp. 256, 190). Lieselotte is a bitch (p. 176) involved with Wetherby, a man who disgusts Theodora. The one well-married woman in the group, Gloria, Principessa dell'Isola Grande, is an illusion created by Mrs Rapallo (herself a fantasy figure); Theodora is evidently maintaining that a happy and prosperous marriage exists only in the imagination. Varvara is engaged simultaneously to two men, Ivanov and Federmann, and so not deeply committed to either. Katina Pavlou undergoes her first sexual experience within the section, to find it repugnant. The other women in the sec-

---

[5] Burrows (1966) writes of Wetherby's 'plans of seduction', but it is clearly Katina who is choosing her partner in a deliberate sexual experience. She is an early version of Kathy Volkov in *The Vivisector*, who turns out to be quite other than the pure spiritual child for whom Hurtle Duffield is searching.

tion—the Misses Bloch, Henriette, Ludmilla—are all confirmed spinsters. The total picture that emerges from these women is that Theodora is clearly hung up in her attitudes to love and sex.

Since everyone wants love, we would do well to try to understand the reasons for Theodora's unresolved conflicts over love and sexuality. What stops her from expressing the one or at least experiencing the other?

Theodora's inability to experience love is the result of the unsatisfactory relationship existing between her mother and her father and of her own unsatisfactory relationship with each of them. She is torn between both parents in a desire to please each, torn between the pine trees and the rose garden at Meroë (male and female symbols respectively, explicitly associated with her father and her mother). Her fantasised engagement as Varvara to two very different suitors proceeds from this conflict: her mother (Anna Stepanovna) would want a prestigious marriage for her, while her father (Sokolnikov) would want a reliable if duller marriage (p. 181). As a child, Theodora found difficulty identifying with the sex of her destructive mother, who constantly denied her any feminine grace. Her alignment accordingly was with her father,[6] whom we see taking her side a couple of times against her mother, who favours Fanny. Theodora consequently does not succeed in attaining a clear sexual identity, without which she cannot give or receive love. Her moustache is the clearest symbol of her sexual ambiguity. But another such symbol is the nautilus (a vaginal symbol and symbol of Theodora herself), within which is contained the sound of pine trees (p. 162). Ultimately the nautilus is destroyed in the wrangling between her parents (Mrs Rapallo and Sokolnikov); when it shatters, 'Theodora herself felt considerably reduced' (p. 225). Theodora varies in her sexual identification. As a child, she thinks of herself on one occasion as a stick versus the white rose

[6] 'Theo should have been a boy, they said', p. 32

Pearl Brawne (p. 38), finding a masculine severity more appropriate for herself than a feminine softness. On another occasion, however, she thinks of herself in more feminine terms, claiming to be a rose, if a lesser rose, from the same stem as Fanny (p. 67). It is worth noting that Fanny, who grows up in much the same environment as Theodora, resolves her difficulties with love by abandoning it: 'Fanny was safe now, she had children and possessions, she could dispense with love' (p. 119). Theodora at the end of the novel is seen as a black rose, having abandoned sexuality and even identity.

Theodora is also hindered in forming a satisfactory relationship with a man by her persisting attachment to her father. Without a satisfactory relationship to her father, she has very little hope of forming a successful relationship with a man. She is most at ease with older men where no direct sexual threat is involved, like the Man who was Given his Dinner or Moraïtis or Huntly Clarkson. Her father in the role of Sokolnikov dominates part 2 because he was on the one hand so unsatisfactory a parent but on the other so very necessary. While he in fact prepared her for little else in life than shooting or reading, he was desperately necessary to Theodora as a potential source of affection and as an ally against a murderous mother. One part of her shows revulsion at his physical aspects and even some contempt,[7] but another part shows affection and protectiveness towards him. Troubled by the feelings he has aroused in her, Theodora remains haunted by him in the 'Jardin Exotique'. These feelings have to be raised again before she can take her leave of the ordinary world. Consequently, in Holstius in part 3, she creates an idealised father-figure in an effort to work through her problems before she finally abandons the struggle. I will discuss the tenor of her conversation with Holstius in more detail near the end of this paper.

---

[7] 'Old men, she decided, should be quietly mopped up before they reach the age of dribble', p. 182

Theodora is also afraid of her mother's resentment if she should take a man. The basic competition is of course over her father. When as Ludmilla she seeks to escape with Sokolnikov through the Russian forests, disguised as a boy in a situation recalling her shooting outings with her father, she is detected and shot—a punishment Theodora no doubt expects for ousting her mother. She certainly felt her mother's hatred and unwillingness to let her marry.[8] Playing cards of an evening, Mrs Goodman would gloat,

> 'This fine lady … is waiting to be kissed. If he can get through. No, no, he won't. He can't …'
>
> But mostly Theodora did not care.
>
> 'Look, it is your game,' she said.
>
> 'It is no fun,' said Mrs Goodman, 'when one's opponent does not try.' (p. 99)

She is quick to cut down Theodora in front of Huntly:

> 'Oh, and this is my daughter Theodora,' Mrs Goodman had said. 'Of course, you will know my younger girl, Fanny Parrott … Fanny is a great favourite. With everyone.' (p. 104)

Mrs Goodman fantasises a younger version of herself as Huntly's sweetheart (p. 105) and resents his interest in Theodora. When she is told of his lunch invitation to Theodora, she reacts with jealous rivalry:

> 'You will go of course,' said Mrs Goodman. She could not wait for the answer, to feel her anger or contempt. (p. 105)

Theodora, however, is not particularly interested in marriage to Huntly. But years before she had definitely been attracted to Frank (p.

---

[8] Mrs Goodman is herself in conflict over what she wants for Theodora—hence the apparent contradiction between her wish to deprive Theodora of any marriage while also wanting a prestigious marriage for her.

58), to the point where she was finally tempted to defy her mother and take him. That is why she took her mother's silver paperknife on the night Frank came courting. In the end, her defiance lost out to her fears: after a highly ambivalent encouraging and discouraging of Frank, she virtually handed him over to Fanny, and returned the knife abjectly to her mother. But the scene with Frank under the apricot tree (pp. 83–85) continues to haunt her, for she had wanted him intensely.[9] It appears emended in part 2 when as Katina she follows Wetherby among the trees at the picnic and states her feelings: 'If you will let me, I shall love you enough' (p. 240).

There are, then, cogent reasons why Theodora is not able to love and be loved. But her concept of love is in the first place distorted. It derives of course from her observation of the relationship between her parents, and is carried over into her own abortive relationships with men. It is reflected in the Wetherby-Lieselotte affair (pp. 207–08, 258), which operates on two levels. On one level the affair records her impression of her parents' marriage and on the other it suggests deeper undercurrents in her own relationship with Huntly than the surface calm would indicate. The Wetherby-Lieselotte affair is filled with hatred, marked by a kill-or-be-killed antagonism, compounded of contempt on the one hand and mutual dependence on the other.[10] Lieselotte and Julia Goodman and Theodora are all stronger-willed than their men and all are finally responsible for killing the relationship. Lieselotte kills Wetherby just before the outbreak of the fire. Julia Goodman's wish to murder her husband is frustrated when he escapes her into the grave. Theodora kills her relationship with Huntly at the shooting gallery; and she had earlier

---

[9] Burrows' (1966) verdict on Frank as 'brutally obtuse' (p. 173) is severe, and not borne out in Frank's appearances as a young man. While he is uninteresting in middle age he was a quite personable and attractive young man.

[10] The unreal, histrionic quality of their conversation indicates how little idea Theodora has of actual conversations between lovers.

dampened Frank's courtship in similar fashion during their shooting contest. With her concept of love so charged with hatred, we can hardly wonder that Theodora feels constrained about committing herself emotionally.

Theodora's experience as a child when she and Fanny, looking for mushrooms, discover Pearl Brawne and Tom Wilcocks engaged in sexual play among the nettles is important as a focus for her sexual curiosity and fears. The outcome of their affair considerably disturbed her, 'the great mystery that had taken place' (p. 39), for the incident keeps recurring in various forms in the 'Jardin Exotique' section. She is concerned with the fate of both the woman and the man in such an affair. Pearl's abandonment by Tom, as Theodora sees it, recurs in Katina's story of her Aunt Smaragda who had an affair with someone who went away (p. 185). Mrs Rapallo, too, tells Theodora about her abandonment by Rapallo 'in a cheap hotel in Munich' (p. 256) directly after Theodora's return with Katina from the sexual experience of the tower. Since Tom is the original abandoning man, he has to be punished. His fate was in reality unclear so that Theodora is free to imagine a violent punishment for him: he is represented as an old landowner dragged several versts to his death in Russia. 'When finally he was picked up by some peasant women who were gathering mushrooms in a wood, for all they knew he was offering his recipe of nettles to God' (p. 213). Particularly interesting here is Theodora's evident need to deny sexual activity on Tom's part, for he is represented as gathering nettles for a medicinal soup. Following her discovery of Pearl and Tom among the nettles, too, Theodora permanently associates nettles, which sting, with sexual activity. As she goes to the tower to look for Katina, she imagines it filled with 'the intolerable, pervasive smell of crushed nettles' (p. 251). And when Katina asks her if she has ever been inside the tower, referring to sexual experience, Theodora dreads, 'in anticipation, the scream of nettles' (p. 252). Katina does indeed confirm that her experience was painful.

Katina's experience was also nauseating, for Theodora further associates rot and emptiness, death and corruption with the tower (pp. 251–53). All these associations go back to her father, the object of pity: 'Once the object of pity accepts, he is lost. The rot has set in' (p. 207). Despite Theodora's lifelong desire to return to Meroë, one objective observer had called it Rack and Ruin Hollow; and it twice reappears in this aspect as the rotting pavilion on Anna Stepanovna's estate.

Sexual desire itself Theodora sees in terms of fire or lightning. On her twelfth birthday she was struck by lightning—almost a kind of puberty rite. As a young woman, she dreams of lightning striking deep, with clear sexual implications: 'She was holding the faceless body that she had not yet recognised, and the lightning struck deep' (p. 80). She wakes to feel hot and suffocated. Mostly, however, she thinks of sexual desire in terms of fire. On her first visit to Huntly, she asks him if he has ever seen a volcano. To fill vicariously the gap in her own life, Katina must discover fire, Theodora decides (p. 238). Katina emerges from the burning Hôtel du Midi 'with her hands outstretched, protecting herself with her hands ... from ... some other fire' (p. 263), probably her experience with Wetherby that afternoon. Her sleepwalking pose calls to mind Theodora walking through the darkened corridor at Meroë after her lightning dream. Theodora evidently fears that the release of sexual passion will be overwhelming, even destructive. Katina's first words after emerging from the fire, in fact, are 'Miss Goodman ... have you ever seen a burning piano?' The piano, like the volcano mentioned above, symbolises Theodora herself.[11]

---

[11] The sexual implications of musical instruments have often been exploited in bawdy comedy. Consider Marlene Dietrich's famous song in *The Blue Angel*, 'They Call Me Naughty Lola':
The boys all love my music,

Because of her fears; Theodora controls her sexual interests by a feeling of repulsion towards physicality. Thus she is repelled by the physical side of Sokolnikov, though she feels considerable affection for him (p. 210). But the chief gauge of her attitudes towards love and sex is to be found in the changing portrait of Wetherby. The initial portrait of Wetherby is neutral. Theodora is at ease with him as long as he is the romantic, consumptive poet à la Keats (p. 173), with his pale face reminiscent of a 'cello (and therefore of Moraïtis). At the picnic however, he predicts that she will dislike him (p. 239), and starts to arouse that dislike when he assumes a sexual role in relation to Katina. Within a very short time, her dislike of him grows to the point where she has to conceal it (p. 244). As he takes on phallic aspects, his squamous hands suggesting the scales of a fish or snake, her revulsion increases (p. 242). What emerges most clearly from the portrait of Wetherby is the fact that Theodora cannot accept the role of sex in love—the man repels her by what to her is his coarseness and brutality and cynicism. She would have been happier with the kind of love described in the poems that Violet Adams was enamoured of (p. 55) and that Katina wrote (p. 227); if Wetherby could have conformed to that image, then he might have lain with his head in her lap and discussed Tennyson and Morris with her (p. 245). But the escalators have carried them apart—life itself, and Theodora's own adult awareness that love is more than just abstract emotion. It is not Wetherby but his creator, Theodora, who is being cynical when she has him say, 'I think I am right in saying of love that the most one can expect is the logical conclusion' (p. 245): brutal, painful, nauseating sexuality. Wetherby tries to get her to confess that 'If I could have loved Katina Pavlou just as she leapt from your imagination, clothed in white … then

---

I can't keep them away,
So my little pianola
Is working night and day.

it might have been different.' As it is, sexuality must run its brutal course. Theodora cannot agree with Wetherby that things might have been different, for ultimately she too knows that romantic love is an incomplete concept. Katina herself, for all the virginal whiteness consistently and strongly associated with her as a romantic heroine, is the seducer rather than the seduced. Theodora cannot quite assign herself through Katina the role of complete innocent.

Theodora's last wrestlings with her problems of love dominate her conversation with Holstius. She finds that 'although he spoke in abstractions, these answered the depths of her being' (p. 292), voicing the central problems that have tormented her throughout her sad life. Holstius is an ideal figure to do so, for he is able to comfort her in a way that makes the explicit raising of the painful problems bearable: he is a recreation of the father she has missed so sorely, endowed with the articulateness of the Man who was Given his Dinner (an articulateness that George Goodman himself quite lacked). Taking up her unspoken thought, Holstius agrees that the expectation of happiness is very thinly divided from the expectation of sorrow. Happiness is equated first with love (p. 292), then with joy (p. 293). When Holstius tells her that she must accept the two irreconcilable halves that have torn her apart, life and death, flesh and marble, we are suddenly given an insight into the crucial part played by her father in her unhappiness, for we have just seen marble specifically associated with her father: 'Death had taken George Goodman and put him under marble' (p. 292).

Holstius' words give a measure of Theodora's insecure and unhappy existence. She has no real belief in the possibility of love, in which alone happiness lies, for she finds it hardly divided from sorrow. Her one love, for her father, could not be fully satisfied because of the blood relationship, yet the loss of this love at his death leaves her with a gap that she has not been able to fill. The figure of Sokolnikov, who dominates the 'Jardin Exotique' section, allows us to see how much he has remained in her mind during all those silent years with her mother in Sydney, years of living death, for she had really died along with him: 'I am dead, I am dead. Meroë has crumbled' (p. 88). Throughout this scene with Holstius, her thoughts return to her father: 'the cloth on the legs of Holstius had the familiar texture of childhood, and smelled of horses, and leather, and guns' (p. 293). Since we see Theodora here in her final struggles with reality ('I have reached a stage where [these tortures] are not bearable'), it would appear that, after all, even Mrs Goodman's hatred is secondary in the destruction of Theodora's personality to her tormented love for her father.

13

Dreams and Visions in *The Tree of Man*[1]

> For, mark you, men *will* dream; the most that can be asked of them is but that the dream be not in too glaring discord with the thing they know. (Olive Schreiner, *The Story of an African Farm*)

Patrick White's chief interest throughout his novels has been in 'burnt ones', emotionally damaged people who lead a lonely existence without a lifeline to other lives. He is reluctant to portray his burnt ones as totally destroyed, but seeks to find for them a compensating value that might give their life some significance. Again and again, he portrays the force that supplements or transforms their blighted personal life as a richer life within the imagination. Those who do not or cannot attain to a rewarding dream life, a life of conscious fantasy, White tends to endow with a visionary quality.

Throughout this article, I use 'dreams' to designate the process of conscious fantasy. 'Dreams' and its cognate 'dreaming' are broad terms, covering longings, aspirations, and memory. Dreaming is a universal process; but when one's personal life is especially unsatisfactory, the dreams need to be richer, and they occupy a larger part of one's existence. Some form of dreaming—mysticism itself can be seen as one form of dreaming—is necessary as an outlet or compensation for stark reality.

[1] First published in 1973, *Australian Literary Studies*, 6(2): 152–66.

When in *The Aunt's Story* Theodora Goodman's life in the ordinary world becomes unbearable, she elects a life completely within fantasy. Stan and Amy Parker, although emotionally undernourished, are not so burnt as Theodora; they do not dream so much as she does because they do not need to and also because they cannot, lacking broad and deep experience. Amy dreams more than Stan, and finds in dreaming some outlet for her frustration. Stan, similarly frustrated, represses his impulse to dream. What then is left in compensation to give significance to his life?

Instead of an indulgence in a dream life like Amy's, Stan is endowed by White with a sense of vision. By 'vision' I mean an experience beyond a human level, something mystical. It is noteworthy that Stan's visionary sense is at its highest when his personal life is particularly empty. His feeling of oneness with nature, during a storm, comes when he and Amy are estranged from one another (pp. 151–52). His great illuminating vision at the end comes, as A.P. Riemer has pointed out, when his life is at low ebb.[2] The principle of compensation is evident in White's thinking: he endows Stan with a visionary sense because Stan cannot dream to any large extent. Both the dreams that White shows Amy indulging in and the visionary sense that he endows Stan with appear to spring from his unwillingness to abandon these burnt ones to a wholly wasted life.

In this essay I am concerned with the relationship of dreams primarily and visions secondarily to the makeup of Amy and Stan, and with the success or failure of these dreams and visions in making their life more bearable. In Stan's case it is particularly necessary to study his life in the imagination at the basic human level of dreaming before going on to

---

[2] 'Thus the Parkers' world has collapsed around them, and both the husband and wife have retreated into themselves and seem to be preparing for the final spiritual annihilation. It is then that Stan suffers a cerebral stroke which seems to rob him of the last remaining vestige of stature and integrity. It is in this desperate and apparently destroyed state that Stan experiences his most magnificent vision of totality'. Riemer (1967), pp. 3–19.

study his higher life of visionary experience, for in his dreams he is seen in human situations that reveal much about his emotional makeup. With a better understanding of his makeup it is possible to suggest very human reasons why he is a visionary. And since the author himself has made Stan a visionary, some evaluation can be made of White's success in conveying the visionary aspects of *The Tree of Man*.

It is their common aloneness that first attracts Stan and Amy to one another. Both have difficulty in dealing with people socially: 'all these people … breathing in the one room' (p. 14). Stan, we learn later, has never had a friend (p. 415), and Amy has neither been loved nor felt affection for any human being (p. 16). As Stan walks her home after their first meeting, she wonders whether the town will still be there in a thousand years, a speculation that of itself shows her proneness to dream; and her comment, 'I shan't worry if it is not', suggests her accompanying expectation of frustration. Their thoughts about this speculative future reveal significant differences between them. Stan's interest is confined to the non-emotional process of trees turning to coal: 'You'd be able to remember the fossils, how they looked when they were walking about.' He is really speaking of people, not trees; his image seems to rise from a sense of the emotional fossilisation that is to take place within him in the course of the novel. Amy's interest is centred in an emotional response, even if a depressed one: 'Perhaps there'd be a fossil or two you wouldn't want to remember.' The two reactions point to basic differences between Stan and Amy: Stan shows strong repression of emotion, while Amy betrays a vague but deep sense of deprivation. Aware of a lack in her life, Amy 'did expect something to happen eventually, because it does, but these expectations were timid and wholly theoretical' (p. 16). Because of their lack of emotional experience, both Stan and Amy are timid dreamers. Neither of them quite believes in the possibility that their dreams could be realised, and each for that reason is angered by their frustration. Stan rejects early any hope that the world of dreams has anything positive to offer him, however, while Amy continues to dream to the end, even though not quite believing in any realisation of her dreams. In consequence, Stan becomes more quietly repressed as the novel progresses, while Amy becomes more restless and bitter.

Stan never indulges in any exotic dream. He is not without impulses towards fantasy; they are simply checked early and strongly. In chapter 4 we see him on the brink of fantasy about the Gold Coast of Africa after his imagination has been excited by the visit of the man with the Magnetical Water. But he quickly rejects the temptation to dream by immersing himself in the practical world of work—angrily, for he cannot believe in the possibilities of wider horizons in his life.

> His Gold Coast still glittered in a haze of promise as he grubbed the weeds out of his land, as he felled trees and tautened the wire fences he had put round what was his. It was, by this time, almost enclosed. But what else was his he could not say. *Would his life of longing be lived behind the wire fences?* So he did begin then with impatience, even passion, to hew the logs that still lay, and to throw aside his axe at the end, with disgust, apparently, for something wood will not disclose. (p. 38; my italics)

Amy is never able to centre romantic fantasies around Stan because of his emotional repression. It is Tom Armstrong who first arouses sexual impulses in her. After meeting him in town one day, she returns home and fantasises being swept off her feet in an overwhelming wave of passion. As she watches Stan sharpen a knife, 'She held her throat up, in the dim cool light of the tree above the well, offering it almost to the gleaming knife, that she would have received with what cry of love' (p. 108). Stan's reaction is merely to be 'pleased with the strong throat of his wife'. Aroused by young Armstrong, she does manage that night to arouse a sexual response from Stan, and the second of their sexual experiences is alluded to.[3] Tom Armstrong appears in another fantasy of Amy's following her first encounter with Madeleine. Despite its sexual content, the fantasy is remarkable more for its propriety than for its abandonment, and is especially notable as the only developed fantasy that Amy centres around herself:

> She began to wonder whether she could have resisted the advances of a lord, if he had driven up, and she was wearing a mauve dress such as she had never owned. What words she would have spoken she had not yet formed, but felt, but knew. As the lord, in shining boots, descended on the grass and smiled at her with the thick lips that had breathed upon her that day, as she mounted the steps of the store. She would have had children perhaps, as well as diamonds from the lord, whose features were permanently and irresistibly those of the young Armstrong. (p. 134)

Amy does not have the emotional and moral freedom, the social or educational background to create extensive fantasies centred around herself, and that is why the figure of Madeleine becomes important to her: through Madeleine she can externalise her fantasies.

Shortly after her two encounters with Madeleine out riding, there is a notable episode in which Amy tries unsuccessfully to cast Stan in the role of romantic lover. The setting, under the mulberry tree, is idyllic:

> Big glistening leaves waved upon their stalks as she worked. There was a continual opening and closing of the tree, an interplay of sky and leaves, of light and shade, so that she was mottled with it, as well as stained by the juice. Then her husband had come, and they stood together, inside the envelope of the shining tree, talking, and laughing at nothing, and gathering fruit. Then she had kissed him suddenly on his surprised mouth, with such

[3] Lovemaking between Stan and Amy is only recorded twice in the whole novel—here and on their wedding night, p. 25. On both occasions the allusion is indirect.

vehemence, she remembered the impact of their teeth, destroying the soft ripeness of mulberries. And he laughed and looked shaken; he did not hold with kissing by daylight. So that she began again quietly to gather the fruit, ashamed of her ripeness and her purple hands. (pp. 149–50)

Projecting her feelings of frustration and rejection onto the leaves, she thinks 'How flat the leaves were afterwards'. Stan's reaction to the mulberry tree incident is very different from hers. His emotions are pallid as he contemplates there 'the goodness and familiarity of her face', and his sexual impulses are startled and transient rather than strong:

> he looked with surprise at her kind of burnt beauty, and she was pressing her mouth into his, they were hanging on each other with sudden hooks. But the desire to grapple with the unknown woman, who was also his wife, quickly dried up. (p. 151)

His embarrassment produces a sense of shame and discouragement in her: 'She continued to be obsessed by … the eyes of her husband, that were at best kind, at worst cold, but always closed to her.' Amy's resentment grows with her increasing sense of failure to allure Stan and of the distances between them: 'He should, but rights, have been chained by the power of her soft darkness. But … he was not. It might have been hard daylight in which they walked' (p. 149). Stan can feel at one with impersonal nature or with an abstract God, but he cannot convey love for a person; indeed, his feelings of closeness to nature and God seem to spring from his human apartness. Later we will examine the validity of his visions of nature and God in their own right. That he should be married to a woman hungry for affection like Amy is disastrous. His goodness is not enough to make up for his coldness—Amy complains to Stan, ostensibly of Mr Forsdyke, that 'It is not enough to be good' (p. 349). Further, she wants to know of Thelma:

> 'But has she *got* him, Stan?'
>
> Looking at her husband's face.

'Has she *got* him?' (p. 357)

The question indicates her own need to possess, for she does not see herself as ever winning love or a man as ever accepting it.

Madeleine, because she is able to touch off fantasies in both Amy and Stan, plays a very special role in the novel. Although their encounters with her are brief, she is more important in their lives than any other person. Amy sees her twice out riding and once through the windows at Glastonbury, but does not actually speak with her till she visits as Mrs Fisher some thirty years later. Stan meets Madeleine when he rescues her from the fire at Glastonbury, and relives the episode years later when he stands on top of the ruined staircase at the second Glastonbury. He senses the identity of the elderly Mrs Fisher even though Amy does not identify her. Madeleine also figures in the mind of both Amy and Stan as they watch the performance of *Hamlet* in Sydney.

To Amy, Madeleine represents a world she will never be able to enter: she will always be on the outside looking in, as during her visit to Glastonbury. It is a world Amy very much desires and needs, so that when harsh reality gives it the lie she becomes bitter. She will not easily accept the reality of Madeleine. Thus she ignores Mrs Frisby's warning, 'She's out of tune. It's all in the eye with Madeleine' (p. 164), and ignores the passage of years in order to see Madeleine in a member of the audience at *Hamlet* (p. 418). The singed hair and dry retching of Madeleine at the fire at Glastonbury finish her youthful novelette about Madeleine. But her fantasies revive at the performance of *Hamlet*, dampened this time by Stan's curt comment: 'Madeleine is by this time an old woman. She would be older than you, Amy. And you are old.' It is a shock for her to meet Madeleine as Mrs Fisher and see at first hand the coquettishness unmodified by the passage of many years.

In Stan, Madeleine arouses rare sexual desire when he meets her in the burning house: 'suddenly he wished he could sink his face in her flesh, to smell it, that he could part her breasts and put his face between (p. 183). Her expressed interest in him, 'And I know nothing about you.

You haven't been able to tell. You won't now', produces only a characteristic closing of himself: 'There isn't anything to tell.' On this occasion the physical fire shrivels any sexual fire within Stan, but years later as a middle-aged man he again stands on the ruined staircase at Glastonbury and pictures Madeleine. Now he 'thought quite distinctly how he would finish this unfaithfulness to his wife if the opportunity occurred' (p. 221). His fantasy is never made more specific than that. It is a half-hearted fantasy: 'he could not remember enough. He could not remember the pores of her skin, the veins in her eyes, her breath on his neck, however hard he tried to.' Mild as this indulgence in fantasy is, it is a rare flight for Stan, who, we have already seen, had early rejected strongly the life of fantasy as leading only to disappointment. As with Amy, his rejection is not simply realistic, but angry. Frustrated at the impossibility of a Madeleine in his life, he takes out his anger on the escaped duck that had brought him to Glastonbury:

> So he swore at the bird. 'I'll get that bastard,' he said …
>
> Then he … picked up a long branch of a tree that wind had torn off, and that he noticed lying, rushed at the now desperately regretful duck, and pressed it to the ground with the fork of the branch, pressed as if he would crush the bird through the earth, out of existence, rather than take it alive.
>
> 'Got the bastard!' he exploded. (p. 221)

We do not see as much evidence of Stan's frustration and anger as we do of Amy's, but this incident is clear evidence that it does exist. It is probably his own dim, frustrated memory of Madeleine at the *Hamlet* play ('If he could remember what he said as they stood at the top of the stairs, but he could not remember one word') that makes him snap at Amy for her memory of Madeleine:

> 'I could swear that that woman with the violets is Madeleine,' said Amy Parker, leaning down …

> The old woman could have bent down and gathered the violets, so fresh was her memory, and dewy.
>
> Then her husband looked at her slowly and said with the brutality of husbands, 'But Madeleine is by this time an old woman. She would be older than you, Amy. And you are old.'
>
> And stupid, he saw. (p. 418)

Stan seems to resent the fact that Amy can still allow herself fantasies, whereas he has repressed his own so deeply that the memory that could feed them has dried up.

Amy's encounters with Leo parallel her encounters with Madeleine, but mark an important further stage in her attitude towards dreaming. White himself consciously links Leo's blue car with Madeline's horse as he first approaches Amy sitting on her veranda: 'In the day of horses and her youth she would have gone down to the gate, but that was not now' (p. 306).[4] Amy had seen Madeleine twice on her horse and once with Stan at the fire. She goes to bed with Leo twice and converses with him on a third occasion, when Stan arrives back to see his car.[5] Late in the novel, in chapter 22, the elderly Madeleine visits Amy, and her visit is paralleled within the same chapter by Ray's visit, which Amy responds to as if it was Leo's. Ray is described in terms that cannot fail to associate him with Leo, notably as flash and pursy (pp. 306, 319, 329, 435). She sees Ray, 'this flash man she had loved' as 'like some commercial' traveller, and in rejecting Ray would appear to be taking out on him the resentment she still feels against Leo. Her last meeting with Leo had ended in frustration: 'So that she was not to come closer to this man, she saw, or perhaps to anyone' (p. 329). In the one chapter, Amy is confronted with the reality that underlay her fantasies about both Madeleine and Leo.

---

[4] Madeleine's is the only horse ever mentioned as passing the Parkers'.

[5] Stan never sees Leo, but during the performance of *Hamlet* fantasises accurately enough 'the big arse of that commercial traveller', p. 419.

In paralleling Leo's visit so directly with Madeleine's, White is underlining the change that has taken place within Amy over the intervening years. The change is implied in the sentence quoted above: once she would have gone down to the gate, 'but that was not now', when she sits and watches 'in lethargy or with irony'. Amy is still a dreamer, but she has become more hopeless and bitter. Dreams themselves are no longer enough for her: she will test them against the reality, convert this potential lover into an actual one. And so she seduces Leo. Because she feels repulsion for him, her romantic expectations of him are bound to be disappointed; there is even an element of self-defeat implicit in her entering upon the brief affair. But she is desperate, for her unfulfilled emotional and sexual needs are so great. The frenzy in her first sexual encounter with Leo points to the powerful part that deprivation and dreams play in her life:

> The man drew from out of her lovely ribbons of appeased flesh. But when she took his skull, and tried to enter it, she could not, but bruised her mouth against the sockets. It was her husband's head. Then she put her tongue, crying, against the mouth ... she was fighting her disgust, and crying for her own destruction before she had destroyed, as she must destroy. Long waves of exquisite pleasure were carrying her condemned body towards that point.
>
> 'Steady on now,' breathed the man's hot breath into her burning ear ... Now he tried to calm this woman, whose passion overflowed the bounds that he knew.
>
> 'Take a hold of yourself,' he laughed ... 'I'm not going to run off and leave yer'. (pp. 310–11)

Amy meets Leo at a time when she is particularly in need of dreams. Their meetings all occur in chapter 18, the long chapter that deals with the distance that has grown up between Stan and Amy, with the 'years of drought' (p. 304).[6] The distance is presented by White through symbolism and through fantasy: Stan's dream one night and Amy's lie. The empty notebook given Amy at her wedding is a symbol of their married lives: unwritten on by Amy, it remains unwritten on by Stan, to whom she gives it.

> So the book remained empty. He went about, ploughing, chopping, milking, reaping, emptying buckets and filling them. All these acts were good in themselves, but none of them explained his dream life, as some word might, like lightning, out of his brain. (p. 304)

Stan himself is troubled by his difficulty in communicating with Amy. His dream one night, sandwiched between Leo's first and second visit, is testimony of the estrangement between him and Amy:

> Stan Parker, who had fallen asleep tired, in a draught, dreamed that he could not lift the lid of that box to show her what he had inside. It does not matter, she said, holding the dishcloth between, to hide. But he could not lift. It does not matter, she said, Stan, I do not want to see ... Grey water was flowing between them. (p. 316)

Amy feels the same distance, with a good deal of resentment. Her one recorded lie follows Stan's dream almost directly and, as a fantasised experience, is likewise to be interpreted as a dream. In answer to Stan's questions about a walk she has taken, she tells how she met an old man:

> 'He was on his way to Wullunya,' she said, 'where he has a block of land. He has pigs, and some poultry, and a citrus orchard. Poor old man, he is walking because his horse went in the feet,

[6] Chapter 18 is the second longest chapter of the novel; it is only slightly shorter than chapter 16.

> back near Badgerys', where he left it. He had been to Bangalay to see his daughter, who is suffering from the quinsy.' …
>
> She turned away, guarding a pulse in her throat, and a coldness for that wave of falsehood which had overtaken her. (p. 318)

Through her lie, she seems to be warning Stan that he is being left increasingly on his own, like the old man, as she goes into a world of her own. She also seems to sense her disintegration ('his horse went in the feet') and may be appealing to him for help in her distress. Her conversation with Stan, on the night of Leo's second visit, about the rats killing the hens appears to reflect the same sense of her disintegration and to appeal to Stan for help:

> 'But what can we *do*?' she said, standing there. 'They ate the head off and tore out the inside. It is a horrible thing, Stan. And if they keep on, now that they have begun, tearing our good fowls to bits—' She could not say more, but waited for him.
>
> He did not know what to do. (p. 323)

Stan is in no state to offer assistance. The Leo interlude ends in emptiness and depression for both Stan and Amy. Amy, after her final conversation with Leo, feels a kind of hopelessness: 'Whatever is to happen now will happen in spite of me, she realized' (p. 330). Stan, seeing Leo's car on his last visit, interprets its presence and feels strong impulses to violence: 'Visions of violence rose up in him like blood, and boiled over. His lips were blubbery as he took an axe perhaps or a hammer, or his own hands gave a quick answer.' But because he habitually stifles his fantasies, these violent impulses are quickly checked and turned inward, becoming suicidal (pp. 322 and 341). Following the Leo affair, both Stan and Amy pitch their lives in a lower key. At night 'they would fall asleep again, because they were tired, *and would not dream*' (p. 342; my italics), for they dare not.

The lives of Stan and Amy are still on this apathetic level when Amy suggests the trip to Sydney, during which they see a performance of

Hamlet. Amy, who remains confused by life to the end (p. 482), no longer believes 'that there is any exit from confusion, except by living it out, though she did once try the other' (p. 413). What 'the other' was is not specified; it could refer to her brief affair with Leo, but may well cover the whole range of her dream life. When she suggests to Stan that they should go to the city before they die, her expectations are no longer high, but she is also not willing to accept that there is no hope left in life: 'Even if we are disappointed, we shall know' (p. 413). Self-consciously, she makes a joke of her suggestion, 'laughing at themselves, while hoping.' Stan shows no emotion at her plan other than to dash cold water on it by asking what good it would do her to sit under the pines and watch the waves come in. Her retort that he would not know, though somewhat hostile, is not inaccurate in view of his rejection of emotional impulses.

Their seeing the *Hamlet* performance during their trip to Sydney is important in indicating that even a potentially evocative experience serves the old couple not as a stimulus to imaginative fantasies but as a door opening to the past. Far from soaring on wings of fancy, both Stan and Amy have very prosaic reactions to Shakespeare. Stan thinks how 'Once he had known an old horse called Hamlet, a bay, no, an old brown gelding, a light draught, that belonged to an old cove, Furneval was it, or Furness?' (p. 416). Amy, during the re-enactment of the death of Hamlet's father, recalls how 'She could not bear glycerine, or hot oil, that they put sometimes for earache from a roaring spoon' (p. 419). In their reactions to the personages of the play, both Stan and Amy are taken back into the past. Ophelia, for instance, takes Stan back to Madeleine at Glastonbury, and Amy to Bub Quigley. And the green-lit ghost reminds Stan of the old green trench coat he had bought back from the war, whereas the only ghost Amy had seen 'was her conscience in mirrors. It ... was quickly got rid of, by not looking at it' (p. 416). So they watch the play together from the circle, the 'gallery of memory' (p. 418).

Although Stan and Amy are not moved by Shakespeare's poetry, the play does touch off a strong emotional response in their personal lives.

Amy shudders for 'the afternoons that had poisoned her' (p. 419) with sexual and emotional frustration. It was this frustration that drove her into tying Ray to her in a mutually damaging relationship:

> I want Stan, I want Ray, said the queen, and I am not sure that I have had anything, that I know enough to have …
>
> The old woman in the gallery sat on, very unhappy. She was sitting on the iron bed, her knee touching that of her young husband. (pp. 419–20)[7]

Stan is not so much disturbed by the play as depressed. We are not clearly told why, but it is probably because of his empathy with Hamlet, whose suicidal impulses reinforce his own. That would explain the strong presentiment of death that he is left with. We have already seen him in suicidal mood in his dream one night (p. 316) and after seeing Leo's car (p. 322, 341). His apparent accident with the gun while out ferreting shortly after their return to Durilgai seems more the expression of a suicidal impulse than a genuine accident. Stan himself, dazed by the nearness of death, thinks of that evening after Leo's visit when he had been suicidal. He is chronically depressed because of his containment of emotion and suppression of life itself.

Amy is not only unmoved by Shakespeare's poetry: she is resentful of it. The resentment, even bitterness, she feels towards poetry, as to words and books generally, is towards it as an entry into a world of fancy that she hungers for but has never been able to find. To Amy

> Life is not talking, it is living. Then this old woman … wondered what she had lived … She would have liked to see, to think of, there and then, some solid instance of living …

---

[7] In the personage of Hamlet Amy fuses both son and husband. In suggesting these oedipal overtones White may have been influenced by similar overtones in the bedroom scene in Laurence Olivier's film of *Hamlet* (1949).

> 'I have never heard so much talk,' she said irritably, almost abusively. (p. 416)

Poetry is cruel to her because through it other people have found what she has not: the distance 'along the road, along which she has been looking all her life' (p. 417). Hence 'books are unpardonable. You cannot go by what is written' (p. 418). To Thelma Amy complains, ' "People are different in books. They would have to be. It would not be bearable". She would have choked herself with her own hair in the mirror' (p. 352).

Books offer to Amy no real entry into a world of dreams more enriching than the reality of life—and Amy is in any case no reader. A more important symbol to her of the means of entry into a life lived within the imagination is wine, which represents the intoxication she would wish. Wine sets her fancies free when as a young woman she visits Glastonbury and catches a vision of Madeleine through the windows:

> As the wine flowed through her veins and sparkled in her head, she could have got up and fumbled through the baize door, to stand before Madeleine …
>
> 'I would like to sit beside her,' she said, 'like she was, sitting in there, under that curtain thing, with the horses. And sit beside her. I would tell her about my dream, if I could remember it. I have never been able to talk about the things there are to talk about … You see, I know quite a lot. But it is not possible to tell'. (pp. 163–64)

But Amy is never really drunk (p. 327), never caught up into the heady world of fancy. When as an old woman she watches *Hamlet*, she has largely given up her dreams out of hopelessness, and so can acknowledge that the wine in the play poisons the queen. Perhaps that is why she herself would like a good cup of tea after the play (p. 421), in a retreat to earthy reality.

On one more occasion, wine represents to Amy her means of entering a fulfilling life of the spirit: the wine that she drinks at the Communion

Service she attends with Stan shortly after their return to Durilgai. But this means also fails and the wine turns to poison (pp. 431–32) like the wine that poisoned Gertrude. The Communion Service, in addition, enables White to make a general comment upon the futility of dreaming. Here he is making the point not only of Stan and Amy, but of the whole congregation, and therefore of people at large. At the service it is the attainment of grace through the Communion wine or prayer that represents entry into the world of the spirit and imagination. 'Tentative faces were waiting for grace to descend' (p. 427) onto the congregation, but it does not, and everybody remains wooden. Stan, who has always maintained a vague faith in God, remains weighted down by leaden reality: 'I cannot pray, he said, not trying, as he knew the hopelessness of it' (p. 429). Amy attends the service for two reasons: out of resentment that Stan might escape her into a world where she cannot follow, and out of her not yet dead hope that some miracle might yet happen to her (p. 426). While not really believing in her own hope, she is angry at its enduring power to disappoint her. When Stan asks her on the morning of the service if she is coming, she becomes 'quite red with anger', and offers a flimsy rationalisation for her wish to attend: 'What would I do after you have gone? You have not heard that car roaring out of the yard, you are always in it' (p. 426). Neither Stan nor Amy attains to an exalted world through the service: he remains empty and she confused (pp. 431–32). And Amy's realisation that it is finally between herself and God (p. 432) stands as a valid summation of the general feeling of aloneness and non-communion among the congregation.

In this novel White shows considerable ambivalence towards the value of dreaming in making life bearable. On one hand he is saying that because life is disappointing, dreams are needed to give it significance. On the other hand he is saying that dreams are bound to disappoint in that life will not measure up to them. There is bitterness accompanying this dilemma: if one does not dream one is left empty and hopeless, and if one does dream one will be disappointed with the realities of ordinary life. In

Stan and Amy Parker White depicts two people frustrated by life, with only a partial alleviation through dreams. Because of their lack of emotional and educational experiences, they are not equipped to dream richly enough to compensate for the drabness of their lives. Further, the figures that their dreams are built on are unfailingly disappointing. Madeleine is cold and out of touch with such physical realities as fire or bees (p. 450); Leo is 'flash' and no great lover; the parson 'did not help matters. He had scrubbed the face of religion till any nostalgia had fled out of it' (p. 427). Thus the bitterness of the novel is compounded and life itself is shown as providing no firm foundation for dreams.

The Tree of Man is a more depressing book than its predecessor, *The Aunt's Story*. It shows the bleakness of the lives of people who cannot enter the life of the imagination completely like Theodora Goodman, in order to find an alternative or supplement to the harsh reality of ordinary life. For Stan, who dreams even less than Amy, the prospect of an outlet for his frustration through fantasy is dim.

But Stan is given a compensating sense of vision, to redeem what is otherwise largely a wasted life. His virtues are sterile, being confined to himself; his goodness does not erase his coldness. His visionary streak is only faintly outlined and receives sporadic attention. It is largely lost sight of in the long central section of the novel, but is revived to reach its fullest expression at the time of his death. There are two sides to Stan's visionary sense, his closeness to nature and his closeness to God.

The closeness to nature intimated in Stan is a derivative theme, harking back to D.H. Lawrence. It is not consistently developed throughout the novel, and is of temporary duration. His oneness with nature is most stressed in the storm scene that follows the incident under the mulberry tree (pp. 149–52). The vision fades quickly as events of the next day resume their course. J.F. Burrows has pointed out the weakness in Stan's feeling of closeness to nature:

> all the claims made for him in this passage are immediately and severely betrayed by events ... Praying to God 'for the sake of

> company', Stan ignores the company within the house. Knowing 'every corner of the darkness … down to the last blade of wet grass', he knows little enough of his wife and children. 'In love with the rightness of the world', he has repressed wrongs he has seen and overlooked wrongs close at hand.[8]

As the early settlement takes on a place name (Durilgai) and goes on to become an outlying near-suburb of Sydney, nature necessarily becomes less important; in fact, the idea of Stan's closeness to nature is dropped less than a third way through the novel.

Nor is Stan's religious vision successfully conveyed. Stan is not shown as a particularly religious man. Early he prays to God from an emotional rather than a spiritual need: because God will understand him without any need on his part to open himself, something he would like to do to a human being but cannot. The scene in which he visits Lola, Ray's mistress, and spreads enlightenment to her (pp. 455–59) is one of the failures in the novel: nothing in their interchange indicates 'that he could light anyone with his own darkness.' The Communion Service is likewise obscure, but does not appear to be a transcendent experience for Stan or anyone else.[9] Stan's final illumination is disappointing. A.P. Riemer asserts that 'Now he is able to perceive that man must find his own divinity, his own and very private grandeur.'[10] If that is the crux of Stan's enlightenment, then he has attained to no greater insight than Amy had already realised during the Communion Service: 'Then she realised it was finally between herself and God' (p. 432). If the gist of Stan's vision is that 'One, and no other figure, is the answer to all sums' (p. 497), then it is a disap-

---

[8] See Burrows (1969).

[9] White's own attitude towards the effects of taking Communion remains elusive: 'So the people were fed by degrees. Some felt their sins go out of them blessedly. Others, though, were stuck with them forever, except that they had received the favour of knowing those sins better', p. 430.

[10] Riemer (1967), p. 13.

pointing fulfilment of his conviction during the Communion Service that 'I shall … eventually receive a glimpse' (p. 432) and to Lola that 'in the end I shall know something [about God]. What else is there that would be any use to learn?' (p. 457).

From both aspects of Stan's visionary sense, closeness to nature and closeness to God, Amy is excluded. Is she then, as White suddenly charges near the end of the novel, 'a superficial and sensual woman, when the last confessions are made' (p. 485)? That would imply that Stan is deeper. Manfred Mackenzie is right, I think, in his interpretation of White's intention in the novel, to develop a conflict between the powers of good and evil.

> These are ambiguously mixed throughout, but gradually essentialize themselves in the spiritual vision of Stan Parker on the one hand, and in the corporeal vision of Amy and her children on the other. In the face of natural process, even as he is overtaken by natural process, Stan remains open to religious experience. By contrast, Amy tries to halt the flux in which she is immersed by 'possessing' it; she must possess her husband, her son, the child rescued by the floods, the 'poetry' of Madeleine's life, Con the Greek, the commercial traveller Leo. She would reify potential being.[11]

But the human values of the novel go contrary to the mystical intention: Amy is not bad enough nor Stan good enough to bear out a simple opposition of good and evil. Until White's flash of dislike for Amy so late in the novel, he had presented her sympathetically, so that it is hard for us to accept his condemnation. And his criticism of her as possessive (pp. 27, 126) is not vindicated by the evidence within the novel, except in her relationship to Ray. Her search for love and her expectations from love seem reasonable enough, especially in the light of Stan's retreat from

---

[11] See Mackenzie (1966).

emotion.[12] To the child she shelters during the flood she seems no more than kind and reassuring; that whole incident of the child's early morning flight is strange and unconvincing. Stan's religious sense is too superficial for him to be considered a spiritual man. He is so repressed that too little of him as an individual emerges to fit him to his role as a visionary. Contrast him, for instance, with the far more articulated visionaries of *Riders in the Chariot*. White's attempts to elevate him are uncertain and ineffective. Stan is even, perhaps, overshadowed in the book by Amy.[13] His apartness strikes one as isolation rather than special destiny. Must one agree that 'only through absolute alienation from social existence can man have a possibility (no more than that) of visionary achievement'?[14] If that is what White is saying, then one is held back from giving an easy endorsement by discerning too clearly the principle of compensation at work.

If *The Tree of Man* is a failure as a visionary novel, on what does its greatness rest? 'The strength of the book,' writes G.A. Wilkes, 'lies in its human relationships … *The Tree of Man* may fill one with trepidation at what it sets out to do, but it stands firm on what in a different way it has achieved.'[15] More specifically, its achievements lie in its depiction of the marital relationship between Stan and Amy; in its portrayal of Amy (next

---

[12] It is impossible not to feel sympathy for Amy in search of love in a passage such as the following: 'Amy Parker touched the cane chair. She had woken from a miserable sleep, only of a minute or two, but clammy. She would have liked to see someone that she loved. But the afternoon was empty', p. 401.

[13] Amy is the focus of the novel in that other people come and go from her. She remains at Durilgai while Stan goes off to the flood and to the war. We hardly see him in the flood, and do not see him during the war, while Amy's life goes on before our eyes. Amy also has more extensive outside contacts than Stan, and is seen more in company.

[14] Riemer (1966), p. 17.

[15] Wilkes (1965).

to Theodora, perhaps White's most successful accomplishment in characterisation); and above all in its depiction of dreams that reveal deep longings and fears. It is his presentation of fantasy that is White's chief contribution to the English novel. *The Tree of Man* is surpassed in his work only by *The Aunt's Story* and *Voss*—by *Voss* in the conveying of a sense of vision, by *The Aunt's Story* in the rendition of fantasy life. Abortive as a visionary novel, *The Tree of Man* is nonetheless highly successful in its exploration of the life of imagination through dreams.

14
THE TREE OF MAN AS A PIONEER NOVEL[1]

When *The Tree of Man* appeared in 1955, it was hailed as the first important novel by an Australian to gain world attention. In a front-page review in *The New York Times Review of Books* James Stern praised it highly, and *The Sydney Morning Herald* was quick to pick up and cite his acclamation in its next edition.[2] There was no thought of placing the novel in a wider context then; but fifty years have passed and our perspective has changed. In this paper I would like to suggest that now we can more fully appreciate White's achievement in *The Tree of Man* from a new perspective, considering it as a pioneer novel and setting it in particular alongside the acknowledged classic American pioneer novel, Willa Cather's *My Antonia* (1918). The comparison of White's work to this older, more established classic offers the bonus of helping us to understand White's overall achievement as it appears to us in this new century.

As a basis for a comparison of the two novels, let me first establish something of the timespan covered within each. The novelists provide evidence for the dating, but do not supply actual dates:

---

[1] First published in 2003, *Antipodes*, 17(2): 149–54.

[2] Stern (1955); 'Australian's Novel Praised,' *Sydney Morning Herald*, 16 August 1955, p. 3.

Cather drew extensively upon her own life in *My Antonia*. She begins and ends her novel with her own years in Nebraska, from the time she was brought there from Virginia as a young girl in 1883 until she left it in 1896, not visiting it again until 1912. She brings her narrator, Jim Burden, from Virginia to Nebraska as a young boy of ten, presumably also in 1883. She traces the story continuously until 1892, when Jim leaves college in Lincoln to go to Harvard at the age of nineteen, and then suspends the story in his absence until he revisits Nebraska twenty years later, enabling us to see the changes in the lives of the principal characters. Antonia tells Jim during that visit that her daughter Martha has a Ford car, no doubt the Model T that was invented in 1908; so one can posit 1912 as the *terminus ad quem* of the novel, the year that Cather herself returned to Nebraska to visit Annie Sadilek Pavelka, her model for Antonia.

The time frame of White's novel is harder to establish, since White is deliberately vague, but there are clues that point to its limits. Working backwards, we note that when Stan is away in France during World War I, his son Ray is thinking of leaving school, so is presumably about fourteen in 1917 and therefore born in 1903. Since Ray was a late child, preceded by a miscarriage, his parents probably married in 1900 at the respective ages of about twenty-five and twenty-three. Stan was born then in 1875, and Amy in 1877. We first see Stan at the beginning of *The Tree of Man* just after he has left home to clear his land, at roughly twenty years old; so the novel commences in 1895. When at the end he dies from a stroke—survived by Ray's son, who appears to be about ten—Stan would be in his late sixties, which places us around 1942. However, World War II is never mentioned, probably because White chooses to maintain his pioneer emphasis throughout the novel. The dates I have suggested would give *The Tree of Man* a time frame from 1895 to 1942.

The early events of *My Antonia* and *The Tree of Man*, then, take place at the same time. Jim Burden and Stan Parker are nearly the same age, and the pioneer periods of their respective regions overlap. Cather, writing in 1918, tells a brief, quick-moving story—in full colour—from 1883 to 1892, then picks it up again for a few memorable days in 1912. White, writing nearly forty years later, tells a long, slowly unwinding story—in shades of grey—from 1895 to 1942. The additional thirty years covered by White's narrative were still a pioneering period for Australia; it was only during the war years, the 1940s, that Australia transformed into an industrial country.

Cather's novel was quickly recognised as a classic and has become an archetype of pioneer novels. It continues to attract respect and affection; it has never been out of print and is easy to find in any large bookstore, in Australia as well as in America. *The Tree of Man* is currently out of stock in Australian bookstores and has to be ordered from warehouses. *My Antonia* is an excellent source to draw upon in formulating one's ideas of the characteristics of a successful pioneer novel; indeed, it provides the basis of what I have to say about pioneer novels.

A pioneer novel has a strong sense of human history—past and future—a sense of history renewing itself in new areas and new lands. It looks at the past as it depicts the establishment of a settlement, but looks more to the future, when continuity is ensured and a noteworthy culture has begun to emerge. Writers like Cather and White who are very conscious of their own role in the creation of a regional culture are particularly concerned with its emergence and establishment. A pioneer novel highlights the concept of growth of the land and its settlers. Since it surveys a part of history to which all of a country's inhabitants will look back, it has at its core a major theme, the 'Big Idea' that some critics, like Louise Adler, consider to be one criterion of the Great Australian (or American) Novel.[3] Both *My Antonia* and *The Tree of Man* are novels

[3] Adler (2001).

with themes that are important to their respective cultures, and indeed to the culture of new countries in general.

The characters in pioneer novels show a common commitment to hard work, a readiness to help others beyond the immediate family, an awareness of being part of a community. Courage, co-operation and endurance are qualities that have brought about survival and guarantee future prosperity. Necessarily there will be some natural and human failures, even tragedies, on the way to success. Flood, drought, storms, fire and blizzards are standard and formidable obstacles of nature, but it is the human tragedies that touch us most—of those unable to adapt to the difficulties or crudities of pioneer life, those who could find no place either in the society from which they sprang or that to which they came. If endurance, survival and growth are central to a pioneer novel, so are the difficulties they come to outweigh. The conclusion of a pioneer novel characteristically reads like a calm time for taking stock, not a final serene resolution.

A pioneer novel is religious at heart; it is animated by a belief in the dignity of human life, the meaningfulness of human endeavour, faith in the future. The forces that operate on the characters and their lives are not blind; a sense of Destiny hovers over the narrative. There is a sense of a world beyond the material, and at times that world will open to communicate with this world. If success in a newly settled area is seen as the outcome of persistent hard work over several generations, it is achieved under the monitoring eye of God. Both Cather's and White's novels speak directly of God or Destiny.

Cather demonstrates a stronger sense of the past and a deeper attachment to her land than does White. Part of the reason lies perhaps in their very different childhoods, different memories. The young Cather spent her early years in a rural environment, first in Virginia to the age of nine, then in Nebraska to the age of twenty, when she moved to Pittsburgh and later to New York City. White also came from a rural background, but spent many of his early years in Sydney, then in England, returning to Australia permanently only in 1948, when he was thirty-six. Cather remained always deeply interested in stories of exploration and early settlement. She inserts into *My Antonia* the incident of the Spanish sword found in a riverbed in Nebraska (no doubt the Republican River), a sword made in Cordova that probably belonged to one of the men in Coronado's 1541 expedition; that would point to Nebraska and not Kansas as the northern limit of Coronado's exploration. The difference is a matter of only a few miles but to Cather, who loved her region, it was important. White shows little interest in the process of the early settlement of New South Wales; his settlers are either there already, or they simply appear and make their living in an unspecified way. Stan is the first to settle in his area, on land left him by his father; later other settlers move in on the periphery, rarely intruding upon his or Amy's consciousness. Neither *My Antonia* nor *The Tree of Man* makes any mention of the indigenes who preceded European settlers. Only their place-names point to non-European origins: Black Hawk (an Indian-sounding name like that of Cather's own Red Cloud) and Durilgai, first given a name at the end of part 1 of *The Tree of Man* (one-fifth of the way through the novel), but not often named thereafter. The real-world model for Durilgai was Castle Hill, twenty miles from Sydney, where White lived when he was writing *The Tree of Man*. It was never the outback, as Ruth Brown suggested,[4] but a rural district now an outlying suburb of Sydney.

Looking to the future beyond the end of her novel, Cather is again more positive than White at the end of his. Cather is careful to emphasise continuity and a certain abundance, if not actual prosperity. The last section of *My Antonia*, 'Cuzak's Boys', tells of Jim's visit to Antonia after twenty-years' absence from Nebraska to find that she now has nine children, and the eldest of these, Martha, has a boy of her own. Antonia's

[4] Brown (1955), p. 861.

children, 'big and little, tow heads and gold heads and brown, and flashing little naked legs', 'come running up together out of the family's fruit cellar', 'a veritable explosion of life out of the dark cave' (p. 249).[5] It is as if they burst from the earth itself; and if the cave represents Antonia's womb, then she becomes a fruitful Earth mother. White in his brief final chapter—really an epilogue—is far less positive. The only human presence there is Stan's grandson, whose name is never used—'a rather leggy, pale boy', frail perhaps like Thelma, his aunt—and even this human presence is subordinated to the trees: 'In the end there are the trees' (p. 498). The rate of human reproduction in *The Tree of Man* is so low in fact that it is insufficient to ensure the continuance of the settlement. Of some twenty characters in the novel who have any importance at all, only Ray and Joe Peabody have any children. Families like the O'Dowds, the Quigleys, and the Gages, and characters like Thelma and Madeleine do not reproduce at all. From the epilogue it appears that White is less interested in the characters he has created than in cycles of life in general.

As serious writers deeply committed to traditional European cultural values, Cather and White do not simply equate success with population growth and prosperity. Both Cather and White look to the emergence of a local culture as nearby cities develop. So Cather shows Jim at a dramatic performance of *Camille* in Lincoln where he attends college, and White shows Stan and Amy at a performance of *Hamlet* in Sydney; but it is Stan's grandson who points to future cultural achievement in Australia. We are told on the final page that he will write a poem, all-embracing in its compass: 'He would write a poem ... but not yet ... He would write a poem of death ... he would write a poem of life, of all life, of what he did not know, but knew ...' (p. 499). The crowning cultural achievement for Nebraska and Australia was already in process: it was what the two authors themselves sought and did attain, a memorable depiction in

---

[5] Cather (1944). Page references in this chapter are to this edition.

literature of their respective communities from early settlement to the emergence of a civilisation there. Both wanted to show their region developing an important culture. When Jim quotes admiringly from Virgil's Georgics, '*Primus ego in patriam mecum ... deducam Musas*' [I was the first to bring the Muses into my country], it is really Willa Cather stating her own literary ambition, making it clear that '*patria*' here 'meant, not a nation or even a province, but the little rural neighborhood' of which she writes (p. 197). And one sees in the boy and his poem at the end of *The Tree of Man* a projected early version of White himself and his literary ambitions, which he articulated in his 1958 essay 'The Prodigal Son': 'There is the possibility that one may be helping to people a barely inhabited country with a race possessed of understanding'.[6]

The establishment of a distinctive culture comes late in the settlement of a region, however. As they portray the early growth of a settlement, when settlers often have to help others in distress, Cather and White show notable differences in their representation of such situations. Cather shows individuals helping other individuals, while White depicts his characters acting in groups, anonymously, to deal with threats to the community at large—flood and fire. So, for instance, the Burdens in *My Antonia* take food to the Shimerdas and Anton Jelinek makes a coffin for Mr Shimerda; but the only personal kindness shown by one of White's characters to another is Mrs O'Dowd's lending a goat to Amy to provide milk for the newly born heifer whose mother has died. The ability to endure hardship is graphically shown in *My Antonia*, where poverty is an abiding way of life for the Shimerdas and, indeed, a number of other characters. White's characters are not called upon to endure chronic hardship. The flood is temporary, in an outlying area, and does not affect any of the characters we know. The bushfire is more vivid and more immediate, and although it damages only the estate of the wealthy Mr

---

[6] White (1989), p. 17.

Armstrong, it stays in our mind because of the fear of fire that is such a strong part of Australian consciousness. Extreme poverty itself has never been characteristic of Australian life as it has been in America, so that adversity rightly appears in White's novel in the form of natural disasters. Dorothea MacKellar's *My Country* (1908), the most famous of all Australian lyric poems, known to all Australian schoolchildren, expresses the Australian ethos that dictates these aspects of White's story:

> Core of my heart, my country!
> Land of the Rainbow Gold,
> For flood and fire and famine,
> She pays us back three-fold.

With her image of gold at the end of the rainbow, MacKellar shows an optimism, a faith in the ultimate generosity of the land that is lacking in White; his characters merely live through potential disasters, then go on with their lives.

Cather and White both tell episodes of settlers' inability to adapt to their more primitive life and of their consequent sad deaths, but such characters and their stories in Cather are vividly realised, while in White the characters are merely outlined and their stories briefly recorded. Mr Shimerda's death by suicide in *My Antonia* is sad and touching; he is established early as a gentle, affectionate misfit, unhappily married and out of place as a Bohemian migrant and a musician in a still unformed culture. His story builds up to his suicide, and the account of his death and the effect of it on his family are sympathetically conveyed. The suicide in *The Tree of Man* of Mr Gage, a painter of extraordinary talent, is reported factually, without emotion; it touches no one deeply, not even his wife. He is seen only once, in a nearly wordless encounter with Amy (pp. 103–04). Stan, when Amy tells him of the suicide, responds with a flat 'Go on', the Australian equivalent of 'You don't say' (p. 291).

At the end of both *My Antonia* and *The Tree of Man*, the characters have gone beyond tragedies to acceptance, with a sense that one cycle is ending and another is beginning. Wandering around Black Hawk at the end of *My Antonia*, Jim comes upon traces of the first road that led north from the town and recalls the night he and Antonia first arrived there:

> This was the road over which Antonia and I came on that night when we got off the train at Black Hawk and were bedded down in the straw, wondering children, being taken we knew not whither ... I had the sense of coming home to myself, and of having found out what a little circle man's experience is.

The Tree of Man begins with trees that are to be felled and ends with trees that are still standing: 'In the end there are the trees ... quite a number of them that have survived the axe'. The dog that the young Stan brought with him at the beginning is replaced in the epilogue by a dog that has recently died. The endings of both novels heighten our awareness that we are ourselves involved in a cycle of history, and in that way we are linked to the past and invited to look beyond ourselves into the future.

Cather and White illustrate well the religious predispositions of pioneer novels. Both authors accept the presence of a God who monitors the lives of their characters and, on occasion, they speak of him directly. Cather chooses not to attach religious beliefs too conspicuously to her main characters, though Jim confides to Antonia that he felt her father's presence when he was left alone with the dead body, and she tells Jim that 'I talk to him and consult him all the time' (p. 237). Cather's strongest statements of faith are made by her minor characters, no less memorable on that account. One is made by Jim's grandmother to Otto Fuchs after his hard-luck story of how, while looking after a woman committed to his care as they travel from Austria to Chicago, she gives birth to triplets and he is accordingly eyed with suspicion by everyone: 'Grandmother told him she was sure the Lord had remembered these things to his credit, and had helped him out of many a scrape when he didn't realize that he was being protected by Providence' (p. 56). The other, more memorable still, is told by Anton Jelinek, who during the

1870 war with Prussia accompanied a priest bearing the Sacrament to dying men:

> the cholera break out in that camp, and the men die like flies … Everybody that go near that camp catch the sickness but me and the priest. But we have no sickness, we have no fear, because we carry that blood and that body of Christ, and it preserve us … All the soldiers know, too. (p. 82)

In the closing sentences of the novel, Jim speaks of Destiny in human lives: 'For Antonia and me, this had been the road of Destiny; had taken us to those early accidents of fortune which predetermined for us all that we can ever be.' Cather's God is protective but leaves the characters free to lead their own lives.

White's God is less conventional than Cather's, for White never accepted organised religion. During the bulk of *The Tree of Man*, organised religion plays a small part; it is only towards the end that it assumes importance, in the Anglican Communion Service that Stan attends with Amy and Thelma. The account of the Communion Service portrays the common difficulty of obtaining spiritual sustenance and uplift from a church service. It is unclear whether Stan attains much enlightenment during the service, but he is elevated above Amy and Thelma by dint of White's repeated mockery of them. When the party leaves the church, it is Stan who leads the way, acquiring thereby a certain authority. The chief function of the scene is to lay a foundation for Stan's final epiphany. One may see White as seeking through the persona of Stan to understand the nature of God, searching finally outside organised religion. Speaking to a young evangelist just before his death, Stan spits and says of the gob of spittle, 'That is God', an observation that seems intended to startle the reader as much as to challenge thought. Perhaps White is saying that God is in everything. Stan's epiphany at the moment of death is not attained within organised religion. Although we are told that 'It was clear that One, and no other figure, is the answer to all sums' (p. 497), the epiphany communicates little to us. (It may well have meaning to White as an expression of his need to integrate his various selves, as Theodora was urged to do at the end of *The Aunt's Story*, but discussion of that is outside the scope of this paper.) However, we are to see Stan as having been brought to this epiphany by God, who concerns himself in the novel chiefly with Stan, paying only intermittent attention to Thelma and to Amy. If Cather's God is compassionate, White's is arbitrary, capricious in his choice of his elect.

From the discussion so far it is clear that Cather has a more positive outlook than White: a deeper interest in the history of her region, a stronger sense of place, a reassuring faith in God (a God who, unlike White's, does not play favourites), a more confident view of the future. She stresses the idea of continuity and growth, whereas White, even as he indicates that the cycles of life will continue, tells a story of decline; whatever growth takes place in *The Tree of Man* takes place offstage and unnoted. It is a depressing story in which the characters pursue their lives doggedly, without direction, until they end worn out, knowing nothing, comprehending nothing. Stan's epiphany comes only at his death; his life is as dreary as anyone else's in the novel. The original title White had intended for the novel was *A Life Sentence upon Earth*, but he came to reject it as too pessimistic; nevertheless, that attitude to life does colour much of the novel. The comparison between *My Antonia* and *The Tree of Man* makes clear White's constant downplaying of any of the positive aspects that attend the pioneer experience; yet the period that he depicts was a time when the foundations of contemporary Australian society were being laid, so that his negative attitude can seem like an accusation against Australia. Understandably, many readers will feel uncomfortable as they read the book.

The Tree of Man is a story of multiple failures, in personal relationships and in personal ambitions, failures in living that do not necessarily come from the difficulties of pioneer life and are extraneous to it. Notably, the relationship between Stan and Amy, never really close, becomes increasingly empty. Thelma summarises their relationship well to her husband: 'Just the business of two people discovering each other by degrees, and not discovering enough, as they live together' (p. 344). And directly after that, we find her husband wondering 'Why did I marry Thelma?' (p. 345). There is an emptiness at the core of *The Tree of Man*, the emptiness of personal unfulfillment.

The character whose failures are most emphasised and who is most consistently accused is Amy. Since she is one of the two main characters, and since she stands accused of a possessiveness that is not really demonstrated, this necessarily results in an unsatisfying quality to the novel. All four parts of the novel end in an incident that highlights a failure of Amy's. Part 1 ends in her failure to keep the lost boy she brings home from the flood. 'She would imprison the child in her house by force of love', we are told, but she fails to do so (p. 96); he simply disappears, without explanation. Part 2 ends with her inability to protect old Fritz against an outburst of anti-German hostility during World War I, so that she has to help him leave Durilgai. Part 3 ends with her failure to reclaim or hold Ray after she meets him secretly in the ruins of the Armstrong estate, to give him money and food. Part 4 ends with her witnessing Stan's death, unable to help him or to keep him: 'she was holding him with all the strength of her body and her will. But he was escaping from her' (p. 497). And so Amy is left alone, accused to the end of destructive possessiveness; but the case against her depends on White's recurrent accusations, not on evidence that he provides. White's severest judgment upon Amy, that 'she was a superficial and a sensual woman, when the last confessions are made', may draw a startled protest from the reader (p. 485), for White will quarrel with his readers as well as his characters.

Why does White keep maligning Amy while implying no criticism of the cold, inaccessible Stan? The answer seems to be that the diminishing of Amy is his way of indirectly building up Stan for his final epiphany and the attainment of a certain mythic stature, for pioneer novels do tend to aspire to a certain mythic status. Even as the protagonists remain firmly rooted in common humanity, they transcend ordinariness to become archetypical representatives of the pioneer community, acquiring a wisdom and a stature beyond the reach of others. Cather readily grants these qualities to Antonia, also near the end of her novel: 'It was no wonder that her sons stood tall and straight. She was a rich mine of life, like the founders of early races' (p. 295). In *The Tree of Man* that dignity is confined to Stan.

White's judgment of both Stan and Amy is arbitrary, but then so are many of his judgments of his characters. He is prone to spend a good deal of effort in mocking a character for reasons of his own that are not persuasive to the reader. This is especially the case with Thelma, upon whom he vents more bile than she merits. He dismisses her finally with the observation that her soul was thin, and yet he allows her a telepathic awareness of Stan's death, probably again to boost Stan's importance. Such arbitrariness is likely to irritate the reader.

But even with the boost to Stan, there is still no affection shown to him, or indeed to any of the characters in *The Tree of Man*. White's lack of sympathy for his characters, which extends far beyond this novel, is quite conspicuous when one sets *The Tree of Man* alongside *My Antonia*. Cather never arbitrarily criticises a character and often provides a kind interpretation for a character misjudged by others, like Ole Benson. Ole was an unhappily married man who would sit for hours and help Lena Lingard watch her cattle: 'All the settlement was talking about it' (p. 125). Years later Lena confides to Jim that 'There was never any harm in Ole. People needn't have troubled themselves. He just liked to come over and sit on the draw-side and forget about his bad luck. I liked to have him [there]' (p. 210). Speaking of Cather, Eudora Welty was driven to exclaim 'How she refreshes the spirit!'[7]

What then do we learn about White's achievement from the comparison with *My Antonia*? We have seen that Cather reaches out to her

---

[7] Welty (1973), p. 3.

readers as fellow human beings with common joys and sorrows, while White maintains a formal distance from his readers. White's writing has negative aspects that will always alienate his readers. One of these is a proneness to sarcasm and derision. At times his derisive remarks are witty, but the wit rarely overrides the derision; in *The Tree of Man* there is far less wit than scorn. When Thelma kisses her father, for instance, we are told that she 'did quite enjoy being an affectionate daughter for its passing novelty' (p. 279). Another of White's negative aspects is his arbitrary elevation of certain characters, often strange, unlikable, or, like Stan, inaccessible, to the closed ranks of his personal Elect. If one asks, will *The Tree of Man* endure, the answer has to be that it can never win a place in the hearts of its readers as *My Antonia* has done; like certain human beings, it will be admired but not loved. *The Tree of Man* will endure as an important work dealing with the pioneer period in Australia, but it is a work that will be studied in universities rather than widely celebrated for its power to touch the heart and uplift the spirit.

We also learn something of White's aims in the comparison with Cather. Whereas Cather's novel resonates with an intense love for her characters and for the land, White's novel keeps a formal distance from both. Cather paints a vivid picture of the Nebraska landscape, its tall red grass, its treelessness at that time: 'Trees were so rare in that country, and they had to make such a hard fight to grow, that we used to feel anxious about them, and visit them as if they were persons' (p. 28). (Nebraska now has more trees than in Cather's time, but there is a park just outside Red Cloud that preserves the Nebraska landscape that she knew, as a tribute to her). White tells us almost nothing of the land around Sydney, other than mentioning stringybarks on the first page and referring to scribbly gums ('the already scribbled trees') on the last; in fact, Sydney itself is never named. White is more concerned with creating a mythic status for his story of pioneer life, with Stan as 'the man' (a sort of Everyman), later 'the father', and Amy as 'the woman', later 'the wife' or 'the mother'. Personal names are rarely used, and then almost exclusively by Amy, that 'superficial and ... sensual woman' (p. 485). In the course of writing this article, I have become convinced that White, unlike Cather, is interested not so much in the development of character or narrative flow as in the establishing of mythic status for his story of pioneer life. The difference between the two authors and their aims is expressed in the very titles of their novels: the personal, affectionate *My Antonia* and the formal, generic *The Tree of Man*. Techniques of myth-making continued to preoccupy White in *Voss* and *Riders in the Chariot*; but that is the subject of another essay in this collection.

AUTHOR'S NOTE

The accent mark that Willa Cather has added to the initial 'A' in her heroine's name, Antonia, presents a problem:

First, Antonia is not a Czech name: it is widespread throughout Europe, and is pronounced in Czechoslovakia, as in other European countries, An-TO-nia, with emphasis on the second syllable.

Second, the accent mark in Czech is used to indicate a long vowel, not an emphasised syllable. English readers are used to interpret an accent mark as the sign of the stressed syllable, as in the phonetic transcriptions in our dictionaries.

Third, Czech words normally stress the first syllable, so that the accent mark over the A of Antonia is superfluous.

Why then does Willa Cather add the accent mark?

Perhaps she heard the name as having two almost equal emphases in its first two syllables, and wished to indicate that. If so, she would have said AN TO nia, much as we say 'lipstick', with its two nearly equal stresses. It would have been important to her, for she cared deeply about Annie Pavetka, her Antonia. She probably did not know that the accent mark in Czech is merely an indicator of vowel length. Who would have told her?—not uneducated Annie.

But Cather failed in her purpose: almost one hundred years later, no one in English calls it 'My AN TO nia': the most common pronunciation, even among educated people, is 'My Anto NI a'. Usage almost always wins out. As W.C. Fields said, 'If at first you don't succeed, give up. No use being a damn fool about it.' Prevailed upon by such wisdom, I have abandoned Cather's accent mark throughout this article, while maintaining the profoundest respect for her literary achievement.

15

STAN'S GRANDSON, THE LOST BOY, AND WHITE'S *ARS POETICA* IN *THE TREE OF MAN*[1]

Three years after *The Tree of Man* was published, Patrick White published his famous essay, 'The Prodigal Son',[2] in which he spoke of the genesis of *The Tree of Man* and *Voss* and articulated his literary ambitions. It is a retrospective statement, clearly spelled out, and it won special prominence from the fact that the essay contained some autobiographical information on the man who had in those two novels firmly established himself as the leading Australian novelist. This undoubtedly important essay has been quoted again and again. But its obvious importance has drawn attention away from an earlier and fuller account of White's literary theory, couched in poetic rather than literal terms: the still unwritten poem germinating in the mind of Stan's grandson at the end of *The Tree of Man* (pp. 498–99). One could call the poem White's *Ars Poetica.*

In a recent article on *The Tree of Man*,[3] I suggested that Stan's grandson is a projection of the young Patrick White, bent on creating an important body of literature for an Australia that he looked upon as culturally barren. The boy is young and his poem seems so nebulous and

---

[1] First published in 2004, *Commonwealth*, 26(2): 71–76.

[2] White (1989).

[3] Beston (2003b).

so ambitious in its concept that we may not take it seriously; but White did intend that we should do so, for he prepared us for it six chapters previously (chapter 20). There the boy is born, unobtrusively assigned a name, Ray,[4] and grows to the age of about six or so. By that time he has established a relationship with Amy and Stan. We are told that his mother, Elsie, 'frequently took her child to Durilgai, to his grandparents' (p. 397). One day there the boy asks Amy for a tin he sees in her pantry, to keep his pencils in, for, he says, he will 'Write things' (p. 400). He does not answer Amy's question 'What sort of things?' but confides to Stan that he will write a poem. He is vague about the theme, but is quite sure that he will write a poem, on a grand scale: 'The boy was stretching his arms … till they were embracing air … "Don't you ever know, Grandpa, about things, because you just know?"' (p. 407). It is only in the final chapter, really an epilogue to the novel, that we learn about the nature and the scope of his future poem.

The impulse to his poem is touched off by Stan's death. It is the boy's assertion of life in the face of death, his first confrontation with the poem that he will ultimately write. A close reading of the projected poem reveals it to have much greater significance than first appears: it emerges as a poetic summary of White's literary ambitions, and even looks at his themes and techniques.

As soon as the boy goes into a creative mode, his mind turns to the practical colour of his view of the world. He has in his pocket a piece of crimson glass that he had asked for from Amy (p. 399), a piece of stained glass from an empty church that was left by the lost boy whom Amy found at Wullunya (pp. 87–98). Now the young Ray lies on his back as he looks through the glass at 'the crimson mystery of the world'. Looking at the world through stained glass is an image that identifies White as a romantic and a religious writer and as such represents an important

[4] 'they called [him] after the father', p. 394.

statement. It can also be a statement of an artist's uniqueness and separateness, as it appears to have been in Patrick White's case. The stained glass was introduced into the novel by the lost boy, who appears and disappears without explanation in what seems an insignificant, puzzling episode, but he is recalled to our attention when he is linked to Stan's grandson a generation later. The lost boy was the same age as Stan's grandson Ray when he acquired the stained glass—about six years old, just old enough to jump down from the dray by himself (p. 91). The lost boy seems to be autogenous, and that points towards his importance, for many artists think of themselves as being self-born entities. The lost boy, I would suggest, is another projection of the young Patrick White, future artist; to both White and the lost boy creativity is a unique way of looking at the world, through a coloured glass of one's own.

Here is the somewhat Rimbaud-like poem as it germinates in the mind of Stan's grandson on the last page of the novel:

> He would write a poem of death. Long words wired for the occasion, marble words of dictionaries, paper words in rat traps would decorate his poem. He was a bit frightened of it. But of course he did not believe in it, not really. He could not believe in death. Or only in passing through a dark hall, in which it is an old overcoat that puts its empty arms around him. Then death is faintly credible because it is still smelling of life.
>
> So he would write a poem of life, of all life, of what did he not know, but knew. Of all people, even the closed ones, who do open on asphalt and in trains. He would make the trains run on silver lines, the people still dreaming on their shelves, who will wake up soon enough and feel for their money and their teeth. Little bits of coloured thought, that he had suddenly, and would look at for a long time, would go into his poem. And urgent telegrams, and the pieces of torn letters that fall out of metal baskets. He would put the windows that he had looked inside. Sleep, of course, that blue eiderdown that divides life from life. His poem was growing. It would have the smell of bread, the rather grey

> wisdom of youth, and his grandmother's kumquats, and girls with yellow plaits exchanging love-talk behind their hands, and the blood thumping like a drum, and red apples, and a little wisp of white cloud that will swell into a horse and trample the whole sky once it gets the wind inside it.

The 'crimson mystery of the world' that the boy contemplates through the stained glass is an acknowledgement that there are dimensions beyond the physical, and the fact that the glass comes from a church window suggests that, to White, creative inspiration is a kind of spiritual impulse. The boy's poem, inchoate through it may seem, embraces a wide range of possible subjects, styles and emotions. It looks at the world of dreams and the material world alike; it can see inherent beauty in the commonplace. As it grows in the boy's mind, he envisions the germ of an idea, 'a little wisp of a white cloud', swelling into a horse that can 'trample the whole sky once it gets the wind inside it'.

Above all, it is the colour and the mystery of the world that excite the boy and inspire him to poetic activity. At first, torn between impotence and a compulsion to write, he contemplates the idea of death, his most recent powerful experience, but that is for him an intimidating theme: 'He was a bit frightened of it'. He is unable to believe in death, to look it in the face and deal with it because it is too final; it is only credible to him when it is 'still smelling of life', like Stan's old overcoat in the hall that he imagines putting its empty arms around him. Nevertheless, he conceives of diction that would be appropriate to his poem of death: long, formal words, dignified, memorable marble words. The 'paper words in rat traps' are not clear. Do they perhaps refer to obituaries in the newspapers and elegies in anthologies, and the perils that attend both?

At an impasse with the idea of death, the future poet turns to the theme of life, and then his poem begins to grow. He still retains something of the young boy who, years before, had told Stan that he would write a poem even though he did not yet know how. His poem, still unborn, will be 'of all life, of what he did not know, but knew', and now he knows much more. It will be of 'all people, even the closed ones', one of the greatest challenges of all, though they 'do open on asphalt and in trains' as their lives 'run on silver lines', and they offer these lives to those whom they will never meet again. He will record his close observations of people from 'the windows that he had looked inside'. He will enter and record their dreams as they sleep under 'that blue eiderdown that divides life from life', the life of fantasy from the daily life in the physical world that constantly impinges upon our senses as we begin each day feeling for our money and our teeth.

'Little bits of coloured thought, that he had suddenly, and would look at for a long time' will go into his poem, like those arresting phrases that are scattered through White's early novels, lighting up the sentences in which they occur. Sometimes the coloured thought is only a word, as when Mrs O'Dowd, facing the great and overwhelming moment of her death, is 'occupied with matters of *minute* importance' (p. 477; my italics). Or four words, as when a man tells how in the bushfire he 'had seen a snake bite on itself before it died, *to hold someone responsible*' (p. 167; my italics). Or five, when Amy, contentedly milking a cow in the early days of her marriage, feels that '*Peace fell into her bucket*' (p. 31; my italics). Bits of coloured thought like these make us aware of how painstaking a stylist White was.

A whole range of intense emotions too will go into the boy's poem, such as would be taken from 'urgent telegrams', and end, sadly, in 'pieces of torn letters' that fall, abandoned, 'out of metal baskets'. It will tell of times when the blood is 'thumping like a drum', in fear or in sexual desire.

The poem continues to grow, embracing such basic human experiences as 'the smell of bread', seeing the beauty in foods like red apples and preserved kumquats (the kumquats become precious stones at the end of chapter 5 in *Voss*), describing rites of passage like flirtation as part of sexual maturing, as 'girls with yellow plaits [exchange] love-talk behind their hands'.

The final image of the power of creativity is an exciting one, 'a little wisp of white cloud that will swell into a horse and trample the whole sky once it gets the wind inside it', and that is why the boy cannot bear the feeling of impotence that it produces in him.

The image is particularly interesting as an adumbration of the song that Voss sings in that novel as he sets out from Jildra into the interior, having received Laura's answer to his proposal. The song is of White's own composition. Regularised, without Voss' embellishments as he sings it, it would appear thus:

> Eine blosse Seele ritt hinaus
> Dem Blau' entgegen …
> Sein Rock flog frei.
> Sein Schimmel mit den Wolken
> Um die Ehre rrrann …
> Nur der edle Rock zu Schaden kam,
> Die Fetzen fielen
> Den Himmel entlang (pp. 202–03)[5]

What the similar images from the two novels both express is a feeling of exultation and confidence quickly succeeded by a feeling of diffidence and failure. As the poem mounted in the boy, we are told, 'he could not bear … what was still his impotence.' The mixed emotions of exultation and fear of failure are common in any artist undertaking a grand enter-

---

[5] [A bare soul rode out
into the blue.
Its coat flew free.
Its white horse was trying to outrace the clouds.
But the fine coat came to grief,
its tatters falling along the sky.]

prise, and were clearly experienced by White himself as he wrote *The Tree of Man* and *Voss*.

The lost boy, who is also a projection of the young Patrick White, reveals what writing meant to White: an assertion of his independence, his uniqueness, and, above all, his separateness from a mother he saw as domineering. That is why the lost boy is depicted without parents or the need for parents; he comes and goes in a world of his own, as the young Patrick endeavoured to do. White intends us to see the boy as escaping Amy's possessiveness, a charge he repeatedly levels at her without ever sustaining it. He is clearly beset by the problem of his own relationship with his mother. Simon During[6] has written about that at some length, and White himself remarked to me when I visited him in 1973, almost twenty years after he wrote *The Tree of Man,* that the more thousand miles between him and his mother, the better. The episode of the lost boy, then, is not merely an unintegrated intrusion into the novel; rather it constitutes a very revealing aspect of Patrick White the man.

The lost boy and Stan's grandson are linked in two important respects. The first and most obvious link is their fascination with viewing the world through stained glass, but the second is also important: their ignoring of the mother figure, Amy. In the episode of the lost boy, it is almost as if he is adopted solely so that he can reject Amy. It is a vengeful fantasy. And Stan's grandson pointedly ignores Amy's question about what will he write; he does not answer but picks at the woodwork, yet he tells Stan freely about the poem he will write! The lost boy finally goes into aloneness, so far as we know, and Stan's grandson too is last seen alone among the trees after Stan's death, unaccompanied by either Amy his mother Elsie, presumably rejecting in advance any comfort they might have proffered.

---

[6] See During (1996).

On a first reading of *The Tree of Man*, one is likely to pass over both the strange episode of the lost boy, left hanging in the air, and the forlorn appearance, at the end, of Stan's grandson, 'a frail, leggy boy' whom we have not encountered over the last fifth of the novel. But both episodes, I have argued, are important. The first points to the role of writing in White's life and to the recurrence of certain themes in his novels, like the struggle between a potential artist or mental adventurer (like Theodora or Voss) and a dominating mother figure. The second episode describes the poem that Stan's grandson will write, telling us a good deal about White's concept of writing and his deep commitment to style. After *Riders in the Chariot*, his style and his interests change so radically that the later novels can be treated as a separate body of work; but for the cluster of three novels, *The Aunt's Story, The Tree of Man,* and *Voss*, which contain most of his greatest work, the epilogue to *The Tree of Man* provides the best description of White's aims and methods that we have.

16
THE THEME OF SPIRITUAL PROGRESSION IN *VOSS*[1]

> How important is it to understand the three stages. Of God into Man. Man. And man returning into God. Do you find, Doctor, there are certain beliefs a clergyman may explain to one from childhood onward, without one's understanding, except in theory, until suddenly, almost in spite of reason, they are made clear. (p. 411)

Laura's doctrine of the three stages of man's spiritual progression, although somewhat cryptic, makes a statement of the central theme of *Voss*. The doctrine is highlighted by the intensity with which Laura utters it, and it is elevated to the status of visionary insight by the fact that it climaxes Laura's severe illness. Frequently in White, severe illness like Laura's, or some kind of 'doffing' of the body, precedes spiritual illumination.[2] It is our aim in this article to clarify Laura's doctrine, and to show

---

[1] Co-written with Rose Marie Beston; first published in1974, *Ariel*, 5(3): 99–114.
[2] The term 'doffing the body' is taken from *Riders in the Chariot*: to the dying Himmelfarb it seems that special illumination is attained only 'by those of extreme simplicity of soul, or else by one who was about to doff the outworn garment of the body.'

how central it is to the novel's theme of spiritual progression by indicating how it is led up to in several earlier scenes. Those scenes involve Laura's analysis of Voss in Mr Bonner's garden (pp. 92–98), Voss' song as he rides into the Australian hinterland (pp. 202–03), and Le Mesurier's poems (pp. 313–17). These scenes, and Laura's pronouncement from her sickbed (p. 411), are regularly spaced throughout the book and are linked with one another, indicating how steadily White had in mind the theme that Laura articulates and how concerned he was with stressing it.

Most simply, Laura's doctrine may be explained as follows:

The first stage, 'God into man', refers to the act of creation, whereby God breathes a spirit into man, and with it some of his own divinity. Further, it is a time of dependence, usually associated with childhood.

The second stage, 'Man', describes the time when man rejects the notion of his dependence and feels strongest, in control of himself and the world around him. At the height of his pride, he assumes the role of God—an illusion he must renounce before he can achieve union with God.

The third stage, 'Man returning into God', involves the renunciation of man's belief that he stands alone and in control. In this third stage, the attainment of humility is crucial before man can be drawn back into God. Humility is reached through the embracing of suffering and the experience of failure. In its extreme form, the attainment of humility means a dissolution of the self.

Laura's doctrine takes its inspiration from the life of Christ. She herself speaks of the three stages as 'certain beliefs a clergyman may explain to one from childhood onward, without one's understanding, except in theory, until suddenly, almost in spite of reason, they are made clear.' And, on the verge of illumination during her illness, she intimates that 'human truths are also divine. This is the true meaning of Christ' (p. 366). In Christ above all, God came into man. As an adult, Christ lived as a man for whom human truths and divine truths were the same. His humble acceptance of suffering, 'Nevertheless, not as I will but as Thou wilt', marks the beginning of his reunion with God. But while the doctrine of spiritual progression is based upon Christ's life, it is explored most fully within the novel with respect to Voss.

The first of the scenes that foreshadow the enunciation of the doctrine of the three stages is the garden scene in chapter 4. In her analysis of Voss there, Laura describes him as caught up in pride. Voss' statement that he believes in a God who is above humility confirms Laura's analysis, for he maintains that people fashion God after their own image (pp. 94–95). His God is necessarily then a projection of himself, above humility: 'Ah, the humility, the humility! This is what I find so particularly loathsome' (p. 96). Laura warns him, 'To maintain such standards of pride, in the face of what you must experience on this journey, is truly alarming', for he may well break without attaining the humility that is essential for a return to God. Laura in her dissection and Voss in his confession here point to his being set in what Laura is to describe as the second stage in man's spiritual progression.

The garden scene has more than one link with the first scene of Laura's illness and illumination. In the first place the garden scene has in common with the later scene an intensely spiritual quality. Laura and Voss are transported out of their bodies, as it were, for the revelations in the garden, and when the revelations are over, 'they realized they had returned into their bodies' (p. 97). And as Laura announces her revelations from her sickbed she is racked by fever and almost torn from her body; her revelations once made, the fever breaks and she returns to her body. The scenes in Mr Bonner's garden and in Laura's sickroom are also linked by White through the reiterated notion of the difficulty of comprehending the simplicity of a great idea. In the garden scene we are told that 'These simple ideas were surrounded with such difficulties, they would scarcely issue out of her inadequate mind' (p. 97). Likewise, as Laura strives to articulate her doctrine at the height of her illness, we are told that she was 'struggling with the simplicity of a great idea' (p. 380).

The garden scene is important for its elucidation of Voss in the second stage of man's spiritual progression. But the song Voss sings as he rides into the interior, away from Jildra, succinctly outlines all three stages in a foreshadowing of Laura's later formulation of them. The song was composed by White himself,[3] and intended to be closely integrated with the theme of Voss' spiritual development:

> Eine blosse Seele ritt hinaus
> Dem Blau' entgegen …
> Sein Rock flog frei.
> Sein Schimmel mit den Wolken
> Um die Ehre ran …
> Nur der edle Rock zu Schaden kam,
> Die Fetzen fielen
> Den Himmel entlang. (pp. 202–03)[4]

We are likely to overlook the significance of Voss' song at the time, largely because Voss follows it by the disclaimer that words have no significance ('Wörter haben keine Bedeutung. Sinnlos!' [Words don't have any meaning. Senseless!]). Further, Voss is happy and confident here, so that the song seems little more than an expansive outburst. Ironically, Voss does not realise the relevance it will have for him.

---

[3] Suspecting that the song was in fact his own, I asked Patrick White if that was so. He replied he had composed it himself, and had the German checked by Curt Prerauer. I have normalised the appearance of the song here, for White writes it to indicate how Voss sang it.

[4] [A bare soul rode out
into the blue.
Its coat flew free.
Its white horse was trying to outrace the clouds.
But the fine coat came to grief,
its tatters falling along the sky].

The bare soul that rides out into the blue represents Voss' soul in the first stage ('God into man'), having newly had life breathed into it by God—hence its bareness. The second stage follows quickly here: the soul becomes 'Man', no longer bare but protected now, clothed in a coat that flies free without hindrance, with all the overtones of mastery and lordship that the coat image suggests.[5] The progression into the second stage is marked by the use of the masculine possessive, 'Sein' [Rock], which can only refer to '*ein* Mann'—man, in the second stage—and not to '*eine* Seele', which would have the feminine 'ihre' as its possessive. At the height of his pride, the man's horse vies with the clouds in the purity of its whiteness, the whiteness being a manifestation of divine power. The song ends, however, with the picture of the fine coat of the rider having to come to grief, its shreds falling along the sky. There is a warning to Voss in the song that life itself may force him to abandon his conviction that he is master of the universe. And so it points to the third stage, when man, humbled now, can approach God.

Frank Le Mesurier's prose poems 'Childhood' and 'Conclusion' flesh out the notions in the three stages that are so spare in Laura's pronouncement. The scene in which Voss reads Le Mesurier's notebook is linked both with the scene in Mr Bonner's garden earlier, and with the scene of Laura's illness later. The connection with the garden scene is clearest when Laura's analysis of Voss there is made '*as if she were reading from a notebook*, only this one was her head, in which her memorandum had been written, in invisible ink, that the night had breathed upon' (p. 83; our italics). The connection with Laura's illness is made chiefly through the oracular nature of both Laura's and Le Mesurier's revelations,

---

[5] The song is borne out literally in the person of the Aboriginal Dugald, whose fine coat does fall to shreds, along with the illusory 'conscience he had worn in the days of the whites', p. 234. When he renounces this false identity, however, he is able to return to his own people and their gods. But if Dugald literally bears out the song, its chief relevance is still to Voss.

attended by fever that has racked the body but passed its crisis. (Although Le Mesurier's poems were written before his illness, they are directly associated with his fever, so that they seem to proceed from this fevered intensity). There is much about Laura and Le Mesurier at times that suggests the role of a medium, through whom the revelation is made. When Laura in the garden bends her head and knows that 'some kind of revelation must eventually take place, terrible though the prospect was' (p. 80), it is as if she is consenting to act as the instrument of a power beyond her control. Laura's name in fact (beyond recalling Petrarch's Laura),[6] suggests the word laurel and so associates her with Apollo, revealer of truth, whose symbol was the laurel. Both her residences, Mr Bonner's house (pp. 29, 57, 167), and the school where she later teaches (pp. 424, 426), are surrounded by laurels. She possesses, we have seen, many of the qualities of a pythoness. And Le Mesurier's name means 'the measurer' (Fr. *Le mesureur*, Ger. *Der Messer*), appropriate to his role as one who gauges what is taking place within Voss' soul.[7] Le Mesurier proves to be startlingly accurate in his poems in gauging what has taken place within Voss' soul in the first and second stages, and in foreseeing Voss' advance into and through the third stage.

The first poem, 'Childhood', provides some explanation of what leads up to the second stage. It enables us to see that stage, when man feels he is in control of the world around, as a defence against his feelings of vulnerability that dominates the first stage. The kind of childhood that

---

[6] White early shows Laura associating herself with the laurel when he tells how she would recall Jack Slipper (who fascinates and frightens her with his sexuality) 'and again see him spit a shiny stream into the molten laurels', p. 57. Her association is one of intercourse with Jack Slipper.

[7] It is also worth mentioning in relation to Le Mesurier's name that German '*Messer*', with only a change of gender (from *der* to *das*), means 'knife'—which would be appropriate to the frequent reference to knives and cutting in Le Mesurier's poems, and to the vivisecting effect of those poems on Voss, pp. 313, 317.

the poem describes is meant to have a validity for childhoods beyond Le Mesurier's own, and for Voss' in particular. Voss' reaction to the poem forcefully establishes its relevance for him: he 'was at once standing in the terrible arena of childhood, deafened by the clapper of his own heart' (p. 313). The poem, indeed, 'turned upon the reader, and he was biting his nails to find himself accused' (p. 315).[8] Shortly before his death, Voss comes to an awareness that his illusions of indestructibility cover a deep sense of vulnerability: 'He himself, he realized, had always been most abominably frightened, even at the height of his divine power, a frail god upon a rickety throne, afraid of opening letters, of making decisions' (p. 384).

Childhood is portrayed in the poem as a time of vulnerability and reliance on others, who hurt rather than help. The child is pictured as an onlooker, troubled, insecure. The phrase 'a white tablecloth is spread to celebrate the feast of children' encourages us to regard the children as devoured rather than entertained, for 'the feast of children' is mentioned in the context of their vivisection: 'when they had opened us with knives, they took out our hearts.' Children, we are told, 'are not expected to think, but are allowed to suffer, and rehearse the future.' They are beset by a sense of their limitations ('I was the prisoner of stone'), of their dependence upon their parents ('they break off their tears and put them in the parents' hands'), of impermanence ('We have not arranged our things, who will not be staying long in this house'), and of vulnerability ('Prayer is, indeed, stronger, but what is strong?'). Only the old see and understand that the child suffers and that he will go on to the illusions of his parents in the second stage, of strength and independence and destructive power.

---

[8] The experiences of childhood recorded here are also remarkably similar to those of Theodora Goodman earlier in White's work and of Hurtle Duffield later.

In the process of their vivisection, children themselves learn to vivisect: 'Children soon forget from whom they have learnt to use the knife.' In consequence they become alienated from mankind and their own humanity. And so they learn to stand alone with their dreams and illusions: 'We run, and flap, and crow, and rise—one foot? Everyone applauds, and pretends, and disperses, unaware that we have flown above the pointed trees. We enjoy the immense freedom of dreams.' Thus the soul is drawn into the second stage of man's spiritual journey, 'Man'.

It is at the height of the second stage that Le Mesurier's poem 'Conclusion' begins:

> Man is King. They hung a robe upon him, of blue sky ... He rode it across his kingdom of dust, which paid homage to him for a season, with jasmine, and lilies, and visions of water ... Fevers turned him from Man into God.

The poem is made up of four verse-paragraphs. Broadly, paragraphs I and II portray man in the second stage in the fullness of his illusions. Paragraph III portrays the transition from the second to the third stage. Paragraph IV repeats and intensifies that transition and makes explicit the achievement of final union with God.

Le Mesurier's poem, like Laura's doctrine of the three stages, concerns Voss more particularly than mankind in general. The poem states more clearly than Laura's cryptic pronouncement later that the second stage, 'Man', does not merely mean that man stands alone but that he regards himself as God, with the earth as his domain and other men as his subjects. Within a few pages after Voss reads this poem,[9] he is shown regarding the desert as his kingdom and the blacks as his subjects. When the party encounters a group of blacks, Voss rides towards them 'sustained by a belief that he must communicate intuitively with these black

[9] Chapter 11, dealing with Laura in Sydney, intervenes between Voss' reading of Le Mesurier's poems and his encounter with the blacks.

subjects, and finally rule them with a sympathy that was above words' (p. 356). Their running away, foretold in Le Mesurier's poem ('afraid of his presence, they had run away'), makes him a 'rejected sovereign'.

In paragraph I, the coat of Voss' song ('der edle Rock') has become a royal robe, made of the blue sky ('das Blaue') covering Voss as he rides into his kingdom. But even as this paragraph portrays man's kingship it simultaneously undercuts that kingship as an illusion. The kingdom is finally one of dust, paying homage to the Man-King only for a season. Whereas paragraph I shows man regarding the earth as his kingdom, paragraph II shows him so far subordinating nature as to regard it as an extension of himself: 'I am looking at the map of my hand, on which the rivers rise to the northeast. I am looking at my heart, which is the centre.' The death of this Man-King has the power to 'water the earth and make it green', when 'trees will spring up, to celebrate the God-head with their blue leaves.'

In paragraph III the illusions begin to fail, and man confesses his inability to subordinate the universe to himself. The kingdom of dust that had for a season paid homage to the Man-King has returned now to dust. The importance of the quest for humility is acknowledged; but humility is like brigalow scrub, difficult and painful to find one's way through (p. 206), and offering only 'a thin shade in which to sit.' The quest for humility resembles the striving for spiritual progress generally. When Palfreyman, for instance, realised 'he had failed that day to pray to God', and so must forfeit 'what progress he had made on the road where progress is perhaps illusory' (p. 137), he too found that humility was his brigalow. The chief growth in spiritual awareness in this verse-paragraph is that 'As I grow weaker, so I shall become strong';[10] it is an awareness

[10] As the ship is being loaded in Sydney Voss looks at Palfreyman and realises Palfreyman is weak. White quickly corrects that view by commenting 'It was only

that corroborates Laura's doctrine that as man abandons his illusions of power he can return to God. As his understanding of ultimate values grows he finds other values become increasingly superficial and transient. To Le Mesurier, his life as a member of an aristocratic society seems now hardly credible—a life of courting rituals, of formal dinners, of elegant displays of wealth: 'As I shrivel, I shall recall with amazement the visions of love, of trampling horses, of drowning candles, of hungry emeralds.' Dissolution becomes a sought-after state[11] as the most complete expression of humility: 'Now that I am nothing, I am, and love is the simplest of all tongues.' It is this ability to experience love, for Harry and for mankind, that Voss attains shortly before his death: 'he loved this boy, and with him all men, even those he had hated, which is the most difficult act of love to accomplish, because of one's own fault' (p. 407). As man returns into God, he necessarily loses his sense of alienation from other men.

Paragraph IV begins with the acknowledgement that man's powers are limited, and depend on a God above him: 'Then I am not God, but Man.' He must suffer in order to attain humility, and must accept that suffering.[12] Le Mesurier has a brief outburst of despair that may recall Christ's own: his 'O my God, my God, if suffering is measured on the soul, then I am damned forever' suggests Christ's 'My God, my God, why hast Thou forsaken me?' But his despair is shortlived, and he prays in acceptance, 'O God, my God, let them make from [my flesh] a vessel that endures.'

---

really through humility that [Palfreyman's] strength was restored to him', p. 103–04.

[11] Theodora Goodman represents the most fully developed illustration of this doctrine in White's writings.

[12] Cf. White's epigraph to *Happy Valley*, from Mahatma Gandhi: 'It is impossible to do away with the law of suffering, which is the one indispensable condition of our being. Progress is to be measured by the amount of suffering undergone … the purer the suffering, the greater is the progress.'

When man is most humbled, when he is reduced to the bare bones,[13] he is closest to God: 'I am God with a spear in his side.' The man Christ has become one with God when his side was opened with a spear. In this fourth verse-paragraph, the similarity between Christ's life and the course of man's spiritual development ordained by God and announced by Laura is made clearest.

In referring to God with a spear in his side, Le Mesurier also appears to foresee the approaching death of Palfreyman, speared by an Aborigine. As Palfreyman advances to his death, all the members of the expedition remember 'the face of Christ that they had seen at some point in their lives, either in churches or in visions, before retreating from what they had not understood, the paradox of man in Christ, and Christ in man' (p. 364). Like Voss immediately before his death, Palfreyman is said to love all men (p. 365), an indication to us that he has attained the humility that is necessary for reunion with God. Judd's account at the end of the novel of Voss with a spear hanging from his side is wrong in fact, but his identification of Voss with Palfreyman has a rightness about it, for both die in humility after having expressed a love for all men. Laura herself is unconcerned whether Judd is speaking fact of not, for she is convinced of a greater truth, that 'Voss had in him a little of Christ, like other men' (p. 474).

In paragraph IV Le Mesurier sees suffering as inevitable, as part of the human condition: 'Flesh is for hacking.'[14] But suffering does serve a positive function, providing a certain nourishment: Le Mesurier's spirit will fill 'the empty waterholes', just as his 'blood will water the earth and make it green.' The suffering of one man is regarded as beneficial to many

[13] In *The Aunt's Story*, Theodora and Moraitis are established as fellow visionaries when Theodora tells him 'I too come from a country of bones.' In a country of bones, a country stripped down to essential values, he agrees, it is easier to see.
[14] Harry Robarts, too, had learned that 'man's first duty is to suffer', p. 102.

as well as bringing union with God for that man. The pre-eminent example of that notion is Christ, whose life forms a pattern for Voss'. When Voss' blood runs out upon the dry earth (p. 419), we are meant to believe that the earth responds to this watering. The last pages of the book can suggest that Voss' sacrifice provides a certain guarantee of the future of Australia, as well as of his own salvation.

After persecution and humiliation comes public honour, which is only an externalisation of the exalted state of the soul: 'They chase this kangaroo, and when they have cut off his pride, and gnawed his charred bones, they honour him in ochre on a wall.' That is true not only of Old Man Kangaroo among the Aborigines, but of Christ among the Christians, and of Voss among the people of Sydney at the Domain ceremony. The spirit of Old Man Kangaroo, of Christ, and of Voss 'has gone out, it has gone away, it is everywhere', in a dissolution that is also supreme fulfilment.[15] In the prayer with which Le Mesurier concludes his poem, the sentiments are those of the soul in the third stage, reunited into God:

> Oh God, my God, I pray that you will take my spirit out of this my body's remains, and after you have scattered it, grant that it shall be everywhere, and in the rocks, and in the empty water-holes, and in true love of all men, and in you, O God, at last. (pp. 316–17)

This prayer is essentially a prophecy that is fulfilled in the death of Voss. When Jackie cuts off Voss' head, White tells us 'His dreams fled into the air, his blood ran out upon the dry earth, which drank it up immediately' (p. 388). He goes on to observe 'Whether dreams breed, or the earth responds to a pint of blood, the instant of death does not tell.' But dreams do breed and the earth does respond to a watering with blood in time so

[15] Near the end of *The Vivisector*, Hurtle Duffield cannot stop himself 'attempting to reach higher … towards total achievement or extinction', fulfilment and dissolution being equated here.

that Laura can announce, again in her role as seer, 'Voss did not die … He is there still, it is said, in the country, and always will be' (pp. 477–78).

There are circumstances surrounding Laura's enunciation of her doctrine of the three stages that compel us to consider her spiritual state as well as Voss'. The arrogance with which she makes her pronouncements indicates that she is locked in the second stage. She speaks from a position apart from mankind, close to that of the God-head. The most startling of her utterances is her judgement of man as a shabby creature:

> man is so shoddy, so contemptible, greedy, jealous, stubborn, ignorant. Who will love him when I am gone? I only pray that God will. (p. 411)

Clearly here she does not include herself in the human race. And when she says 'Who will love him when I am gone? I only pray that God will' she is first of all talking not merely of Voss but of man generally and then making slighter claims for God's love than for her own. Likewise she had declared herself earlier in her illness 'willing to give up so much to prove that human truths are also divine' (p. 395), thereby assigning herself a great power beyond that of ordinary human beings. There she was speaking of giving up Mercy, which to her represents a great sacrifice—not because she loves Mercy, one feels, but because she regards the child as an abiding symbol of her Virgin Motherhood. In spite of her statement, Laura proves unwilling to relinquish that role and associate herself with the human race. That is why she will not look at the comet (p. 399) that travels towards the Southern Cross (p. 414). When Voss fears 'some final torment of the spirit' that he might not be able to endure (p. 385), he also does not dare for a time to raise his eyes towards the comet, but when he regains the courage to accept his final ordeal he does look up, to see 'the nails of the Cross.' Laura cannot renounce her pride to embrace, like Voss, the humility that is necessary for her to return into God.[16]

Because her arrogance is more directly expressed at the height of her illness, it makes clearer the special position in which Laura has long held herself: apart from and above mankind. The least position that she has ever accepted or will ever accept is that of equality with Voss. The acceptance letter that she wrote to Voss (pp. 197–99) is especially characterised by the sense of a contest in which she is determined to best him and remain equal with the God-head.[17] Even her telepathic message to Voss at the beginning of her illness suggests a contest in which she will not be less than him: '*Even if there are times when you wish me to,* I shall not fail you' (pp. 381, 387; our italics). Such an interpretation is strengthened by the occurrence of the italicised phrase just before the onset of her illness, in a context of competitiveness. Tom Radclyffe, dancing with Laura at the Pringles' ball, reminds her that the fact that she has been hurt does not mean that others will be, 'Even though you may wish it' (p. 345); and he is right, we think, that Laura is so concerned with maintaining her ascendancy.[18]

In spite of these instances that compel us to an awareness of Laura's lack of humility, White is generally highly protective towards Laura.[19] Usually he removes her from judgement by the principles that she enun-

[16] Beatson (1970) sees Laura's concern for Voss during her illness as 'the unearthly love of a saint for an erring soul'. Beatson's article is interesting, but the three stages he discusses do not strictly correlate with the stages that Laura describes.

[17] See chapter 19 this volume.

[18] An earlier occurrence of the phrase, in a letter that Voss writes Laura, also strongly suggests the contest between them: 'I cannot kill myself quite off, *even though you would wish it*, my dearest Laura', p. 231; our italics.

[19] White is defensive towards all his visionaries, guarding them from criticism. With Laura, and with Theodora and Stan earlier, he elevates their visionary qualities and plays down their alienation or hostility.

ciates. Even in the scene of her illness, at the same time that he indicates she lacks the humility necessary to proceed to the third stage, he also elevates her by associating her with Christ. Her suffering is linked with Christ's,[20] and her Crown of Leeches recalls Christ's Crown of Thorns. Elsewhere White discourages us from relating the pythoness to the truths that she reveals.

There is a marked discrepancy in White's attitude towards his two main characters. Although both Voss and Laura are presented as beings apart from the rest of mankind,[21] between God and man, Voss is brought closer and closer to humanity and Laura is removed further and further from it as the novel proceeds. White reminds us that Voss is finally man, but he leaves us somewhat in awe of Laura. A phrase used of Voss near his death, 'the man who was not god' (p. 404), is not paralleled by any similar phrase used of Laura, and would in fact be inappropriate. White does not allow anyone in the book to diminish Laura, to induce humility in her. Tom Radclyffe and Colonel Hebden confront her with certain truths, but White plays down the justness of their accusations.

At the Pringles' ball Tom accuses Laura—after considerable provocation—of living off her imagination, and goes on to ask her what she expects of Voss (p. 347). White makes snide jabs at Tom, concerning his insecurity and shaky masculinity and malice, and invites sympathy for Laura's great distress;[22] he does not endorse Tom's indirect accusation that

---

[20] 'Dear Christ, now at last I understand your suffering', p. 410.

[21] In the garden scene, Voss comments to Laura that they were unwise 'to flounder into each other's private beings', p. 97. Laura smiles with pleasure at the word 'beings', probably because their encounter has been more like one of supreme beings than mere humans.

[22] Her 'face was shrunk to the extent that it resembled a yellow skull', p. 347.

Laura has not come to successful terms with the ordinary world.[23] Yet we see Laura, after confessing that Voss is lost, proceed to bear out the truth of Tom's accusation by writing a letter that she knows cannot possibly be sent to Voss. In the letter, too, written essentially to herself ('If you, my dear [Johann Ulrich], cannot hope to benefit, it is most necessary for me'), Laura comes close to admitting the inadequacy of her adjustment to the realities of life: 'How strong one was, how weak one always is!' (p. 350).

In his two scenes with Laura, at Mrs De Courcy's and at the Domain ceremony, Colonel Hebden presses the literal truth about Voss on Laura, and once accuses her of no longer respecting the truth (p. 473) and again White plays down the justness of the accusation. Again White makes snide jabs at Laura's challenger, concerning Hebden's snobbery and superficiality and calculatedness, and again he invites sympathy for Laura's distress (she is filled with 'a dry, burning misery' on the one occasion, and feels as if her lifeblood might gush from her mouth on the other). White does not endorse Hebden's accusation, which is ultimately the same as Tom's, that she lives off her imagination. He implies rather that Hebden's desire to know the facts betrays an inferior kind of understanding of Voss and his expedition, when set against Laura's. While it is true that facts never do tell the whole story, it is not true that 'The air will tell us' what the story signifies, as Laura claims at the end of the novel. But Laura is allowed the last word, not only at the close of the novel, but against her assailants generally.

Laura is a dominating character, threatening to dominate the novel, especially since she figures importantly in the fifty pages after Voss' death. Nevertheless, she does not succeed in shifting the focus of attention away

---

[23] When White alludes to 'The truth that [Tom] had let loose', he is referring to the truth that Tom draws out of Laura, that Voss is lost, not to Tom's remark about her living off her imagination.

from Voss to herself. In the section that follows Voss' death, we are concerned still with the nature of the man Voss and the effect of his expedition on the people who inhabit Australia. The question of Voss' spiritual progression is never lost sight of for long. That progression, expressed in general but cogent terms in Laura's doctrine of the three stages, is the central theme of the novel.

17
ALIENATION AND HUMANISATION, DAMNATION AND SALVATION IN *VOSS*[1]

I should explain at the outset that the terminology of damnation and salvation is Patrick White's; the rendition of them into more general concepts, alienation and humanisation, is my own. The term damnation, too, is used throughout the novel, while its opposite, salvation, is hardly used at all. Thus Laura and Le Mesurier both speak of damnation, including themselves among the damned. The term salvation occurs very rarely in the novel, though it is reinforced by the use of 'rescue', used of Laura's role towards Voss in the garden scene and by Voss himself in his native language ('*rette mich nur!*' [save me]).[2] The terminology is of course religious, but gets its chief significance in psychological or, still more generally, in human terms.

The emphasis in White's terminology (though not necessarily in *Voss* itself) is negative, on damnation, and so I will define the two terms in that order. Damnation means to White the perpetuation of an individual's alienation, isolation from mankind. It does not imply any moral judgment on White's part, nor are we invited to look askance at the damned; rather is it an acknowledgement that the makeup of the

---

[1] First published in 1971, *Meanjin*, 30(2): 208–16.

[2] 'Salvation', though, is used on p. 227. 'Rescue' occurs on p. 97 and in Voss' prayer on p. 415.

damned one is such that reintegration within the human race is no longer possible—if, indeed, it ever was possible, considering the fears and limitations of the adult person. Not infrequently in White, 'the burnt ones' are burned so badly early in life that they simply develop inevitably into damned ones. Which is the case with Laura.

Salvation would accordingly mean reintegration within the human race and hence abandonment of one's notion of special separateness. To certain of White's characters this is never a problem. If they were firmly entrenched early within humanity, then they remain so—like Mrs Judd, for instance, or Mrs Poulter of *The Solid Mandala*. Some, like Mrs Godbold, are saved even to the point of having a special vision or of being destined to be riders in the chariot. But reintegration is not even an issue for those who were always integrated. We are here in *Voss* faced with White's most detailed study of the journey towards salvation of an initially lost soul. The incompleteness of Voss' salvation may well be the reason for White's avoidance of that positive term in the novel. In this article I propose to examine the process by which Voss moves along the path towards salvation, and the reasons for his salvation and for Laura's damnation. Mostly I will use the terminology of alienation and humanisation, but will need intermittently to return to White's terminology.

That Laura is to be regarded as lost in perpetual alienation (that is, damned) and Voss as finally advanced on the way towards humanisation (saved) should perhaps first be demonstrated. The alienation of Laura, being a completed process, is easier to demonstrate than the humanisation of Voss, which was still in process at the time of his death, and which would doubtless have continued had he been given time. Although he is seen as lost by Mrs Bonner and Rose Portion and later by Mrs Sanderson, he is well on the path back to humanity even before he is captured by the Aborigines. We should beware of taking Laura's statements about him near the end as valid evidence against his progress towards humanisation. She is still, several years after his death, projecting her own state onto Voss, and herself suspects as much:

> I do know ... that Mr Voss had some very undesirable, even horrible qualities ... one wonders whether one has not interpreted them according to what one knows of oneself. Oh, I do not mean what one knows. What one suspects! (pp. 438–39).

Laura is lost early and late, and is seen as drowning by both Palfreyman and Dr Badgery. Palfreyman saying farewell to her at the wharf 'received the impression of a drowning that he was unable to avert, in a dream through which he was inevitably sucked back' (p. 117);[3] and her refusal of Dr Badgery is so definite and so hopeless that even he 'could not have rescued her from that sea' (p. 349). This image of drowning associated persistently with her contacts with men provides one measure of Laura's alienation. Her conversations with Palfreyman and Badgery indicate an increasingly hopeless attitude towards life. Speaking enviously to Palfreyman of those who can make such journeys, despite the dangers, she declares: 'I would welcome dangers ... One must not expect to avoid suffering. *And the chance is equal for everyone. Is that not so?*' (my italics). Some years later Dr Badgery expounds the same philosophy: 'The past is desirable, more often than not, because it can make no demands, and it is in the nature of the present to appear rough and uncharitable. *But when it comes to the future, do you not feel that chances are equal?*' (my italics). Laura recants, in fright and despair, admitting that her life is already utterly beyond her control.

Another measure of Laura's alienation is provided by a comparison between her clash with Voss in Mr Bonner's garden and her clash with Colonel Hebden at the Domain ceremony in Voss' honour. Although it is hard to say who maintains the ascendancy in the earlier contest, where

---

[3] There is a textual problem here in that the drowning referred to could be Palfreyman's. But in that case we would still be left with the fact that Laura manages to attract certain kinds of men to her—to their injury, for she can give them nothing in return.

accusation counters accusation and offensive is met with counter-offensive, Laura is in control at least initially and does uphold the struggle. In the later contest Colonel Hebden 'towered above her, with his … burning desire for truth … Was he, then, the avenging angel? So it appeared, as they struggled together' (p. 470). When he implies that he is no longer so impressed by her respect for truthfulness as he was years ago, her retort is cynical: 'If I am less truthful now, it is owing to my age and position.' Whereas the garden scene ends in something of a stalemate with a consequent change of subject ('Is it not really very cold?') and a laying down of weapons ('We were unwise … to flounder into each other's private beings'), the Domain scene ends in Laura's agonised defeat: '"Leave me", she strained, out of her white mouth, "I beg of you, Colonel Hebden!"' The woman who had wielded the powerful weapon of truth in order to put Voss on the defensive is now herself defensive when faced with a truth she does not want to confront. With a diminished ability to deal with her problems, Laura has all but given up the struggle. She can relate to people only as a schoolmistress, within the realm of ideas and ideals.

It is significant that although we see many of Voss' dreams and fantasies we catch only a glimpse of Laura's during her fever. Their fantasies bear witness to their conflicts, their fluctuating impulses towards and away from integration within the human race. In Voss' case the conflict is chronic but progressively resolved; in Laura's it is more acute coming to a head on the night of the Pringles' ball for Belle and breaking as a 'brain fever' but abandoned when the crisis is past: 'It is over.' She survives her fever and the conflict that induced it by retreating from personal relationships. The pear blossoms, symbol of feminine fertility, which she had Belle carry as her wedding bouquet turn to rotted pears in her sickroom. On the last page of the novel we find Laura pinning her hopes like Chekhov's three sisters on the impersonal future of the country; for her as for them there is no personal future.

Voss' s fantasies are the most important single indication of his development towards humanisation. The central conflict that recurs in them, the 'perpetual question which grappled him as coldly as iron' (p. 227), is the choice between humanisation through love ('the ring of gentle gold') and alienation through a delusion of divine separateness ('the crown of fire').[4] His first dream, which occurs after he receives Laura's answer to his proposal, reveals his wishes and his fears: 'Two *zusammen* should gain by numbers, but lose in fact. Numbers weaken. The weaker is stronger, O Vooooss' (p. 201). There is even in this dream a sexual fantasy in which he and Laura are 'swimming so close they were joined together at the waist', a more full-blooded element than we ever find in Laura, whose strong sexual fears never allow her any sexual fantasy.

Within Voss' fantasies, the change in Laura's role gives evidence of his growth in humanisation. Not that his development is by any means a steady continuum: it diverges and can even regress, without however stemming the insistent advance towards humanity that is taking place within him. In his earlier fantasies he subordinates Laura to himself, but in his later ones he sees her in the main as stronger, even filling a protective role, taking his weaknesses from him. In his first dream he makes Laura 'humbly grateful' and pictures her in a kneeling position (p. 201). After shooting Gyp he consoles himself with an image of Laura as dog-eyed love. But when reminded disturbingly of his vulnerability by the mule kick, he sees Laura as 'the wife from whose hands he would accept salvation, if he were intended to renounce the crown of fire for the ring of gentle gold' (p. 227). It is chiefly after he reads Le Mesurier's poems,

---

[4] Rock and fire are associated with Voss a number of times, most clearly in his power fantasy, p. 67. His realm is the desert, and that is probably why he is so upset at the Bonners' on reading the German poem describing the sea rushing nearer and nearer, presumably threatening his domain.

an experience almost as disturbing to him as the contest in the garden with Laura, that she becomes a stronger figure in his fantasies. The prose poems confront him with truths about himself and expose his delusions of divinity much more directly and more deeply than Laura's earlier analysis. Voss' rejection of them with '*Irrsinn!*' [crazy stuff!] is accordingly more violent than his rejection of Laura's earlier remarks with 'I am aware of no similarity between us'. Now, in his distress, Laura comes to him during the night 'and held his head in her hands, but he would not look at her, although he was calling: Laura, Laura' (p. 317). But it is his last dream that offers the strongest evidence of his ultimate humanisation: in it the lilies which he and Laura pick are

> the prayers, she said, which she had let fall during the outward journey to his coronation, and which, on the cancellation of that journey, had sprung up as food to tide them over the long journey back in search of human status. (p. 418)

As the expedition advances Voss' arrogance and delusions of divinity become replaced by a realisation of his human limitations. His delusions of grandeur are made evident early in the novel. To Mr Bonner, possibly just because that man is his patron, he is unusually boastful, maintaining in chapter 1 that, rather than consult the map of Australia, he will first make it. No doubt, too, he is only part joking when he apologises for the ship's delayed departure from Sydney by confessing that he has not yet learned to influence the wind (p. 124). That his delusions spring from a sense of his alienation, from fears and angers, is clear from a violent power fantasy that he entertains when Mr Bonner refers somewhat slightingly to the possible failure of the expedition:

> None, [Voss] realized with a tremor of anger, was conscious of his strength. Mediocre, animal men never do guess at the power of rock or fire, until the last moment before those elements reduce them to—nothing. (p. 67)

His sense of his divinity is strongest at Jildra and directly after leaving there. Surveying the goats with Boyle, he projects onto a she-goat recognition of 'his secret, that he was, in fact, only in appearance man' (p. 185). Likewise he sees the other members of the expedition as sensing his divinity and becoming dependent on him (p. 188). To him they are not a help but an encumbrance, for they 'could prevent his soaring towards the apotheosis for which he was reserved' (p. 190). Even after such a disenchanting catastrophe as the capsizing of the raft Voss still retains delusions of divinity, being reconciled to suffering only 'along with men' (p. 302).

Voss renounces his divinity when he is captured by the blacks. Very likely it is the blacks' ability to reject his sovereignty, despite his efforts to 'communicate intuitively with these black subjects, and finally rule them with a sympathy that was above words' (p. 356), that leads him to renounce his sovereignty generally. So he is able to respond to Harry's exclamation, 'Good Lord, sir, what will happen? ... Lord, will you not save us?' with a denial of his Lordship: 'I am no longer your Lord, Harry' (p. 390). Asked by Le Mesurier what his plan is, he admits simply that he has none 'but will trust to God' (p. 403)—surely a radical change in his attitudes!

When he can feel love for Harry 'and with him all men, even those he had hated, which is the most difficult act of love to accomplish, because of one's own fault' (p. 407), then he must be regarded as firmly on the road to salvation within humanity. Laura now enunciates her doctrine that when man has learned he is not God he is nearest to being so (p. 411) and Voss realises consciously that he has always been 'a frail god upon a rickety throne' (p. 414). Abandoning the throne to Christ, he can pray in the language of his youth, '*O Jesus ... rette mich nur! Du lieber!*' [O Jesus! ... save me! Dear God!].

We are not told much about why Voss and Laura are as they are.[5] That is not particularly White's interest in this novel, and is perhaps not essential to an overall understanding of their makeup. We do know, however, that Voss' life with his family was unhappy. When Mr Bonner offers to take responsibility for his family, Voss evidently tightens and responds with a strong rejection of it:

> My family ... It is long since I corresponded with them. Do you not think that such arrangements of birth are incidental, even if in the beginning we try to persuade ourselves it is otherwise, and are grateful for the warmth, because still weak and bewildered? We have not yet learned to admit that destiny works independently of the womb. (pp. 119–20)

He stands alone, an alien in his isolation and anger; it does not surprise, then, to find him maintaining that 'Most of us have committed murders' (p. 25). Laura's situation as an orphan seems crucial in accounting for her makeup; indeed, we are told little else about her. We may guess that her abandonment by her parents (as she would likely have seen their deaths) has made her resolve to allow no one else near enough to her to subject her to the same experience; much of her relationship to the Bonners, anyway, is bent on demonstrating to them, hurtfully, how little she needs them.

---

[5] Except in *The Aunt's Story*, White is not much interested in the causes of the destruction wrought upon his burnt ones. Not only is he uninterested in showing the causes of destruction: this can be one of his main areas of weakness. From Zack Johnson (*The Aunt's Story*) through Ray Parker (*The Tree of Man*), Laura Trevelyan, and Waldo Brown (*The Solid Mandala*) to Hurtle Duffield (*The Vivisector),* there is a series of disturbed characters whose hostility seems either largely unaccounted for or quite out of proportion to what causation we can see. Weakest in this respect is *The Vivisector*, in which, despite a portrait of Hurtle Duffield covering his lifespan, we are given no more clues to his coldness than to those of Laura's, whom we first meet as an adult.

More important than the causes of the alienation in Voss and Laura, however, are the traits in them that enable the one to abandon his isolation but that confirm the other in hers. There are from the outset some key differences between the two. For all his defenses, Voss is more reachable than Laura, more open to influence from other people and consequent modification of his own makeup. Mrs Sanderson, the most analytical and articulate of the three women who sense he is lost, realises that he is 'asking to be saved' (p. 162).[6] Laura; on the other hand, stands always at a distance and believes steadily in her own damnation, actually helping to bring it about herself. Underneath Voss' delusions of divinity there is a real attempt to learn human reactions, an effort that continues throughout the novel. Thus he imitates Sanderson's benevolence and Judd's ministrations to a sick colleague. It is significant that in his first dream he hears 'All human obligations are painful, Mr Johann Ulrich, *until they are learned, variety by variety*' (p. 201; my italics). As the expedition is near total failure, he can admit that he is human and fallible. Laura, however, can only resolve the conflict underlying her fever, a conflict between humanisation and alienation, by denying that any conflict exists and by turning from human emotions. It is this, and not her choice of profession or her material position, that makes her a failure among her circle so that Belle has to apologise for her ('a headmistress must adopt a certain attitude').

Voss also lacks Laura's bitterness. He is accordingly able to confess to Sanderson his envy of those who have the ordinary things in life: 'It is not for me, unfortunately, so, to build a solid house and live in it the kind of life that is lived in such houses … Honest people can destroy most effectually such foundations as some of us have' (p. 141). Laura on the other hand needs to disguise, from others and herself, her envy of material

[6] Mrs Bonner, p. 31, and Rose Portion, pp. 171–72, as mentioned, are the other two.

values by suggesting disdain for them.[7] Lacking Laura's bitterness, Voss is also free from her bitchiness. There are many occasions when Laura is sharply cutting, and with little or even no provocation. As an example, let me cite her retort to Dr Badgery after she has refused his offer to dance with her:

> 'I do not blame you,' he replied. 'I am never surprised at any person not wishing to dance. It is not sociable, for one thing. It is not possible to jig up and down and express one's thoughts clearly at the same time.'
>
> 'Oh', said Laura, 'I had always been led to understand that the expression of thought was the height of unsociability.' (p. 340)

Voss' antagonism is focused mainly on Judd, whom he feels to be a special threat, because Judd is not dependent on the approval or subordination of others to find his own strength. To others, like the Bonners or the Sandersons, he can be hostile or rude,[8] though that is less from a desire to hurt them than from a fear of accepting kindnesses and an unwillingness to be indebted. As Mr Sanderson perceives, 'Rocks will not gash him deeper, nor sun cauterize more searingly than human kindness' (p. 149).

Although Voss and Laura are both frightened, insecure people, the defenses that they erect against imagined threats to their identity are different and so affect differently their development. Laura's defenses lie in unapproachable rigidity or in flights into idealism. Voss' defenses,

---

[7] Most notably, Laura suggests superior disapproval to Una Pringle about marrying well ('I would not marry stone') and to Mr Bonner about Voss ('He does not intend to make a fortune out of this country, like other men. He is not all money talk').

[8] He rejects the Bonners' invitation to dinner with an obviously manufactured excuse and later refuses the offer of a ride home. His rudeness to the Sandersons is averted only by Palfreyman's fainting.

centred around his delusions of divinity, are less unyielding, whether to people or to circumstance. It appears that it is Beethoven's Ninth Symphony that is running through his mind in chapter 6 as he rides to visit Judd, imagining all creation bowing before him as GOTT [GOD] (p. 154):[9] but he is presumably also aware that the same text pronounces the need to call another's soul one's own in order to belong to the brotherhood of man—

> Ja—wer auch nur eine Seele
> Sein nennt auf dem Erdenrund!
> Und wer's nie gekonnt, der stehle
> Weinend sich aus diesem Bund.[10]

And it is this desire to win another's love and so belong to the league of mankind that becomes stronger in him as the novel progresses: 'Wer ein holdes Weib errungen, / Mische seinen Jubel ein!' [He who has won a lovely woman, let him join in with his rejoicing!].

---

[9] The text is Schiller's '*An die Freude*'. The imperfectly remembered part running through Voss' mind is especially the third stanza:
Und der Cherub steht vor Gott.
Ihr stürzt nieder, Millionen?
Ahnest du den Schöpfer, Welt? (32–34)
[And the cherub stands before God.
Do you fall on your knees, you millions?
Do you sense the Creator, O World?]
It is line 32 that climaxes his ride through the bush: 'Voss was jubilant as brass. Cymbals clashed drunkenly … Yes. GOTT … It rang out shatteringly, like a trumpet blast', p. 154.

[10] [Yes—whoever can call one soul his on this planet!
And let him who has never been able to do that
steal weeping out of the League of Mankind!]

Another important difference between Laura and Voss is that we find them repeatedly assuming the roles, one of schoolmistress, the other of pupil, in their relationship to the people around them. From beginning to end of the book, Laura holds class with people, in severe and preachy style. In this schoolmistress role she has stopped learning and has little room for development. Voss is no tractable pupil: he resists before he accepts, and is commonly the bright pupil bent on contesting primacy of place with his teacher. But he continues to learn human reactions, however reluctantly, throughout the novel, 'variety by variety'. The conversation between Laura and Voss in Mr Bonner's garden has already something of an antagonistic teacher-pupil quality about it. After manipulating Laura into a teacher role ('And in my instance, what does your imagination find?'), Voss finds that he cannot meet her on equal terms, and so has recourse to an earlier lesson he had learned from Brother Müller at Moreton Bay. Brother Müller had pointed out to him, 'you have a contempt for God, because He is not in your own image' (p. 54); now Voss parrots the remark as an accusation against Laura: 'Atheists are atheists usually for mean reasons … the God they have abandoned is of mean conception … Easily destroyed, because in their own image' (p. 95). Despite his initial resistance Voss does learn under tuition and so continues to develop. He struggles throughout the novel with the issues Laura raises in the garden but with increasing acceptance of their validity. Likewise, despite his immediate rejection of Le Mesurier's poems as '*Irrsinn!*', his final dream cancels his journey to his coronation and so accepts Le Mesurier's judgment that it was 'Fevers turned him from Man into God' (p. 315).

With Laura, White seems to be saying that her development is from the potential to the actual schoolmistress. The striking similarity between the conversations at the end of the opening and concluding chapters confirms Laura's alienation: in both scenes she holds class, enunciating principles in a way that puts down the people around her (specifically Mr Bonner and the Englishman), and concludes in an evasive retreat. One might be tempted on first reading of either scene to regard Laura's principles as noble until one reflects first, that idealism, like goodness, can be used as a club to elevate oneself and diminish others, and that idealism is not usually accompanied by such hostility as Laura shows towards her audience; second, that Laura's principles are distressingly vague and difficult to substantiate, while the values of those she is attacking have at least a healthy practicality about them.[11] It is probably a sense of her hostility and, consequently, her assailability that leads her on both occasions to beat a retreat before her monologue can become a debate:

> Though presently, when they had got up from the table, she went away to her room. (p. 32)

> By which time she had grown hoarse, and fell to wondering aloud whether she had brought her lozenges. (p. 478)

Her hostility is clear in her attack on Judd's airiness concerning Voss' leaving his mark on the country ('"How?" repeated Miss Trevelyan. Her voice was that of a man. She dared anyone.'), for she is herself guilty of the same airiness later that day: ' "Voss did not die," Miss Trevelyan replied. "He is there still, it is said, in the country, and always will be" ' (pp. 477–78).

Not all the causes of the ultimate destinies of Voss and Laura lie within their own characters. External events and even chance do play their part in the salvation of the one and the damnation of the other. But the external plays overall a very secondary role. It is true, for instance, that the failure of Voss' expedition progressively humanises him; but more important in the determining of his fate is the fact that his mind was oriented towards humanisation from the beginning. He is able, for

[11] Una Pringle does marry well and does not appear unhappy like Laura in the concluding chapter. One should be wary of too easily agreeing with Laura and labelling Mr Bonner's honesty as gross materialism: 'this is the country of the future. Who will not snap at an opportunity when he sees one? And get rich.'

instance, to respond warmly finally to the Sandersons, whereas Laura resists any warmth or even acknowledgement of friends. To Palfreyman's remark that friends of hers are approaching she retorts, 'Friends? … I know nobody very well. That is, of course, we have very many acquaintances' (pp. 104–05). Life itself would have modified the more grandiose of Voss' illusions; and we should also bear in mind that he elects for humanisation by proposing to Laura before he leaves Rhine Towers. Could Laura have been humanised had she been less of an isolated intellectual in mid-nineteenth century Australia, less of an 'insect-woman' confined to domestic activity, able to embark as a man upon an expedition like Voss? The answer is a clear negative. In the first place White makes it clear that Laura, though intelligent, is less than brilliant,[12] and that again like Chekhov's three sisters, she uses her education to guard her apartness. Had she been a man, her strong sexual fears would have remained, merely taking a different form. We see evidence of these fears,[13] but never any sexual fantasy. Voss, on the other hand, has at least the dream of himself and Laura joined together at the waist. Even within her confined, domestic life, opportunities present themselves to Laura to become less alienated, but she foils them from her own makeup. She avoids Dr Badgery, a worthy suitor, using Mercy's slight indisposition as an excuse not to go on a picnic that he attends, and behaves antagonistically towards him at the ball. Circumstances that would humanise most others are turned by Laura into occasions of further alienation. Her adoption of Mercy does not soften her in any way; instead she draws the child into her own isolation, very likely ruining Mercy's chances of a

---

[12] See the second paragraph of chapter 4.

[13] The most striking of the passages indicating Laura's sexual fears is this: 'The incident with the German in the garden had been indescribably ugly, untidy, painful. She could not help recalling that, and, in doing so, there came into her mouth a bad taste, as of blood oozing, as if she had lost a tooth', p. 130.

happy marriage.[14] We never see Laura in a loving scene with Mercy either as baby or young woman, not even to the degree of the brief affectionate scene between Mrs Bonner and the child (p. 393). The one conversation that Laura has with the grown Mercy has an asperity and sarcastic cast to it. It is not circumstance but a bitter hopelessness that damns Laura from the start. She already sees herself as irrevocably damned in the garden scene with Voss, and feels that her life is beyond her control when Dr Badgery makes his tentative proposal. At the height of her fever she states a principle that guides her sad life: 'nothing can be halted once it is started'.

Voss' death occurs some fifty pages before the end of a 450-page novel. These last pages deal chiefly with Laura, but also with a number of characters we have met earlier in the novel, such as Belle, Tom Radclyffe, Topp and Miss Hollier, Willie Pringle, and Dr Kilwinning. None of them has changed much over the twenty years that have elapsed since Voss' death. For none of them does this much matter except for Laura. Her life is in no way fuller, and is likely even emptier than at the time of Voss' death. She has a stern apartness about her. Her most notable virtue is her sense of justice, a quality that never by itself won love; indeed, we are told that she liked to be disliked. Laura could never have married successfully and probably not have married at all.[15] Voss, in time, probably could

---

[14] Mercy appears as a child dressed in green, on which White comments, 'It was not what one would have chosen for a child', p. 426. It seems Mercy is being deprived of a normal childhood to serve Laura's needs. And Mercy as a young woman is quietly but habitually snubbed by the circle Laura moves in. What contacts, then, are left for this girl rumoured to be Laura's illegitimate daughter?

[15] When Belle speaks of Palfreyman implying some attraction between him and Laura, Laura angrily ruins a sketch she is making, evidently upset at the idea of marriage. Her 'marriage' to Voss is safe in that it exists only in fantasy; and it is surely significant that she writes to him on the night after she has admitted to Tom Radclyffe that he is lost.

have; his last dream has in it a sense of togetherness with Laura. And perhaps the ability to love and be loved within marriage is a fair test of the degree of integration within or alienation from humankind, of salvation or damnation.

18

WILL *VOSS* ENDURE? FIFTY YEARS LATER[1]

The question 'Will *Voss* Endure?' was recently asked me by a longtime friend of mine, and my attempt to answer it has touched off this essay. The question is a good one, for almost fifty years have passed since the publication of that work in 1957. One is aware that not much does survive long in our fast-changing world; values change faster and faster, and accordingly many great literary works of the past seem to have less and less relevance to us. I have read *Voss* many times over the last fifty years and have read it again recently in order to suggest an answer to my friend's question. My own response to *Voss* seems to be a common one now, and since it has bearing upon the likely ultimate place of *Voss* and Patrick White within Australian literature, it is worth considering. My answer shows a marked ambivalence: on the one hand, *Voss* still impresses me as a great novel and on the other, it gives me less pleasure every time I read it. In the course of this essay, I would like to look at both aspects in some detail: the greatness of the novel and the qualities that alienate the reader from it.

What makes *Voss* a great novel? Essentially, it is its undertaking of themes of great significance in its culture: the exploration of the heart of a land only recently settled and, more abstractly and more importantly, of a new culture still in formation. These two themes are closely linked,

---

[1] First published in 2003, *Antipodes*, 17(1): 50–54.

each reinforcing the other. They are developed with an intensity unmatched elsewhere in White's writings and are conveyed in a style that is often highly poetic and even memorable. With all his idiosyncrasies, White is one of the great stylists of the twentieth century. Quite simply, reading *Voss* represents the kind of challenge to one's intelligence that only great novels are able to offer.

Stories of exploration of the interior of the continent are a vital part of Australian consciousness: every Australian child from Patrick White's generation (he was born in 1912) through at least the 1970s has had his imagination fired by the stories of the nineteenth-century explorers. (In the 1980s, massive migration from continental Europe and from Asia diminished a sense of Australia's past—and that is one factor that will affect the abiding interest of young Australians in White's novel.) Voss' story is based mostly on the explorations of Leichhardt, but also incorporates elements of the journeys of Eyre (the spearing of Palfreyman) and of Burke and Wills (the poorly organised aspect of the expedition and the unknown fate of the explorers), and it is the more evocative for suggesting all these explorers. Fascination with the heart of Australia has not diminished but, rather, grown: one of the most distinguished books to be published in Australia as the twentieth century ended, Roslynn Haynes' *Seeking the Centre*, deals with the growing importance of the heart of Australia to its mythology and culture.

But the themes of geographical and cultural exploration of a young country were not chosen by Patrick White merely because of the importance of explorations in Australian history. They have a vital significance for White himself, and that is why the book is so intense. One could argue convincingly that in no other novel of his is he so ardently committed to making the cultural map of Australia, that is, to establishing Australia as a significant presence on an imagined cultural map of the world, not just a large unit of physical geography. Through the persona of Voss, in the opening chapter of the novel, he declares 'I am compelled into this country' (p. 23). When Mr Bonner asks Voss if he has studied the map and he retorts, 'The map? I will first make it', we should understand that what is really being talked about here is White's ambition to put Australia on the cultural map (p. 26). It is a startlingly ambitious undertaking, so ambitious that White will accuse himself repeatedly of arrogance. *Voss* is a highly self-critical work, a project that tears White apart, for he will not allow himself to feel any gratification for what he really succeeded in: putting Australia on the cultural map.

It is in his essay 'The Prodigal Son', written when he was forty-six (hence in 1958, the year after *Voss* was published), that White talks most explicitly about the cultural deadness of Australia in the 1950s:

> In all directions stretched the Great Australian emptiness, in which the mind is least of possessions, in which the rich man is the important man, in which the schoolmaster and the journalist rule what intellectual roost there is, in which … muscles prevail, and the march of material ugliness does not raise a quiver from the average nerves. (p. 157)

No doubt White's disappointment at the failure of *The Aunt's Story* to elicit any notable reader interest when it was published in 1948 contributed to the bleakness of his picture of the Australian cultural landscape. He even abandoned writing for nearly seven years before beginning another novel, *The Tree of Man*, with the very positive aim of filling the cultural void by writing about an ordinary man and woman while seeking to 'discover the extraordinary behind the ordinary, the mystery and the poetry which alone could make bearable the lives of such people, and incidentally, my own life since my return' (p. 157). Although *The Tree of Man* was highly successful, White refers to its success only glancingly ('How it was received by the more important Australian critics is now ancient history'), for he still had not achieved his aim of transforming the cultural map of Australia. He goes on in 'The Prodigal Son' to talk in fairly general terms about the genesis of *Voss* and ends by making a statement that expresses succinctly his artistic aims in both *The Tree of Man* and *Voss*, the central novels of his literary career: 'There is the possibility that one may be helping to people a barely inhabited country with a race possessed of understanding' (p. 158).

Although *Voss* tells the story of a geographical expedition, it is the cultural exploration that engages White's heart and mind. That he wasn't much interested in the geographical aspects of the exploration of the Australian interior is clear from the very vagueness of the geographical details in *Voss*. Newcastle is named several times, but only as a destination; Rhine Towers is described in idyllic rather than realistic terms, being modelled upon the White family estate of Belltrees in the Hunter Valley; and all we know of Jildra, in the Darling Downs, is that it is surrounded by a sea of grass. Beyond that, we have almost no sense of locality or of distance, only of weather or seasons (flood and drought). Perhaps the outcrop of rocks where Turner and Angus die is meant to suggest the Olgas in the Northern Territory, but there is only the description of them as 'cruelly salient rocks' that form a citadel to suggest that possibility. Colonel Hebden makes the same journey as Voss' party, 'at least twice', but nothing more is conveyed of the geographical features (p. 452). The journey in *Voss* is into the country of the mind.

White's cultural ambitions in this novel become clear through his identification with Voss at times, with Le Mesurier at others. In one of Voss' early pronouncements we can recognise White's aims as they were expressed in 'The Prodigal Son'. 'Every man has a genius', says Voss, 'though it is not always discoverable ... But in this disturbing country ... it is possible more easily to discard the inessential and to attempt the infinite' (p. 38). White is aware of the price to be paid for his ambitions. Voss' warning of the consequence of attempting the infinite is an acknowledgement by White of the agony his writing caused him at times: 'you will have the flesh torn from your bones, you will be tortured probably in many horrible and primitive ways.' But, he consoles himself, 'you will realize that genius of which you sometimes suspect you are possessed' (pp. 38–39).

Le Mesurier is also an important guide to White's cultural ambitions in his exploration of Australia—to his hopes and fears and delusions. Le Mesurier represents the more intellectual and sensual side of White: he is well educated, rather a snob, disposed to wallow in the gutter or to whore under the trees—pretty much the kind of life that White confessed to living in New York City in 1941 in his autobiography *Flaws in the Glass*. Le Mesurier articulates clearly the ambivalence that White feels about himself, and gives voice to the desire to bring forth something beautiful that drives them both:

> this colony is fatal to anyone of my bent ... How can I make a fortune from merino sheep, when at the same time there is a dream of gold, or of some inland sea floating with tropical birds? Then, sometimes, it seems that ... all the worst evil in me is gathering itself together into a solid core, and that I shall bring forth something of great beauty. This I call my oyster delusion. (p. 106)

When he is ill, Le Mesurier states one of White's guiding principles in the novel, a concept that keeps recurring: 'The mystery of life is not solved by success, which is an end in itself, but in failure, in perpetual struggle, in becoming' (p. 289). The theme of personal failure runs through all of White's novels, linking them as no other theme does. Le Mesurier announces it with a perception that his illness is intended to heighten. Having enunciated the doctrine, he goes on to associate himself with Voss as an exemplar of it: 'Of course we are both failures' (p. 290). The association between Le Mesurier and Voss and White himself is especially marked in Le Mesurier's two Rimbaud-like prose poems that Voss reads while Le Mesurier is delirious: 'Childhood' (pp. 313–15) has its origin in White's memories of his own childhood, and 'Conclusion' (pp. 315–17) reveals his cultural aspirations, his fears of rejection and of overreaching. 'Conclusion' ends with the most heartfelt of White's prayers:

> O God, my God, I pray that you will take my spirit out of this my body's remains, and after you have scattered it, grant that it shall be everywhere, and in the rocks, and in the empty waterholes, and in true love of all men, and in you, O God, at last. (pp. 316–17)

This prayer that his spirit may be in the rocks and empty waterholes and in love for all men expresses White's desire, not just Le Mesurier's, to dissolve and disappear into the arid Australian landscape while also transcending dissolution to nurture its inhabitants. It is a moving statement of White's ambitions in writing *Voss*.

The themes of exploration of a new land and its culture have the scope characteristic of a great novel, and these themes are developed in a style which has an appropriate dignity and grand seriousness. White consciously cultivates a style that is consistently formal and elevated: 'Places yet unvisited can become an obsession, promising final peace, all goodness' (p. 135); and 'Palfreyman realized he had failed that day to pray to God, and must forfeit what progress he had made on the road where progress is perhaps illusory' (p. 137).

The formality of the style distances the novel from the reader, discouraging intimacy in order to gain respect. *Voss* is a *vous* novel, almost never a *tu* novel. As in *Moby-Dick*, there are a number of usages that are Elizabethan or Biblical, inevitably recalling Shakespeare or the King James Bible. One of these Elizabethan usages is the frequent use of 'did' + infinitive instead of a simple past tense: 'It did amuse him to be hated' (p. 88); and 'He himself did also behave with jolly or grave precision' (p. 111). As in many other great works of literature, there are continual suggestions of destiny driving the main characters and events, and one noteworthy stylistic device that White calls upon to reinforce the idea of destiny is his frequent use of 'So' at the beginning of a sentence with the meaning of 'accordingly' or 'thus': 'So they advanced into the country which now possessed them' (p. 208); and 'So it was come to pass' (p.

470). Before the grand seriousness of White's style one frequently stands in awe.

But if this formal dignity is impressive it is also off-putting and is one of the factors responsible for the ambivalence many readers experience as they read the novel: *Voss* is a great novel that is held at arm's length from the reader, a novel that one is not permitted to love.

The distance is there from the start: even as we meet the two main characters in the opening pages, we find them repeatedly referred to impersonally as 'the young woman' and 'the German'. Voss and Laura are never really made sympathetic as protagonists and they are quite unsuitable as central figures in a love story. In the opening chapter of the novel, both Laura and Voss are depicted as unapproachable. It is a chapter in which White makes derogatory remarks about all the characters, but he is particularly unsympathetic to Laura and Voss. Laura is closed, almost impenetrable, concerned with behaving according to established rules. In his first full-length portrait of her, at the beginning of chapter 4, White is more sarcastic than admiring of her. Her achievements, beyond a dedication to self-improvement, are made to seem rather mediocre:

> No one in that household could write a more appropriate note on occasions of mourning, or others calling for tact, in that version of the Italian hand which courts the elegant while eschewing the showy. She was the literate member of the family ... more by instinct than from concentrated study ... [Her] knowledge of the French tongue [was] modest, though sufficient ... (p. 80)

Like all of White's protagonists, she is a tangle of troubled emotions, 'beset by all kinds of dark helplessness' (p. 80); like them too, she shows no warmth. She takes the Bonners' kindness for granted, without returning any affection. 'I was never yours, except at moments, and by accident', she announces to them, hurtfully, in their final scene together (p. 429). On several other occasions she is unprovokedly bitchy to them. One of the most notable of these is when she takes it upon herself to allot the best room in the house to Rose to have her baby there; when they protest at the ingratitude of 'one who has been treated as a daughter', Laura retorts, 'When one is unhappy, one does forget … Threats and injustices overshadow all the comfortable advantages' (p. 240). Bitchy remarks, in literature as in life, stay in one's mind. Mr Bonner's final remark to her in the novel, when she rejects his kindly suggestion to leave the life of a spinster schoolteacher that she has chosen, is that she is behaving 'Like some foolish nun' (p. 430). It is a verdict upon her, an expression of his disappointment in her, and may recall his similar observation upon Voss that he too is 'something of a disappointment' (p. 84). White is rarely kind in his evaluations of his characters, but tries to conceal that by distributing his criticism among a number of characters, usually minor ones like Mr Bonner here. Another example of this habit is the sailor's remark about Laura at the wharf as Voss is about to depart from Sydney: 'That one is a sour-faced lass', he says, thus reinforcing the impression of her severity (p. 109). We do not need to see Mr Bonner's judgment upon either Laura or Voss as merely his own, for it expresses the same kind of attitude that White repeatedly shows towards his characters.

Voss in the opening chapter is even more ill at ease than Laura and shows no social graces. As he and Laura sit 'in almost identical positions, on similar chairs' on either side of the window, they seem almost like two bookends (p. 14). Mrs Bonner intuits early that 'he is already lost … His eyes cannot find their way' (p. 31). His arrogance is alienating, but what is still more alienating is his conspicuous rudeness in refusing hospitable gestures: the invitation to dinner at the Bonners' and the ride home from Potts Point, and, later, the offer of accommodation by the Sandersons at Rhine Towers.

If Voss and Laura do not engage our sympathies as protagonists, neither are they acceptable as the central figures in a love story. White is successful in establishing links between them early in the novel, but these are abstract and do not hold up against the need for evidence of human love. What links the two characters from the beginning is that while they stand apart from the other characters, they stand apart in similar ways. Less socially oriented than the others, they obviously feel superior, being more attached to ideas and ideals and less concerned with materialistic values. They both have a sense of a special destiny that is always there within them on some level of awareness. Further, they have in common religious values that set them apart in an anti-religious society. (Consider Dr Kilwinning's embarrassment at Laura's discussion of religion during her brain fever.) This last is especially important to White, for the religious values that they hold are very much his own.

Other than these links, there are no clear indications of a strong sexual or emotional attraction between them on the few occasions they meet in Sydney. On one occasion we see Laura staring at the hairs on Voss' wrist, an indication of a certain sexual curiosity, but there is nothing about Laura to arouse sexual interest in Voss; the stress, rather, is on her off-putting qualities and mannerisms. Even in a novel in which there is very little physical contact between people, the relationship between them is remarkably free of physicality. Nearly halfway through the novel, White himself comments on the slightness of their acquaintance. When Voss begins his second letter to her (a letter she never receives), White comments on the address, '*My dear Laura*', as surprisingly intimate, 'as if he knew her' (p. 230; my italics). Here the temptation to be sarcastic, which White rarely resists, overpowers his rational judgment as he is preparing to elevate the two to near mystical lovers. In being frequently sarcastic to both Voss and Laura, White deprives them of the dignified status they need to attain before they can ascend as spiritual lovers. Jane Austen, by being satirical towards her characters, effectively eliminates the element of passion in their love stories, but White goes further than Austen: he is sarcastic and at times even belittling, and thus stifles a basic warmth. He is not affectionate towards his characters, and they are not affectionate toward one another.

The course of the Voss-Laura relationship can be seen to fall into five chief stages:

Among their four meetings in Sydney, the longest and most important is the meeting in Mr Bonner's garden. Far from laying the basis of a romantic interest, it provides Laura with the opportunity she has been seeking to hurl accusations at Voss, accusations he defends himself against with only limited success.

There is a short series of letters that they write to one another, though each receives only one; the other three (one of them left unfinished) never reach their goal. In these letters Laura continually tries to put Voss on the defensive, and he to cast her in a subordinate position. Curiously, it seems to matter more to the writers of these letters to set down their preoccupations in writing than that the intended recipient should read and react to them: they write essentially to themselves or at one another. 'But write, I must', says Laura in her third letter. 'If you, my dear, cannot hope to benefit, it is most necessary for me' (p. 350).

After the expedition leaves Jildra, Voss and Laura each indulge in fantasies of the other. They do not however engage with the real person; Laura, for instance, is never the 'dog-eyed love' of Voss' imagining (p. 285). This is the stage in which the two are raised by White to telepathy—though of ambiguous import, as I discussed in a 1972 article in *Quadrant*[2]—and near mystical closeness.

The relationship changes radically when Voss is captured by the Aborigines and Laura endures her brain fever. At this stage both turn to Christ for salvation. Voss becomes softer, renouncing the notion of his divinity and acknowledging his vulnerability as he cries 'O Jesus, rette mich nur! Du lieber!'[3] Laura experiences a kind of epiphany as she understands the three stages 'Of God into man. Man. And man returning into God' (p. 411); but it no way softens her, for we see her becoming stiffer, more staid, a very proper schoolmistress.

---

[2] Chapter 19 in this volume.

[3] 'Oh Jesus, save me! Dear Lord!' p. 415.

Finally, in the last scene of the novel, Laura denies to Colonel Hebden that she ever really knew Voss other than having met him on a few brief, insignificant occasions. In her criticism of him as a mixture of good and bad—more bad, it seems, than good—she perpetrates a virtual betrayal of his memory. It is at once a denial of the significance of her own life and a reduction of Voss' expedition to insignificance. Whatever sympathy we feel for Voss and Laura at the end of the novel is not for two people thwarted in the fulfilment of their love, but for two people who never achieved fulfilment within themselves. Such characters do not make for a compelling love story.

As we try to assess the enduring nature of *Voss*, we always have to face a division in the novel between negative and positive values: on the one hand the novel is weighed down by misanthropy and a whole cast of characters who fail in life, while on the other it is elevated by strong spiritual and cultural aspirations. The division takes its rise in White himself, and he transmits it to the reader: he cares little about Voss personally (or, indeed, about any of his characters), but cares intensely about Voss' mission for Australia. White sees Voss as an overreacher, like himself, and that too has its negative and positive aspects: Voss (and White) must fail, of course, but in an inspiring undertaking that cannot be forgotten. And Voss' failure is softened when set alongside the failure of the other characters. Laura at the end is a reduced figure, a thorny middle-aged woman walking heavily over the grass; Le Mesurier has slit his throat when reality has not matched his dreams; Judd (Judas?), who abandoned Voss' party, has lost his entire family, his land, and to some extent his mind; Hebden, who makes the same journey as Voss, at least twice, simply wastes his time and effort. Voss' (and White's) ultimate achievement will be left for the future to assess; if it is still uncertain, it will continue to inspire. At the moment of Voss' death, we are told that 'His dreams fled into the air, his blood ran out upon the dry earth, which drank it up immediately. Whether dreams breed, or the earth responds to a pint of blood, the instant of death does not tell' (p. 419). The notion of the sacrificing of blood as fertilising a country is commonly accepted in myth and religion, and is seen as the ultimate sacrifice for the good of a community.

At the outset of this article, I suggested that *Voss* is a highly self-critical work in which White will not allow himself any gratification for his attempt to put Australia on the cultural map. He will not even acknowledge to himself that he may be successful. White was not an arrogant man. Whatever impulses he felt towards arrogance were continually and strongly checked by his awareness of the need for humility. That is why the theme of humility is stressed throughout *Voss*, his most ambitious work. He was a deeply religious man and stated that quite unambiguously to Craig McGregor in an interview published in *In the Making* in 1969:

> Religion. Yes, that's behind all my books. What I am interested in is the relationship between the blundering human being and God. I belong to no church, but I have a religious faith; it's an attempt to express that, among other things, that I try to do. (p. 218)

His critics and researchers have ignored that confession of faith as possibly embarrassing in an anti-religious country like Australia, but we cannot appropriately do so as we endeavour to understand Voss and White.

For Voss and for White, the striving has been everything; it is a noble striving that must compel our admiration. Laura is essentially voicing this theme when on the last page of the book she rises from her own mediocrity to defend Voss and her adopted country. She becomes again, briefly, the Laura who first impressed us as she contended with Voss in Sydney, regaining her earlier authority to curb a sarcastic English visitor ('we are in every way provided for, by God and nature, and consequently, must survive'), and going on to assert that 'Voss did not die … He is there still, it is said, in the country, and always will be. His legend will be written down, eventually, by those who have been troubled by it' (pp.

477–78). When she proclaims that Voss has merged with the country as an enduring part of its history, and that his story will necessarily be recorded in the course of time, she is urging his aspiration and his striving, not the historical achievement of his expedition. When her listener insists on historical accuracy, asking how Voss' story can be recorded when we do not know the facts, she replies with a vague but strong affirmation that cannot be dismissed: 'The air will tell us.' She speaks for her creator White, who has faith that the air will testify to the enduring value of his novel, *Voss*.

Australia has changed radically since White wrote *Voss*. No one then could have envisioned the enormous changes that would take place in the late 1980s and especially in the 1990s. White did not live to see the greatest changes, for he died in 1990. It seems reasonable to state that he would not have written 'The Prodigal Son' with its description of Australian dullness at the end of his life, when that description was no longer valid—but he himself had been an important factor in the cultural changes in Australia.

White wrote within an Anglo-Celtic population, in which the Anglo was dominant (that is why he allows himself to make sarcastic references to the Irish at the end of *Voss*), but in the 1980s and 1990s large-scale migration from continental Europe and from Asia quickly diluted that racial admixture and the deep-rooted Protestant-Catholic antagonisms that accompanied it. As a result of the migration, Australia became cosmopolitan rather than parochial, European rather than British in character, Catholic more than Anglican (Church of England); it embraced diversity instead of prescribing conformity. But it was the Age of Computers in the 1990s that most rapidly brought Australia out of marginality into the mainstream, and this was perhaps the greatest change of all. No one should underestimate the degree to which feelings of marginality dispose a people towards defensiveness and resentfulness; but those aspects of Australian culture, which were so blatant until the 1990s, now hardly impress themselves upon foreign visitors.

Two years after *Voss* was published, in 1959, jet travel became common, greatly reducing Australia's geographical isolation and the sense of remoteness from the centre of things. (I flew by propeller plane from east-coast America to Australia in 1958, a flight that took two days, with an overnight stop in Hawaii, and returned by jet in 1960.) In retrospect, the arrival of the jet inevitably meant that *Voss*, which deals with the continuing exploration of a continent only recently occupied by Europeans, would be consigned for a time to oblivion. If in the late 1950s Australian readers perceived it as an historical novel with strong and vital links to the contemporary culture, most Australian readers now look upon it as an historical novel set in the mid-nineteenth century: the links to the present have been broken. The awareness of convict origins that weighed upon Australians of the 1950s, implicit in the presence of Judd in *Voss*, has gone: the past is shrouded in fog, the present is all-encompassing, the future is vague but vaguely good. The Australia of the late 1950s exists only in the memories of those who lived there at that time, as did I. But the cultural map that White created in *Voss* from his own exploration of the country of the mind, wrought in extraordinarily beautiful relief, will endure.

Reputations of creative artists notoriously come and go, being subject to the changing interests and tastes of different generations, and White is no more immune to this tendency than any other artist. During his lifetime, he stood like a colossus over what was then the small body of important Australian literature, but he is now pretty much ignored. The fluctuation of his reputation is unremarkable: consider the course of Herman Melville's. During his lifetime (1819–91), Melville was known chiefly for his Polynesian romances *Typee* and *Omoo*, largely because of the late nineteenth-century fascination with the South Sea islands, which drew Robert Louis Stevenson and Paul Gauguin to live there. *Moby-Dick*, a later work, was widely considered to be incoherent and unreadable, and from the 1860s until his death in 1891, Melville sank into obscurity, appreciated by only a small group of admirers until the revival of interest in him in the 1920s. White's reputation is presently in abeyance, though he has never been regarded as unworthy of serious critical attention. The awarding of the Nobel Prize of 1973 drew attention to him, but the laurels soon withered, for Australians have always been uncomfortable with rare achievement in fields other than sports. In the current period of neglect, it is important to draw attention from time to time to the enduring aspects of his work that I have discussed in this essay.

Author's Note

Since this essay has dealt with changes in late-twentieth-century Australia—indeed, has been inspired by them—it may well be of interest to readers to know something of my own background that drew me to the topic.

I first went to America in 1955 on a Fulbright Scholarship to Harvard University. I returned to Australia in 1958, but could not complete my doctorate (on twelfth-century French literature) there, and returned to America in 1960 on the Saltonstall Pacific Fellowship from Harvard. As a medievalist, I understandably stayed in the land of better libraries. In 1970, I was awarded a very generous Postdoctoral Fellowship from the University of Queensland to write on Patrick White. My wife taught there first as a senior tutor, then as a lecturer. In the time we lived in Brisbane and later in Perth it was clear that for her, even with a PhD and an impressive publication record, only a limited career path was open in those anti-feminist times. Disenchanted, we returned in 1976 to America, where my wife went on to become a university president. We did not return to Australia until 1990, but what a change we encountered then from what we had experienced! Australia, we felt, had passed us by; I was lost in the pace of growth and troubled by my awareness that the Australia I had known no longer existed, that my memories of it were only memories. But that visit prepared us for a longer and more open-minded visit in 2000, when we loved it. The country was efficient, affluent, neither defensive nor jingoistic. Wanting to feel reconciled to the land I had loved as a child, I resumed Australian citizenship this year while continuing to hold American citizenship. After a six-week stay in Australia early in 2002, we bought a condo in Coffs Harbour, where we spent half the year, spending the other half in Santa Fe, until 2006, when we moved permanently to Australia, to Coffs Harbour.

19

VOSS' PROPOSAL AND LAURA'S ACCEPTANCE LETTER: THE STRUGGLE FOR DOMINANCE IN *VOSS*[1]

The relationship between Voss and Laura in Patrick White's novel is complex and confusing. During their actual meetings it betrays an antagonistic rivalry as each seeks to subordinate the other, but during their separation it suggests a mystical closeness. In this article the aspect of their relationship that I want to establish more definitely is their struggle for dominance, an aspect that most critics to date have overlooked[2] in favour of the more attractive, though vague, indications of their closeness. I will endeavour finally to explain the curious fact that White, who presents early such strong evidence of the antagonism between his two main characters, should be willing to discount this evidence in the latter part of the novel and present them almost as saints of love.

I have chosen to focus my attention on Voss' s proposal and, more especially, Laura's answer because these reveal with unusual fullness and clarity the struggle for dominance that is going on, conflicting with their common desire to express some kind of love for a like soul. These letters

---

[1] First published in1972, *Quadrant*, 16(4): 24–30.

[2] Brissenden (1959) refers to 'The two lovers, Voss and Laura', and accepts 'some form of telepathic communication' between them. Wilkes (1967), too, writes of Laura's effort 'to save Voss through love'.

are particularly important in that, being written, they are without the inhibitions that attend a physical confrontation, and they bear the weight of deliberate thought (Laura's letter, she stresses, was written after 'the deepest possible consideration'). In their letters, the writers make their points without danger of interruption or immediate challenge. Accordingly, the correspondence provides even better evidence of what is going on between Voss and Laura than did their vehement collision in Mr Bonner's garden (chapter 4), where each assaulted the other with the weapon of truth, a weapon so powerful that the contest was of brief duration, exhausting the contestants: 'We were unwise … to flounder into each other's private beings' (p. 97).[3] These letters comprise the final communication between Voss and Laura: she does not receive his answer to her letter. Henceforth, they deal with each other only in fantasy.

Why does Voss propose to Laura? An immediate answer, and a valid one, would be that he has been softened by his recent observations of the warm and stable relationship between the Sandersons and between the Judds. A less immediate but probably more profound answer would be that Voss at the time of writing is about to embark into the Australian wilderness, a desert where he has to confront the disturbing image of himself that Laura has raised in the garden scene:

> 'You are so vast and ugly,' Laura Trevelyan was repeating the words; 'I can imagine some desert with, rocks, rocks of prejudice, and, yes, even hatred. You are so isolated. That is why you are fascinated by the prospect of desert places, in which you will find your own situation taken for granted, or more than that, exalted … I am fascinated by you … *You* are *my* desert!' (p. 94)

Laura in this passage has not merely perceived their common isolation and associated destinies, but has also set herself above Voss as his observer: '*You* are *my* desert!' He could not in the garden and he cannot in his letter directly refute the truth of Laura's pronouncement. By pro-

---

[3] White (1957a). Page references in this chapter are to this edition.

posing to her, however, he is indirectly repudiating her declaration of his isolation and capacity for hatred. Further, he is endeavouring to oust her from her superior post by making her an associate rather than a hostile observer. His letter of proposal is in part a re-engagement of their contest for ascendancy.

For there is little expression of love in his letter. It was written with constraint only after he had discharged the demands of all other correspondence and it is restrained in its expression of his feeling. Striking is his omission of any tenderness, whether in himself or in her. (The letter recalls another famous letter of proposal, which may be its model: Casaubon's to Dorothea in *Middlemarch.*) He praises only Laura's 'moral strength and discernment' (p. 163)—curious praise, that may imply a fear of her strength and a suspicion of his weakness. Underneath his stated admiration there is something of alarm at her strength, so that he is careful to stress his own superior destiny: 'The gifts of destiny cannot be returned. That which I am intended to fulfil, must be fulfilled.' In the accomplishment of his destiny she can only be a companion, implicitly subordinate; from his mission, he asseverates, he will return to her the victor, no doubt over the rest of humanity (including her) as well as over the Australian continent. The possibility that she might pray for him is disturbing to him—indeed, he emphatically entreats her not to, for such a role would acknowledge her superiority and the existence of a God to rival himself.

Although Voss sees his letter of proposal as couched in 'such personal terms', it must surely strike many of us as lacking in personal passion. Yet it is a softer letter than Laura's answer, and does plead for human acceptance. He betrays a fear of her ability to reject him, asking apologetically for her answer 'if you are so agreeable', and he hardly dares to make stronger claims upon her interest in him than to acknowledge her 'friendliness, and sincere interest in *our* welfare' (my italics). For all his attempts to elevate himself at her (and God's) expense, he needs to protect himself from the hurt of possible rejection by implying a 'Let's be friends anyway' correspondence in which he will keep her informed about the flora and fauna encountered on the expedition. In his second letter, written after her answer but never received by her, he feels confident enough of her acceptance to drop this defensiveness: 'If I have not described every tree, every bird, every native encountered, it is because all these details are in writing for those who will not see beyond the facts' (p. 232). The proposal itself, however, is impersonal and tentative, written by a man afraid of tenderness and of rejection, afraid of his own subordination in a close relationship and therefore determined to subordinate the one whose love he would gain. It is a letter that ends impersonally in the implicit denial of the very personal purpose for which it is written. Already in Voss there is becoming clear the same conflict which we are presently to find in Laura: the need to maintain a godlike self-sufficiency clashing violently with the need for human affection.

Understandably, Laura does not show anyone Voss' proposal. Even were she not a girl who in her isolation keeps very much to herself, it is hardly a letter she could be proud of. It does not testify to a warmth in her that the Bonners could recognise; neither does it glow with a warmth in the writer that she could happily share with them. Mr Bonner is right in detecting in Laura 'signs of unusual dismay' on receiving the letter.[4] Like Voss, she delays writing her answer. How much effort it has cost her to write, how much it has disturbed her, is clear from the contradiction she does not even notice in her opening sentence: 'I must *hasten* to thank

---

[4] When Laura is aware of a man's sexual attraction to her or of sexual impulses within herself, she reacts with fear and repulsion. Of the passages in the book that indicate her sexual fears (see, for instance, p. 77), the clearest is this: 'The incident with the German in the garden had been indescribably ugly, untidy, painful. She could not help recalling that, and, in doing so, there came into her mouth a bad taste, as of blood oozing, as if she had lost a tooth. She bit her lip, and was reminded of his rather pointed teeth as he stood talking that morning at the wharf', (p. 130). Likewise, when Dr Badgery makes his tentative proposal, she is conscious of his 'rather blunt, white teeth, *set in a trap*, in his crisp beard' (my italics). The fear of being bitten, or of losing a tooth, is a common expression of sexual fears.

you for your letter, which arrived at its destination *several days ago*' (my italics). When she mentions the possibility that her delay might make him suspect an 'utter unwillingness' on her part to reply, she is betraying an unwillingness, even if it stops somewhere short of being utter.

And Laura's answer is devastating, however much Voss needs to blind himself to it. With a fright that expresses itself in anger at his proposal, she writes an acceptance that is tantamount to a declaration of war:

> Dear Mr Voss,
>
> I must hasten to thank you for your letter, which arrived at its destination several days ago, by Newcastle packet. If the length of time needed for mine to reach you, should make you suspect an utter unwillingness on my part to reply, you must take into account great and exonerating distances, as well as the fact that I have been compelled by the substance of what you have written to give it the deepest possible consideration. Even after such thought, I confess it is not clear what answer one in my position would be expected to return, and since it is one of my most stubborn *weaknesses* to try to reach conclusions without the benefit of advice, I must, I fear, remain at least temporarily confused.
>
> Your letter was unexpected, to say the least of it: that anybody possessed of your contempt for human frailty should make so unequivocal a proposition to one so well endowed with that same frailty! For, on at least one memorable occasion, you did not attempt to conceal your opinion that I was a person quite pitiably weak in character. Having formed a similar estimate of myself, I could not very well reject your judgement, even though the truth one has perceived is, if anything, more distasteful when confirmed by the mind of another, a mind moreover, that one has held in some esteem. That you made me suffer, I cannot deny, but the outcome or purpose of that suffering still remains to be understood. In the meantime, if nothing else, my lamentable frailty does accuse my arrogance.

Arrogance is surely the quality that caused us to recognize each other. Nobody within memory, I have realized since, dared so much as to *disturb* my pride, except in puppyish ways. Men, I am inclined to think, are frightened if their self-importance does not impress. You, at least, were not frightened, but ignored me so coldly that I was the one to become alarmed—of my insignificance and isolation.

So, Mr Voss, we have reached a stage where I am called upon to consider my destroyer as my saviour! I must take on trust those tender feelings you profess, and which I cannot trace clearly through the labyrinth of our relationship. Can you wonder that I am confused? All the more since I have remained almost morbidly *sensitive to the welfare* of one whose virtues do not outweigh the many *faults* I have *continued to despise.*

Now the question is: can two such faulty beings endure to face each other, almost as in a looking-glass? Have you foreseen the possible outcome? And have you not, perhaps, mistaken a critical monster for a compliant mouse?

I, personally, to assume a most unseemly candour, would be prepared to wrestle with our mutual hatefulness, but mutually, let it be understood. For I do respect some odd streak of humanity that *will* appear in you in spite of all your efforts (after reading poetry, for instance, or listening to music, while your eyes are still closed), just as I regret most humbly my own wretched failures to conquer my unworthiness.

Only on this level, let it be understood, that we may *pray together* for salvation, shall you ask my Uncle to accept your intentions, that is, if you still intend.

In any event, Mr Voss, I do thank you once again for your kind letter, and shall intercede as ever for your safety and your happiness.

Your sincere,

Laura Trevelyan (pp. 197–99)

Voss' proposal has thrown her. Her contempt for 'puppyish' men, none of whom had 'quite dared' (p. 18) to propose to her, has not protected her in this encounter. Now she is left insecure, unable to trust her own instincts, unable to turn to others for assistance, unable to fall back upon a personal code of conduct that she has worked out for herself: 'I confess it is not clear what answer one in my position would be expected to return.' Sadly, Laura cannot speak from her own heart; and suddenly we are afforded a fleeting vision of her final aloneness, 'going away, heavily, a middle-aged woman, over the grass' (p. 474). Confused, she turns upon the man responsible for her confusion in anger, derisive and defiant. Her sarcasm, clear evidence of her anger, manifests itself in such phrases as 'to say the least of it', 'So, Mr Voss', and 'I must take on trust those tender feelings you profess'. She reacts to the proposal as an attack and is 'prepared to wrestle', even to launching a counterattack of her own. Her warning of the possible outcome of their contest is defiant, but is also, perhaps, a perverse plea for his acceptance of her shortcomings: 'Have you not, perhaps, mistaken a critical monster for a compliant mouse?' Her concluding sentence, however, is outright defiant, without any ambivalence. She has ignored Voss' injunction, *'do not pray for me'*, with a final needling assertion of her own superiority: 'In any event, Mr Voss, I … shall intercede *as ever* for your *safety* and your happiness' (my italics).

Laura's letter is charged with resentment at imagined injuries. She expresses her chagrin at an accusation Voss never made, that she is 'a person quite pitiably weak in character', and to nurse this unjustified grievance she contrives to overlook his unwritten tribute to her 'moral strength and discernment'! She charges him, too, with having ignored her coldly, overlooking her own cold and condescending reception of him in chapter 1. This proneness to grievance-collecting, which Laura shows evidence of elsewhere in the novel,[5] is one mark of her alienation

[5] Laura's whole relationship with the Bonners is tainted with a resentment for which we can see no good reason. When Mrs Bonner understandably protests at

and of her inability to give or receive love deeply. Her resentment at Voss' having 'ignored' her would proceed from his not having held her in awe. Up until now, she has used this awe to keep men at a distance, and without this defence she is frightened and angry. The deeper fright that underlies her anger emerges from time to time despite her attempts to conquer it.

But perhaps the most important aspect of Laura's letter is that we see her here in a letter written after 'the deepest possible consideration' reacting to their relationship as to a contest. Her letter serves to recapitulate and highlight the rivalry that has existed between them from the beginning. From this contest only one can emerge the victor. Accordingly, Laura cannot refuse Voss' proposal, a tightening of the bonds that already bind them. He has challenged her very identity, for, as she later writes, '*Two cannot share one throne*' (p. 256).[6] She must contend with a rival deity, even if she has misgivings about the consequences of their own self-deification: they must 'wrestle with (their) mutual hatefulness', troubled by doubts that under their mask of superiority lies ultimately perhaps only 'insignificance and isolation'.

These two beings, godlike in their own desperate estimation, are basically aware of the humanity in themselves that they would deny. 'Arrogance', writes Laura, 'is surely the quality that caused us to recognize each other'; but arrogance is only their attempt to convey a

---

Laura's assigning Rose Portion the best room for her confinement, and chides her with forgetting the kindness done her, Laura retorts with a cutting 'When one is unhappy, one does forget ... Threats and injustices overshadow all the comfortable advantages', (p. 240). Laura's resentment seems to proceed from no better source than that she was not physically born to the Bonners: 'I was never yours ... except at moments, and by accident', (p. 429).

[6] On the surface, Laura is speaking of Voss and Christ as contending for the throne. Essentially, however, she is speaking of Voss and herself: 'I do attempt, continually, to humble myself. Do you also? ... *Two cannot share one throne* ... Let us understand this, and serve *together*.' By diminishing her own challenge to the godhood, she hopes to encourage Voss to lessen his.

superiority that hides the alienation they feel from common humanity. Believing early that she is damned as an alien from humankind, Laura is rawly sensitive to any attack on her apartness or even to any human approach to her ('Persistent touch was terrifying to her', p. 131), and is far too prone to see in Voss 'the same fate approaching someone else' (p. 96). They are what their pasts have made them. Had she or Voss the security to make a free choice, they would no doubt prefer to align themselves with humanity—a course that, painfully, gradually becomes available to Voss as the expedition advances—and would want the normal love of two human beings for one another. Laura does confess, grudgingly, to respecting 'some odd streak of humanity that *will* appear' in Voss in spite of all his efforts to master it. But though she is drawn to this softer side of him she is frightened of the same softer side of herself, regretting 'most humbly my own wretched failures to conquer my unworthiness', an unworthiness that keeps her somewhat short of the godhood to which she aspires. She will not concede, however, that Voss is closer to that godhood than she. If necessary, she will gladly cut herself down to near lifesize in order to bring him down to the same level as herself: 'Only on this level, let it be understood, that we may *pray together* for salvation, shall you ask my Uncle to accept your intentions.' On more than one occasion, she castigates herself in order to diminish Voss along with her. In the garden scene she had spoken of their mutual pride and common damnation, and in this letter she writes of their mutual hatefulness and common arrogance. There is no humility in her admission, only a camouflaged attack. Knowing that she has cut to the heart of his illusions, she accepts his intentions of marriage with a challenge that is also, perhaps, a plea: 'that is, if you still intend.'

Laura certainly feels herself threatened by Voss' proposal. Here is the man whom in Mr Bonner's garden she had endeavoured 'to rescue (let us not say, subdue)' (p. 97) overthrowing the relationship she had tried to control, subordinating her now by the offer of marriage. He was to be her desert (p. 94), her dominion, but instead he offers companionship in a dominion of his own. That she is right in sensing the contest is demonstrated by a remark in his second letter: 'At the risk of incurring your serious disapproval, I will raise you up to … my side' (p. 231). It is not surprising then that she should try to cut him down and should gloat over any sign of weakness in him: 'that anybody possessed of your contempt for human frailty should make so unequivocal a proposition to one so well endowed with that same frailty!' She taunts him with assuming the role of her saviour. Although he never did accuse her of being 'quite pitiably weak', as she charges, she retorts that he has provided her with no new insight, 'Having formed a similar estimate of myself'. She will yield to no one her role of pythoness.

So Laura is thrown into considerable conflict by Voss' letter: she would both reject and accept him at the same time. Again and again, we are confronted by the contradictions in her: her defensiveness and her aggressiveness, her fear of love yet strong need of it, her denial of 'tender feelings' in their meetings yet fear that his proposal might be withdrawn ('that is, if you still intend'). In the very middle of her letter, she admits her conflicts and for a brief moment softens: 'Can you wonder that I am confused?'

The inevitability of the relationship between Voss and Laura was determined before his letter of proposal. Since two cannot share one throne, they collide convulsively in Mr Bonner's garden; indeed, the earth reels between their legs (p. 96). The relationship is not so much one of love as one of antagonism, in which each is preoccupied with the maintaining of his identity, his principle of existence. Since this principle of existence for each lies in the disguising of his alienation as a godlike superiority, he must best any rival in the field. But neither Voss nor Laura entirely believes in his or her divinity. Both, being human, need love or at least sympathetic understanding, and so each is drawn to the other out of this need for understanding and some safe form of love. (Their later letters, shamefacedly tender, show this need more clearly.) The two sides of their attraction, the need to prove their self-sufficiency and even superiority on the one hand and the need to experience human affection on the other, act against each other, so that their relationship is necessarily vehement, electrically charged with conflict. There can be no satisfactory resolution to the conflict: one or the other of the two clashing aspects has to weaken. Voss has already opted for the path towards humanisation by writing the letter. He has become aware before leaving Jildra that 'Obsessed by the struggle between their two souls, they had threatened each other with the flashing weapons of abstract reasoning, while overlooking the common need for sustenance' (p. 203). Laura, however, is terrified at the path open to her. Soon, with her adoption of Mercy, she is to retreat into a divine Virginal Motherhood: since affection is also involved in caring for the child, she is accordingly able to realise some kind of a coalition between her warring selves. Mercy's name is ironical, however, for she is made to perpetuate Laura's remove from the rest of mankind.[7] Laura cannot accept a reciprocal love between man and woman, and is left at the end with her illusions of Voss. We see her in the last pages of the book as a defensive, insecure spinster, whose safety lies in lozenges. In a sarcastic exchange with a visiting Englishman, she answers his insistent questions about Voss with an evasive 'The air will tell us', and then conveniently becomes hoarse, 'wondering aloud whether she had brought her lozenges' (p. 478).

Laura was always without hope, believing in her damnation even while maintaining her divinity. 'In the absence of a rescue party, she had to be strong' (p. 6), but her strength is spurious and evaporates as the novel proceeds. In her letter to Voss, we have a concentrated expression of the fears that drive her further away from human contacts into a world of her own within the spirit. There she survives with a certain dignity at least: ' "I will not go. I am here. I will stay." Thus she made her covenant' (p. 474).

Why does White, having provided such evidence of antagonism between Laura and Voss, end by suggesting a kind of mystical closeness between them? In the first place, it should be pointed out that the actual evidence of closeness is quite slight; that is why White is driven into

---

[7] Ray's name in *The Tree of Man* is similarly ironical, for he brings no ray of sunshine into Amy's life. When he rejects her love, which he feels to be possessive, he makes her life still emptier.

coddling the frail relationship. We see much more of Voss preoccupied with his fantasies of Laura than of Laura preoccupied with fantasies of Voss—Laura soon becomes more involved with her adopted child than with Voss. There is further a wide disparity between the Laura of Voss' fantasies, loving and consoling, and the Laura of reality, cold and aloof. It is a fantasy that Voss grows close to, not the reality. Laura pours out her love for Voss only in a letter written after she has admitted to Tom Radclyffe that he is lost: it is easier for her to love a memory than a man. Finally, the evidence of closeness amounts to a paralleling of incidents or situations (e.g., Voss is kicked in the stomach as Laura vicariously brings forth a child, and Laura's hair is cut and she is bled as Voss is decapitated) and to one instance of verbal telepathy: 'I shall not fail you. Even if there are times when you wish me to, I shall not fail you' (pp. 381, 387). The incidents surrounding the telepathic words, however, are so different as to suggest an incomplete communication.[8] And, more important, this one instance of telepathy is ambiguous in its import. Laura is expressing not only her dedication (I shall not fail you = I shall not let you down) but also her lingering determination not to be bested (I shall not fail you = I shall not be less than you, even if at times you want me to be). The telepathic message is as much ambivalent as it is intense!

I have mentioned at the beginning of this article that Voss and Laura are shown during their meetings as engaged in a battle for dominance, but are presented during their separation as attaining a mystical closeness. We can best understand their relationship when we see it as one instance of a recurring pattern in White's novels: the elevation to visionary status of characters when they are unable to relate to others on a human level. This pattern had already revealed itself in the two novels that precede *Voss, The Aunt's Story* and *The Tree of Man.* Theodora Goodman is confirmed as one of White's elect (Holstius 'laid his hands on', sacramentally as it were) when she opts for a life lived within the imagination, abandoning her identity in the ordinary world. And Stan

[8] See Kiernan (1971), pp. 121–22.

Parker is shown as closest to nature and to God when he is most estranged from his wife and his children. The same pattern occurs with Miss Hare and Himmelfarb in *Riders in the Chariot* and with Arthur Brown in *The Solid Mandala.*

White is unwilling to allow the lives of his isolates to be utterly wasted, and so he compensates for their human failures by according them a special sense of vision. As his characters become more isolated and less attractive, they become more eligible for visionary status. Thus Laura loses the beauty she possessed as a young woman and becomes positively ugly (p. 465) in order to preside at Belle's party like a pythoness at her tripod. White's novels do not merely vindicate his isolates, but glorify them. The highest illumination that any of them attains is that 'One, and no other figure, is the answer to all sums' (p. 497)—a celebration, I feel, of *aloneness* rather than of monotheistic faith.

In order to glorify his isolates thus, White has to distort the evidence of their alienation from the rest of humankind. This he does by understressing their human failures and eccentricities on the one hand, and by highlighting their spiritual pretensions on the other. Since he assumes the role of an intrusive author, frequently pronouncing upon his characters and life values generally, he can more easily direct the reader towards accepting his pronouncements. Rodney Mather has pointed out that *Voss* is an exercise in self-projection;[9] but he does not go on to note that the image projected contains elements of contempt and of glorification. In an interview with Craig McGregor in 1969, White stated, 'All my characters in my books are myself, but they are a kind of disguise.'[10] In creating Voss and Laura, he seems to have expressed a contempt for their human qualities as unpleasant, and a glorification of their spiritual qualities as so refined that they can maintain a mystical closeness during their physical separation.

---

[9] Mather (1963).

[10] McGregor (1969), p. 221.

This split in values whereby White presents his visionaries as lost in human terms and illuminated in spiritual terms is a fundamental weakness in his thinking. It is difficult for us to overlook the failure of his visionaries to operate in human situations, in view of the extraordinary claims that he makes for them in the realm of the spirit. The greatest literature has to rest on acceptable human values, not on a highly arbitrary personal ethic. The conflicting values that White sets forth in *Voss* do not allow reconciliation; the novel will accordingly continue to resist a simple, logical interpretation.

Section 4
Thematic Studies of White's Novels

20
Why are Epiphanies so Prominent in Patrick White's Novels?[1]

Epiphanies are a prominent feature in White's novels over a period of twenty-five years, from *The Aunt's Story* in 1948 to *The Eye of the Storm* in 1973. The epiphanies that occur at the end of a novel are the major epiphanies; they are reserved for the main character or characters, like Stan Parker at the end of *The Tree of Man*. Their position at the end draws attention to their importance, and they have accordingly been the subject of a good deal of critical commentary. It is not my purpose to offer another interpretation of the major epiphanies in White's novels, or to assess their validity as John Colmer did in his definitive study of that aspect nearly twenty years ago.[2] And I am not concerned with the minor epiphanies, intimated rather than developed, that are scattered throughout the course of White's novels.[3] My aim is to examine the function of the major epiphanies and to suggest reasons why White indulged in so

---

[1] First published in 2006, *Aumla*, 105: 109–21.

[2] Colmer (1987), pp. 70–76.

[3] The minor epiphanies are normally experienced by secondary characters, like Mr Gage's vision of the ant in *The Tree of Man* or Ruth Joyner's exaltation as she listens to Bach in Ely Cathedral in *Riders in the Chariot*. They have little impact on their novel.

many over so long a period that a concluding epiphany becomes a sort of final signature to a White novel.

There is not complete agreement among critics on which of the novels end in an epiphany. I acknowledge four such novels, which are in fact the four most commonly agreed upon: *The Aunt's Story, The Tree of Man, Riders in the Chariot,* and *The Eye of the Storm.*[4] No one sees an epiphany in *Voss,* only a spiritual maturing. Hurtle Duffield's vision of an intense indigo in *The Vivisector* seems too slight to constitute an epiphany, even as an image of God, and Ellen Roxburgh's contemplation of the inscription 'God Is Love' in Pilcher's chapel at the end of *A Fringe of Leaves* is slighter still, a message that has been repeated to us since we were children. Cecil Hadgraft rejects an epiphany for Ellen on the grounds that she is a 'slightly stolid', decent woman: 'She almost represents the triumph of the ordinary.'[5] John Colmer also concludes that she 'incorporates herself anew into the social fabric … At the end there are no ecstatic affirmations, no lonely apocalyptic visions'.[6]

A number of critics have tried to explicate the epiphanies, from varying viewpoints and with varying plausibility. The two most notable and most sympathetic, Karin Hansson in 1984 and Carolyn Bliss in 1991, suggest a pattern of development in White's epiphanies, but the patterns

---

[4] Thomas Michael Stein agrees that 'Mit Mrs Hunter im *ES* endet die Reihe der Visionärfiguren in Whites Oeuvre … In *FL* und *TA* stehen mit Ellen Roxburgh und Eddie Twyborn Charaktere im Vordergrund, die zwar einer Identitätskrise ausgesetzt sind, deren Ziel es aber nicht ist, zu religiös-metaphysischen Erkenntnissen vorzustossen.' [With Mrs Hunter in *ES* the series of visionary figures in White's work comes to an end … In *FL* and *TA* Ellen Roxburgh and Eddie Twyborn stand in the foreground as characters who are indeed exposed to a crisis of identity but whose goal is not to advance to religious or metaphysical awarenesses.] Stein (1990), p. 235.

[5] Hadgraft (1977), pp. 34–46.

[6] Colmer (1987), p. 75.

that they discern are different.[7] Some critics, like J.D. Heydon in 1966, have from the beginning been unsympathetic in their response to White's epiphanies; his is an important essay, but was published in the short-lived *Oxford Review,* and so did not attract critical attention.[8] Recent critics, now that White's prestige is no longer overwhelming—his reputation was declining from around 1980, and he died in 1990—are more vocal in expressing irritation at his illuminates and their epiphanies.[9] David Tacey in 1986 charged that White 'has been playing bully to the critical establishment since the 1950s', and spearheaded the movement against White that has grown over the last twenty years: 'we are all so terrified of his frequent attacks and smarting words that critical judgement has been silenced.'[10]

What, more precisely, are we to understand by the concept of an epiphany in White's novels, and just what are the principal epiphanies? How did he arrive at the concept, and why did he return again and again to the representation of an epiphany? We should bear in mind that White himself did not use the word 'epiphany' until *The Twyborn Affair* in 1979, after the term had become a commonplace in White criticism[11] and after he had ceased to portray them—but more of that later.[12]

---

[7] Hansson (1984), Bliss (1991).

[8] Heydon (1996).

[9] Colmer (1984), Wolfe (1990).

[10] Tacey (1990), pp. 61–63.

[11] Beatson (1980).

[12] There White says that in certain circumstances lust can become an epiphany (p. 417), perhaps in grudging deference to D.H. Lawrence, who repeatedly shows sex as an ecstatic, transforming experience. But 'Lorsque White évoque le corps au cours des relations sexuelles, l'union charnelle ne représente le plus souvent à ses yeux qu'une manifestation d'animalité,' writes Geneviève Laigle. 'Selon White, le mot "amour" est souvent employé à tort pour désigner le désir qui possède deux êtres et les pousse à se conduire comme des bêtes en rut, sans qu'il y ait la moindre lueur de communication entre eux sur un plan spiritual.' [When White

An epiphany in White is a partial opening into a world beyond this one, offering the reassurance of a higher state of awareness in an existence that continues after death. It is a two-way process, an interaction between a higher power and the character. It is not just sent as a grace from God: the character has to have attained a certain state in order to be able to open himself or herself to the epiphany. Each of White's illuminates experiences a different epiphany, in accordance with his or her makeup. Normally the epiphany is attained near the end of a character's life or effective life. Theodora and Ruth Godbold, both in their fifties at the end of their novel, continue to live on beyond their epiphany, the former passively, the latter unobtrusively. Elizabeth Hunter's epiphany during the cyclone comes in direct response to her most destructive course of behaviour at the age of seventy, when she drives her daughter away, humiliated in sexual competition for the attention of Edvard Pehl—who is, furthermore, asexual. Elizabeth lives on for another fifteen years, but her defeat of Dorothy is the last significant action that she takes; after that, she is restricted by the author to her usual manipulation. At the end of her life, her memories of her experience during the cyclone return to assume a renewed significance.

What are the principal epiphanies? In *The Aunt's Story* there's Theodora's communion with the sententious Holstius on two occasions. 'You cannot reconcile joy and sorrow', Holstius tells her during their first meeting:

> Or flesh and marble, or illusion and reality, or life and death. For this reason, Theodora Goodman, you must accept. And you have

---

focuses on the body in the context of sexual relations, the physical union to him is merely a manifestation of animal behavior. According to White, the word 'love' is often wrongly used, designating rather an urge that takes control of two human beings and drives them to behave like animals in heat, without there being the least glint of communication between them on a spiritual level.] Laigle (1985a).

> already found that one constantly deludes the other into taking fresh shapes, so that there is sometimes little to choose between the reality of illusion and the illusion of reality. Each of your several lives is evidence of this. (p. 293)

On their second meeting he is briefer and more cryptic, telling her that 'true permanence is a state of multiplication and division' (p. 299). In *The Tree of Man* there's Stan's epiphany just before his death: 'It was clear that One, and no other figure, is the answer to all sums' (p. 497). In *Riders in the Chariot* there's the communal epiphany experienced by the illuminates at Himmelfarb's deathbed as they restage a contemporary Australian version of the Deposition. One assumes that the actors are aware of their parallel to the Deposition and are deeply moved in spirit by their experience: that is what constitutes their epiphany. Its nature is not directly articulated as Theodora's and Stan's are, though Mrs Godbold observes that 'Mr Himmelfarb, too, has died on the Friday' (p. 493). White endeavours to play down the parallel just because it is so blatant: 'Although her remark was so thoughtfully spoken, its inference was not conveyed to anybody else. Nor had she intended exactly to share what was too precious a conviction' (p. 493). In *The Eye of the Storm* Elizabeth Hunter has a double epiphany, a softer one which has not had much attention from critics, and a harsher one which, giving its name to the novel, has always commanded full attention. The softer one is a vision of her soul as the flaw in an emerald—though even that can still suggest the notion of beauty that can betray at any moment—while the harsher one is a vision of herself as the eye in a cyclone of her own creation, surrounded by the destruction she has wrought. This is the epiphany that she attains to during her actual experience of a cyclone. White's offering of a softer version of her illumination along with a severe one may well spring from a need to temper his account of her destructive side because of a certain identification with her: he portrayed both Elizabeth, a version of his own mother, and himself as having flaws that appeared in an emerald or a looking glass (a notion that is explicit in the title of his 1981 autobiography, *Flaws in the Glass*).[13]

I have mentioned earlier that there are a number of minor epiphanies scattered throughout White's novels. In themselves, they are not especially important, and they are immediately identifiable by the fact that they occur within the course of the novel, not at its end; but it is worth pointing out that major and minor epiphanies alike serve to keep the novels oriented towards a dimension beyond the material. That is as true of Mr Gage's vision of the ant as of Stan's final epiphany. Laura's epiphany of the three stages of man during her brain fever is a minor one, merely a convenient restatement of the main theme of the novel: 'How important it is to understand the three stages. Of God into man. Man. And man returning into God' (p. 386). Gerald Wilkes observed that any effort to get a religious message out of this will fail;[14] its primary function is to anchor *Voss* to a world beyond the material one as the novel moves towards its conclusion. The minor epiphanies automatically lack the emphasis and the solemnity of the major epiphanies that conclude the novels.

Let us consider reasons why the major epiphanies experienced by his special elect loom so large in White's novels. There is a complex of reasons working together: White's religious beliefs, his elitism stemming from his privileged family background, his sense of his literary weaknesses and his attempts to deal with them, and, most important, the impulses of his own psychic makeup. For White continually projects on to his illuminates his own difficulty in reconciling mind and body.[15]

---

[13] Laigle (1987) draws attention to White's oedipal fixation.

[14] Wilkes (1967).

[15] 'Êtres de chair, asservis à leur corps, les personnages de White n'en ont pas moins une dimension spirituelle, et le plus grand mystère de l'homme réside probablement, aux yeux de l'écrivain, dans cette étrange union d'une pitoyable envelope charnelle et d'un esprit qui rêve de s'en dégager' [Creatures of flesh and

Theodora's epiphany, in which she is enjoined to reconcile flesh and marble—the temporal and the eternal, ultimately body and spirit—is a version of White's own quest and a prototype of all the other epiphanies.

White's portrayal of epiphanies strikes us most immediately as an expression of his religious faith, his affirmation of communication between this world and the world beyond. And religious values, it is well established, are an important part of his thinking. In an interview with Craig McGregor in 1969 he acknowledged that religion is behind all his books:

> What I am interested in is the relationship between the blundering human being and God. I belong to no church, but I have a religious faith ... Whether he confesses to being religious or not, everyone has a religious faith of a kind ... I believe that God does intervene ...[16]

In *Flaws in the Glass* twelve years later, still asserting his 'spiritual self', he told how it 'always shrank in contact with organized religion' because of 'the sterility, the vulgarity, and in many cases the bigotry of the Christian churches in Australia' (pp. 74, 146). One may suspect, however, that his expressed dislike of religion in Australia was determined more by his chronic dislike of Australian values generally than of its religious beliefs specifically.[17] When one considers how reluctant most Australians are to acknowledge any religious belief publicly, White's statements of faith are remarkably strong.

---

blood, at the mercy of their bodies, White's characters none the less have a spiritual dimension, and the greatest mystery of mankind to him is probably that strange union of a pitiful covering of flesh and a spirit that dreams of getting free of it]. Laigle (1985a), p. 270.

[16] White (1989), p. 19.

[17] Laigle (1985b), through her analysis of the paintings of Mr Gage, Alf Dubbo, and Hurtle Duffield, defines White's religious beliefs more fully and more clearly than does White himself.

Nevertheless, religion was not a significant factor in White's first representation of an epiphany, Theodora's in *The Aunt's Story.* He was led to it rather through his reading of Olive Schreiner's *The Story of an African Farm* (1883), from which he takes his epigraph to part 3 of *The Aunt's Story.* To David Marr he spoke of Olive Schreiner with admiration. The idea appears to have come from the chapter 'Waldo's Stranger' in Schreiner's novel—one of the most anthologised passages of English prose, her allegory of the Search for Truth—in which a stranger who appears on the farm interprets Waldo's carving, gives sententious advice to Waldo, then goes his way. Introduced only for this particular scene, the stranger is endowed with an extraordinary understanding of the carving and of Waldo. For Waldo the encounter is unforgettable, quite like an epiphany experienced by one of White's characters. As the stranger rides away, 'Waldo waited till the moving speck had disappeared on the horizon; then he stooped and kissed passionately a hoofmark in the sand.'[18] The role of the stranger is similar to that of Holstius in White's novel, the chief difference being that Holstius is not a realistic figure like Waldo's stranger but a fantasy figure of Theodora's creation. As such, however, he can be assumed to be familiar with all the details of the fantasy life she created in the 'Jardin Exotique' section of the novel, and can therefore appropriately give her the advice (sententious like that given to Waldo) that constitutes her epiphany.[19]

What seems to have led to the strong religious element in White's epiphanies from *The Tree of Man* to *The Eye of the Storm* was his own epiphany at Castle Hill just before Christmas in 1951, when he slipped in the mud and was confronted by his own vulnerability. 'As he clambered

---

[18] Schreiner (1976), p. 173.

[19] Beston & Beston (1975). My wife Rose Marie and I discussed the incidents in the 'Jardin Exotique' section of *The Aunt's Story* as taking place within Theodora's mind in chapter 10 in this volume.

to his feet cursing', reports David Marr, 'he sensed a Presence about him in the storm'.[20] The incident is recounted in his conversation with Gerald Wilkes and Thelma Herring and again in *Flaws in the Glass*,[21] and is seen by some as a lesser version of St Paul's epiphany on the road to Damascus. When one considers the strong religious convictions instilled in the young Patrick by his Scottish nanny Lizzie Clark, it is not surprising that he should later have re-embraced a religious outlook. And, likely, his partner Manoly Lascaris' strong faith also played a part in White's change of heart. In any case, Stan Parker's epiphany is religious in nature, and the restaging of the Deposition in *Riders in the Chariot* even more so. With the central character in *The Eye of the Storm*, he raises a basic Christian question, the matter of her eternal salvation; but then Elizabeth is a version of his own mother. He resolves the question in her favour, allowing her to bestow a transfiguration upon her favourite acolyte, Mary de Santis, at the very end of the novel.

White's elitism, an expression of his family and personal background, also played an important part in his interest in epiphanies and his arbitrary assignment of them to certain characters. His epiphanies are reserved for the favoured few that he chose for highly personal and arbitrary reasons, to the exclusion of the bulk of humankind; indeed, the bulk of mankind is meant to be excluded. His family was wealthy, and he had the benefit of a privileged education, with special tutors even before he attended Cambridge University.[22] He accordingly developed certain patrician attitudes, which find expression in 'The Prodigal Son', a sense of his superior cultural values and a disdain for values other than his own and for the ordinary Australian. Like his much admired Stendhal, White

---

[20] Marr (1984), p. 86.

[21] Herring & Wilkes (1973), p. 144.

[22] There was a sign in the driveway of Belltrees, the White family estate near Scone, when I visited it in 1973, 'Be Careful of Grandchildren.'

wrote 'To the Happy Few', the dedication with which Stendhal closes *La Chartreuse de Parme.* His aim to give 'the theme and characters of *Voss* what Delacroix and Blake might have seen, what Mahler and Liszt might have heard' can strike one as pretentious: the evocative mysticism of Blake and the broad expanses of Mahler are appropriate for *Voss,* but surely not the brilliant colours of Delacroix and the surface glitter of Liszt.[23] His disdain for 'the Great Australian Emptiness' is patronising, but mild compared with the scathing contempt he shows for popular taste and suburbia in his next novel, *Riders in the Chariot.* We the readers are permitted to look on and accept White's epiphanies, but not really invited or expected to understand their exact nature. This is especially true of the minor epiphanies, which are flashed before us and then withdrawn, hardly allowing us time to contemplate them. And we are in no way encouraged by White to think that we ourselves would ever be granted an epiphany as members of his elect. White's novels are always held at arm's length from the reader; author and reader are never on intimate terms.

From a literary viewpoint, the major epiphanies serve to give a lift, an impact to the novels where they most need it, namely, the end. Without them, the novels would end drearily and lamely. Plot is not White's forte, as he himself was aware: to Craig McGregor, he observed 'I don't think any of my books have what you call plots ... I always think of my novels as being the lives of the characters'.[24] To his cousin Peggy Garland he wrote concerning *The Tree of Man* in 1952, 'It has no plot, except the only one of living and dying. But perhaps that is because I am no good at plots'.[25] When he has taken his characters' lives to the point where he will

[23] White (1968). Later, in 1960, he tried to vindicate his choice of Delacroix and Liszt to Geoffrey Dutton, but his self-conscious attempt betrays a sense that his initial remark in that famous essay was ill-advised, Marr (1994), p. 169.

[24] White (1989), p. 21.

[25] Marr (1994), p. 87.

leave them, the end of the novel, it is as if he has nothing further to say that will engrave the novel on our memory. His characters are not happy people, any more than their author, who, we should remember, suffered from frequent bouts of very severe asthma, a depressing, frightening condition, incurable and recurring, always lying in ambush. Critics have quite underestimated the effect of this on White, but anyone who has seen or suffered a severe attack of asthma will know immediately whereof I speak. The novels end in an overall sense of tiredness, a kind of emotional exhaustion, so that the final lift given by the epiphany is very much needed. White's endings are never energetic; he endeavoured instead to invest them with a certain solemn dignity.

Consider how the novels I am discussing would end without the final epiphany. Theodora, instead of experiencing two emotionally intense visits from Holstius at the end of *The Aunt's Story,* would be merely taken away to a mental home in New Mexico, a sad, lost, crazy woman. Stan Parker, without any charged interchange with an itinerant evangelist at the end of *The Tree of Man,* would just die peacefully in his garden on a day like any other, in his late sixties, after an unremarkable life. The re-enactment of the Deposition around the figure of Himmelfarb *is* the epiphany in *Riders in the Chariot* . It is the only means of bringing all four illuminates together, however briefly, and giving them an exalted significance they lack individually; afterwards, they go their separate ways and drop out of life. Elizabeth Hunter, without the memory of her epiphany fifteen years ago that keeps pushing into her mind in her final hours in *The Eye of the Storm,* would die quietly on a commode—Cleopatra denigrated. Stripped of the spiritual overtones of the epiphanies that conclude them, the novels fall flat.

White, as said earlier, never used the word 'epiphany' until *The Twyborn Affair* (1979), by which time the word had become standard in White criticism. The term became part of twentieth-century literature through the influence of James Joyce, whom White greatly admired early in his career. Joyce defined his concept of an epiphany in *Stephen Hero* as 'a sudden spiritual manifestation'; epiphanies, he said, 'are the most delicate and evanescent of moments.'[26] *Stephen Hero,* although written in 1907, was published only posthumously in 1944, but the concept of an epiphany that Joyce had defined permeated his works. A typical story in *Dubliners* leads up to an epiphany or is itself an epiphany, its *raison d'être.* That is not true of White's epiphanies, which, although they are integrated into their novel, are not really an essential part of its theme. White found in Joyce's epiphanies a device that he found useful, but by avoiding the term and by modifying Joyce's concept, he endeavoured to play down the question of influence. Early in his career he expressed strong admiration of Joyce, but in later life remarked that it was easier to read about Joyce than to read him[27]—but that too can proceed from a desire to discount his debt to Joyce. White was sensitive about the influence upon him of other writers. When I published an article on the influence of *Madame Bovary* on *The Tree of Man* in the *Revue de Littérature Comparée* in 1972, he wrote to me rather irritatedly, but did not altogether dismiss the connection.[28]

White's own psychic makeup impelled him to portray the various epiphanies: through them he is able to give literary expression to his personal obsessions and offer a vindication of them. His own dichotomy between mind and body and his deep need to reconcile them is manifested in his main characters.[29] Whenever he speaks of the body in his novels, it is to draw attention to its most repulsive aspects. The exigencies of the body prevent his visionaries from achieving the timelessness of

---

[26] Joyce (1944), p. 211.

[27] Marr (1994), p. 292.

[28] John Beston (1972a), see chapter 2 in this volume.

[29] The apparent discrepancy between Stan's epiphany of One as the answer to all sums and Holstius' doctrine of permanence as a state of multiplication and division can be resolved by considering both epiphanies as expressions of White's deep need to reconcile his body and his spirit.

pure being that they so ardently long for.[30] True life begins for them only when the bonds of flesh are broken: the destruction of their physical being allows them a greater intensity of perception, opening the door to the ultimate truth that they attain to in an epiphany. That is the substance of Le Mesurier's prayer in his poem 'Conclusion':

> O God, my God, I pray that you will take my spirit out of this my body's remains, and after you have scattered it, grant that it shall be everywhere, and in the rocks, and in the waterholes, and in true love of all men, and in you, O God, at last. (p. 297)

Le Mesurier, a secondary character, is not raised to visionary status, but here he is a stand-in for Voss and ultimately White himself.[31]

So if Theodora is able to maintain a life with the spirit, it is because she has given over the care of her bodily needs to a mental home in New Mexico. Stan experiences his epiphany immediately prior to his fatal heart attack. At the end of *Riders,* Mary Hare, always a pantheist, dissolves into nature, and Alf Dubbo dies after feverishly recording his vision in paint. Elizabeth Hunter is buffeted and stripped half naked by a force stronger than herself in order that she can arrive at a sense of her essential self. The visionaries are granted their supreme revelation when they no longer have the strength to struggle or when they relinquish the will to do so.

For all Patrick White's fascination with epiphanies, they remain vague and fail to enlighten or move us. Yet White was more at ease in portraying an epiphany than in fleshing out a close personal relationship. None of his novels concludes with the achieving of a close, meaningful relationship—characteristically they end with the renunciation of a relationship—but a number of his novels end with an epiphany. One comes to suspect that for White, the portrayal of an epiphany came to be

---

[30] Laigle (1985a), p. 273.

[31] John Beston (2003a), see chapter 18 in this volume.

a substitute for a sense of personal fulfilment, his characters' or his own. The two novels before *The Aunt's Story, Happy Valley* and *The Living and the Dead,* ended in aborted relationships, and, largely because of that, are lacking in vitality. (Elyot Standish's rather brutal rejection of Connie Tiarks in *The Living and the Dead* stands out conspicuously as a failed relationship.) With White's first representation of an epiphany in *The Aunt's Story* and with the epiphanies that conclude the novels that follow, the mood of his endings lightens somewhat. Theodora has ruined any potential relationship with Frank Parrott and Huntley Clarkson, but her final communion with Holstius suggests the possibility of a continuing life within the imagination; like the black rose that glitters and trembles on her hat, she leads a life of her own. Stan and Amy become increasingly distant from one another with the passage of the years, soothed by habit rather than energised by love, but Stan goes acceptantly into the next world, comforted by his epiphany: 'It is all right', he says (p. 497). Neither Mary Hare nor Alf Dubbo ever experiences love, and Himmelfarb and Mrs Godbold do not seem to miss their dead spouses; but they all achieve a kind of fulfilment in their last days or hours. Elizabeth Hunter seems happiest when she is in Sydney and her husband is at Kudjeri, for her feeling for him is one of obligation rather than love. Her fulfilment seems to lie in facing and surviving a force stronger than herself, one that can command her respect and respect her. In her epiphany at the eye of the cyclone, there is no grace involved: what is operating is almost a confrontation of wills as she and God seem to take each other's measure. When she dies, her death is represented as the withdrawal of her will to live rather than as an act of God. For all these characters, failure to experience fulfilment in a loving relationship is masked by an epiphany offering an alternative fulfilment.

Although the lack of love in White's novels is closely connected to his preoccupation with epiphanies, it is a connection that has not been hitherto commented upon. When we see the epiphanies as a substitute for close personal relationships, they make clearer what is White's fundamental weakness: an inability to portray human love. Geneviève Laigle sums up the repeated situation in White's novels thus:

> quelle que soit la nature des relations qui unissent les personnages de White, qu'il s'agisse d'amis, des parents et de leurs enfants, de frère et soeur, d'amants ou de couples légitimes, jamais la communication ne parvient à s'établir de façon satisfaisante, et chacun finit par renoncer à comprendre l'autre et à en être compris. L'âme d'autrui est perçue comme un gouffre ténébreux, où on craint de s'aventurer, ou comme un labyrinth dont on est incapable d'atteindre le centre.[32]

The question can even arise, did White himself experience a sustained love? David Marr records the historian Manning Clark's impression of White when he first met him in the late 1950s: Clark saw 'the face of a man who wants something he is never going to get … Perhaps it was simply a hunger for ordinary communion with the human race.'[33] White's tribute in *Flaws in the Glass* to his lifelong partner, Manoly Lascaris, is brief and impersonal: it refers only to Manoly's 'immense moral strength' and casts him in the abstract role of 'the central mandala in my life's hitherto messy design' (p. 100). Then, in a shift of focus from Manoly, White accuses himself of a 'jealous, not to say violent nature.' He does not establish either Manoly or himself as a warm hu-

---

[32] [whatever the nature of the relations that connect White's characters, whether they are friends, parents and their children, brother and sister, lovers or married couples, communication never succeeds in establishing itself in a satisfactory way, and one of the parties finally gives up trying to understand the other or be understood by the other. The soul of the other party is seen as a dark gulf that one fears to enter or as a maze whose centre one cannot reach] Laigle (1989), p. 266. In this long work, Laigle establishes herself as the most acute analyst of White's personality structure.

[33] Marr (1991), p. 354.

man being; what seems to emerge again is Manning Clark's man who hungers for something he is never going to get.

Epiphanies are normally solitary experiences, but are not necessarily detached from any relation with other people as they regularly are in White. White's epiphanies are solipsistic. (For Theodora and Stan, for example, the rest of the world does not come into consideration; for Mrs Godbold and Elizabeth Hunter, their relationships with the people around them remain unchanged after their epiphany.) The epiphanies are not really heartfelt; they are blurred, revealing the same hollowness that they attempt to cover. White did, as his Nobel Prize citation stated, introduce a new continent to literature, but he did not extend its humanity.

21
Mythmaking in Patrick White's Novels

'We have often heard that White is a myth-maker', remarked David Tacey in a 1986 article.[1] But in fact very little had been written before then on myth in association with White other than by Tacey, who from 1983 undertook a series of psychological analyses of myths that he discerned in White. Earlier writers who noted White's use of myth were Thelma Herring in 1965, Manfred Mackenzie in 1966, Patricia Morley in 1972, and myself in 1976.[2] Herring drew attention to White's use of the *Odyssey* in *The Aunt's Story*, Mackenzie showed how White paralleled the lives of the characters with the seasons in *The Tree of Man* in accordance with mythic patterns of human existence, Morley linked White's divine fools to the Perceval legend in the Arthurian story,[3] and I discussed White's use of stylistic techniques proper to myths in two novels, *The Tree of Man* and *Voss*. The chief difference between these early studies and Tacey's articles is that the former see White consciously drawing freely upon aspects of myth—stylistically, structurally and thematically—while Tacey is concerned with archetypal mythic patterns that welled up in White's unconscious, outside his control.

Tacey stated his central position in 1985, proclaiming that

---

[1] Tacey (1986), p. 192.

[2] Herring (1965); Mackenzie (1966); Morley (1972); John Beston (1976).

[3] Morley (1972), pp. 92–93.

> White criticism tends to go astray by focusing on the author's stated intentions and claims, instead of paying careful attention to the novels themselves. It is disturbing to see how often commentators suspend critical judgement in order to make way for the author's views.[4]

But such an extreme position is itself disturbing insofar as it discounts the importance of White's conscious control and aims. John McLaren was one critic who objected early to Tacey as dogmatic, wondering whether, 'in trusting the tale rather than the teller, he does not force their structure into his own preconceived patterns'.[5] Tacey maintained his stance, however, and in 1988 published a book-length study of White's psyche and the novels as representations of White's unconscious.[6]

Tacey sees White as 'not so much a myth-maker, as an artist who is himself made by mythic impulses'.[7] His interpretation of White's unconscious is at times persuasive: he is no doubt right, for instance, that White's mother Ruth stands behind his fiction as the Mother Goddess 'and is responsible … for the mental anguish of the author'[8] but she is more important as an impulse to his creativity than as a presence in the novels that he actually published (with the exception of *The Eye of the Storm*). Tacey's assertion that White's novels 'are not products of his conscious mind but spring up, as it were, from the creative unconscious' goes too far.[9] One cannot ignore, as Tacey did, the importance of White's conscious control over his material, his ultimate literary reworking of his material in accordance with aims that he stated in 'The Prodigal Son'[10]

---

[4] Tacey (1985), p. 267.
[5] 'Introduction' in McLaren (1995), p. vi.
[6] Tacey (1988).
[7] Tacey (1986), p. 192.
[8] Ibid., p. 193.
[9] Tacey (1983), p. 165.
[10] White (1989), p. 5.

and pursued over a period of twenty-six years, from *The Aunt's Story* (1948) to *A Fringe of Leaves* (1976).

The myths that White uses in his novels are consciously drawn from literature or history or even from films, and are not the same as those that Tacey points to as revealing of White's psyche. White turned to myth to provide him with a framework for his narratives and to elevate their dignity, thereby helping him to achieve his chief goal as a writer, which was to enrich the culture of his native country, Australia:

> Because the void [the Great Australian Emptiness] I had to fill was so immense, I wanted to try to suggest in [*The Tree of Man*] every possible aspect of life through the lives of an ordinary man and woman. But at the same time I wanted to discover the extraordinary behind the ordinary, the mystery and the poetry which alone could make bearable the lives of such people, and incidentally, my own life since my return [to Australia] ... Above all I was determined to prove that the Australian novel is not necessarily the dreary, dun-coloured offspring of journalistic realism ... There is the possibility that one may be helping to people a barely inhabited country with a race possessed of understanding.[11]

The close link between White's use of mythmaking techniques in *The Tree of Man* and *Voss* and his aim in those novels of raising the cultural level of Australia is clear in that quotation from 'The Prodigal Son'. (One should bear in mind that the concept of culture shared by White and his audience of the 1950s was that of a high level of achievement in literature and the arts. It is in this sense that 'culture' is used throughout this article, not in the broader sense that developed later from Raymond Williams' studies.)[12] What needs to be stressed—and it is the main theme

---

[11] Ibid., pp. 13–17.

[12] Williams (1961) and (1981).

of this article—is the continuance of the link between White's mythmaking and his cultural goals over the next eighteen years, representing a more enduring commitment to Australia on his part than could have been anticipated in 1958, and more than is fully realised even now. After *A Fringe of Leaves* in 1976, White was no longer concerned with the goal of raising the cultural level of Australia. The Nobel Prize in 1973 confirmed his success in that, and his own interests changed along with changes in Australian culture. But during the years from his 1958 essay to *A Fringe of Leaves*, mythmaking became something of a stock in trade for White, a resource he increasingly mastered to give weight to his work and, beyond it, to Australian literature.

What are we to understand by the term myth? Myth has been defined and redefined during the last century, without much gain in precision. Most basically, myths are archetypal stories that attempt to give significance to human existence within the universe. Some widespread and most immediately recognisable myths are creation myths, fertility myths, journey myths (often to the other world), myths of scapegoats and sacrificial death. Myths recur across cultures and keep recurring within a culture: 'Every myth we know has both a past and a future'.[13] Myths orient people towards the metaphysical; they represent 'a disclosure of unprecedented worlds, an opening on to other possible worlds which transcend the established limits of our actual world'.[14] Some kind of relationship between human beings and higher powers is therefore often implied or involved, though this is less true of very recent myths. The relationship that White most commonly suggests is that of a destiny assigned to his characters by a higher power.

There have been attempts to distinguish between myths, folklore, legends and sagas, but the distinctions fail because of inevitable

[13] Munz (1973), p. 7.

[14] Ricoeur (1991), p. 490.

overlapping. And there have been attempts to unify the study of mythology by means of a single approach—for example, psychological (Freud and Jung), theological (Ricoeur and Cupitt), anthropological (Frazer and Campbell), archetypal (Frye), Marxist (Voloshinov), linguistic (Saussure and Cassirer), or structuralist (Lévi-Strauss and Barthes)—each approach claiming its interpretation as the key to understanding myth; but none has gained universal acceptance.[15]

White does not actually create myths; instead, throughout his career, he takes stories from both ancient and modern times that resonate strongly within Western cultural consciousness and infuses them with a high seriousness and formal dignity appropriate to mythmaking. In *The Tree of Man*, *Voss*, and *A Fringe of Leaves*, he uses archetypal stories from Australian history and links them to myths in literature. To speak of White's mythmaking is to imply both the nature of the stories that he is drawing upon and the ways in which he raises the stories to mythic or near-mythic status. The first four novels in which White demonstrates his characteristic mythmaking appeared in chronological sequence over a period of fourteen years (1948 through 1961). After a gap of twelve years, he produced another two successive novels, *The Eye of the Storm* and *A Fringe of Leaves* (in 1973 and 1976), that again use archetypal stories and mythic techniques.

White draws upon both ancient myths (whether primitive or Biblical myths, myths from ancient Greece and Rome or the Middle Ages) and modern myths (archetypal stories from recent, even contemporary history). There is a basic difference between the two in that the former normally tell stories of gods, while the latter tell stories of extraordinary

---

[15] Sigmund Freud (1919); Carl Jung & Carl Kerenyi (1963); Don Cupitt (1982); Sir James Frazer (1963); Joseph Campbell (1959); Northrop Frye (1957); Valentin V. Voloshinov (1973); Ferdinand de Saussure (1983); Ernst Cassirer (1979); Claude Lévi-Strauss (1979); Roland Barthes (1972).

people who are a familiar part of the history of a country (for instance, frontiersmen like Davy Crockett or Kit Carson in the US, and explorers like Burke and Wills or Leichhardt in Australia). White appears to have a greater sense of freedom and to feel more personal involvement when he deals with modern myths. It is the exploration and settlement of Australia that most engages his imagination, probably because he himself came from a rural background, and grew up in a pioneer period. And the less complex society of pre-industrial Australia—that is, before World War II—provides a more suitable background for his mythic stories.

There is a wide variety of myths in Patrick White's novels, evidence of the extent of his interest in myths and the literary uses to which they could be adapted. There are primitive myths (a comet as omen and blood sacrifice in *Voss* (pp. 375–91, 394),[16] old, well-known European myths (the *Odyssey* in *The Aunt's Story* and *A Fringe of Leaves*, the Tristan story in *A Fringe of Leaves*), Biblical myths (the Chariot of Ezekiel and the Crucifixion in *Riders in the Chariot*), literary myths from Shakespeare (allusions to Hamlet in *The Tree of Man*, Lear and Cleopatra in *The Eye of the Storm*) and Stendhal (the figure of Sanseverina paralleling Elizabeth Hunter in *The Eye of the Storm*), and popular myths from Hollywood movies (recognisable scenes from *The Cabinet of Dr Caligari* and *Rebecca* in the 'Jardin Exotique' section of *The Aunt's Story, Gone with the Wind* in *The Tree of Man, Citizen Kane* in *Riders in the Chariot,* and *Lifeboat* in *A Fringe of Leaves*).[17] Laurence Coupe emphasised that 'the mythic and the literary are not so far apart as is often supposed', for 'literature is a means of extending mythology'; and Joseph Campbell further acknowledged the power and speed of movies to create myths.[18]

---

[16] White (1957a).

[17] John Beston (2004c).

[18] Coupe (1997), p. 4; Campbell (1988), pp. 15–16.

Most importantly, however, White makes extensive use in *The Tree of Man*, *Voss* and *A Fringe of Leaves* of stories that stand out in Australian history, myths of exploration and settlement. It is mainly White's use of these Australian myths that will be discussed in this article, for they are the most direct expression of his aim to build a strong cultural identity for his country. It is not just Voss but White the author who is 'compelled into this country', Australia (p. 23). The map that Voss wants to be the first to make represents for White the opening up of Australian cultural territory that he himself will continue to explore, and whose terrain he will mark out for others to follow. When one considers the state of Australian literature in the late 1950s one could justly compare his achievement to that of Virgil 2000 years ago when he claimed '*Primus ego in patriam mecum ... /Aonio rediens deducam uertice Musas*'.[19] That the *Georgics* lay close to White's heart is clear from Austin Roxburgh's deep attachment to them in *A Fringe of Leaves.*

White's most important myths are national in scope: they have their roots in Australian history, in the exploration of the continent, in interaction between Aborigines and stranded whites or escaped convicts, in the settlement of the land and the development of a distinctive Australian culture. The myths were already there in the Australian consciousness before White began to write; they were part of the milieu in which he grew up. (Stan Parker, for instance, has many of the qualities that Russel Ward spelled out as characteristically Australian in his *The Australian Legend.*)[20] What White undertook in his fiction was a deliberate process of revitalising archetypal Australian stories, raising them to a new awareness in the national consciousness, and telling them with a high degree of literary sophistication in order to enable them to occupy a

[19] ['I am the first to bring the Muses from the heights of Aonia into my country'] Virgil (1988), 3.10–11. All translations in this article are my own.
[20] Ward (1958).

role in Australia parallel to that of myths in other cultures. His interest in myths was no doubt heightened by his long association with his partner in life, the Greek Manoly Lascaris, whom he first met in Egypt during the war years. It was a Greek myth, the *Odyssey*, that provided a framework for White's first major novel, *The Aunt's Story*.[21] The genesis of *The Aunt's Story* lay partly in White's own experience of Europe and America, and his attitude to the Australia he had newly returned to, in 1946. White had lived in England since 1932 and was in America during the early part of World War II, in 1939 and 1940. Theodora's odyssey reflects aspects of White's own journey to Europe and America. As an odyssey of the mind rather than of place, it offers a free-flowing compendium of White's memories and impressions of European culture; the American section is briefer, for Theodora is in transit.[22] Theodora's journey is also an elevated version, given mythic overtones, of the Australian ritual of 'going overseas', and so the story draws on sources from both Greek myth and Australian tradition. For many Australians of the twentieth century the journey to Europe represented a ritual, a sort of cultural coming of age; the ritual journey was extended to America when America emerged as Australia's defender in World War II.

Theodora's personal odyssey is one of rejection, escape, and a search for self-discovery—rejection of her past, escape from her mother (dead only in fact), and an attempt to create an identity of her own in which she is a central figure in the lives of the fantasised figures she surrounds herself with in the Hôtel du Midi. When her fantasies grow to threaten her new identity, she destroys them in a conflagration and moves on to America, where she finally cuts her ties to her past. For Theodora there is

---

[21] White's turning to the *Odyssey* was reinforced by his admiration of James Joyce's *Ulysses* at this time, an admiration that he abandoned later in his life, saying it was easier to read about Joyce than to read him. See Marr (1992), pp. 145, 449.

[22] John Beston (2004b).

no return home; she will spend the rest of her days in a mental home in New Mexico. With his own reaction to Australia still undetermined after fourteen years' absence, White may have felt reluctant to treat the subject of homecoming; homecomings have always been dangerous, in myth and in life. From *The Tree of Man*, written seven years later, it is clear that his response to Australia during that period was negative. If he left a Europe that he described as a 'spiritual graveyard',[23] he had come to a land that he looked upon as a cultural desert, but one which he strove to make fertile through his creation of a body of highly sophisticated literature.

As Theodora prepares to retire into her life within the mind, she is comforted and guided by the fantasy figure of Holstius. On the most basic level, Holstius is a recreation of Theodora's father consoling his agitated daughter; on a more literary level, he is a male Athena who has appeared earlier in other guises, as the Syrian, the Man who was Given his Dinner, and Moraïtis. The appearances of these Athena-like figures link Theodora to Odysseus, thereby heightening her dignity and her stature: in spite of her apparent isolation, she is watched over by mythical forces. On her twelfth birthday, she had already been marked out by the gods as special when she was thrown down by lightning but survived unhurt. The Man who was Given his Dinner appears that same day, and comments, 'No girl that was thrown down by lightning on her twelfth birthday, and then got up again, is going to be swallowed easy by rivers of fire' (p. 45).[24]

Between the publication of *The Aunt's Story* (1948) and *The Tree of Man* (1955), seven years elapsed. Discouraged by the public reception of *The Aunt's Story*, White turned from writing while continuing to farm his property at Castle Hill some twenty miles outside Sydney. But he had

---

[23] White (1989), p. 14.
[24] White (1948b).

time during this period to contemplate the Australian cultural scene and to determine what he wanted to achieve within Australian literature. *The Aunt's Story* was a highly ambitious novel, as are his next three novels, but the direction of his ambitions changed radically, towards Australian stories. In *The Tree of Man* and *Voss*, which followed one another more quickly than any others among his novels, he sought to bring Australia out of what he saw as its cultural immaturity by using and elevating two myths of national importance. The first, *The Tree of Man*, tells an archetypal pioneer story of a family that experiences flood, drought and fire and sees its area grow from a pioneer settlement to near suburbanisation. The second, *Voss*, tells a story of exploration by a man whose expedition fails and who is never found again, another archetypal pattern well established within the history of Australian exploration. Stories of the exploration of the continent are a more vital part of the Australian consciousness than are stories of the exploration of North America within the American consciousness. Every schoolchild in Australia is familiar with stories of Australian exploration, so White was able to rely upon the idea of exploration without having to be precise about the geography of Voss' expedition.

The Tree of Man, then, is White's first attempt to treat a specifically Australian myth. It covers a period from around 1900, when Stan Parker arrives to take up his claim on the land left him by his father, to the early 1940s, when Stan dies.[25] White places his story of an Australian settlement within the wider framework of the archetypal story of settlers in a new country, treating the period of the novel as if it were pre-industrial, but in fact Australia had already entered a period of rapid industrialisation during the latter years of the story.

---

[25] I suggest a dating of the time covered by the novel in chapter 14 in this collection.

The Tree of Man is recognisably an archetypal pioneer novel, but its plot is commonplace, unable by itself to support the mythic quality that White would wish it to achieve. He raises the novel to its mythic level by his extensive use of certain formalising stylistic devices: casting the characters in universal rather than individual roles and highlighting the role of destiny in the characters' lives. Stan and Amy, the names we use for the two main characters, are rarely used by White; early in the novel, they are referred to as 'the man' and 'the woman'—that is, Everyman and Everywoman. When their names are used, Stan and Amy are mostly referred to by their full names, Stan Parker and Amy Parker; their last name, Parker, is generic, a substitute for 'settler'. Eschewing the intimacy of first names, White consistently maintains a formal, abstract quality throughout the novel. This is also true with the main characters in *Riders in the Chariot*, *The Eye of the Storm*, and *A Fringe of Leaves*. We contemplate his central figures and the novels themselves at a respectful distance, as onlookers.

To heighten the mythic quality of his story, White interjects observations on the role of destiny in acknowledgement of a higher power directing the course of events, independent of the intentions of the characters. It is an aspect of myth that he uses again in *Voss*, *Riders in the Chariot*, and *The Eye of the Storm*. The characters in *The Tree of Man* live out a recurrent situation in human existence, the settlement of a new area. They are part of a wider plan that is directed by higher powers. It is Stan especially who voices the notion of destiny:

> he knew … there was nothing to be done. He knew that where his cart had stopped, he would stop. There was nothing to be done. He would make the best of this cell in which he had been locked … He had tried his hand at this and that … But he had

> not continued to do any of these things for long, because he knew that it was not intended. (pp. 7–8)[26]

It is not his personal destiny, his success or his failure, that is of prime concern; if he were to fail in this settlement, others after him would succeed. His acceptance of destiny gives him at times a passive quality. 'It would never occur to him', we are told, 'that what must be, might not' (p. 24); but if that reduces his heroic stature, it augments the role of destiny. *The Tree of Man* is a mythic story in which the story of the settlement of a new land is more important than that of the characters who are its agents; and the cycle of flood, drought and fire (chapters 7 and 12) which they live through is an ordained part of life in eastern Australia. The notion of destiny is important in the ethos of a young country; it was articulated in conspicuous form during the 1840s in the United States in the doctrine of Manifest Destiny.[27]

In *Voss* White goes back a half-century before *The Tree of Man* for his subject, to the mid-nineteenth century: the book is based largely upon the expedition of Leichhardt in the late 1840s.[28] *Voss* is a more ambitious work than *The Tree of Man*—it is even a driven work, born of many forces operating within White: his experiences in the North African desert during World War II, his readings in Australian history in London during the war, his readings in French and German literature at the University of Cambridge, and his increasing commitment to Australia after his return there, all these coming together in his growing literary ambition. For his overreacher Voss, he found his inspiration in larger

---

[26] White (1956). Page references in this chapter are to this edition.

[27] The phrase 'Manifest Destiny' was first used in print in 1845 by John L. O'Sullivan, editor of the influential *Democratic Review*. Initially it referred to the expansion of US territory across North America, but quickly came to mean a belief in America's destiny to lead the world in spreading freedom.

[28] Day (2003), pp. 131–33.

than life figures on the contemporary world scene (like Hitler) and in literature (Satan, Tamburlaine, Faust, Captain Ahab). The closest literary analogue to Voss is Melville's Captain Ahab: both these overreachers are driven by their will. 'This expedition ... of yours', pronounces Laura, 'is pure will' (p. 74).

Voss represents White's most serious and sustained effort to tell a story of mythic dimensions that can stand alongside the established myths of Western civilisation, myths that it draws upon in its turn. It combines two archetypal stories, one Australian and one European, the story of an explorer who is also an overreacher. The overreacher is a mythic figure who has his origins in European and American literature, appearing at a time of cultural explosion in his particular country; in *Voss* White has introduced the figure of the overreacher into Australian literature. The famous overreachers of Western literature are all giant figures who conceive of themselves as superhuman. Their failure is inevitable, for they challenge the highest principles of order, but even in failure they attract our admiration. Death itself does not diminish them.

Although it is the story of Voss' expedition that propels the novel forward, it is the concept of the overreacher that engages White's main interest. We learn little of Voss' plans to explore, nothing of his discoveries. Neither does Colonel Hebden, the first to retrace Voss' steps, give any account of the terrain traversed. The geography of exploration plays little part in the novel, and discovery none at all. Why, one may ask, is White more interested in the concept of the overreacher? The answer that presents itself reveals a good deal about White the artist and his literary aims for Australia. In his ambition to make the literary map of Australia, like Voss making a physical map of the heart of Australia, White saw himself as an overreacher, and his literary ambition frightened him even as it spurred him on.

The role of destiny, an important element in mythmaking, is a strong force in *Voss* as in the preceding novels, but in an enduring tension that is a major theme in the work. For Voss' concept of his destiny, forged within his own powerful will, is opposed to the destiny that he would have achieved under the guidance of higher powers. This conflict can obscure the workings of the higher destiny that run through the novel. Voss certainly feels under the rule of destiny, but will not acknowledge its source, referring to it only in passive or impersonal constructions: 'I am compelled into this country' (p. 23) or 'It is intended that I will lead an expedition into the interior' (p. 38). Is he thinking of the force of his own will, or is he deferring to a supernatural being (God)?

If Voss feels ruled by his own will, we the readers are continually reminded that the course of his life is guided by a Christian God. There are frequent reminders of God and prayer in the novel: in discussions between Voss and Laura (pp. 94–97), and Voss and Brother Müller at the Moravian Mission near Moreton Bay (pp. 53–54), in the presence of Palfreyman as a man of strong faith in the expedition, the celebration of Christmas in the desert (pp. 209–21), Laura's epiphany of the three stages of God into Man, Man, and Man returning into God (p. 386), and in others still. As the expedition goes on and failure seems inevitable, Voss' concept of his own willed destiny yields before his sense of a higher destiny. 'I do not withdraw … I am withdrawn' (p. 404), he acknowledges then, meaning probably that while he has not yet quite relinquished his will, he recognises that stronger forces are operating upon him. Shortly before his death he utters a heartfelt prayer, '*O Jesus … rette mich nur! Du lieber!*' [Save me, Jesus! Dear Lord!] (p. 415), an expression of faith in a God upon whose mercy he now depends.

As with the earlier novels, one should consider the circumstances of White's life and the cultural ethos of Australia at the time he wrote *Riders in the Chariot* to understand what he was doing in that novel. In an important departure from his earlier novels, *Riders in the Chariot* acknowledges the flow of postwar migration to Australia: two of the main characters (Himmelfarb and Mrs Godbold) are migrants, and White himself, returning to Australia from England in 1946, could be considered part of that movement. The country was undergoing a racial and cultural restructuring in the years after World War II, and it is the Australia of this period that White is depicting in this novel. Although it was published in 1961, *Riders in the Chariot* deals with events that took place in the late 1940s, when Himmelfarb arrived in Australia from Palestine. The events of White's 'contemporary' novels regularly take place ten to fifteen years before the date of his writing about them; he clearly felt more comfortable with the near past than the immediate present.

In their racial origins and religious beliefs, the four Riders in the Chariot—the four who in Ezekiel bear the Throne of God (1.4–28)—reflect the changes in Australia since White's return: Himmelfarb is a Jew from Germany, Mrs Godbold is a Methodist from the fen country (probably Cambridgeshire) of England, Mary Hare is a pantheist of second-generation Australian birth, and Alf Dubbo is an Aborigine of an Anglican upbringing that he has discarded. The inclusion of an Aborigine reflects a developing sense in White's Australia of an Indigenous population even as European migration poured in. The names of the riders are humour names, adjusted to the personality and creed of the particular rider. Himmelfarb means heavenly blue, Godbold is self-explanatory, a hare (for which Mary is named) is identified for us as a sacrificial victim (p. 104), and Dubbo is an Aboriginal place name (a town in central New South Wales). The name Dubbo has no religious overtones, but it establishes Alf in Australia more firmly than the others.

Riders in the Chariot shows the same concern as White's earlier novels with adding a mythic dimension to Australian culture, this time with myths from the Old World, of a more spiritual nature. White takes two Biblical myths, one Old Testament (the Chariot of Ezekiel) and one New Testament (the Crucifixion and Deposition), and relocates them in Australia to stage them there. With the Old Testament account of Ezekiel's Chariot is fused the classical myth of the chariot of Apollo/

Phaeton, as painted by Odilon Redon;[29] but White's notion of the Chariot is his own, neither quite that of Ezekiel nor that of Redon. Although the novel ends in a re-enactment of the Crucifixion and Deposition, the most important myth is the one that gives its name to the novel, the myth of Ezekiel's Chariot. The Chariot is a symbol indispensable to the novel, a way of marking out the four riders as special, whether a *zaddik* (Himmelfarb, p. 108, perhaps also Miss Hare, p. 173), a saint (Mrs Godbold, p. 545), or a visionary artist (Alf Dubbo).[30]

White endows each of the four riders with the transcendental quality of a mythic figure. He seeks to convey a breadth of vision embracing four different religious viewpoints while also suggesting something in common between them. What the riders have in common seems to be an acceptance of their role as sacrificial victims and their need to suffer. Himmelfarb, himself a sacrificial Christ figure, tells Mary Hare that a hare is considered a sacrificial animal in some cultures (p. 104), establishing that link between them. Mrs Godbold is committed to a life of service and sacrifice (p. 275). Alf Dubbo is portrayed as a silent victim, used by whites for their own purposes—by the Reverend Calderon, Mrs Spice, Hannah and Mr Mortimer. He never shows resentment, withdrawing instead into his own integrity and nurturing within himself a creative vision that will express itself as an act of faith.

Like so many myths, the novel aspires to deal with the grand theme of good versus evil (p. 474). It is here that White is weakest: his concept of both good and evil is too superficial to support the weight of other mythic elements in the novel. The good characters, the four riders (also called 'the illuminates') do not touch the lives of a wider humanity, and

---

[29] Redon produced a series of paintings, *Le Char d'Apollon*, between 1905 and his death in 1916. His interest in mythic subjects from around 1895 would be one reason why White was attracted to his work.

[30] White (1961b).

the evil characters, Mrs Jolley and Mrs Flack and her son Blue, are merely petty: vulgar, mindless and spiteful. But evil has dimensions that reach far beyond the petty, dimensions that White does not explore. White's notion of the outcome of the contest between good and evil, that evil burns itself out (p. 172), is also weak; it is not even as forceful as the popular notion prevailing in our own times, that good will emerge triumphant, but at great cost to itself. This is the vision common in Hollywood films, of which the mythmaking *Star Wars* and Tolkien trilogies are notable examples.

In *Riders in the Chariot*, as in the previous novels discussed, White sounds the theme of destiny heavily, though not for all the illuminates. It is confined almost exclusively to Himmelfarb, the main illuminate; one can detect hints of it with the other illuminates, but White does not draw attention to it. The role of destiny in Himmelfarb's life is the stronger for his own passivity: many of the most important events in his life are recounted in the passive voice. So he feels impelled towards Liebmann (p. 135), whose daughter he is to marry, and she is incorporated into the destiny that directs his life: when he proposes to her, she acknowledges that she knew from the beginning they would marry, but that her role as wife would be a 'minor part she would be given to play' (p. 140). As anti-Jewish feeling emerges in Germany and his brother-in-law Ari leaves for Palestine, Himmelfarb does nothing because he 'had received no indication of what his personal role might be' (p. 161). Speaking to Mary Hare after his arrival in Australia, he declares that it 'will be made clear … what link we provide in the chain of events' (p. 337)—a chain that culminates in the Deposition scene, when the four illuminates finally appear on stage together.

It is the symbol of the Chariot that links the four figures, who else have little in common, and whose lives touch one another only fleetingly. Each has a different concept of the Chariot, however, so that the Chariot, a frail link in itself, has to be periodically brought in and highlighted in the novel. There is a structural and a thematic need therefore to bring the four illuminates together at the end, and that is done not through the Chariot but through the Deposition scene, where the two Marys (Ruth Godbold and Mary Hare) hold the dead Christ (Himmelfarb) while the St John figure (Alf Dubbo) looks on from a distance (p. 490). (Alf had earlier been associated with St John, when the Reverend Calderon read to him from the Gospel of St John.)

The Chariot is introduced tentatively into the lives of each of the illuminates. Although it achieves somewhat more definition as the novel goes on, it never becomes a clear image. Himmelfarb, the chief illuminate, first finds the Chariot in books (pp. 171–73); he draws it for his wife before he sees it, and explains it as the Throne of God, but she is not familiar with the symbol (p. 151). Mary Hare's interest in the Chariot is awakened by her father's enigmatic allusion to it (p. 25), but she does not see it until the eve of Mrs Jolley's arrival, a warning to her of the advent of evil (p. 40). Alf's acquaintance with the Chariot mirrors that of Patrick White himself: he first sees a reproduction of one of Odilon Redon's *Le Char d'Apollon* series, and later superimposes on that the account of Ezekiel's Chariot in the Old Testament (p. 398). The passage from Ezekiel is quoted for us from the Bible that Alf leaves open in the washroom at the factory where he works (p. 348). Alf never actually sees the Chariot; his painting of *The Chariot-thing* is a creative and spiritual outburst representing for him a proof of the Absolute (pp. 387, 513–15). With Mrs Godbold the first mention of the Chariot is in one of her hymns, associated with the triumph of good (p. 257). We are not told that she ever sees it, only, at the very end, that she 'had her own vision of the Chariot' (p. 549), a vision that is not conveyed to us. But what Himmelfarb draws, what Mary sees, what Alf paints, what Mrs Godbold pictures is never really clear. We are asked to accept an idea of four figures very different from Ezekiel's four living creatures, riding in a Redon Chariot, supporting a non-literal Throne of God. The importance of the Chariot is not as a pictorial representation, but as a symbol of a divine presence that presides over human existence and that interests itself especially in these elect figures whom it has picked out in the newest of New Worlds, Australia.

Riders in the Chariot represents perhaps the ultimate in what White could claim for Australia in his attempt to give it a body of myth: the translation of the spiritually elect to Australia from the Near East and Europe. Neither of his two novels of the decade following *Riders in the Chariot* achieves mythic status. *The Solid Mandala* (1966) depends upon a symbol that has a limited emotional resonance for his readers and conveys an essentially simple idea, that of totality, with unnecessary complexity. Early critics of *The Solid Mandala* were in general more conscientious than enthusiastic, while recent White critics tend to discuss it fleetingly or not at all.[31] *The Vivisector* (1970) deals with an unattractive subject, that of the artist who uses the lives of people around him as a source for his art. It evoked the disapproval of the members of the committee awarding the Nobel Prize in Literature and killed White's chances of receiving it that year.

But in the two novels which he published in the mid-1970s, *The Eye of the Storm* (1973) and *A Fringe of Leaves* (1976), he returned to an interest in mythic characters and themes, if not with the same intense commitment to raising the cultural level of Australia that he had in *The Tree of Man, Voss* and *Riders in the Chariot.* In *The Eye of the Storm,* the first of these two later novels, he created in Elizabeth Hunter a fictionalised portrait of his own mother that would endow her with mythic status. While there are a number of mythical elements that serve to bolster the status of Elizabeth Hunter, the story itself is not an archetypal one that has relevance to the history and culture of Australia as did *The Tree of Man, Voss,* and *Riders in the Chariot.* It is most meaningful to

---

[31] Beatson (1976) offers the most extended discussion of the novel. Laigle (1989) considers it only intermittently in her long and perceptive study. Edgecombe (1989) and Steven (1989) do not discuss it at all.

Patrick White himself, but in the hands of this artist takes on dimensions beyond the purely personal.

White clearly thought of his mother as a more powerful, dynamic person than he was himself, and in this novel yielded, even capitulated, to her as such.[32] He was aware that he will be remembered for his literary achievement, not for his personal qualities, but he believed that the memory of his mother, through the persona of Elizabeth Hunter, ought to endure, and he sought to ensure that through the extraordinary portrait he has created of her. He raises her to mythic status by associating her closely with famous figures from French and English literature: Stendhal's Sanseverina, Shakespeare's Lear and Cleopatra. And he grants her an almost mystical epiphany that gives its name to the novel.

The mythologising of Elizabeth Hunter is a highly personal matter for Patrick White, charged with ambivalence. She is both greatly admired and greatly feared, at times almost hated. If there is any one attitude that prevails towards her, it is awe. The character with whom she is most conspicuously linked is Sanseverina, the chief female character in Stendhal's *La Chartreuse de Parme* (1839), one of White's favourite novels.[33] Sanseverina, who is referred to many times throughout *The Eye of the Storm*, is the most brilliant figure in the court of Parma, a beautiful,

---

[32] See John Beston, 'The Making of the Artist in Patrick White', *Commonwealth Novel in English* 1.1 (1982), 86–93; Laigle (1987); Tacey (1988), p. 97. Beston argues that 'in apotheosizing Elizabeth Hunter White has capitulated to the destructive mother that she represents' (pp. 86–87). Laigle (p. 55) and Tacey (p. 97) discuss an image of a male symbol (fire) or a male figure being absorbed into a female symbol, water. Laigle, however, sees White as accepting absorption into the mother in order to acquire her strength: 'La relation dominant-dominé abolie, le fils accède à la toute-puissance de la mère.' [The relationship between the controller and the controlled having been abolished, the son takes on the power of the mother].

[33] Marr (1991), p. 127.

intelligent, energetic and resourceful woman who far eclipses the prince himself; indeed, he compromises himself to keep her at his court. She fascinates Stendhal and keeps drawing the focus of his novel back to herself, even though the adventures of her nephew Fabrice form the bulk of the novel. She is greatly admired by Elizabeth Hunter's mild-mannered husband Alfred ('What a dazzler of a woman, the Sanseverina!' p. 200)[34] and by her insecure daughter Dorothy, who recognise in her the strong qualities of another Elizabeth, without Elizabeth's destructiveness. Elizabeth herself perceives the similarity, but will admit no competition and so shrugs off Sanseverina with a dismissive remark (p. 200). When Dorothy observes that she finds Sanseverina 'dishonest in some respects' (p. 225), Elizabeth senses that the accusation is directed against herself and retorts with a quick defence of Sanseverina that is really a defence of herself: 'Everyone is more or less dishonest … dishonest with themselves, I mean. This—Sanseverina was no more dishonest than any other beautiful woman, or—or jewel. An emerald isn't less beautiful, is it? for the flaw in it?' (p. 225). Sanseverina provides White with a useful literary model, a sort of touchstone, to control his attitude to his mother: she provides a means of stabilising the portrait of his mother, which continually threatens to run out of control.

There are two Shakespearian characters, Lear and Cleopatra, with whom Elizabeth is also associated, and they are associations that also add to her status. She is such a powerful Lear—a sort of Queen Lear—that Basil is unable to compete with her, and cannot play the part of Lear on the English stage ten thousand miles away. Like Lear, she arouses strong emotions in her audience (she is usually onstage, pp. 33–34) and in her retinue, intimidating them, winning some loyalty, but inviting affection only from the Tom Fool character, Lottie Lippmann. The story runs roughly parallel to Shakespeare's play, for Elizabeth is betrayed by her

[34] White (1973).

two children, a drag Goneril (Basil) and Regan (Dorothy), who manoeuvre her out of her money and seal their pact in a night of incest.

The association of Elizabeth with Cleopatra is less strong than that with Lear but is still important. Like Cleopatra, Elizabeth clings to the image of her beauty, even though for her at eighty-six that is long gone; she loves to be made up by one of her nurses, all of whom are called acolytes (pp. 75, 117, 151, 276), and dons a purple wig for special company. Her death in heavy makeup, upon an elaborate commode that resembles a throne, its arms carved like swans' heads, will recall the death of Cleopatra, seated upon her throne in regal attire. In linking Elizabeth to three famous literary analogues, Sanseverina, Lear and Cleopatra, White is giving her a mythic status. All three, like Elizabeth, are imperious, strong-willed characters, memorable but not especially sympathetic.

By *The Eye of the Storm* White had largely mastered techniques belonging to mythmaking. One encounters again in *The Eye of the Storm* references to destiny, a fate determined by a power beyond the human; and one confronts again the concept of an epiphany like that experienced by some of White's earlier mythic figures, but here the epiphany is of central significance and conveyed more clearly. These concepts of destiny and an epiphany raise the novel to a metaphysical level, envisaging a world beyond the material, as in myths of the classical world.

The theme of destiny is confined in *The Eye of the Storm* almost exclusively to Elizabeth. If it is sounded less frequently and less forcefully with Elizabeth than with earlier mythic figures like Himmelfarb or Voss or Theodora, it is because Elizabeth is so imperious, so much in control of her own life and the lives of those around her, that she leaves little room for the workings of destiny. Elizabeth's will and her destiny are in conflict, like Voss' earlier. It is her experience at the eye of the storm that gives her a sense of a force greater than herself and that leads her in time to acknowledge that she may have a destiny: 'perhaps you are reserved … for other ends' (p. 334). During the eye of the storm she is brought to face her small, lonely place in the world and to confront her own destructiveness. As she emerges from her bunker during the calm of the storm and looks at the wreckage around her, she realises that it is 'no worse than any she had caused in life in her relationships with human beings' (p. 425), a wreckage that will resume on the island and in her life after the calm has passed.

Her greatest illumination during the eye of the storm, however, comes through the image that flashes upon her, of herself as the flaw in a jewel: 'She was … a flaw at the centre of this jewel of light' (p. 424). It is an image that recurs in her final weeks of life, after Basil and Dorothy have returned to Australia. When she recalls the eye of the storm, she thinks of her 'enormous, gaping, at times agonizing flaws' (p. 334). These flaws are part of her emerald identity and do not preclude some kind of transfiguration, which in fact she is granted at the end of the novel.

The Eye of the Storm is the only one among White's novels where the eternal fate of a character is an important theme—but then Elizabeth is a version of his own mother, so that the issue is important to him personally. The question, 'Are regenerative states of mind granted to the very old to ease the passage from their earthly sensual natures into final peace and forgiveness?' is asked fairly early in the novel (p. 73). The mere posing of the question implies that White feels there is a need for such regeneration (a rebirth of hope, a renewal of the soul) for his mother at least, too powerful a figure, whatever her flaws, to fade into insignificance. As Elizabeth eases out of life, she draws upon her experience years before at the eye of the storm in order to leave her sensual nature and pass into peace. That she makes that transition is clear on the final page of the novel, where her spirit offers a benison to Mary de Santis gathering roses in the early morning. As the light swells and birds swarm around her, Mary herself becomes transfigured:

> The light she could not ward off: it was by now too solid, too possessive; herself possessed.

> Shortly after she went inside the house. In the hall she bowed her head, amazed and not a little frightened by what she saw in Elizabeth Hunter's looking glass. (p. 608)

In *The Eye of the Storm* Patrick White has granted mythic status, even a final transfiguration, to his mother, setting her spirit to rest and leaving to Australian literature one of its most memorable character portraits.

In coming to terms with the influence of his mother on his life in *The Eye of the Storm*, White threw off one of his most oppressive burdens. The award of the Nobel Prize in Literature later that same year (1973) seems further to have disposed him more kindly to life at large. *A Fringe of Leaves*, published three years later (1976), also has a woman at the centre of the story, not an intimidating figure like Elizabeth Hunter but one who is sympathetic and accessible. Ellen Roxburgh, like Elizabeth, is another hunter/seeker, but with a more clearly defined goal: the search for a love that is emotionally and sexually fulfilling.

As in the novels already discussed, White is concerned here with linking his main character to myth, thereby elevating her status. His award of the Nobel Prize in Literature largely confirmed his success in raising the cultural level of Australia, but his desire to create larger than life characters remained undiminished. If Ellen herself is of common birth and impelled by the universal human desire for emotional and sexual fulfilment, she is given a dimension far beyond the ordinary through a variety of mythic themes with which she is associated. There are myths from literature (*Madame Bovary*, the Tristan story, the *Odyssey* and Dante's *Inferno*), from the Bible (Adam and Eve figures) and from history (Eliza Fraser's ordeal, also in 1836).

As an unfulfilled young dreamer, Ellen has something in her of Emma Bovary, the archetypal romantic dreamer. The link with *Madame Bovary* is directly established in her sexual encounter with Garnet Roxburgh when they ride into the bush (p. 116);[35] it parallels closely Emma's seduction by Rodolphe when they ride into the woods (2. 9). Ellen is also linked to the Tristan story as a young girl in Cornwall, living near Tintagel. She would dream of being sent a god: 'Out of Ireland, according to legend' (p. 50). The legend is the Tristan story, but she knows it only vaguely and inaccurately. There is no indication that she even knows the names of the legendary lovers, but the name Tintagel stays with her as a shortcut to her romantic aspirations (pp. 277, 346). Myth, Ellen knows, can belong to Cornwall—and she herself will achieve a certain mythic status in Australia. Later she unknowingly enacts part of the Tristan story in her life with the escaped convict Jack Chance in the Australian bush: the episode in the Tristan story is his life with Iseult (now often called Isolde, from Wagner's opera) in the forest of the Morois. Although the lovers are in continual flight, reduced to the bare necessities of life, their apartness from other society has an idyllic aspect for them in that they are immersed in one another.[36]

In one respect Ellen and Jack go beyond Tristan and Iseult to evoke the myth of paradise lost: they are both naked except for the fringe of leaves around Ellen's waist, and so conjure up an image of Adam and Eve after their loss of innocence.

The fringe of leaves seems like a minor detail in the novel, but it gives its name to the novel and so invites interpretation. The function of the vines, the fringe of leaves wound around her waist, is not to serve as a modesty screen but to conceal the wedding ring Ellen has threaded onto the vines. The wedding ring is primarily a talisman that protects her during her life with the blacks and leads her back to white civilisation,

---

[35] White (1976a).

[36] White would have read Joseph Bédier's *Le Roman de Tristan et Iseut*. Bédier's is the only complete version of the Tristan story that tells of the lovers living in the open forest, changing location from day to day.

when she loses it, no longer needing it; myths and fairytales alike are full of such talismans. The extraordinary garment also provides a vivid way of remembering Ellen as the Lady of the Fringe of Leaves, very much as we remember the heroine of Alexandre Dumas fils as the *Dame aux camélias*: the image becomes more evocative than the personal name.

At the most basic level, Ellen's adventures belong within the framework of an archetypal journey myth. She re-enacts an odyssey that has links with both Homer's epic and Dante's *Inferno*. It is a journey story that we have already encountered with Theodora in *The Aunt's Story*, but *A Fringe of Leaves* is closer than *The Aunt's Story* to the *Odyssey* in its narrative structure as it tells of the wanderer's travails at sea and on land in the course of a long sea voyage to return home. Ellen, like Theodora, is cast as a mythic wanderer, helped and encouraged at a critical stage by a male Athena figure; for Ellen it is Jack Chance. At the end of her odyssey Ellen will have a homecoming rather like that of Odysseus: she will have a spouse again (Mr Jevons), and the three children she has lost will be replaced by three new stepchildren.[37]

Ellen's odyssey also has links to Dante's journey into Hell (*Inferno*), an odyssey in which Dante was guided by Virgil, the voice of reason. As Ellen and the crew of the *Bristol Maid* enter upon their journey into Hell, Austin, Ellen's husband, clings to his copy of Virgil, who exhorts courage and offers a picture of rural harmony. Austin quotes from the *Georgics* just after the ship leaves Sydney (p. 34):

> felix qui potuit rerum cognoscere causas,

[37] Most critics agree that Ellen will marry Mr Jevons, but no one has noted the corroboration of that impression by his spilling tea on her lap, a clear sexual reference.

atque metus omnis et inexorabile fatum
subiecit pedibus strepitumque Acherontis auari.[38] (2.490–92)

Ellen's association with Virgil is through Austin, but White's references to Virgil do convey a grand seriousness to the crew's experiences and especially to those of Ellen, the protagonist of the story. It is Ellen that the above lines from Virgil allude to. She understands the cause of her ordeal to be her adultery with Garnet; by adapting to her ordeal, she survives.

Ellen's experiences at sea and later on land have an important connection with historical fact that has become part of Australian mythology. They are based upon the actual experiences of Eliza Fraser, who was shipwrecked off the Australian coast in 1836.[39] In fact, Fraser Island off the Queensland coast is now generally thought to be named after her (it may originally have been named after her husband, but he is forgotten while her fame has grown). Her place in Australian history was reinforced some fifteen years or so before White's novel by Sidney Nolan's series of Mrs Fraser paintings (1957–58). It was Sidney Nolan in fact who first interested White in her story.[40]

Although *A Fringe of Leaves* is White's best-told narrative, it is by no means simply an adventure story: his overall concern is with Ellen's development. Her character as a woman of mystery is established in the opening chapter in a conversation between two women who have just met her in Sydney. The account of Ellen's experiences from the time she leaves Sydney until she returns to the European settlement at Moreton Bay shows those possibilities given free expression. The last section of the novel deals with her reintegration into white society and establishes her

---

[38] [Happy is he who has been able to understand the causes of things, who has rejected all fear, spurning inexorable Fate and the roar of the insatiable river Acheron!]

[39] See Davidson (1990); McNiven, Russell & Schaffer (1998).

[40] Marr (1991), p. 378.

again as a woman of mystery, like most of White's characters at the end of his novels. If Ellen's search for emotional and sexual fulfilment is a common story, one that is not inherently mythical in its theme, White has presented that theme with a protagonist that he makes larger than life and invested her particular story with a wide range of mythic associations that continue to dignify the Australian culture he deplored as sterile in the 1950s.

There is a continuity in White's literary aims and methods in his major novels that overrides his constant shifts in subject, setting and period. That continuity becomes clearer in a broad discussion of his novels such as has been undertaken here. White found early, in *The Aunt's Story* (1948), that using aspects of myth imparted structure and dignity to a work that lacked a strong narrative and an extended character portrayal. When he surveyed the uninspiring cultural landscape of Australia after his return in 1946 and resolved to enrich it, he drew upon the subjects and techniques of myth to heighten his ambitious works. His historical novels (*The Tree of Man*, *Voss*, and *A Fringe of Leaves*) were able to sustain both the themes and the techniques of myth, in fact were strengthened by the combination. In *Riders in the Chariot,* however, he strained Biblical myths to their limits. Later, in *The Eye of the Storm*, although the story itself is not mythic, he found that the techniques of mythmaking that he had mastered were brilliantly suited to the creation of the larger than life portrait of his mother.

Patrick White's use of the subjects and techniques of myth in his major novels helped him to create the most distinguished body of literature produced by an Australian author. If he viewed Australian culture of the 1950s through the patronising eyes of an Australian from a landed family who had become a cultivated but uncompromising European, his commitment to enriching Australian culture was admirable. With the international recognition of his extraordinary achievement, initially through the glowing front page review of *The Tree of Man* in the *New York Times Book Review*,[41] he attracted an audience for Australian literature on a scale that no one previous had done, helping to accelerate the renaissance in Australian literature that we have all witnessed.

[41] Stern (1955), pp. 1, 13.

22
WHITE'S STYLE*

> I bet your tastes and style ... won't remain fixed—not if you're any good. (Hurtle Duffield in *The Vivisector*)

As late as 1991, when the field of White scholarship was already well developed, Carolyn Bliss pointed out that the subject of his style was its most neglected area.[1] There were few studies of White's style at all before the 1980s. The earliest essay purporting to study White's style, by Harry Heseltine (1963), does not really discuss style at all, but lists and analyses recurring images.[2] Erwin Koch-Emmery (1973) draws attention to White's sense of sound (intonation, alliteration, and rhythm) in his prose, but attributes it quite unnecessarily to White's study of Middle High German and not to his innate sense of sound.[3] An overlooked article by Jean Crowcroft (1974) offers a brief but balanced overview of White's

---

* All references in this chapter are to the following editions: White (1939), (1941), (1948c), (1956), (1957a), (1961a), (1966), (1970), (1973), (1976a), (1979) and (1986).

[1] Bliss (1991).

[2] Heseltine (1963).

[3] Koch-Emmery (1973). Koch-Emmery deals with alliteration and assonance on stressed words or syllables, but English itself has always been given over to this habit. And there is abundant evidence that White was strongly interested in music and aware of the cadences in his writing.

style.[4] My own essay of that time (1976) examines stylistic devices that White uses to impart a mythmaking quality to *The Tree of Man* and *Voss*, but they are devices that he uses hardly at all in later works.[5]

The first extended studies by trained linguists of White's style were written in Germany, by native English-speakers with a language background similar to that of White. (White studied French and German literatures at Cambridge University in the 1930s.) The first, by Hilary Heltay (1983), analysed White's use of the English definite and indefinite articles, demonstrating in the process what a careful stylist White was.[6] The second, by Gordon Collier (1992), analysed White's style in great detail in just one novel, *The Solid Mandala*.[7] Both Heltay and Collier offer extended analyses but their studies are narrow in focus, and both writers tacitly assume that White's style was constant during his nearly fifty-year career. It was not, and my aim in this essay is to demonstrate that although certain stylistic features do recur throughout his novels, his style varies markedly in accordance with his aims and his mood and his thematic interests as they changed throughout his life.

In general, it is the linguists who have defended White's stylistic usages against criticism and gone on to laud his experiments. People who read two or more foreign languages are used to encountering and accepting and even adopting language habits different from standard English practices, as are poets—and White is often thought of as a poet in prose. Poetry, after all, was his first literary medium. He admitted to being saturated in Rimbaud, an important influence on him.[8]

---

[4] Crowcroft (1974).

[5] John Beston (1976).

[6] Heltay (1983).

[7] Collier (1992). As a kind of appendix Collier takes a brief look at *Riders in the Chariot*.

[8] John Beston (2005). See chapter 3 in this collection.

It is the linguists who have the clearest idea of what is meant by White's style; non-linguists tend to have only a vague idea of what it embraces. My concept of it in this discussion includes White's vocabulary, his levels of usage, and his sentence construction and syntax. The nature of White's recurring vocabulary is an important aspect of his style, for it reveals a great deal about his chief preoccupations. His levels of usage vary from a deliberately enervated prose (in *The Living and the Dead*) to a highly poetic prose (in *The Tree of Man* and *Voss* and later in *A Fringe of Leaves*), depending on his purpose. White's sentences are carefully constructed and balanced, but he has an unusual fondness for sentence fragments, which he uses very precisely. In all areas—language, levels of usage, sentence construction and syntax—he plays with standard usages and creates usages of his own, and if these are sometimes idiosyncratic, that is not unusual in a writer so conscious of style.

These are the chief aspects of his style that I will discuss throughout this essay. I am concerned primarily with conveying a picture of how they vary in individual novels: I discuss his style as it changes chronologically in accordance with his themes, with the kind of novel that he wanted to write at a particular time. Nearly twenty years after his death, with the perspective that time bestows, it is possible to discern five groups within his novels that reflect his changing interests and his personal development.

1939–41: His first two novels, *Happy Valley* and *The Living and the Dead*, were written in this period.[9] Both books are carefully composed but subdued, restrained rather than adventurous. They are weighed down by the author's dissatisfaction with the human condition, a dissatisfaction that is highlighted by the negative vocabulary. *Happy Valley* conveys a transparent dislike of Australia, while *The Living and the Dead* portrays England as an Eliot-like wasteland in which the living seem hardly differ-

---

[9] Heltay (1983).

entiated from the dead. Even in these apprentice novels, however, White is a skilful stylist.

1948–61: This is White's greatest period, when he produced the dazzling *The Aunt's Story*, followed by three works with grand, aspiring themes: *The Tree of Man*, *Voss* and *Riders in the Chariot*. *The Tree of Man* and *Voss* are highly poetic, carefully wrought works, achieving a richness and complexity in style that White did not attain again until *A Fringe of Leaves*, which he wrote in an expansive mood after being awarded the Nobel Prize in Literature. *Riders in the Chariot* oddly fluctuates between visionary concepts and a derisive attitude to contemporary Australia and its inhabitants, and accordingly manifests two contrasting styles, one dignified and the other sarcastic.

1966–73: The three novels of this period, *The Solid Mandala*, *The Vivisector* and *The Eye of the Storm*, show a self-preoccupation in White during an unsettled, introspective period in his life. In *The Solid Mandala* he strove to understand divisions in his own personality: between the living spirit and the dead intellect. In *The Vivisector* and *The Eye of the Storm* he further sought to understand the sources and nature of his own creative gift, a gift that in the previous period had drawn world attention to him. The style of the first two novels is abrasive, and the third is strongly negative.

1976: The only novel here forming a group in itself is *A Fringe of Leaves*, White's calmest and least-flawed novel, written when he felt vindicated and fulfilled by being awarded the Nobel Prize in Literature in late 1973. It does not have the ambitious themes of *The Tree of Man* and *Voss*, however; it does not aspire to mythological status, being content rather to recount an historical legend.

1979–86: The two novels of this final period, *The Twyborn Affair* and *Memoirs of Many in One*, are somewhat bizarre works, dealing with confused identities. They resume White's attempts in *The Solid Mandala*, *The Vivisector*, and *The Eye of the Storm*, and even, much earlier, in *The Aunt's Story* to represent his different selves and understand his own identity. As White's health declined in these last years of his career as a novelist, his control of style weakened. There are a good many instances of unclear, confused writing in *The Twyborn Affair*, while *Memoirs of Many in One*, written mainly for White's own amusement, makes no effort to create a distinctive style.

White's first two novels, *Happy Valley* and *The Living and the Dead*, are depressing, almost without relief. The dissatisfaction with the human condition that pervades them recurs throughout White's work, varying in degree and in kind; here it is at its most intense. There is no humour in *Happy Valley*, and little in *The Living and the Dead*. In Adelaide Blenkinsop's dinner party in *The Living and the Dead*, however, there is an adumbration of the kind of comedy of manners that White develops and indulges in later in his career, in Cherry Cheeseman's party for Dorothy in *The Eye of the Storm* most notably and the Winterbothams' party in *The Twyborn Affair* less protractedly. It consists in *The Living and the Dead* of a series of derisive, cerebral observations on people in a social context, betraying a view of social intercourse as 'the rape of the ear' (p. 203).

The vocabulary of both books is negative from their very beginnings, and the opening pages are a good indication of what is to follow. In the first few pages of *Happy Valley* we find 'listless' twice within a few lines, 'cold', 'vaguely', 'dribbled', 'dull', 'grey slush', 'lost', 'dumbly', 'pain', 'straining' and 'tearing apart'. On the second page we are confronted by the image of a man crucified on a dead tree, the first of a number of Goyaesque images in White,[10] and shortly thereafter read the numbed account of a baby

---

[10] The bloated body of a dog in *The Living and the Dead* and in *The Eye of the Storm* and of a cat in *The Twyborn Affair*, the dead man upside down in a tree in *The Tree of Man*, the rotting bodies of Turner and Le Mesurier in *Voss*, the crucifixion of Himmelfarb in *Riders in the Chariot*, the mutilation of Waldo in *The Solid Mandala*, the bird impaled on a branch in *The Eye of the Storm*, finally Eddie Twyborn's hand blown off in *The Twyborn Affair*.

born dead: 'It was like delivering a cow … When she moaned it was almost like the lowing of a cow. And that same bewildered stare' (p. 12). The second chapter begins with words like 'empty' and 'aimless', 'groaned' and 'laboured' (pp. 22–23), and so it continues until we are told that 'In Happy Valley the people existed in spite of each other' (p. 28). The vocabulary of the opening page of *The Living and the Dead* is as negative as that of *Happy Valley*: words like 'confused', 'drifting', 'dim', 'dark' and 'empty' culminate in 'a shapeless, directionless well of fear', and the same negativity continues throughout the chapter. The mood of the opening sentences is deliberately subdued: 'Outside the station, people settled down again to being emotionally commonplace. There was very little to distinguish the individual feature in the flow of faces.' Within a few pages a drunk is run over by a bus and probably killed, in a kind of parallel to the crucified man at the beginning of *Happy Valley*.

If the dreary content of these first two novels operates against our engagement with them, we are nevertheless compelled to admire White's skilful control of style so early in his career. In *Happy Valley* he uses short sentences, in *The Living and the Dead* longer sentences, both to suggest the lack of direction in the lives of the characters. The two opposing kinds of sentence, short and long, convey distinctly different moods: the short sentences of *Happy Valley* stress the lack of energy, the monotony in the lives of those who live there, while the longer sentences of *The Living and the Dead* emphasise the drawn-out quality of meaningless existences spent in an enduring limbo. The vocabulary in the dinner party scene in *The Living and the Dead* is one of futility—there are clusters of words like 'dull', 'desultory', 'bleakness', 'nonentity', 'condescension' (p. 198)—while the complex sentences there suggest the enclosed, rule-bound complexities of artificial social behaviour: 'In the comparatively twilit depths faces announced a wall, the faces of portraits, and the formations of furniture, like baroque grottoes, offering no shelter from the conversation' (p. 198).

From his first novel, White was unusually fond of sentence fragments, a stylistic habit that bothered conservative critics unwilling to recognise just how much they are part of our normal thought processes. Fragments, with or without subjects or objects, are common in conversation and in informal writing (like letters to friends); it is only in highly formal contexts that they may seem inappropriate. White uses them freely, thoughtfully, and confidently. His most common sentence fragments begin with conjunctions like 'and', 'but', and 'or'; by creating a separate sentence they give distinctness to the piece of information that they convey. 'Because' as the introduction to a sentence fragment is not especially common in these two novels but by *The Aunt's Story* was to become one of White's favourite stylistic habits. He uses it colloquially, often as a sort of diffident remark accompanying a personal confidence: 'I shall be a painter, he said. Because you had to do something ...' (*LD*, p. 32). But it is sentence fragments of only a few words that White uses most effectively, to suggest a character's half-expressed thoughts, thoughts that we can fill out ourselves. So in *Happy Valley* Oliver Halliday refuses a breakfast that is offered him before he leaves after an all night delivery with a two-word explanation: 'His wife' (p. 15).

Sentence fragments abound in stream of consciousness passages, and it may well have been the opportunities to play with their evocative fragments that attracted White to this stylistic device from his first novel. One of the more notable such passages in *Happy Valley* occurs after Hagan kisses Sidney Furlow:

> Because something happened that was something dirty and she had wanted something dirty to happen all the time she had ridden past Hagan hoping not to happen because she was afraid ... because as you see I am dirty I have always been am crying from my mouth his mouth pressed and feeling him. (pp. 185–86)

Quickly mastering the techniques of stream of consciousness, White refined upon them in later novels by portraying the freer streams of unconsciousness in dreams, like those of Elyot Standish (p. 284), Stan Parker (p. 316), Voss (pp. 149, 200–01, 287), or Hurtle Duffield (pp. 108–09).

There are flashes of poetry in both early novels, pointing towards White's more intense cultivation of a poetic prose in his next period. We see already in these early novels strong evidence of his interest in experimenting with language, in his creation of his own adverbs. In *Happy Valley* he attaches '-ly' to adjectives of colour: 'silverly' ('the railway line dribbled silverly out of the mist', p. 9), 'pinkly' ('the lip of an old man hung pinkly down', p. 50), and 'whitely' ('The dining-room table was a round mahogany pond with the sauce-boat pushing whitely into port', (p. 75); 'whitely' appears again in *Riders in the Chariot* (p. 280). In his next period, he extends his adverb creation beyond colour, to words like 'sulkily' (p. 10) and 'shallowly' (p. 67) in *The Tree of Man*, 'shadowily' (p. 102), 'surlily' (p. 107), 'solidly' and 'naggingly' (p. 309) in *Voss*. But his favourite created adverb, from *The Aunt's Story* (p. 70) on, was 'uglily', an ugly form for an ugly word; it reappears in *Riders in the Chariot* (p. 18), *The Solid Mandala* (p. 70), *The Vivisector* (p. 99), and *The Eye of the Storm* (p. 22). White liked to play with inflections, was obviously fascinated with the sound and shape of these words. Later, in *Voss*, he used the comparative inflection in 'honester' (p. 100) and the superlative in 'silentest' (p. 147).

The seven years that passed between *The Living and the Dead* and *The Aunt's Story* worked to produce a radical change in the direction of his work and his style. Perhaps the seriousness of his war experiences in World War II helped him to realise that *The Living and the Dead* represented a dead end in its triviality and negativity. *The Aunt's Story* is not a positive novel—there are no happy novels in the White corpus—but it has his first substantial theme and vibrates with an emotional energy that one does not find in the earlier novels. The central idea, the portrayal of a schizophrenic woman, made heavy demands upon White's imaginative resources, and he met them with an impressive array of stylistic devices.

The core vocabulary in *The Aunt's Story* is one of waiting, a waiting that intensifies from part 1 to part 2. There are four uses of *wait* (-ing, -ed) in the first four pages of part 1, and the sense of waiting is highlighted in the opening sentence by the 'at last' of 'But old Mrs Goodman did die at last'. Part 2 emphasises the state of waiting even more: there are sixteen occurrences of *waiting* in its first nine pages. For Theodora the waiting is an expression of her indecision, her passivity, her helplessness perhaps before the course of her life: 'If she left the prospect of freedom unexplored, it was ... from not knowing what to do ... But now freedom ... possessed Theodora' (p. 10). Her will to action has already been broken, and she cannot respond to opportunities that offer themselves. By part 3 the sense of waiting, and hoping, has disappeared, and the prevailing vocabulary becomes one of anxiety, a common condition in White's chief characters. On the first page alone we find 'blared', 'belting', 'frail', 'complained', 'frustration', 'distance', 'a weight', 'exhausted', 'distressed', 'nervous', 'small', 'destroyed', 'dumped', 'consumed', 'could not understand': Theodora Goodman 'had retreated into her own distance and did not intend to come out' (p. 269). Centred on notions of indecision and anxiety, the vocabulary of *The Aunt's Story* points to White's careful structuring of the work: he never loses focus on Theodora's progressive loss of control.

The Aunt's Story represented a grand and original undertaking, with a style designed to suggest dimensions beyond the concrete and the everyday. As a means of suggesting Theodora's state of mind, White uses metaphors abundantly. Mostly the metaphors are short but incisive, as in the remarks that Theodora 'closed doors' behind her (p. 113) or 'continued to wait with something of the superior acceptance of mahogany for fresh acts' (p. 141), but others are more extended and more memorable. The most brilliant metaphor in the novel, and White's most brilliant metaphor altogether, is developed around the idea of a musical score seen and heard as Theodora crosses America by train to the accompaniment of the trumpeting of ripe corn, the metallic sound of the advancing train, or the reeds of human voices (p. 269). Telephone lines appear as musical staves and houses become musical notes as she progresses (p. 273). White also employs a good many anthropomorphic expressions to draw attention to the fluid world in which she lives, where the boundaries between the senses dissolve. So in the early pages of the book the sound of bells 'gropes' through the afternoon and 'snoozes' in the leaves of a tree (p. 10), a house has 'eyes' (p. 23), roses are 'serious' and have smooth 'flesh' (pp. 22–23). Textures, abstract concepts, sounds take on physical qualities: night can 'solidify' and a soul can 'fade' (p. 200), music can 'drip' and cover the walls with a 'moisture' of sound (p. 174). In such a world Theodora's imagination can flow.

With so many opportunities for poetic usage and for the continual interchange of the five senses, White did not much concern himself with word creations of his own in *The Aunt's Story*. He refers however to a group of '*stareful* people' (p. 47) and at times extends usages as in labelling the meek Mrs Parrott's remarks as 'pale things' (p. 37) or referring to 'the beige women' of England (p. 145). He maintained a fondness for verbs with an unstated object or for incomplete sentences we can complete ourselves. So Theodora's 'hands searched' as she tries to think of an answer (p. 283). And passersby noticing groups of visitors in the Goodmans' garden look 'To see whether the Goodman girls' (p. 67). The sentence is not finished with 'might have a suitor'.

The sentences in *The Aunt's Story* are characteristically long: ample and dignified, evenly paced, subdued in keeping with a serious subject. There are few sentence fragments in *The Aunt's Story*, especially as compared to the other novels.[11] White's fondness for clause-sentences, too, is less marked in this novel, but those beginning with 'Because' clearly establish themselves here as his favourite among such constructions. They cluster in the closing pages of the novel as Theodora tries to retain some grip on reasoned behaviour (see, e.g., pp. 292, 294, 296, 298, 300–02).

In *The Aunt's Story* White established himself securely in a poetic mode. He always felt the work to be one of his masterpieces, but it was

[11] *Memoirs of Many in One* is full of sentence fragments, being told in the first person as the colloquial outpourings of a manic elderly woman.

not popular: people were puzzled by what they saw as the bizarre 'Jardin Exotique' section, and often stopped reading there. White himself noticed that copies in the libraries were unstained after half way through. In his next two novels, he turned to themes of central interest to the people of his native country and to himself: a story of pioneer settlement in *The Tree of Man* and of early exploration of Australia in *Voss*. He was at the height of his powers and, in dealing with these subjects, was more accepting of Australia than ever again, with the single exception of *A Fringe of Leaves*. Dissatisfied with the cultural and spiritual level of Australia after his years in Europe, he set about creating myths for it, based on its own history and on his personal faith. His style is accordingly directed primarily towards the achieving of effects similar to those in myths, and it is these techniques that I focus on in my discussion of these two novels.[12]

In order to give the novel a timeless and universal quality appropriate to myth, White uses a variety of stylistic devices, some drawn from Renaissance English (the English of the King James Bible and of Shakespeare), some from contemporary English. Taken from Renaissance English are such practices as the use of simple past tenses instead of continuous forms, omission of the article, and the lack of contractions in conversation. The contemporary usages, certain conjunctions and regionalisms, are specifically Australian, in keeping with the story of pioneers in Australia.

White's frequent use of the simple past in *The Tree of Man* instead of the past continuous of modern English recalls Renaissance English: 'Birds looked from twigs' (p. 3), 'Thin clouds flew' (p. 20). But he would have been predisposed to the usage through his study of French and German at Cambridge; indeed, some sentences reflect French or German constructions: 'But no bird fell' (p. 10), 'It [rain] fell always' (p. 67), 'Here am

[12] See Beston (1976) in chapter 21 in this collection.

I' (pp. 69, 90).[13] In his omission of the article at times, too, White again adopts an older or a poetic usage: 'Birds babbled' (p. 4), 'Fowls flew' (p. 44).

The ordinary contractions in conversation—pronoun + verb (I'm, I've) and verb + negative (don't, can't)—are infrequent in *The Tree of Man*. The uncontracted forms endow the story with a certain timeless quality, removing it from its historical setting in the late nineteenth century and early twentieth century, by which time the contractions were already common. They give it a formal dignity and establish it in a framework appropriate to mythmaking:

> 'I am not putting up any lunch,' she said, watching her husband …
>
> 'That is right,' he answered. 'They would not like that'. (p. 373)

Side by side with these older usages White deliberately employs a number of colloquial contemporary usages, some specifically Australian, that help to create an Everyman story set in Australia. So we find 'only' or 'though' at the beginning of a sentence or clause used with the meaning of 'but', 'still' used for 'nevertheless', and Australianisms like 'whinge' (p. 11), 'rootle' (p. 484), 'slithery' (p. 26), and 'to poddy' (p. 59):

> But there were no neighbours. Only sometimes … you might hear the sound of an axe … Only very distant. (p. 11)
>
> 'There,' she said. 'We shall soon be happy.' Though she had begun to doubt. (p. 88)
>
> Still, the draper had managed to get three rollicking girls. (p. 13)

[13] The 'of which' constructions that bothered a number of critics are for *Voss* a literal translation of the genitive plural of his native German, *deren*: 'There were certain books, for instance. He would interrupt his study of which … ' [*er wurde sein Studium deren unterbrechen*].

When he uses specifically Australian colloquialisms, White is most accepting of his Australian origins.

To convey the mythic aspect of Stan and Amy Parker, the central figures, White uses two main stylistic devices. His most common device is his habit of referring to them throughout as 'the man' and 'the woman', terms that project them into archetypal roles. When Amy and Stan are together in a scene, Amy is often referred to as 'his wife' and Stan as 'her husband', and when they become parents they become 'the father' and 'the mother'. The other device through which White elevates them to mythic status is his use of their full names, 'Stan Parker' and 'Amy Parker', a designation that gives them an added dignity. Only rarely are they called Stan or Amy in accordance with common narrative practice.

The vocabulary of *The Tree of Man* is negative, as in the three preceding novels. It is most noticeable at the beginnings of the four parts of the novel and also at the very end, in the final short chapter. At the beginning of part 1 we find 'scrub', 'cold', 'frost', 'bald', 'stuck', 'sighed', 'loneliness', 'longing', 'brooding', 'black'. Part 2 begins with similar negativity in words like 'dust', 'grit', 'waste', 'crushed', 'lose', 'censure', 'awkward', 'dishonesties' (p. 101), and part 3 begins with words like 'chaos', 'violence', 'destruction', 'lost', 'mud', 'exhaustion' and 'longing' (p. 203). But it is at the end of part 4, in the last two pages of the novel, that the most negative vocabulary occurs: 'poor land', 'ugly mass of scrub', 'whips', 'ashen', 'died', 'maggots', 'dusty', 'death', 'scraggy', 'breaking', 'suffocate', 'fright', 'frightened', and 'torn'.

Yet the overall effect of the novel is not depressing, for there are strong counters throughout to the negativity of the vocabulary. In *The Tree of Man* White emphasises the cycles of life and death, the recurrence of the seasons and the alternation of flood and fire in Australia. He accepts continuity in nature more readily than continuity of human beings: 'in those parts the earth predominated over the human being' (p. 206). It was probably his ambivalence towards Australia that made him so reluctant to show growth in Durilgai (there is a conspicuous absence of children), but he does endorse the notion of achievements to come, as in the 'unborn poem' that Stan's grandson will write one day (p. 499). And there is always in *The Tree of Man* a sense of life as filled with mystery that challenges and eludes the everyday and the ugly. We are continually made aware of a sense of destiny, of things appointed. It appears stylistically in many ways. At the beginning and end of the novel, it is conveyed through the frequency of impersonal constructions, 'There is' and 'There was': 'There was the sound of tin plate' (p. 4), 'There was the young man her son' (p. 6), 'there was always the joy and excitement of brought things' (p. 12), 'In the end there are the trees', (p. 498) 'in the end, there was no end' (p. 499). Some impersonal force, whether directing or merely observing, lies behind whatever is being stated.

The Tree of Man has more short sentences, often in sequence, than any other of White's novels. A short sentence or sentence fragment can exist as a paragraph in itself:

> Amy Parker did not speak.
>
> She mixed the scones.
>
> Breathing. (p. 442)

The general effect of the short sentences is to give a certain authority to the telling by paring it down to simple statements. Such passages sound firm and factual, as in the telling of a saga. These things happened in the past and were intended to happen:

> [the man] knew also there was nothing to be done. He knew that where his cart had stopped, he would stop. There was nothing to be done. He would make the best of this cell in which he had been locked. (p. 7)

Telling a tale that was meant to be, the short sentences in the novel contribute to the pervading sense of destiny.

If *The Tree of Man* relates a myth of a nation's development through the embracing of a common destiny, *Voss* relates a myth of an individual's quest for extraordinary achievement through rejecting a normal destiny and imposing his will upon the order of things. Voss is a recognisable mythic figure, an overreacher, bent on contesting the limits of being.[14] His pursuit of a destiny of his own making is highlighted in the early chapters of the novel through a number of stylistic devices, one of which is his use of passive and impersonal constructions: 'I am compelled into this country' (p. 23); 'I am pursued by this necessity' (p. 36); 'It is intended that I will lead an expedition into the interior' (p. 38). If these passive constructions can initially suggest a force external to Voss, we quickly realise that the force is in fact his own will, which he sees as greater than himself.

An important way in which White conveys the tension between Voss' idea of his destiny and the destiny he would normally follow is through a highly individual use of auxiliary *did*. In ordinary usage *did* as an auxiliary has either an emphatic or a concessive aspect, but in this novel it repeatedly emphasises the clash of destiny against Voss' will (an assertion *of* a pre-existing order against human will) or of Voss' will against destiny (an assertion of human will *against* a pre-existing order). Early in the opening chapter we are told that after he has wrung freedom from his parents and is leaving Germany, 'he did wonder at the purpose and nature of that freedom' (p. 16): he is lost because he has rejected the destiny that would be his without having replaced it by one of his own making. When he has determined his destiny, he feels that human emotion would weaken his pursuit of it, but at times 'the immensity of his presumption did accuse him' (pp. 204–05). As he becomes weaker during the course of

[14] His mythic antecedents are Lucifer within Christian myth, Faust (in Marlowe and Goethe) and Captain Ahab (in Melville) within literature. White certainly associated Voss with Goethe's Faust, which may be why their names are similar. The scene in Mr Bonner's garden where Voss and Laura discuss religious beliefs represents a memory of the scene in Marthe's garden where Faust and Gretchen discuss religious beliefs.

the expedition, he yields increasingly to his human destiny: 'he did begin to falter, and was at last openly wearing his sores that he had kept hidden' (p. 387).

Reinforcing the conflict between Voss' attempt to create his own destiny and the natural course of destiny itself is the strong tension throughout between chaos and order, a tension that is reflected stylistically in a number of ways. The high number of short sentences and the frequency of one-sentence paragraphs contribute to the sense of chaos. When Laura receives Voss in the opening pages, for instance, movement, sound and behaviour contend against each other:

> She was the expert mistress of trivialities. The distressed German was rubbing the pocket of his jacket with one hand. It made a noisy, rough sound.
>
> He began to mumble.
>
> 'Thank you,' he said.
>
> But grumblingly. (p. 13)

Countering the movement towards chaos and fragmentation that keeps surfacing in the book are the forces of order and reason. The large number of 'because' sentences illustrate White's attempt to impose logic and stability upon a world in continual upheaval: 'Because he was rich and among the first to arrive, he had acquired a goodish slice of land' (p. 135). Likewise, the frequent 'so that' sentences suggest a course of events moving in ordered sequence, according to logic: 'So that after the midday halt ... Voss called his men and divided his strength into several parts' (p. 202). If, according to White, 'Order does prevail' (p. 14), the novel shows instead that upheaval and mutability continue to threaten.

Several stylistic characteristics contribute to the sense of a complex world always undergoing change. The very frequent occurrence of 'begin to'/'began to' suggests a world in process or in inchoate state. There are six instances of it in the first chapter alone (pp. 13, 14 twice, 16, 25–26).

And there are many sentences beginning with 'as', which tend to point to things in process: 'As the sun mounted, the skin was tightening on their skulls' (p. 208). The many 'but' sentences, too, suggest a world of forces in contention: 'She might have elected to share her experience with some similar mind, if such a mind had offered. But there was no evidence of intellectual kinship in any of her small circle of acquaintance' (p. 12).

An important aspect of *Voss* that marks it off from the earlier novels but that looks ahead to the following novels is the sense of distance between its characters and between the novel and its readers. The distance between the characters is there from the very beginning, first between Laura and Rose, then between Laura and Voss; they do not seem to look at one another, only at objects in the room. Throughout the novel characters talk *at* one another, not *to* one another. Overwhelmingly the conversations in *Voss* are between two people, not wider groups, but they do not conduce to intimacy and do not even seem much concerned with communication. They often have a mildly accusatory or defensive aspect:

> 'I came on foot,' [said] the German …
>
> 'From Sydney!' she said.
>
> 'It is four kilometres, at most, and perhaps one-quarter.'
>
> 'But monotonous.'
>
> 'I am at home,' he said. 'It is like the poor parts of Germany. Sandy.' (p. 13)

But the chief factor that produces the sense of distance in the novel is White's habit of continually interrupting the conversations with large blocks of commentary of his own between a remark uttered and the response to it. These blocks can be half a page or longer, and they are frequently filled with complex sentences. Such intrusions not only distance the characters from one another and the novel from the reader but also remove the creator from the work as he becomes so caught up in his observations and the complex sentence structures in which he houses them that he is less immediately concerned with the characters and the story. The sentences are at times quite Proust-like, as when the Bonners and their guests return from church as Laura converses with Voss:

> crowding in, resuming possession. Such solid stone houses, which seem to encourage brooding, through which thoughts slip with the ease of shadow, yet in which silence assumes a sculptural shape, will rally surprisingly, even cruelly to the owner-voices, making it clear that all the time their rooms have belonged not to the dreamers, but to the children of light, who march in, and throw the shutters right back. (p. 18)

Since White is an extremely careful stylist, one has to consider why he holds the novel at arm's length from the reader. The answer may have to do with his aim of creating a myth around an overreacher and a strong-minded woman who will not accept a role inferior to his. They, and the novel built around them, are removed to a plane of existence beyond that of ordinary mortals and we must watch across the gulf that separates us, the distance inviting respect. They stand like two colossi 'with their legs apart ... the better to grip the reeling earth' (p. 96) beneath them. One reads *Voss* with a certain awe.

In *Riders in the Chariot* White turned from historical myth to religious myth, from the exploration of Australia to the Biblical Chariot transporting the Throne of God to Australia. He is again treating a theme of high seriousness and, as in *Voss*, maintains a distancing of the characters and the novel itself from the readers. It is White's most directly religious work, but it has inset within it passages of derisive satire of the Australia to which he would convey the Throne of God. There are two contrasting styles in the novel, then, the main one directed towards the promotion of spiritual values and the other towards the mockery of whatever White hated at the time in Australian society. Both the spiritual and the satirical style have finer differences within them as White focuses on the specific object of his approval in the former case or of scorn in the latter. The spiritual style, associated with Mary Hare, Himmelfarb, Mrs

Godbold and Alf Dubbo, his four illuminates, is dignified and rather formal on the whole, but all four are portrayed with stylistic features that distinguish them from one another in keeping with their vastly different backgrounds and concepts of God. The satirical style is associated with three groups: the malicious gossips Mrs Jolley and Mrs Flack, the renegade Jews Harry and Shirl Rosetree, and the society ladies who meet at a luncheon in the final chapter. These three groups—the trouble-making gossips, the renegade Jews, and the society ladies—have less in common with one another than the illuminates do and show correspondingly a wider range of stylistic characteristics appropriate to the nature and social class of each group.

In *Riders in the Chariot*, unlike the other novels, the vocabulary provides few clues to the essence of a character. Nor does the sentence length or the frequency of sentence fragments tell us much more. Since he was promoting a highly individual religious theme, White probably did not want to overload the novel with stylistic experimentation. His chief stylistic concern is with choosing an appropriate diction for each character: its tone, its formality or informality, its literary level. And he avails himself of metaphor and imagery to depict character and convey his theme, as he did in *The Aunt's Story*; indeed, the central concept of the novel is itself a metaphor.

White was on the whole less at ease with his illuminates than with his anti-visionaries. His illuminates are all marginalised, and their links to the Chariot and to one another are tenuous and manipulated (Mrs Godbold, for instance, knows it only from a hymn). They do not come together to form small groups as the anti-visionaries do. Himmelfarb, a German Jew, is an academic in his early profession, passive and withdrawn in personality, and so is presented respectfully in formal language, with melancholy overtones. Alf Dubbo, a half-caste Aborigine of extraordinary talents, is presented in language that is neutral, for various constraints were operating upon White in portraying an Indigenous Australian. Mrs Godbold is kind and polite, but in ways common to most of humanity—the greatest claim made for her is that she wipes up someone else's vomit, something that nearly all of us have done at some stage—so that she lacks a strong individuality. Her conversation is laced with moral terms and she is ruled by duty (p. 282). It is Miss Hare, a sort of latter-day Theodora Goodman, who receives most stylistic attention. The sentences associated with her are jagged and erratic, like her course from the post office to Xanadu at the beginning of the novel (pp. 12–13), and in sentences like this:

> The slope, gentle at first, climbed to abrupter terraces, with dispensations of ferns and moss, and soft, rotting carpets, and there the trees, it seemed, grew straighter, taller and invariably she would turn dizzy if she stared too long upward at their scintillating crowns. (pp. 22–23)

All the illuminates are assailed in some way: Mary Hare is torn at by blackberry bushes (p. 7), Himmelfarb wears clothes that do not fit him (pp. 335–36), Mrs Godbold is prone to minor accidents (p. 305), and Alf repeatedly allows himself to be misused by the people around him. They are inward turned, unassertive, and the vocabulary in which they are represented is generally nondistinctive. It is only when they make their final appearance that White elevates them by according to each of them a vocabulary of transfiguration. Mary's disappearance is told of in a series of present participles: as she is 'being dispersed' she is 'entering her final ecstasy', 'walking and walking' but 'never arriving' (p. 493), suggesting the continuity of a timeless existence. Himmelfarb's soul carries him forward as it flows on a stream towards the source of existence (pp. 490–91). Alf experiences the ecstasy of a vision of the Chariot that he expresses in paint, then dies as his blood overflows his hands, gilding them 'with his own gold' (p. 515). Mrs Godbold is surrounded by images of light, gold, jewels and music as the novel concludes (pp. 550–52).

The chief means by which White indicates his rejection of his various anti-visionaries is through derision. Stylistically, he conveys this in the case of the suburban housewives Mrs Jolley and Mrs Flack and the desperately conformist Rosetrees by underlining their poor speech habits (like 'strickly' for 'strictly') and their bad grammar. So Mrs Jolley is damned when she uses a triple negative in 'You do not know me … any more than you don't know nothing at all' (p. 59), Mrs Flack when she says 'you was' and 'they was', and Harry Rosetree when he protests 'I done nothink' (p. 228).

More effective is White's cultivation of a highly polished style of his own and a precisely targeted wit to demolish the social pretensions of the three society women meeting at a luncheon near the end of the novel. If one is disturbed by the malice of his wit, one is also arrested by its brilliance. It looks back to Adelaide Blenkinsop's dinner party in *The Living and the Dead* and ahead to Cherry Cheeseman's dinner party in *The Eye of the Storm*. As the three ladies advance to their desirable table, we are told that while they cling to the chromium handrail 'to prevent their heels pitching them head-first at their goal … the cutlery on all the tables seemed to applaud their arrival' (p. 537). Their bizarre hats are mocked rather than praised when they are called 'amusing', and they themselves are diminished by being alluded to by the shape of their hats rather than their names: the Volcano, the Bon-bon and the Crab-shell. White locates social pretension in insecure human beings in order to heighten his deflation of it and of them: so the Volcano smiles 'for the blinding bulbs of two photographers, and because she was trying to ignore the arthritis in her knees' (p. 538). He dismisses the women finally as superfluous: 'each of the three tried to remember where she should go next' (p. 545). Social satire produced some of White's most brilliant, and most unsympathetic, writing. It became a hallmark of his style in his later novels.

In some respects, *The Solid Mandala* is an extension of *Riders in the Chariot*. There is the same split between illuminate (Arthur) and anti-visionary (his twin brother Waldo), and the same idea of the illuminate having special access to a higher world through an esoteric symbol: the Chariot in the earlier novel, the mandala here. But in the five years between *Riders in the Chariot* and *The Solid Mandala*, White's negative attitudes hardened, his mood darkened, and his style grew more derisive. The brief opening section entitled 'In the Bus' begins with an amusing, if unkind, account of two uneducated housewives travelling into the city to spend the day 'muckin' around the big shops' (p. 11). Its broad humour (chiefly focused on the hysterical Mrs Dun) is intended to lighten the tone of the rest of the novel. But the section that follows, entitled 'Waldo', immediately propels us into Waldo's mind, his sour outlook upon others, his proneness to project onto them his own worst qualities. His opening remark accuses his brother Arthur of his own unhealthy habit: 'Put on your coat, and we'll go for a walk … Otherwise you'll sit here brooding' (p. 23). Most of this section, which occupies some two thirds of the book, records what is taking place within Waldo's mind, for he does not initiate personal interaction. *The Solid Mandala* has the least conversation in White's novels. The vocabulary is heavily and consistently negative and the sentences are usually long, advancing the narrative only slowly in order to reflect Waldo's sense of feeling trapped (pp. 23, 76, 83, 145–46). When he is excited and flustered, however, the sentences are short or fragmented, as when he puts on his dead mother's dress. On that occasion he dislodges a lamp, which breaks:

> He kicked at the pieces. And went back.
>
> To the great dress. Obsessed by it. Possessed. His breath went with him, through the tunnel along which he might have been running. Whereas he was again standing. Frozen by what he was about to undertake. (p. 193)

While White does use long sentences to suggest Waldo's brooding, he makes use in this novel of an additional new and effective device: long, monotonal paragraphs that record Waldo's obsessiveness. When Dulcie Feinstein plays the *Moonlight Sonata*, for instance,

> Waldo at once knew how wrong he had been to encourage her to make an exhibition of herself. Needn't have accepted, of course, if she hadn't wanted to. But it was going to be a heroic struggle.

> Not in the beginning, not in the *Adagio what's-it.* There she could lay the atmosphere on, and did, in almost visible slabs. Dulcie's ever so slightly hairy arms were leaning on the solid air, first one side, then the other ... (pp. 134–35)

And so the paragraph continues. At times White arranges the long paragraphs in a series (see, for instance, pp. 53–54, 75–76, 78–79, 106, 116–18, 191–93). He continued to experiment with style throughout his career in order to achieve a specific effect.

Arthur's vocabulary in his section of the novel ('Arthur') is positive or, more precisely, unresentful. He recognises, for instance, that his employer's wife, Mrs Allwright, does not like him, and leaves it at that: 'It did not disturb him ... nor that she should continue to dislike' (p. 226). His distinctive way of thinking of people is to attach a 'who' phrase to their name as a way of attributing a role to them. So we find him thinking of 'the person who was Mother's Uncle Charlie' (p. 217), 'Mr Allwright, who didn't say an awful lot' (p. 222), 'Waldo who knew how to think' (p. 229), 'Mother who knew better than anyone how things ought to be done' (p. 229). The phrases are always acceptant, not critical, of others, and serve to heighten the contrast between him and Waldo.

Mrs Poulter in the opening section of the novel ('In the Bus') exhibits uneducated speech habits: slurred speech ('payshow' for 'patio') and bad grammar ('mightn't of', 'wouldn't of', 'we was' and 'they was', 'we come' for 'we came'). In *Riders in the Chariot* those speech habits would have marked her out as an anti-visionary like Mrs Jolley or Mrs Flack. When she reappears in the final section ('Mrs Poulter and the Zeitgeist') she shows the same speech mannerisms, and in addition her preoccupation with material comforts is emphasised:

> They had bought the plastic awnings for the front. She had the electricity, she had the phone ... She had the radio, but no longer used it all that much, not since they got the telly ... You couldn't complain. Not with the electric frying-pan—never used her oven

now … If she didn't have any friends … she didn't need any. (p. 295)

That combination of uneducated speech and material concerns does not condemn her here; instead, she is elevated in this final section into one of White's saints, performing charitable deeds similar to those of Mrs Godbold. At the very end of the novel, after she has experienced the shock of finding Waldo's mutilated body and has seen Arthur taken off to a mental home, she quietly gives her husband his dinner and then turns 'to do the expected things, before entering her actual sphere of life' (p. 216). In attributing a special inner life to her—even if grudgingly, in the concluding sentence, where it is not developed—White severed the link he had forged between uneducated speech and moral flaws in *Riders in the Chariot*. But he still cannot resist the temptation to make fun of uneducated people.

The family that Hurtle Duffield is born into in *The Vivisector* is poorly educated, of low social status and speech habits to match. It is not for their speech habits that White takes Hurtle out of his family, however, but for artistic reasons: Hurtle's talents, he believes, would not have come to fruition in that environment. White gives Hurtle different speech habits as he moves up in society. As a very young boy, he speaks in short sentences and sometimes reflects his family's uneducated usages ('edgercation', 'droring', 'we was') but never drops the final '-g' in his verbal forms ('I'm reading'), a carefulness in speech that is intended to draw our attention to his superior intelligence. His diction and his syntax improve quickly and his sentences become longer when he lives with the Courtneys. When he asks his stepfather, 'Shall I be able to touch one [a sheep]?' he uses a 'shall' form he has picked up from the Courtneys; even among educated people, 'shall' was already rare in early twentieth century Australia.

White himself varies the diction with which he tells of Hurtle's development as he goes through life. The sentences he uses to tell of Hurtle's life as a boy are mostly of the subject + verb + object type. But once

Hurtle becomes an adult, estranged from humanity at large by his way of life as an artist and by his own personality, White uses specific linguistic devices to emphasise the sense of distance between Hurtle and the people around him. One of those devices is an extraordinarily high number of sentences beginning with adverbial clauses or phrases, thereby deferring the subject and so diminishing the force of the main statement of the sentence:

> As he continued gently stroking paint to life under the eyes of this *voyeuse*, he and [she] could have reached one of the peaks of their relationship' (p. 315); 'In spite of the warning in the letter, he hadn't been prepared for such a ruthless departure' (p. 356); 'At some point he was infected with her [sexual] appetite, and took over. (p. 363)

White also frequently uses participial phrases at the beginning of sentences to defer the main statement and weaken its force. Here is a sentence in which the main statement is twice removed, first by a participial phrase, then by an adverbial:

> Moving across the room, back to the crush of tepid blankets waiting for him in his bed, he knew the real source of his gloom was the probability that Kathy would *not* come before Rhoda was installed. (p. 469)

White uses linguistic devices to indicate that life happens to Hurtle at a remove.

Hurtle is in many respects a projection of White himself, and that may be why White used him as a medium for a brilliant display of verbal pyrotechnics. Hurtle's two strokes, marked by speech fragmentation and confusion, give White opportunities for the kind of word play that he loved, similar to that in dream sequences in his earlier novels but more refined in technique, for Hurtle remains conscious enough to edit his thoughts. The first stroke affects Hurtle's hearing as well as his vision for a time: 'The colours vibrating. Too vivid … Noises too tambourines great bong gongs of brass never got the clap ever and o-boes good word the bells bells bells' (p. 571). The fact that he 'never got the clap' comes to his mind reveals his sense of never quite getting the approval he wanted and also betrays a feeling of limited sexual fulfilment, freedom from a venereal disease representing the most notable aspect of his sexual life. The second and fatal stroke comes as he finishes his greatest painting, having captured the celestial indigo (N-D-G-O) he has striven for beyond himself, using a gift that came from outside himself: that would explain his omission of the two personal I's. 'This is this iss hizz Miss the paint iss' (his masterpiece), he hears Don remark (p. 642). He is again distracted by noises in his head, as during his first stroke: 'Why all the hissing and whizzing might piss it out', he fears, but immediately decides it will not—'no the INDIGO decisive it'. Carping criticism by art critics 'hissing and whizzing' will not diminish what he knows is his masterpiece. Hurtle's alternating hopes and doubts of eternal life are suggested in his interpretation of Rhoda's 'My dear-rest Lord' as referring to a God in whom he can rest. They occupy his own final moment of consciousness: 'Too tired too end-less obvi indi-ggoddd'. Too tired for anything else, he can accept that he will rest either in endless oblivion or in God in heaven ('indi-ggoddd'). There is a conciseness and fluency and confidence in these passages depicting Hurtle's strokes that White never surpassed.

The vocabulary at the beginning of *The Vivisector* is not negative; it is concerned rather with establishing the intelligence and curiosity of the young boy Hurtle, who is constantly asking questions. But the epigraphs to the novel, from Ben Nicholson, William Blake, Saint Augustine and Rimbaud, convey a powerful sense of the agony of the artist in his life-long quest for understanding and truth. The epigraphs cast a shadow over the whole work. They are filled with a vocabulary of frustration and suffering, qualities that the novel illustrates abundantly: 'searching', 'Cruelty', 'Jealousy', 'Terror', 'Secrecy', 'forged in Iron', 'a fiery Forge', 'a Furnace seal'd', 'hungry Gorge', 'hate', 'great Invalid', 'great Criminal', 'great Accursed One'. They anticipate the image of the 'crook-neck white pullet'

(p. 7), a metaphor for the creative artist as an aberration in early twentieth-century Australia, alienated from his own family and from society at large:

> the white crook-neck thing, white, too, about the wattles, stood around grabbing what and whenever it could, but sort of sideways.
>
> 'Why're the others pecking at it, Pa?'
>
> 'Because they don't like the look of it. Because it's different.'

The rest of the book carries the weight of that metaphor: the artist is different and is exploited by others. But White also portrays the artist as exploitive in turn: the artist is vivisector as well as vivisected. It is a concept more negative than insightful, and ultimately demeaning to the idea of creativity.

In *The Eye of the Storm* White continues trying to understand his artistic gift, this time in terms of his family background. Having a wider perspective than in *The Vivisector*, he is less self-preoccupied: *The Eye of the Storm* tells the story of the family in which he grew up, sometimes modified in its details, sometimes disguised. White himself is represented in the persona of Sir Basil, but the novel is centred on his elderly mother and controlled in all its aspects by his ambivalence towards her, reflecting the intense relationship that governed his life. Whether in competition with his mother, deferring to her, or hating her, White was never able to assert his independence of her.

White's revisiting of his family in this novel, when he was in his early sixties and his parents and sister were dead (his mother the most recently, in 1963), unleashed negative emotions in him. *The Eye of the Storm* is in fact the most consistently negative of his works. The narrative is an accretion of episodes that move one after another towards a sense of failure: Dorothy's marriage to the French prince, Flora's relationship with Snow, her affair with Basil and her final abandonment of nursing, Mary de

Santis' visit to Basil, Dorothy and Elizabeth's competition for Edvard Pehl's interest, Basil and Dorothy's visit to Kudjeri.

White's attitude throughout is one of derision, and the vocabulary is one of distaste or aversion, complaint or accusation. Words like 'mangy', 'grotty', 'muzzy', 'frowsty', 'slommacky', 'grubby', 'wheezy', 'surly', 'horse-faced', 'wrung-out' and 'stumpy' abound. People are recorded not as speaking but as 'clucking', 'daring', 'protesting', 'insisting', 'gasping', 'moaning', 'nattering', 'wheedling', 'whinging', 'bashing', 'announcing', 'complaining', 'blubbing' and 'glugging'. White even creates derisive words of his own. It is human clumsiness and vulgarity that he emphasises as his characters paddle 'in the shallows of social intercourse' (p. 64): they do not move regularly but 'stumble', 'stagger', 'slam around', 'flounder', 'totter', 'sway', 'tittup', 'lurch', 'stomp', 'lounge about' or 'plonk down'.

At the centre of this imperfect world, however, there is one force that belongs to a higher dimension: Elizabeth herself, and that is despite the destructive qualities that he attributes to her. There are hints throughout that she is marked out for a kind of transfiguration: at the very beginning where she is described as lying in 'a bloom of moonstones' (she is regularly associated with gemstones), at the climax of the novel where she confronts God at the eye of the storm, and in her Cleopatra-like death elevated upon the throne of her commode. Lottie Lippmann's cabaret song shortly before her death sums up Elizabeth's role. In this '*Welt für leere Laffen/Ein Zirkus mit dressierten Affen*' [world of dull nerds, a circus with its trained monkeys], we are assured through Elizabeth's very existence of the power of regeneration: '*Am selben Platz wo sie verwelken/Da wachsen wieder andere Nelken*' [in the same place where carnations wither, others grow again] (pp. 444–45).

But White is far more concerned throughout with destruction than with elevation. He continually analyses and exposes the pettiness of his characters and their frequently irritating ways of behaving. In this most analytical of his novels, it is almost always the uglier side of human motives that he points to. (It is no coincidence that 'uglily' is the favourite adverb of his own creation, appearing here on page 22 as in most of his novels.) Only once in the work is 'compassion' attributed to a character, to Dorothy as she approaches Basil's wound at Kudjeri, their old family home, where they shortly afterwards sink into an incestuous episode (pp. 525–27). *The Eye of the Storm* is a tortured novel, but the torture is of White's own creation.

White extends his disdain for his cast of characters to himself in his portrait of Sir Basil, knighted for his talents as an actor (for which read 'distinguished writer') while remaining an ineffectual adult male, especially in the presence of his mother. We are reminded throughout the novel that the ultimate obstacle to his ability to master the role of Lear is her own more assured command of it. The first meeting of mother and son in the novel is described in the vocabulary of a scene in the theatre as Basil endeavours to drive his mother into the role of an understudy. While they both acquit themselves well as actors—

> probably neither of them was more than formally conscious of an audience: which is how it becomes on those evenings when all the elements of a performance, on either side of the footlights, are perfectly fused. (p. 123)

—neither emerges as a fully developed human being. Basil's competition with his mother inevitably suggests White's own relationship to his mother, a thwarted attempt to best her, a relationship that directs the course of this novel.

Since *The Eye of the Storm* is a brooding, obsessive novel, acutely and negatively analytical, it is not surprising that White's sentences are longer than usual. Although he was in general not much disposed to a Proustian mode of writing, he was occasionally seduced into it here as, intermittently, elsewhere. There are a number of Proustian passages of long, highly structured sentences laced with abstractions: the analytical style characteristic of Proust matches White's own sustained analysis of his cast. As Dorothy prepares to go to Cherry Cheeseman's dinner party, she decides on her Patou black dress,

> of such an urbane simplicity it had often ended by scaring the scornful into a bewildered reassessment of their own canons of taste. And the diamonds; everyone must bow to those: their fire too unequivocally real, their setting a collusion between class and aesthetics. (p. 286)

But the more poetic Patrick White can never be altogether suppressed, and there are memorable passages of sheer lyricism and subtle cadences scattered throughout, as in the account of Flora Manhood's return home at dusk:

> Night was still in its brown stage: the sound of feet was not yet divorced from plodding bodies; you could still read the makes of cars, whereas in another quarter of an hour, all would be swallowed up in a great rubbery volume of traffic. If the lit windows of houses offered a human belief in permanence, the oil refineries ablaze down Botany way suggested other worlds, other more demoniac values. (p. 176)

Heaven and hell are never quite out of sight in White's worldview.

In the last four serious novels of his career, *The Vivisector*, *The Eye of the Storm*, *A Fringe of Leaves* and *The Twyborn Affair*, White is noticeably more prone to reflection and analysis than to the use of conversation. He removes himself from his characters in his preference for analysing them rather than showing them interacting: it is as if his faith in human interaction had declined. The conversations in this novel become depersonalised through the reduced frequency and force in them of the pronoun 'I'. Even when the characters use 'I', the 'I' may convey little that is personal: expressions like 'I'd say', 'I'm sure', I don't know', 'I don't doubt that …' and 'I should have thought that …' gloss over essentially impersonal statements. 'I' phrases that soften an unpleasant fact or announcement, as in 'I can't answer for [the water's] purity' or 'I've got a disappointment for you … Basil has been delayed at Bangkok' (p. 26), also express no real personal involvement on the speaker's part. The only character in *The Eye of the Storm* who uses 'I' freely is the formidable Elizabeth, and with her it is an assertion of self rather than a desire to communicate.

In *The Eye of the Storm* White saw almost nothing positive in human motives as he repeatedly peeled away layers of social pretension to expose the self-concern beneath. The main story, paralleling *Lear*, highlights the theme of betrayal, of parent by children, but White plays a number of variations upon the theme of betrayal: Flora Manhood betrays both Col and Basil by sleeping with Basil, Basil betrays Mary de Santis by getting her drunk, and Arnold Wyburd betrays Elizabeth by stealing the star sapphire, perhaps in retaliation for her seduction of him as a young man. And there are ten pages of sustained derision aimed at social masquerade in his account of Cherry Cheeseman's dinner party for Dorothy (p. 288f). The derision begins from the moment Dorothy arrives to find several of the company swaying on their heels,

> the level of alcohol in the Georgian tumblers clamped against their waists tilting, and in one case spilling down a pale blue front.
>
> The pale blue lady, crimson to purple in the cheeks, was her hostess, Dorothy de Lascabanes saw: pretty, glossy Cherry … swollen into a festive turkey. (p. 290)

And White proceeds to strip the layers from all the guests. The one kindly guest, the elderly Lady Atkinson, who delights in her grandchildren, is totally unaware of their extreme sadism: 'Last week they pulled the legs off a clutch of live chickens, and poked out their eyes with sticks. But that isn't what Grannie sees' (p. 297). At this dinner party, White the writer becomes White the vivisector.

In *A Fringe of Leaves* he continues to remove layers of white European civilisation from his protagonist Ellen Roxburgh, stripping her literally naked and subjecting her to all the hardships of unaccommodated man. Only the wedding ring that Ellen has threaded onto the fringe of leaves she wears around her waist remains to tie her to the social rank and moral values that were hers before the shipwreck. But even as White continued stripping away the layers from the body and soul of his characters in *A Fringe of Leaves*, he simultaneously gave himself over with obvious pleasure to the stylistic possibilities offered by the story. Perhaps his being awarded the Nobel Prize in Literature in 1973, between the completion of *The Eye of the Storm* and the undertaking of *A Fringe of Leaves*, helped him look more positively upon the world; it was certainly an immensely gratifying vindication of his dedication to literature over a period of nearly forty years.

There is no single style in the novel; rather, there are three different stylistic modes, each adapted to the successive stages and locales of the story. First there is the highly formal nineteenth-century style of the story of Ellen's youth and marriage and visit to Australia; this stage ends in the wreck of the ship in which she is returning to England. The second stage is rendered in a simpler style, closer to that of the 1970s, as it tells of Ellen's life with a tribe of Aborigines and her escape with the convict Jack Chance, who helps her to return to a white settlement. The third stage is narrated again in a somewhat formal style, less formal however than the style of the first stage, as it records Ellen's reintegration into white civilisation, a process in which she no longer needs the wedding ring she has lost. It is as if she is tired now, ready to accept life on its own terms, without undue concern for the layers of European civilisation. Her layers having been stripped off, she is in the process of healing. She will have a new marriage, financial security again, and three foster-children to replace her three children by Austin that she had lost.

Although the action of *A Fringe of Leaves* takes place only twelve years before that of *Voss* (in 1836 against 1848), the style suggests nineteenth-century usage more strongly than does that of *Voss*. White cultivated a dignified, formal style in *Voss*, but did not have the same steady concern there with achieving a specifically nineteenth-century quality: he was concerned rather with heightening the mythic aspects of the novel and for that purpose chose to use a style reminiscent rather of the King James' Bible. There is no mythologising in *A Fringe of Leaves*; Ellen is not, like Voss, an overreacher. Accordingly, the 'So' sentences of *Voss*, which are frequently used to convey a sense of destiny ('So they advanced into that country which now possessed them', p. 208), become ordinary result clauses in *A Fringe of Leaves* ('So she sat back and allowed the rain to drench her', p. 197). In seeking to recreate a formal early nineteenth-century literary style in *A Fringe of Leaves*, White was endeavouring to dignify and enhance his well-told but, in comparison with *Voss*, unpretentious narrative—and he clearly enjoyed the stylistic experimentation. He availed himself of such nineteenth-century mannerisms as precisely balanced sentences, old subjunctive constructions, and the avoidance of colloquial contractions in speech; and he again used frequent participial phrases and deferred subjects to establish a formal distance to his narrative, as he had in *The Vivisector*.

White was fond of balanced sentences from the beginning of his career, but he never used them so liberally as here, and his style is the more formally precise accordingly. His 'if' sentences, which early became one of the trademarks of his style, remain one of his favourite forms of balanced sentences: 'If his mouth had tightened, his ordinarily gaunt, erect head lolled softly on his shoulders' (p. 14). But he has a wider range of balanced sentences in this novel, beginning most commonly with 'as' or its alternates 'while' (pp. 9, 19, 24, 32), 'whereas' (p. 299), and 'although' (pp. 17, 33, 41). White also occasionally uses a subjunctive construction now in disuse to impart a nineteenth-century quality to his story: the 'had' construction as in 'had she wanted to' (p. 179). A formal construction even in the 1830s, the period in which *A Fringe of Leaves* is set, it has become almost obsolete in modern usage: the example quoted, 'had she wanted to', would be replaced by an 'if' construction, 'if she had wanted to'. But it is still common in literary German (*hätte sie gewollt*), and that may be why it occurred to White to use it so frequently (see, e.g., pp. 41, 57, 74, 136, 151, 191, 253, 262).

White avoided contracted forms of verb and pronoun (like 'I'll') or verb and negative (like 'don't') in *Voss*, his other nineteenth-century novel, but did so less consistently there than in *A Fringe of Leaves*. These contractions were not common in the early nineteenth century—say, in Jane Austen's novels—but rapidly accelerated in usage in the latter half of the century. In both *Voss* and *A Fringe of Leaves* the uncontracted forms serve to convey White's commitment to historical accuracy in speech, but they take on an extra dimension in *A Fringe of Leaves*, where they act as indicators of social rank and education and so point to the differing layers of culture in the characters. Austin, from an aristocratic family, almost always uses the older, formal uncontracted forms, and Ellen endeavours to follow his example when she marries Austin. In her life with Jack in the bush, however, she drops them along with all the social layers that she had acquired since her marriage. She resumes the formal lack of contractions when she returns to white civilisation late in the novel: 'I shall do my best to behave as I am expected to' (p. 351).

In keeping with his desire to maintain a formal quality to the novel, White again uses devices he found effective in *Voss*, *The Vivisector*, and *The Eye of the Storm*, sentences beginning with participial phrases. Such sentences are a ready means of raising the literary level of the language; they are in fact amongst the most literary constructions in English. French in origin, they entered written English after the Norman Conquest without ever quite making it into spoken English, and so remain one of the boundaries between the written and the spoken language. They occur most commonly in *A Fringe of Leaves* in the first, formal stage of the novel, where hardly a page of the narrative goes by without one (e.g., pp. 59–61, 64, 67). Present and past participial constructions alternate in quick succession: 'On waving good-bye to her departing callers Mrs Roxburgh went below', where, 'Seated the other side of the table, … she resumed her work' (pp. 22–23). From French, too, come

White's occasional triplets—groups of three adjectives, three noun phrases, or three verbs. These are a feature of Old French romance that one finds in Joseph Bédier's *Le Roman de Tristan et Iseut*, which White used for Ellen's dreams of Tintagel and her life with Jack in the forest. So Captain Purdew 'gave orders in a level, aged, but disciplinary voice' (p. 183); Miss Scrimshaw in 'her brown gown, her padded hair, her bobbled shawl, stood looking out' (p. 373); a young woman 'of noticeably Irish countenance, black frowzy ringlets, and [thick] lashes ... greeted the stranger jauntily' (p. 373). White liked his acquisition of triplets, which have an inherent charm, and went on to use them freely in *The Twyborn Affair*.[15]

A device that White availed himself of to give a sustained formal quality to the style of *A Fringe of Leaves* is his use of deferred subjects. Being deferred, a subject (an action, a personage, or an emotion) is removed to a distance where we can observe it without being invited to share in it, much as we experience a myth or legend. Some pages are packed with deferred subjects:

> In the second year of their marriage she conceived ... Even to those aware of the train of events, young Mrs Roxburgh did not look less handsome ... From carriage or chaise she returned her acquaintances' greetings ... On days when she took little walks through the grounds her mother-in-law might accompany her. Grown infirm since the tragedy, old Mrs Roxburgh hung on her arm ... (p. 76)

---

[15] Instances of triplets abound in *The Twyborn Affair*: 'Mrs Golson was jolted, swayed, tossed onward in her ... motor-car'. See also pp. 14, 23, 29, 35, 40, 45–46, 53–55, 71, 75, 83, 88. White's fondness for triplets late in his career illustrates his continued readiness to accept a new stylistic influence. And he remained romantic enough to be charmed by Bédier's masterly version of the great love story.

White's use of deferred subjects in this novel is an effective way of heightening the sense of a past in which legends were created.

Being formal in its style, *A Fringe of Leaves* is inclined to long sentences, which are most noticeable in the first stage of the novel. There are passages so carefully structured that they virtually announce formal style, like the account of Ellen and Austin preparing to abandon their cabin:

> They began to scale the floor of the listing cabin, clinging with one hand to their sole article of luggage, with the second, clawing at any support offered by furniture or fitments, and after the same fashion, once through the doorway, navigated what had been the saloon. Neither would have admitted to the other that water had penetrated, when there it was lying before their eyes, oozing and lapping, an antithesis of ocean—a black, seeping treacle which the plush table cloth failed to stanch, while a teasel-shaped flower they had brought back on an afternoon at Sydney Cove was too light and withered to have been sucked under as yet. (p. 169)

There are passages so complex in their correctness that they recall Proust, but without Proust's finesse:

> From their perch they sat looking back at the one who had them in his keeping and who, they hoped, was possessed of benign wisdom and superhuman powers in spite of resembling an old, moulted member of the same species, Adam's apple working above a dirty collar, blue-red flesh thinly stretched over such bones as were visible, and deposits of salt on drooping lids and in the corners of disillusioned eyes. (p. 174)

At times White overwrites and then his sentences become clogged:

> In the course of the day, incoming tribes joined those already encamped, who greeted the new arrivals with bursts of wailing, to signify joy it would seem, whereas [Ellen] had only ever sensed in the chorus at morning and evening the doubts and forebodings of a troubled spirit. (p. 278)

If in his last few novels White fell into the error of overwriting occasionally, he was also capable of quite memorable poetic passages, like the death from drowning of the boy Oswald: 'His arms were raised several times, fists clenched, lips protesting against the mystery of divine prerogative, before the sea put a glassy stopper in his mouth' (p. 215). White's descriptions of death and the transition to another dimension in fact are amongst the finest passages in his novels.[16] Essentially a religious writer, White can express touchingly a profound human need in time of distress: 'She would have liked to pray, but found the vocabulary and the necessary frame of mind for prayer, wrecked inside her' (p. 173). And every so often he creates an arresting metaphor, as in his description of the mizzen mast falling during the shipwreck: 'It fell, broken, bumping, lanyards torn out by the roots. The canvas leaves of the great tree were carried away, to boil like dirty washing in the surf' (p. 178).

Despite its unusual subject matter, *The Twyborn Affair* is a continuation of *A Fringe of Leaves* in structure and in style: both novels fall into three parts, each with a style appropriate to its story. The three parts of *The Twyborn Affair*, however, are specifically labelled 'parts': they do not flow into one another as the three stages of *A Fringe of Leaves* do but rather resemble three separate novellas, linked chiefly by the same protagonist but eluding a clear integration.[17] They are set in three different countries (France, Australia and England), in each of which the protago-

---

[16]White's account of the death of Alex in *Memoirs of Many in One* lifts that novel from a certain flippancy to high seriousness: 'I was hypnotized by what I saw as the moment when the last of human frailty makes contact with the supernatural. "Is it this—then?" she whispered, whether in horror, or ecstasy' (p. 183).

[17] The main theme of the novel is Eddie's relationship with his mother: her name, Eadie, links her closely to him in all three of his names, and she appears in all three parts, becoming reconciled to him at the very end. White's failure to suggest a direct connection between Eddie's sexual identities and his relationship with his mother has left many readers with only a vague idea of what the novel is about.

nist has a different name (Eudoxia, Eddie and Eadith) and a different mode of sexual expression. As Eudoxia he is the lover (in drag) of an elderly Greek man; as Eddie he is the unenthusiastic sexual partner of one woman and one man, on two occasions with each; and as Eadith he is the owner of a London brothel in an assumed feminine identity, constantly involved with other people's sexual activity but refraining from any of his own. (His taking the young Philip, Gravenor's nephew, to bed is an anomaly in a novel of anomalies.)

The vocabulary of *The Twyborn Affair* is on the whole less negative than that of most of its predecessors, for White in his post-Nobel years was less alienated than hitherto. Writing in the late 1970s as an established figure in a more liberal society, he was able to give rein to his sexual fantasies in a way that had not been possible earlier. He was older and in uncertain health, too, and conveys less energy in *The Twyborn Affair* than in any of his works since the early *Happy Valley* and *The Living and the Dead*. He is less concerned with finding targets for his derision: although he intermittently mocks his characters, the predominant mood of this novel is one of unfulfilment rather than negativity. The vocabulary continually suggests uncertainty, but uncertainty is a milder aspect of unfulfilment than outright alienation.

The opening pages of the novel are filled with words expressing uncertainty, establishing that as the dominant mood of the novel: 'ventured', 'teetered', 'tentatively', 'carefully', 'embarrassing', 'defence', 'non-committal', 'intimidated', 'inferior', 'trembling', 'regrettably colonial', 'unacceptably foreign', 'neglected' (pp. 11–13). But the nervous tautness of the opening is followed quickly by a sort of lush decadence when Eudoxia and her elderly lover appear a few pages later. Suddenly we are swimming in the senses, especially of colour and smell:

> the elderly man, a stroke of black and yellow, ivory rather, in a silver landscape, and ahead of him this charming young woman ... leading her companion through the rambling maze, the carnation tones of her dress dragging through, catching on, fusing

> with those same carnations which she reflected, while absorbing something of their silver from the lavender and southernwood surrounding her. (p. 14)

From the very outset White sets up these two clearly differentiated styles that will alternate throughout the novel according to whether the protagonist has a male or female identity. One could call them loosely the male style and the female style. The first is associated with Eddie's life as a male, with his parents in part 1 (in flashback) and in part 2 when he returns to Australia, and with his life as a jackeroo there. And it is the style in which the appearances of a succession of minor characters throughout are recorded. The second style is associated with Eddie's life as Eudoxia in part 1 and as Eadith in part 3, where the decadence takes on an additional hothouse quality from being confined indoors, in a brothel.

In either style, there is a definite deterioration in this late novel in White's stylistic control. Flawed writing erupts sporadically throughout the novel. In the dominant style, associated with Eddie's life as a man, there are passages that are variously overwritten, cluttered, abstract and vague, or constantly shifting in focus. There are long sentences that get tangled in the tendrils of their modifiers or lose their way in a maze of their own creation:

> turning at last in the direction of the suppliant she trained on her a pair of eyes, normally piercing and lustrous, but now so far shuttered by the lids, they might not be prepared to illuminate more than half a secret. (p. 17)

In the lush secondary style, associated with Eddie's life as a woman, there are Swinburnian passages that are given over to their own excesses, luxuriating in an overload of adjectives and emphasis on the senses. The mention of Swinburne's poems as among the books Eddie finds in his old room when he returns home in part 2 (p. 150) suggests that Swinburne formed part of White's own reading as a young man; and Swinburne comes frequently to mind in the novel:

> the landscape would respond, the brown, scurfy ridges, fat valleys opening out of them to disclose a green upholstery, the ascetic forms of dead trees, messages decipherable at last on living trunks. (p. 161)

Whatever is sensual in the novel lies not in the treatment of sex, which is really quite restrained, but in an abandonment to a highly sensual style. It is a stylistic indulgence that White did not repeat in his next novel, *Memoirs of Many in One.*

White's stylistic control is particularly prone to fall apart when one of his characters faces a situation where he or she lacks confidence. The first such situation occurs at the beginning of the novel, as Joan Golson is out for a drive with her English chauffeur, in whose presence she feels inferior:

> As she imagined sharing with her friend Eadie Twyborn her experience of the previous day, Joan Golson found herself straining against upholstery still new enough to give out some of the perfume of leather, raising herself to the extent where her little motoring parasol might be carried off by the blast created by impetuous motion, while she parted the knotted gossamer protecting her face from wind, grit, and suicidal insects, to anticipate the pleasures of what she hoped to re-discover. (pp. 13–14)

One is forced to reread the sentence. The initial 'as' is ambiguous: does it mean 'at the same time as' or 'because'? And is it the upholstery or the veil covering her face that is hindering Joan from experiencing her anticipated pleasures? The sentence is filled with various implied threats—the persistent smell of leather, the possibility of the parasol being blown away, the incommoding veil, the wind, grit, and insects—but they are disparate and none of them is singled out for emphasis. In the clutter of impressions, what finally is the main fact being conveyed?

In the male style of part 2, which tells of Eddie's life as a man, the passages that are most confused and vague are those that occur in situations where Eddie feels lacking in confidence. When he returns to his home after years of unexplained absence, he goes to meet his father in the garden at dusk, wondering ineffectually if he has made a mistake planning the meeting there. White's style is clumsy in structure and unclear in its metaphor: 'Face to face in the dim light favoured in this house might have been less unnerving, underwater shapes drifting harmlessly around as they took each other's measure. Too bad if a predator appeared' (p. 155). One can read 'Face to face' as the subject of 'favoured' before realising that 'favoured' is not a verb but a past participle used as an adjective. The unclear referent of 'they' in 'they took each other's measure' pulls one up as one checks if it refers to the underwater shapes or the two men in the garden. The metaphor of the two as harmless, wary sea creatures is inappropriate in a garden, inconsistent, and further confused by the mention of a third creature, a predator, that has no parallel in the garden where only the two are meeting. White is a master of stream of consciousness technique, but this is not stream of consciousness: it does not directly take place in Eddie's mind, and does not have the series of phrases flowing into one another in an association of ideas that is characteristic of that technique.

The most extended stretch of overwritten descriptions in the novel, however, is that telling of Eddie's nervous arrival in the Monaro district to become a jackeroo (pp. 175–78). He faces a completely different way of life and the uncertainties of existence as a male. The section is too long to analyse, but passages will leap out at the reader in their oddities. This early sentence is a classic example of White's sporadic failure in the novel to maintain a clear focus: 'Rocks, not strewn, but arranged in groups of formal sculpture suggesting prehistoric rites, prevented monotony taking over the bleached foothills'. It implies direct human intervention and human qualities in a scene from which human beings are removed.

The sense-saturated passages are found especially in parts 1 and 3, in which Eddie lives as a woman. In part 1 the chief such passage is the description of M. Pelletier about to see the naked form of Eddie/Eudoxia, which arouses him sexually (pp. 70–74). The flood of senses recorded in the passage is touched off by M. Pelletier's nervous tension over whether the figure is male or female. The situation is erotic, and if the smells with which the passage is saturated are unpleasant ('tortured sheets and sleeping bodies, a full *pot de chambre* and the dregs of a tisane', 'damp newspapers, mildewed cigarettes, and coffee brewing on a spirit lamp') and the colours in which it is painted are drab and unattractive (oily black, grey, dead green, dark against dark), that is because of White's proneness to link sexual desire and nausea.

There is another similar passage in part 2, as Eddie is returning as a man to Australia by boat (pp. 133–37). With his senses stimulated by the colours of the Mediterranean (periwinkle, gold and hyacinth), he looks back with some longing to the south of France where he was a woman, and evokes its scents (thyme, pine, carnation and rose). He is in a state of some nervous uncertainty as he is making a transition from one continent to another and from a female to a male identity. This passage, like the one just discussed, heightens the eroticism of a situation associated with androgyny by steeping it in the senses, and, as in the first passage, quickly undercuts the lush style by a disparaging reference to the fancy dress ball that is about to be held on board, implicitly a sneer at Eddie's life in drag. If the colours of the Mediterranean and the scents of Provence are exciting, the dun colours and synthetic perfumes that White associates with the sexual impulses of human beings in this scene are less than pleasant.

There is a measure of the decline of White's stylistic control in this late novel in his unsuccessful reuse of a metaphor he had used to telling effect thirty years earlier in *The Aunt's Story*. The metaphor tells of the growing threat of World War I in Europe, heightening the threat by opposing the denial of it by the cultured world (represented by libraries) and the fomenting of it by the daily newspapers: 'outside the novels from the library, history was telling a story, only faintly at first, but growing in importance and alarm, until they had begun to put it in the morning paper, in serial form' (p. 94). In *The Twyborn Affair* White presents the same metaphor in a confused, cluttered, overlong sentence:

> Protected by their pink shades the candle-flames stood erect on their island-tables of the Grand Hôtel Splendide des Ligures as the clientele munched, gobbled, sucked up their soup ... while any larger-than-life passions, and the mythic war promised by the newspaper prophets and reinforced by [the librarian] Miss Clitheroe's well-informed sources, were dismissed to a safe distance from this illuminated stucco folly inside its perimeter of slatternly palms, box borders, and regimented marigolds. (p. 70)

The passage gives pre-eminence to candle-flames on tables located, we are told at the very end, in a pretentious hotel; human emotions and any notion of an imminent war are reduced to secondary importance. What most emerges from the passage is White's difficulty in this novel in focusing on the main impression and keeping it clear of distracting details.

White's last novel, *Memoirs of Many in One*, is largely a comic indulgence on his part. As the title suggests, it deals with the several lives within the one person, an interest of White's ever since his first major novel, *The Aunt's Story*, where he first uses the phrase 'several lives' (p. 74). The central section of that novel gives form to those lives in a series of fantasies set in a sort of enchanted garden in a French hotel. The notion of divided or multiple personality—'several lives'—is central in *The Solid Mandala* and again in *The Twyborn Affair*, where the phrase is again used in the text (p. 336). In all these works White takes one character and fragments it in an externalisation of his attempt to understand the many-sidedness in his own creativity, which constantly drew upon different facets of his personality. In *Memoirs of Many in One* he takes a character of his own creation, Alex Gray, and uses the fiction of himself as editor of her memoirs in an attempt to give significance and order to the very different lives he endows her with: 'I I—the great creative ego—had possessed myself of Alex Gray's life … and created from it the many images I needed to develop my own obsessions, both literary and real (p. 192).' Some of her identities are based on reality, like her vain, theatrical persona as the actress Dolly Formosa who travels with a theatre group throughout rural Australia; and some are purely literary, like the manic Alex who gate-crashes a party in Sydney and rides a horse through the assembly in the style of Brünnhilde in *Götterdämmerung*. Alex is always under threat of being tied into a straitjacket, and is finally sent, like Theodora in *The Aunt's Story*, to a mental home, where she dies.

Memoirs of Many in One in fact can read like a version of the kind of fantasy life that Theodora might have led in New Mexico if there had been a part 4 of *The Aunt's Story*. The chief difference is that White treats Alex as a self-deluded and devious comic character, whereas he portrays Theodora with dignity and seriousness (her name, after all, is Goodman), according her as much sympathy as he ever extends to any of his characters. *Memoirs of Many in One* is not a serious work: it is a flight of fancy that White allowed himself at the end of his career as a novelist, and he spent less care on its structure, characterisation and style than in any previous novel. He even makes fun of himself as Suor Angelica's theatrical aunt in Puccini's opera of that name.

There are broad differences in style in the novel, chiefly between that of Patrick the editor and that of Alex the memoirs writer. Both use the first person, but Patrick uses it restrainedly, almost minimally: he is there to give a context for Alex's memoirs, not to tell his own story. He portrays himself as unobtrusive but elusive, teasing the reader with glimpses of the distinguished writer. He assigns to himself a vocabulary of diffidence, of lack of direction or purpose ('boring', 'inverted', 'delicate', 'superficially', 'frayed', 'flowing', 'faintly'), whereas Alex uses the first person frequently and assertively, establishing herself as vain, self-centred and attention-demanding. She tells of her activities with a prodigal use of phrases that present her in a flattering light ('lithe', 'youthful', 'animated', 'natural glow of health', 'I move magnificently') or that convey the ineffectuality of those around her ('silly', 'pathetic', 'no help', 'sulky little thing'). She records much conversation (which keeps her in the spotlight), but, as in *The Eye of the Storm*, there is no sense that the conversations achieve communication between the people conversing. Her style characterises her well, but it is a familiar, colloquial style that has little distinctive and nothing experimental about it. *Memoirs of Many in One* does not sustain the image of White as the careful craftsperson that his previous novels convey. If one can accept the notion of Patrick White enjoying a romp at the end of a distinguished career, then this is that romp.

Style is one of the most reliable sources of information about an author: an author can control revelation of himself through his characters and story line, but he is seldom aware of what his style reveals. What, then, does the study of White's style show about the man, his attitude to life, the world around him, humanity at large?

White's vocabulary reveals a sense of anxiety and uncertainty in so many of his characters. The sense of anxiety is particularly strong in *The Aunt's Story* and in *The Twyborn Affair*, but it appears in other novels also, like *Voss*. The recurrence of this state points to the same condition within White himself. White was by no means the confident writer assured of his genius, and the stony reception he gave to so many people may well have been defensive. He was a man divided. One of his most common themes is that of the divided personality, the 'several lives' that lie within a person and that person's desire to unify them. Stylistically the divisions appear in the opposed styles I have discussed in this essay: the split between the spiritual and the derisive style in *Riders in the Chariot*, between the obsessive, closed style of Waldo and the more open style of Arthur in *The Solid Mandala*, between the male and female styles in *The Twyborn Affair*. These divisions in style strongly reinforce the sense of

White as a man divided in himself that one may gather from *The Aunt's Story*, *Voss* and *The Solid Mandala*.

White's style also reveals his increasing turning away from conversation to reflection and analysis in his later novels, from *Riders in the Chariot* on. His characters engage in little communication in their conversations; mainly, they disagree, criticise or correct one another, defend themselves, or complain. In *The Eye of the Storm* this sort of antagonism is conspicuous from the beginning. The first meeting of Elizabeth and Dorothy consists of a series of implicit accusations and protests. When Elizabeth asks concerning Dorothy's flight, 'Did they feed you properly, darling?' Dorothy answers 'Yes. I saw to that: I travelled Air France … none of your Qantas plastic.' To which Elizabeth responds 'Oh, but darling—Qantas—the best in the world!' (p. 66). And the alienation between the members of the Hunter family extends to Elizabeth's nurses and her cook, who bicker constantly and complain without seeming to know they bicker and complain. The first conversation between Flora Manhood, Sister Badgery and Lottie Lippmann has Flora referring to Elizabeth as Mother Swizzlestick and Sister Badgery protesting at the term, Flora asking Lottie how she can be content as a cook after her career as a cabaret singer and Lottie complaining that her career ended with the gas chambers of Nazi Germany—though she was never sent there (pp. 82–83).

The persistent failure of White's characters to achieve communication reflects his own lack of faith in human communication, an inconsistency in an essentially religious novelist. It is a flaw he must on some level have sensed, and it was probably to cover this weakness that he turned from conversation to an increasingly analytical mode of narration. This habit sets the characters and the works themselves at a distance from the reader, a distance that is reinforced by other stylistic characteristics, like the frequent shifting of the subjects of sentences away from the beginning. White's technical control was as assured as ever in these later novels, but the fact that they are held at arm's length from the reader virtually assures that, with the exception of *A Fringe of Leaves*, they will never gain the acceptance that his earlier novels have.

What this study has most significantly revealed about White's style is how painstakingly he worked upon it. The creation of an original style preoccupied him throughout his career and is one of his most notable achievements. In plot, theme and characterisation his achievements are deeply impressive, but they vary—the plot of *The Tree of Man*, for instance, is thin, the characterisation in *The Solid Mandala* is one-dimensional and the theme of *The Twyborn Affair* is unclear. But he was consistently dedicated to creating a unique style, continually adapting it to character, situation, and theme. On the first of the two occasions I visited him in 1973, I remarked, 'To me, you're one of the great stylists in English.' His whole face softened, and he said from his heart, 'Thank you'.

Bibliography

Adler, Louise (2001). 'The Great Australian Novel'. *Sydney Morning Herald*, 'Spectrum' (13 Oct): 4, 5.

Alain-Fournier (1971). *Le Grand Meaulnes*. Paris: Fayard.

Bart, B.F. (1966). *'Madame Bovary' and the Critics*. New York: New York University Press.

Barthes, Roland (1972). *Mythologies*. Trans. Annette Lavers. New York: Noonday.

Beatson, Peter (1970). 'The Three Stages: Mysticism in Patrick White's *Voss*.' *Southerly*, 30(2): 111–21.

Beatson, Peter (1980). *The Eye in the Mandala. Patrick White: A Vision of Man and God*. New York: St Martin's Press.

Berrichot, Paterne (1897). *La Vie de Jean-Arthur Rimbaud*. Paris: Mercure de France.

Beston, John (1971a). 'Patrick White's *The Vivisector*: The Artist in Relation to His Art'. *Australian Literary Studies*, 5(2): 168–75.

_____(1971b). 'Alienation and Humanisation, Damnation and Salvation in *Voss*.' *Meanjin*, 30(2): 208–16.

_____(1971c). 'Love and Sex in a Staid Spinster: *The Aunt's Story*.' *Quadrant*, 15(5): 22–27.

_____(1972a). 'The Influence of *Madame Bovary* on *The Tree of Man*.' *Revue de Littérature Comparée*, 46: 555–68.

_____(1972b). 'Voss' Proposal and Laura's Acceptance Letter: The Struggle for Dominance in *Voss.*' *Quadrant*, 26: 24–30.

_____(1973). 'Dreams and Visions in *The Tree of Man.*' *Australian Literary Studies*, 6(2): 152–66.

_____(1974a). 'The Influence of John Steinbeck's *The Pastures of Heaven* on Patrick White.' *Australian Literary Studies*, 6: 317–19.

_____(1974b). 'The Family Background and Early Years of Patrick White.' *Descent*, 7: 16–29.

_____(1976). 'Mythmaking in Patrick White: A Stylistic Approach to *The Tree of Man* and *Voss.*' *Echos du Commonwealth,* 3: 134–41.

_____(1979). 'Three Conclusions: *Buddenbrooks, The Aunt's Story* and *Voss.*' *Literary Half-Yearly*, 20(1): 134–41.

_____ (1982). 'The Making of the Artist in Patrick White.' *Commonwealth Novel in English* 1.1: 86–93.

_____(2003a). 'Will *Voss* Endure? Fifty Years Later.' *Antipodes,* 17(1): 50–54.

_____(2003b). '*The Tree of Man* as a Pioneer Novel.' *Antipodes*, 17(2): 149–54.

_____(2004a). 'Stan's Grandson, the Lost Boy, and White's *Ars Poetica* in *The Tree of Man.*' *Commonwealth*, 26(2): 71–76.

_____(2004b). 'Patick White and Theodora Goodman in New Mexico.' *Antipodes*, 18(2): 171–73.

_____(2004c). 'Films and Patrick White.' *Southerly*, 64(3): 176–79.

_____(2005). 'Patrick White and Rimbaud.' *Commonwealth,* 27(2): 99–110.

_____(2006a). 'Why are Epiphanies so Prominant in Patrick White's Novels?' *AUMLA*, 105: 109–21.

_____(2006b). 'Willa Cather and Patrick White.' *Antipodes*, 20(2): 164–68.

Beston, John & Beston, Rose Marie (1972). 'The Black Volcanic Hills of Meroë: Fire Imagery in Patrick White's *The Aunt's Story*'. *Ariel*, 3(4): 33–43.

_____(1974). 'The Theme of Spiritual Progression in *Voss.*' *Ariel*, 5(3): 99–114.

_____(1975). 'The Several Lives of Theodora Goodman: The "Jardin Exotique" Section of Patrick White's *The Aunts Story.*' *Journal of Commonwealth Literature*, 9(3): 1–13.

Birns, Nicholas (1999). 'Weird White: The Allusive Dynamics of Literary History in *The Twyborn Affair.*' *Zeitschrift für Anglistik und Amerikanistik*, 45(3): 219–25.

Bliss, Carolyn (1991). 'Patrick White: Vision and Visions.' In Robert L. Ross (Ed.), *International Literature in English: Essays on the Major Writers*. New York: Garland.

Brissenden, R.F. (1959). 'Patrick White.' *Meanjin*, 18(4): 410–25.

Brown, Ruth (1995). 'The Country, the City, and *The Tree of Man.*' *Modern Language Review*, 90(4): 861–69.

Burrows, J.F (1966). ' "Jardin Exotique": the Central Phase of *The Aunt's Story.*' *Southerly*, 26(3): 152–73.

______ (1969). 'Stan Parker's *Tree of Man.*' *Southerly*, 29(4): 257–79.

Campbell, Joseph (1959). *The Masks of God.* New York: Viking.

Campbell, Joseph & Bill Moyers (1988). *The Power of Myth.* Betty Sue Flowers (Ed.). New York: Doubleday.

Cassirer, Ernst (1979). *Symbol, Myth, and Culture: Essays and Lectures of Ernst Cassirer, 1935–45.* Ed Donald P. Verne. New Haven: Yale University Press.

Cather, Willa (1913). *O Pioneers!* Boston: Houghton Mifflin.

______ (1923). *A Lost Lady.* New York: Knopf.

______ (1927). *Death Comes for the Archbishop.* London: Heinemann.

______ (1946). *My Antonia.* Boston: Houghton Mifflin.

______ (1994). *My Antonia.* New York: Random House.

Collier, Gordon (1992). *The Rocks and Sticks of Words: Style, Discourse and Narrative Structure in the Fiction of Patrick White*. Amsterdam: Rodopi.

Colmer, John (1984). *Patrick White*. New York: Methuen.

______ (1987). 'Duality in Patrick White.' In R. Shepherd & K. Singh (Eds), *Patrick White: A Critical Symposium*. Adelaide: CRNLE, pp. 70–76.

Coupe, Laurence (1997). *Myth*. New York: Routledge.

Crowcroft, Jean (1974). 'Patrick White: A Reply to Dorothy Green.' *Overland*, 59: 49–53.

Cupitt, Don (1982). *The World to Come*. London: SCM.

Davidson, Jim (1990). 'Beyond the Fatal Shore: The Mythologization of Mrs Fraser.' *Meanjin*, 49(3): 449–61.

Day, Alan (2003). *Historical Dictionary of the Discovery and Exploration of Australia*. Oxford: Scarecrow.

Docker, John (1974). *Australian Cultural Elites*. Sydney: Angus & Robertson.

During, Simon (1996). *Patrick White*. Melbourne: Oxford University Press.

Edgecombe, Rodney (1989). *Vision and Style in Patrick White*. Tuscaloosa, Alabama: University of Alabama Press.

Eliot, T.S. (1920). *Poems, 1920*. New York: Knopf.

Flaubert, Gustave (1951). *Madame Bovary*. Paris: Dumoulin.

Flynn, Christine & Paul Brennan (Eds) (1989). *Patrick White Speaks*. Sydney: Primavera.

Foster, Joseph (1972). *D.H. Lawrence in Taos*. Albuquerque: University of New Mexico Press.

Frazer, Sir James (1963). *The Golden Bough*. London: Macmillan.

Freud, Sigmund (1919). *Totem and Taboo*. Trans. A.A. Brill. London: Routledge.

Frye, Northrop (1957). *Anatomy of Criticism: Four Essays*. Princeton: Princeton University Press.

Gangas, Spiros (1993). *The Cabinet of Dr Caligari* [review]. Edinburgh University Film Society Program 1993–94. Available at: www.eufs.org.uk/films/the_cabinet_of_dr_caligari.html.

Geismar, Maxwell (1942). *Writers in Crisis: The American Novel Between Two Wars*. Boston: Houghton Mifflin.

Gibson, Robert (2005). *The End of Youth: The Life and Work of Alain-Fournier*. Exeter: Impress.

Hadgraft, Cecil (1977). 'The Theme of Revelation in Patrick White's Novels.' *Southerly*, 37(1): 34–46.

Hansson, Karin (1984). *The Warped Universe: A Study of Imagery and Structure in Seven Novels by Patrick White*. Lund: Gleerup.

Haynes, Roslynn D. (1998). *Seeking the Centre: The Australian Desert in Literature, Art and Film*. Melbourne: Cambridge University Press.

Heltay, Hilary (1983). *The Articles and the Novelist: Reference Conventions and Reader Manipulation in Patrick White's Creation of Fictional Worlds*. Tübingen: Narr.

Herring, Thelma (1965). 'Odyssey of a Spinster: A Study of *The Aunt's Story*.' *Southerly*, 25(1): 6–22.

______ & G.A. Wilkes (1973). 'A Conversation with Patrick White.' *Southerly*, 33(2): 132–43.

Heseltine, Harry (1963). 'Patrick White's Style.' *Quadrant*, 7(3): 61–74.

Heydon, J.D. (1996). 'Patrick White.' *Oxford Review*, 1: 33–46.

Hope, A.D. (1956). 'The Bunyip Stages a Comeback.' Review of *The Tree of Man*. *Sydney Morning Herald* (June 16): 15.

Huxley, Aldous (1965). *Brave New World & Brave New World Revisited*. New York: Harper.

Joyce, James (1944). *Stephen Hero*. Theodore Spencer (Ed.). New York: New Directions.

Jung, Carl & Kerenyi, Carl (1963). *Essays on a Science of Mythology.* Princeton: Princeton University Press.

Kiernan, Brian (1971). *Images of Society and Nature: Seven Essays on Australian Novels.* Melbourne & London: Oxford University Press.

Koch-Emmery, Erwin (1973). 'Theme and Language in Patrick White's Novels.' *Wiener Beiträge zur Englischen Philologie*, 75: 136–46.

Laigle, Geneviève (1985a). 'Patrick White et le Corps Humain.' *Etudes Anglaises*, 37: 266–76.

______ (1985b). 'L'Oeuvre 'Picturale' de Patrick White.' *Commonwealth* (Paris), 8: 107–17.

______ (1987). 'Patrick White et l'Empreinte de la Mère.' *Commonwealth* (Paris), 9: 92–98.

______ (1989). *Le Sens du Mystère dans l'Oeuvre Romanesque de Patrick White.* Paris: Didier.

Levin, Harry (1963). *The Gates of Horn: A Study of Five French Realists.* New York: New York University Press.

Lévi-Strauss, Claude (1979). *Myth and Meaning.* New York: Schocken.

Mackenzie, Manfred (1966). 'Apocalypse in Patrick White's *The Tree of Man.*' *Meanjin*, 25: 405–16.

Maclean, Marie (1973). *Le Jeu Suprème: Structures et Thèmes dans Le Grand Meaulnes.* Paris: Cotri.

Marr, David (1991). *Patrick White: A Life.* Milson's Point: Random House.

______ (1994). *Patrick White Letters.* Chicago: University of Chicago Press.

Mather, Rodney (1963). '*Voss*' [Review]. *Melbourne Critical Review*, 6: 93–101.

McAuley, James (1959). '*The Aunt's Story*' [Review]. *Quadrant*, 3(4): 91, 93.

McGregor, Craig (1969). *In the Making.* Melbourne: Nelson.

McLaren, John (1995). *Prophet from the Desert: Critical Essays on Patrick White*. Melbourne: Red Hill.

McNiven, Ian, Lynette Russell & Kay Schaffer (Eds) (1998). *Constructions of Colonialism: Perspectives on Eliza Fraser's Shipwreck*. London: Leicester University Press.

Miller, Alice (1979). *Das Drama des begabten Kindes*. Frankfurt: Suhrkamp.

Morley, Patricia (1972). *The Mystery of Unity: Theme and Technique in the Novels of Patrick White*. St. Lucia: University of Queensland Press.

Munz, Peter (1973). *When the Golden Bough Breaks: Structuralism or Typology?* London: Routledge.

Murray, Nicholas (2003). *Aldous Huxley: A Biography*. New York: St Martin's.

Noël, Jean-Claude (1966). *George Moore, l'Homme et l'Oeuvre (1852–1933)*. Paris: Didier.

Ovid (1966). *Les Metamorphoses*. Ed. and Trans. Georges Lafaye. Paris: Belles Lettres.

Ricoeur, Paul (1991). *A Ricoeur Reader: Reflection and Imagination*. Ed Mario J. Valdes. New York: Harvester Wheatsheaf.

Riemer, A.P. (1967). 'Visions of the Mandala in *The Tree of Man*.' *Southerly*, 27(1): 3–19.

______ (1980). 'Eddie and the Bogomils—Some Observations on *The Twyborn Affair*.' *Southerly*, 40(1): 12–29.

Rimbaud, Arthur (1972). *Oeuvres Complètes*. Antoine Adam (Ed.). Paris: Gallimard.

Saussure, Ferdinand de (1983). *Course in General Linguistics*. Trans. R. Harris. La Salle, IL: Open Court.

Scheck, Reed (1989). *Railroads and Railroad Towns in New Mexico*. Santa Fe: New Mexico Magazine.

Schreiner, Olive (1990). *The Story of an African Farm*. New York: Viking.

Stein, Thomas Michael (1990). *Illusions of Solidity: Individuum und Gesellschaft im Romanwerk Patrick Whites*. Essen: Verlag Die Blaue Eule.

Stern, James (1955). 'The Quiet People of the Homestead' [Review of *The Tree of Man*]. *New York Times Book Review* (14 August): 1, 13.

Steven, Laurence (1989). *Dissociation and Wholeness in Patrick White's Fiction*. Waterloo, Ontario: Laurier.

Tacey, David (1983). 'Patrick White: The Great Mother and Her Son.' *Journal of Analytical Psychology*, 28: 165–83.

______ (1985). 'Patrick White's *Voss*: The Teller and the Tale.' *Southern Review*, 18(3): 251–71.

______ (1986). 'In the Lap of The Land: Misogyny And Earth Worship in *The Tree of Man*.' In P.R. Eaden & F.H. Mares (Eds), *Mapped But Not Known: The Australian Landscape of the Imagination*. Netley, SA: Wakefield, pp. 192–209.

______ (1988). *Patrick White: Fiction and the Unconscious*. Melbourne: Oxford University Press.

______ (1990). 'Patrick White: The End of Genius.' in Peter Wolfe (Ed.), *Critical Essays on Patrick White*. Boston: G.K. & Hall, pp. 60–64.

Tillet, Margaret (1961). *Reading Flaubert*. London: Oxford University Press.

Turnell, Martin (1950). *The Novel in France*. London: Hamilton.

Virgil (1988). *Georgics*. Richard F. Thomas (Ed.). New York: Cambridge University Press.

Voloshinov, Valentin V (1973). *Marxism and the Philosophy of Language*. Trans. L. Matejka and I.R. Titunik. Cambridge, MA: Harvard University Press.

Ward, Russel (1958). *The Australian Legend*. Melbourne: Oxford University Press.

Welty, Eudora (1973). 'The House of Cather.' In Bernice Slater & Virginia Faulkner (Eds), *The Art of Willa Cather*. Lincoln: University of Nebraska Press, pp. 3–21.

White, Patrick (1939). *Happy Valley*. London: Harrap.

______ (1941). *The Living and the Dead*. London: Routledge and Sons.

______ (1958). *The Aunt's Story*. London: Eyre & Spottiswoode.

______ (1956). *The Tree of Man*. London: Eyre & Spottiswoode.

______ (1957). *Voss*. London: Eyre & Spottiswoode.

______ (1961). *Riders in the Chariot*. London: Eyre & Spottiswoode.

______ (1966). *The Solid Mandala*. London: Eyre & Spottiswoode.

______ (1968). 'The Prodigal Son.' In Geoffrey Dutton & Max Harris (Eds). *The Vital Decade: Ten Years of Australian Art and Letters*. Melbourne: Sun Books, pp. 156–58.

______ (1970). *The Vivisector*. London: Cape.

______ (1973). *The Eye of the Storm*. London: Cape.

______ (1976). *A Fringe of Leaves*. London: Cape.

______ (1979). *The Twyborn Affair*. London: Cape.

______ (1981). *Flaws in the Glass: A Self-Portrait*. London: Cape.

______ (1986). *Memoirs of Many in One by Alex Xenophon Demirjian Gray*. London: Cape.

______ (1989). *Patrick White Speaks*. Christine Flynn & Paul Brennan (Eds). Leichhardt, NSW: Primavera.

Whitman, Cedric (1963). *The Iliad: Homer and the Homeric Tradition*. Massachusetts: Harvard University Press.

Wilkes G.A. (1965). 'Patrick White's *The Tree of Man*.' *Southerly*, 25(1): 23–33.

______ (1967). 'A Reading of Patrick White's *Voss*.' *Southerly*, 27(3): 159–73.

Williams, Raymond (1961). *The Long Revolution*. London: Chatto & Windus.

______ (1981). *Culture*. London: Fontana.

Wolfe, Peter (Ed.) (1990). *Critical Essays on Patrick White*. Boston: G.K. & Hall.

Index

www.ingramcontent.com/pod-product-compliance
Lightning Source LLC
LaVergne TN
LVHW020040110826
845155LV00029B/568

* 9 7 8 1 9 2 0 8 9 9 3 7 0 *